Jobs Aren't Enough

Jobs Aren't Enough

Toward a New Economic Mobility for Low-Income Families

ROBERTA REHNER IVERSEN
ANNIE LAURIE ARMSTRONG

TEMPLE UNIVERSITY PRESS
Philadelphia

For each of the twenty-five families in this book, and for our families
—RRI and ALA

Roberta Rehner Iversen is Associate Professor in the School of Social Policy & Practice at the University of Pennsylvania.

Annie Laurie Armstrong is the founder of Business Government Community Connections, a research and evaluation firm in Seattle.

Temple University Press
1601 North Broad Street
Philadelphia PA 19122
www.temple.edu/tempress

Library of Congress Cataloging-in-Publication Data

Iversen, Roberta Rehner.
    Jobs aren't enough : toward a new economic mobility for low-income
families / Roberta Rehner Iversen and Annie Laurie Armstrong.
        p.   cm.
    Includes bibliographical references and index.
    Contents: Are jobs enough for economic mobility?—From the old to the new economic mobility—The parents: their backgrounds, lives, and locations—The children: their lives and worlds—Workforce development: systems and networks—Yesterday's firms and today's families: connects and disconnects with Michele Belliveau—Children's schools, parents' work, and policy: alignment and misalignment—Jobs aren't enough: toward an agenda for family economic mobility.
    ISBN 1-59213-355-X (cloth : alk. paper)
    ISBN 1-59213-356-8 (pbk. : alk. paper)
    1. Working class—United States.   2. Poor families—United States.
3. City dwellers — United States.   4. Social mobility—United States.
5. United States—Social policy—1993–   I. Armstrong, Annie Laurie 1950–
II. Title.

HD8066.I94 2006
305.5′130973—dc22

                                                    2005046668

2   4   6   8   9   7   5   3   1

Contents

Foreword

SUSAN GEWIRTZ, *Annie E. Casey Foundation*

MORE THAN ONE out of four American working families (9.2 million families) now earn wages so low that they have difficulty surviving financially and providing a secure future for their families. Twenty million children live in these families (Waldron, Roberts, & Reamer, 2004). As stated in our 2005 *KIDS COUNT Data Book* essay, the Annie E. Casey Foundation has "long believed that the most powerful approach to altering the future of our nation's most disadvantaged kids is to enhance the financial security of their parents in the present" (Annie E. Casey Foundation , p. 5). At the same time, there has been growing media and scholarly attention to the changing economy due to globalization, demand for workers with higher skills, decreasing wage mobility at the lower end of the wage scale, and the increasing percentage of jobs that do not offer health benefits or paid sick leave. And although there is a sense of growing insecurity even among middle-class workers, low-wage workers and their families are particularly vulnerable to these labor market forces. Recent publications have chronicled the struggle of long-term welfare recipients to join the mainstream economy and the challenges facing workers who work at jobs that pay the minimum wage.

In 1998, when the research described in this book was begun, there was considerable and important research being initiated related to the impacts of welfare reform on families and on the effectiveness of welfare-to-work programs. The families in the Casey Foundation's multicity, multiyear Jobs Initiative include adults who have been on welfare, but also those with a long history in the low-wage labor market, men and women returning from incarceration, single-parent families, and two-parent working families. The Annie E. Casey Foundation, through its grant-making strategy related to connecting adults to good entry-level jobs with career paths, was particularly interested in learning more about the intersection of employment training, family, work, and community. With its Jobs Initiative as the setting, the Casey Foundation supported in-depth ethnographic research to help understand family economic mobility, the impacts of adult employment on children's lives, and the ways working families connect with their communities. The research that started in two cities, Milwaukee and Seattle, soon led to an expanded research study in all five demonstration sites with twenty-five families.

Jobs Aren't Enough places the twenty-five families of this research squarely in the context of low-wage workers across the United States who are struggling to get ahead, meet the needs of their children, and find a workable balance among the many demands on their lives. The families in this book were motivated to seek out employment and training programs, to work full time, and were generally placed in or hired by firms that offered health-care benefits. The starting wage for participants in the Jobs Initiative averages $9.41 per hour (personal communication, Metis

Associates, May 2005), thus placing their wages above welfare leavers whose median hourly wage is $8.06 (Loprest, 2003) and well above the earnings of minimum-wage workers.

By examining the lives of these low-wage working families, this research illustrates the particular vulnerabilities of families whose earnings begin to make them ineligible for critical work supports such as child-care subsidies and government provided health-care benefits. It also demonstrates the tenuousness of their employment as they lose good paying jobs in sectors such as manufacturing during the 2001 recession or see their wages reduced through reduced work hours and overtime. Although in some ways and for some periods of time a few steps above America's lowest paid workers, these families are just like the 9.2 million working families struggling to make ends meet and to provide a secure future for their children. They are in similar jobs, their children are in struggling schools, and their families provide both support and added financial burdens. This research clearly demonstrates the challenges that all workers in low-paying jobs face in moving toward family economic stability.

Rooted in five years of in-depth ethnographic research, *Jobs Aren't Enough* offers important lessons and a theoretical framework for workforce development professionals, students planning to enter the related fields of sociology, urban studies, social work, economics and political science, and for decision makers who can influence the policies and practices affecting low-wage working families. The framework offers readers a view that looks beyond simple notions of blaming low-wage workers for their failure to rise to the middle class and the equally flawed thinking that places all responsibility on society and government policies. Taking a more complex view based on rich data, *Jobs Aren't Enough* urges us to think about how the family as a whole intersects with the critical institutions that can either aid or hinder the achievement of family economic success. In this analysis firms, schools, workforce development programs, families, community supports, and public policy all play an important role and need to be understood individually and as they relate to one another as a first step in helping families move toward stronger financial futures.

This research sheds new light on the challenges facing workers in low-wage jobs and provides analysis relevant to practitioners, policymakers, and researchers committed to addressing the problems of urban poverty. The family stories, for example, reveal the existence of a "life-stage mismatch," by which well-meaning and well-designed workforce programs may place individuals into good paying entry level jobs in physically demanding occupations that might not be a good fit for a forty-year-old with health problems, family responsibilities, and time constraints in moving up the career ladder. *Jobs Aren't Enough* also highlights the impact depression has on job seekers' performance in training and at work and how employment with adequate wages and the availability of ongoing work supports may reduce those symptoms. The research also demonstrates a greater need to focus on career management and reemployment services. Career mobility is becoming increasingly difficult for low-wage earners, and for even those workers who may start in a good job in a sector with strong wages and benefits, this analysis suggests that their ability to translate this opportunity into a clear upward pathway is not automatic or guaranteed. It is worth noting, however, that despite the multiple challenges facing these twenty-five families, over a three-year period their incomes show an 18 percent increase on average over their initial post-training wages, three times the average 6 percent gain reported for other low-income earners (Andersson, Holzer, & Lane, 2005). Yet as the stories behind the numbers suggest, these wages are not high and steady enough to guarantee family economic mobility.

It is clear that for many families it will be necessary to combine human capital strategies with publicly funded work supports such as the Earned Income Tax Credit, food stamps, and health-care and child-care benefits. The families in *Jobs Aren't Enough* vividly illustrate the difference these benefits can make for a struggling family and the consequences for adults and children when these benefits are removed as earnings increase. In fact, these families are particularly vulnerable to the loss of work-supporting benefits as wages fluctuate due to reductions in overtime, during short gaps in employment, and as income rises just above eligibility levels. This research also adds nuance to recent findings that suggest positive benefits for younger children when their parents are working and income is increased. The family stories described here demonstrate that although work, which brings increased earnings and positive adult role models, can have a favorable influence on family functioning and child outcomes, children are very much affected by the ups and downs of parents' work and instability in family income. Furthermore, as working parents put in overtime and pursue educational and training opportunities to further their career mobility, time with children may be sacrificed. The interactions or noninteractions among social institutions are most palpable as families try to balance work, child care, school, and time with family.

Jobs Aren't Enough presents a theoretical framework that urges readers to look beyond the individual institutions of family, school, workforce development, firms, and policy, and to understand how these relate to each other. It also suggests that we already know a great deal about approaches that work and have the potential to increase family economic opportunity. For example, we know that good paying jobs and benefits matter and that publicly supported work supports make a real difference for adults and their children. We also know that effective workforce development efforts require partnerships among employers, community-based organizations, the public sector, and educational institutions. The great challenge therefore is whether we can create the public will to implement the policies and practices that can assist the growing numbers of American families who work and want to provide for their families but are still unable to move out of poverty.

REFERENCES

Andersson, R., Holzer, H. J., & Lane, J. I. (2005). *Moving up or moving on: Who advances in the low-wage labor market?* New York: Russell Sage Foundation.

Annie E. Casey Foundation. (2005). *Kids count data book 2005.* Baltimore, MD: Author.

Loprest, P. J. (2003). *Fewer welfare leavers employed in weak economy.* Washington, DC: Urban Institute.

Waldron, T., Roberts, B., & Reamer, A. (2004). *Working hard, falling short: America's working families and the pursuit of economic security.* Baltimore, MD: Annie E. Casey Foundation.

Acknowledgments

JUST AS FAMILY economic mobility in the twenty-first century requires collaborative institutional networks, we could not have conducted the research or written this book without a rich network of contributors. We are deeply grateful to each of you.

The vision, encouragement, and facilitation of Robert Giloth and Susan Gewirtz at the Annie E. Casey Foundation, other enthusiastic and wise Foundation colleagues, and the extended support of the Foundation in the form of grants for independent research made this book possible. Although the views presented here, as well as any errors, are the authors' alone and do not necessarily represent the views of the Foundation, Susan's and Bob's sustained involvement in the ethnographic project increases the possibility that the families' experiences in and after the Foundation's national workforce demonstration program, the *Jobs Initiative*, will increase labor market opportunity and economic reform in the five research cities—Philadelphia, New Orleans, Milwaukee, St. Louis, and Seattle—and in other cities as well.

We are grateful to the demonstration site directors, Margaret Berger-Bradley, Darryl Burrows, Lee Crean, Laura Dresser and Carolyn Schultz, Dianne Hanna, Steve Holt, and Tom Rhodenbaugh for providing access to their informative and helpful staff members and to their workforce development partner organizations and institutions; to colleagues at Abt Associates and the New School University for sharing program evaluation findings; and ultimately to the extended family members, friends, work supervisors and colleagues, children's school administrators and teachers, local policy board members, social and human service organization staff, and others associated with the families' efforts to move up through work. Most important, the site directors and their affiliated program partners provided access to the twenty-five families at the core of this book who gave generously of their time in hopes that the lessons from their experiences will result in changes that improve the chances of families like theirs to support their families through wage work.

The research and writing of the book could not have occurred without the field and analytic expertise of the research team. First, the onsite ethnographers: Annie Laurie Armstrong in Seattle, Miriam Isabel Barrios and Melissa Burch in New Orleans, Kathe Johnson and Dr. Diane Michalski Turner in Milwaukee, Larry Morton in St. Louis, and Dr. Cynthia Saltzman and Michele Belliveau in Philadelphia. Second, the doctoral research analysts: Mona Basta, Michele Belliveau (also co-author of Chapter 6), Dr. Robert P. Fairbanks, Jr., Dr. Min Park, and Sarah Suh. Third, the competent transcribers: Christine Holmes at Penn and the staff at Bernard Z. Schantzer's firm in Philadelphia.

Our research and this book were not only made possible but also significantly enhanced by colleagues in the School of Social Policy & Practice at the University of Pennsylvania. In particular, Richard J. Gelles, dean, who provided continuous encouragement, faith and flexibility, and Lina Hartocollis, associate dean, who gave unstintingly of her time, back-up help, friendship, and scholarly expertise. The additional support from countless administrative staff members and faculty colleagues at the School enabled this book to be completed.

The *Jobs Aren't Enough* manuscript was enriched by a cadre of academic, professional, and corporate readers who helped us to hone our arguments, checked for accuracy, gave generously of their substantive knowledge, and believed that this book is important. We particularly appreciate the guidance, scholarly respect, wisdom, and perspective of our two editors at Temple University Press: editor-in-chief Janet M. Francendese and former senior acquisitions editor Peter Wissoker. We also appreciate the professionalism and efficiency of the production, marketing, and editorial staff at and associated with Temple Press, as well as the guidance of the Hatcher Group.

Other members of this vital cadre include the anonymous readers of the prospectus and final manuscript; Karen Berry; Steven Feldman; Dianna Finnerty; Linda M. Fischer; Carol Gregory; Mark Granovetter; Barbara Fogg Grove; Joe McGeehan; Alex Osterneck; Martin Patchen; Nancy Hagen Patchen; Lauren M. Rich; Mary Jane Vujovic; and members of the Vermont group. Chris Gurnee deserves special thanks for his extensive help in manuscript preparation. Special thanks also to Julia Koschinsky and Paul Stern for data preparation and technical assistance and to Andy Sherwood for supplemental data. Frank F. Furstenberg, Jr., Kathryn Edin, Leslie B. Alexander, Naomi B. Farber, Kenneth Gergen, and Mary Gergen have been shepherds throughout.

Finally and essentially, we could not have written this book without the incredible and sustained support, guidance, humor, patience, and encouragement of our family members and friends near and far who remained so, despite little contact over the years of research and writing. Roberta Iversen's much-loved family gratefully includes Gudmund Iversen, dear husband, infrastructure provider, and constant fan; John and Doris Rehner; Jack and Chris Rehner; Torborg Iversen; Reidun Iversen; Kirsten, David, Anna and Glenn Wysen; Chikako, John and Chisato Iversen; Gretchen Iversen and Luke Walker; Eric Iversen; and Catherine Hatch. Annie Laurie Armstrong's much-loved family includes Myles, Celina, and baby Isabella Armstrong, who was born during the time we worked on this book.

1   Are Jobs Enough for Economic Mobility?

THE STORY

Twenty-five parents, their fifteen spouses or partners, and their sixty-six children in Philadelphia, Milwaukee, New Orleans, St. Louis, and Seattle let us share their lives from the late 1990s to mid-2003 to learn about low-income families and economic mobility. During this time we also talk with and observe at least one thousand auxiliaries associated with the families' mobility efforts. Through these contacts we learn that the families' attempts to move up economically through work both mesh and clash with the characteristics and conditions they encounter in workforce development programs and systems, firms, children's schools, and public policy.

The story begins with the families. Over the years, the families' infants enter child care and preschool, their preschool children progress to elementary school, their elementary-age children move up to middle school, their teenagers enter or complete high school, and new babies are born. The parents go to their children's basketball games, concerts, school conferences, and special education meetings. They go to the grocery, to the laundromat, to grandparents, to neighbors, to community centers, and to church. They tend to children with asthma, developmental delays, and school performance problems. They take children to doctors, go to doctors themselves, and worry about aging parents. The parents read to their children; the children read to their parents. The parents help with math homework and oversee school projects. They counsel children about conflicts with peers and give birthday parties.

At the same time the parents move up, down, and laterally in their jobs. Some take courses after work hours to try to upgrade their positions. Others wish they could. On the job they commune with coworkers, strive to get along with supervisors, and worry about how to make more money. They work overtime, get second or third jobs, and survive—at times relatively well and at other times barely—on sometimes-rising, sometimes-falling, but generally too-low wages. Many "do without" to provide enriching after-school or summer activities for their children and wish they could afford home computers and build assets and savings. Some make progress on these goals, but many do not no matter how hard they try. They make decisions they later question and mistakes they later rue about work, parenting, job training, and expenditures.

In many ways these families are like most other families in the United States, but they are different at the same time. In the richest large country in the world, they work full time year round, but they still do not earn enough to support their families. In this they are like one out of four other families in twenty-first-century America (Waldron, Roberts, & Reamer, 2004), most of whom work at full-time jobs that keep the country running but do not pay living wages.

Spending their childhoods and teen years in impoverished urban neighborhoods means that many of the parents receive too little education and have too few skills for today's jobs (Holzer, 1996). Most of their underfinanced, embattled urban schools yield poor-quality education, and their high school diplomas translate into eighth-grade reading level at best. These schools often fail to diagnose their learning disabilities or identify family problems that influence their dropping out of high school. Some complete their education in a foreign country, in one case a four-year college degree, to find that American firms do not recognize these accomplishments. Many seek vocational training in for-profit institutes that does not lead to a job and leaves them in debt. Policy prohibitions about debt then disqualify them from further education funding.

Other parents are immigrants and political refugees from war-torn countries who find that their new communities offer few acculturation or language services. This lack of services leaves them ill-equipped to navigate the dangers of low-level jobs, the medical system, and community programs for their children. Still other parents grow up in families who suffer from substance abuse, mental health problems, or domestic violence. Some struggle with bouts of depression themselves, which may result in alternating welfare and low-paid work. A few parents make serious mistakes in their youth or young adulthood, such as selling or taking drugs. Whether the cause is perceiving or experiencing few legitimate opportunities in the labor market or simply making wrong choices, they spend time in prison or rehabilitation facilities to compensate for these wrongs. Rehabilitation notwithstanding, felony incarceration may block or limit their access to housing subsidies, financial aid, and other opportunities that they need to move ahead.

At the same time, the parents, and indirectly their children, contend with a labor market that relies increasingly on contingent labor and with firms that offer inadequate wages and limited or too costly nonwage benefits, like health insurance. Despite the fact that the families contribute to the national well-being through production and taxes, they live in a country that denies subsidy assistance to many immigrants and refugees, disproportionately incarcerates African Americans and Hispanics, and puts time and allotment limits on transitional public assistance. Without adequate wages, benefits, and work supports, past history and current social and labor market conditions intersect to limit the families' economic mobility in a country that prides itself on meritocracy, a "second chance" after rehabilitation, and opportunity for all.

The story continues with the auxiliary contacts who further illustrate that economic mobility is highly complex. We learn this from instructors, administrators, and colleagues in the families' education and job training programs and institutions, often attending classes alongside the key parents[1] and following them as they navigate training, jobs, and family responsibilities. We learn this from neighbors, friends, extended family, faith leaders, human service workers, civic leaders, and policymakers in the families' neighborhoods and cities and observe how these varied community actors aid or constrain family economic mobility. We learn this from coworkers, managers, supervisors, CEOs, and labor leaders at the families' seventy-four firms as we accompany the parents through their work days and overnight shifts. We learn this from over 120 days spent with teachers, administrators, and students in the children's child-care facilities, preschools, and elementary and secondary schools, observing how children and faculty alike learn and simultaneously cope with impoverished and embattled environments.

The fact that these families identify labor market, education, and public policy institutions that do not but *could* facilitate mobility is a significant impetus for this book. In short, *Jobs Aren't Enough* argues that multiple social institutions influence contemporary economic mobility: in particular, the traditional institutions of the family and the labor market (firms) as they intersect with the institutions of education (public schools and workforce development) and public policy. As such this book is an exposé of *intersections*—their presence and more often their absence in the world of public beliefs about human and institutional behaviors and policy solutions to human and institutional problems that exist in the form of contained, unconnected silos. We focus here on intersections *between* the institution of the family and other social institutions as well as on intersections *among* these institutions in different forms, intensities, and geographies.

We note at the outset that our research in New Orleans took place before Hurricane Katrina wreaked its havoc on the city and its surrounds. We address the particular implications of this disaster for the New Orleans families in the Afterword.

WHAT DO WE MEAN BY FAMILY, ECONOMIC MOBILITY, INSTITUTIONS, LOW INCOME, AND THE CONTEXT OF CAPITALISM?

First, we define family, economic mobility, institutions, and low income as used in this book. We then briefly discuss the economic system of capitalism as the context for the old mobility experiences of the families and institutions here and as the potential context for a new economic mobility.

FAMILY

Definitions and conceptualizations of "family" range from a strict view of biologically or adoptively related parents and children residing together to a constructionist view of whomever one considers "family" is family. In this book we tend toward the latter definition, privileging the way in which the respondents define their family constellation in their particular emotional, economic, spatial, and meaning-centered contexts. We also conceptualize family as "a social group, and social institution, with an identifiable structure based on positions and interactions among people who occupy those positions" (Gelles & Levine, 1999, p. 405). As such, families are agents of socialization and cultural reproduction: in effect, navigational vehicles for older and younger members alike. More broadly, we conceptualize all persons as "familied," meaning that every person's life holds others who are significant to them along the dimensions of structure and meaning that influence daily work, decisions, and social being.

ECONOMIC MOBILITY

By "economic mobility," which we call either mobility or economic mobility, we refer specifically to the phenomenon of moving forward financially through wage work. "Labor mobility" is the term commonly used in economics for how people move between jobs and occupations. "Social mobility" and "occupational mobility" are the terms commonly used in sociology (Breiger, 1990; Granovetter, 1995). We use the term economic mobility for several reasons. First, our concern is with the ability of low-earning parents to support their families through wage income, defined by the Census Bureau as "money income before taxes, exclusive of noncash benefits and employer-provided fringe benefits" (DeNavas-Walt, Proctor, & Mills, 2004, p. 1). For our purposes, social mobility is too closely aligned with social status, class, and systems of occupational ranking, and labor mobility focuses on individual workers, not on workers as parents or members of families. Second, economic mobility suggests an emphasis on the worker–family labor market interface and is thus more descriptive of our inquiry than is occupational mobility which addresses prestige criteria that are not relevant here. Economic mobility is also more consistent with the theoretical heritage of economic sociology which is the body of theory we draw upon and aim to extend.

Mobility has generally been viewed and explored as a microeconomic phenomenon; however we argue that mobility is both micro- and macroeconomic. In Weberian terms, we look at economically conditioned phenomena, those that partly—but only partly—can be explained through the influence of economic factors, and economically relevant phenomena, those that are not economic in themselves, but that influence economic phenomena (Weber, 1904/1949, p. 65). Historic examinations of "family" mobility focus on intergenerational patterns (Blau & Duncan, 1967), whereas more recent ones have begun to look at intragenerational patterns (Warren, Hauser, & Sheridan, 2002). Our focus on the family as a *generational institutional unit* affords exploration of the dynamic intersections within families as well as between families and other social institutions—intersections that have both intra- and intergenerational implications for economic mobility.

INSTITUTIONS

Although some might call the spheres of family, education, firms, and the state systems, we characterize them as social institutions. So doing we draw attention to the fact that institutions have structure. All involve aspects of authority and loyalty and are constituted and molded by policies and laws. All thus inherently intersect with one another, even if bureaucracies and funding streams do not acknowledge or attend to these intersections. In Brinton and Nee's (1998, p. 8) definition, institutions are "webs of interrelated rules and norms—formal and informal—that govern social relationships." In contrast, systems are contained entities that form a unity or organic whole in which the "relationships and interactions between elements explain the behavior of the whole" (Grint, 1991, p. 137). From a systems perspective, variation rests within rather than between, which tends to result in deterministic conceptions and atomistic silos. From a social institution perspective, variation occurs dynamically in the nexuses of the intersecting components.

LOW INCOME

In the United States, wage and salary earnings are the primary source of income for many families (McCall, 2000), particularly those like the ones in this book. However, definitions of "low income" vary and the term is often used synonymously with the term "working poor" (Gitterman, Howard, & Cotton, 2003). Briefly here, as we discuss this at length in Chapter 6, the most common metric used to define low income is 100 percent of the federal poverty level (FPL)—commonly called the poverty line, even though many scholars and policymakers view 200 percent of the poverty level as the minimum income that families need to meet their basic needs (Waldron, Roberts, & Reamer 2004). Others define low income more generously in terms of the median national income (Gitterman, Howard, & Cotton, 2003), which at $44,686 in 2004 dollars (Fronczek, 2005) is the equivalent of about 300% FPL. Still others assess income adequacy in terms of an alternative poverty metric such as the Self-Sufficiency Standard (Pearce, 2000, 2001; Wider Opportunities for Women, 2001, 2004).

We explicitly focus on wage income alone in the discussion of "low income" here, as the dominant metric to assess economic mobility and family well-being over the long run is what a parent can earn. Although transitional subsidies and wage supports mediate low incomes in the short run, we argue that earnings are ultimately the key to economic mobility. Accordingly, *Jobs Aren't Enough* uses what we consider to be a relatively conservative definition of low income—200 percent or less of the federal poverty level—a definition that, if anything, underreports the constraints that millions of working parents confront in their attempts to support their families through work.

For example, according to census analyses for 2004, thirty-seven million Americans live in families with incomes below 100 percent of the poverty level (Cadena & Sallee, 2005). In addition, the number of Americans with low incomes (below 200 percent FPL) increased by seven million between 2000 and 2003 (Ku, Broaddus, & Wachino, 2005), and by an additional 1.6 percent between 2003 and 2004 (Fronczek, 2005). In 2003 about 24.3 percent of Americans, essentially one in every four workers in the labor force, earned less than $9.04 an hour, which results in an annual income that just reaches 100 percent poverty for a family of four, even working full time year round (Mishel, Bernstein, & Allegretto, 2005). Especially pertinent to the families here, in 2002 more than one in four (27.4 percent) working parents with children in the United States was classified as low income by earning less than 200 percent of the federal poverty threshold (Waldron, Roberts, & Reamer, 2004). From another perspective, more than one in four children living with married parents is considered low income (Koball & Douglas-Hall, 2005). Thus from any vantage point, families with low incomes are widespread across the United States.

THE CONTEXT OF CAPITALISM

Although a review of the contested definitions and critiques of capitalist economic and social organization is beyond the purpose and scope of this book (see, e.g., Bowles & Gintis, 1987; Braverman, 1974; Edwards, 1979; Hart, 2005; Lafer, 2002;

Wacquant, 2002), many consider capitalism to be the dominant way of organizing the economy, legally, politically, and socially in today's world (Swedberg, 2003, p. 54). As such, it forms part of the context for the families and other institutions here.

Common definitions of capitalism incorporate some variation of the theme that it constitutes an organization of economic interests that allows for the "pursuit of profit, and forever renewed profit" (Weber, 1904/1949). According to some, the commodification of and control over the labor process by employers under capitalism is the established route to such profit (Edwards, 1979; Marx, 1867/1978). On this view authority, exploitation and power hold sway and profit-making trumps other organizational aspects of firms such as investment in training and reciprocity relations. A contrasting approach to the general nature of capitalism is what Swedberg (2003, p. 57) calls "the economists' traditional definition of the economy as consisting of production, distribution, and exchange." Although all economies involve these three factors, capitalism is distinguished from other economic systems primarily by the fact that distribution is organized as exchange in the market rather than as reciprocity or redistribution. Presciently, in *Economy and Society* Weber (1922/1978) speaks not of a single capitalism but of capitalisms: rational (or modern) capitalism, political capitalism, and what can be termed traditional commercial capitalism. Leicht (2002) echoes this perspective almost a century later in his global perspective on "capitalisms" as do Hall and Soskice (2001) in their discussion of "varieties of capitalism," Esping-Anderson (1990) in his configuration of "three worlds of welfare capitalism," Eisenstadt (1963/1993) in his identification of different "capitalist regimes," and Nee and Swedberg (2005) in their presentation of "the many forms and varieties" of contemporary capitalism.

Although some see capitalism as the cause of all labor market ills, we view capitalism as a social form that is historically based, nondeterministic, thus one in which practices and structures can be altered, at least at micro- and mesolevels of the labor market. Newman (2002, p. 1590) concludes similarly that "reformist struggles over government policies within capitalist states can change the fate of the poor for the better." Fundamentally, institutions are rule-governed social constructions (Nee, 2003); thus we argue, as does Miller (1999, 2003), that greater fairness and cooperation and increased economic mobility are possible through the reconstruction of contemporary labor and other social institutions, even in a market economy. In effect, social and economic relations are processes in perpetual construction and reconstruction, as Braverman (1974) suggests earlier and as Swedberg (2003, p. 63) underscores: "No single form of governance—including the market—is responsible for the way that a national economy works." As Bowles and Gintis (1987, p. xiii) hold, "The view that there is an ineluctable conflict between moral and material incentives, between cooperation and competition, or that one of these modes can operate effectively in the absence of the other, is a quaint and anachronistic aspect of our intellectual heritage. Finally, Heilbroner (1999, p. 320) argues that "Economic vision (here we might add economic sociology) . . . could become the source of an awareness of ways by which a capitalist structure can broaden its motivations, increase its flexibility, and develop its social responsibility."

In this vein we are intrigued by the notion of an economic system in which *household and profit* matter (Weber, 1922/1978). Although Weber refers to large capitalist households of antiquity in his discussion, we argue that it may be worth reexamining this prioritization with an eye toward householding *and* profit making in contemporary firms. In this construction, household would not refer solely to consumption, as in Weber's formulation and in Aristotle's earlier one (Swedberg, 2005), but to taking joint responsibility for keeping the property (the firm) intact and for allocating profits equally to meet the interests of all the involved social actors. This reformulation is akin to Swedberg's (2003, p. 6) argument that because institutions are "durable amalgamations of interests *and* social relations," analysis of the capitalist economic system must take the interests of both individuals and corporate actors into account (Swedberg, 2004). Hart's (2005, p. xli) similar position is that "By creating a new, more inclusive brand of capitalism, one that incorporates previously excluded voices, concerns, and interests, the corporate sector could be the catalyst for a truly sustainable form of global development—and prosper in the process."

We hold that laws and policies currently upholding the modern economic order *can* be changed, prevailing political standpoints *can* be changed, and social perspectives in current ascendancy *can* be changed. As we discuss further in Chapter 8, however, all require significant change in what we refer to as the "public will."

PLAN OF THE BOOK

Jobs Aren't Enough is an ethnographic rendition of the experiences of families who are trying to transition from prior economic disadvantage to family-supporting wages through work. Their journeys and our previous work on occupational attainment and workforce development lead us in this initial chapter to question why and how economic mobility is still limited for so many in twenty-first-century America. The immediate context is the lived experience of low-income families trying to move up through work and the daily realities of how they and other social institutions (firms, workforce development, schools, and public policy) intersect to foster or obstruct their mobility goals.

The situation facing us and the families is thus. Scholarly and policy interest in urban poverty in the 1990s and early 2000s is primarily focused on welfare reform, particularly on the assessment of how different types of welfare-to-work programs move single mothers into the labor market, thereby lowering the rolls and costs of public assistance. Little notice is paid to the fact that increasing numbers of *two-parent working families* are poor (Annie E. Casey Foundation, 2001a, 2004). Even though rates of child poverty decrease slightly in the early 2000s, from 43 percent in 2000 to 40 percent in 2001 (Child Trends, 2003), two in five American children remain poor according to the most stringent measure of poverty—at or below 100 percent of the federal poverty line. Similar to other states, Wisconsin reports a 20 percent increase in child poverty between 2000 and 2003 (Dresser & Wright, 2004). Why is this occurring? Why are so many parents unable to support their families through work? This book as a whole implicates multiple intersecting social institutions in the persistent limits to family economic mobility.

The story continues in Chapter 2 with social theory because what the populace thinks, believes, and assumes about economic mobility forms the lattice for the relevant actors, social structures, and practices and policies in organizations and institutions.

FROM THE OLD TO THE NEW ECONOMIC MOBILITY

Chapter 2 first presents what we call the *old paradigm for economic mobility*. In this paradigm, jobs are the expected way for families to get ahead financially in the United States. Yet by the early 2000s over one in four parents works full time year round but does not earn enough to support his or her family. Explanations for this often split into two poles: the "it's their own fault" view and the "it's society's fault" view.

Holders of the "it's their own fault" view believe that opportunity, meritocracy, and initiative are realities in today's America, thus any deviation from the open terrain of mobility must be the person's fault. In effect these persons are viewed as atomistic, individually or personally responsible actors who are thus classified as the "nondeserving poor." Less extreme holders of the "own fault" view, especially those who remember the Great Depression or the civil rights period of the 1960s, may acknowledge—albeit hesitantly and carefully—that life events outside the control of individuals sometimes happen. The company goes out of business, the father becomes disabled from a work injury, or the mother leaves an abusive partner. These individuals are then classified as the "deserving poor," even though holders of this view still tend to believe that atomistic, responsible actors can overcome these happenstances through initiative if they "just put their minds to it."

Holders of the "it's society's fault" view perceive seismic shifts in the socio-economic landscape over the past several decades, such as shifts in the structure, practices, and geography of the labor market and firms; shifts in welfare and workforce development policy that curtail eligibility and skill training in favor of rapid job attachment; shifts in how the demography of contemporary workers matches the characteristics of contemporary firms—what we call a *life-stage mismatch* (Iversen, 2002)—and shifts that show increasing rates of child poverty in working households. The most extreme "society's fault" proponents believe that capitalism determines immobility; thus the economic chances of low-income working families cannot improve without radical reconstruction of the country's political economy. The more moderate "society's fault" proponents seek a middle ground between individual and societal responsibility, understanding that people sometimes make mistakes, wrong choices, or face structural conditions such as inadequate housing, poorly funded schools, inadequate wages, or discrimination that constrains or blocks their opportunity or initiative. More moderate proponents are also more likely to believe that the children of poor parents should not be made to suffer for a parent's limitations or for social structural constraints.

These are simplifications of the worldviews of the American populace to be sure, but they suggest the landscape of assumptions, beliefs, and theories that underlies the structure and practices of the contemporary institutions of social reproduction that are germane to economic mobility—the family, workforce development, firms, children's schools, and the state through its public policies. The voices in this book, all of whom inhabit these institutional spheres, show us how the old paradigm limits or precludes economic mobility for families without prior economic advantage.

These voices also point to the need for a *new paradigm for economic mobility* that we sketch out in Chapter 2, especially as firms and other institutions face the forces of globalization and restructuring, however great or small these forces actually are. To maintain our country's historic philosophical principles and economic productivity, we argue that concepts from economic sociology form the framework for a new paradigm that our ethnographic findings laminate. In effect, a new paradigm for economic mobility fosters foundational American principles that are obscured by geographic and political dispersion and by neoliberal reliance on the market to solve all ills and needs: principles of interdependence, fairness, equity, and real opportunity.

Understanding that economic mobility is a thoroughly relational process leads toward the establishment of genuine trust and reciprocity in the intersecting relationships among education and workforce development institutions, workers and firms, as well as among families, firms, and children's schools. Successful mobility outcomes thus require developing and extending social and cultural capital along with human capital, as the weak ties of social networks (Granovetter, 1973) and the sanctioned credentials that result from institutionalized cultural capital (Bourdieu, 2001) merge with human capital attainment to form a legitimizing signal for those who make mobility-influencing decisions about hiring, promotion, layoff, and termination.

Finally, understanding that economic mobility is increasingly dynamic and variable, and that choice and decision processes involve both cognitive and emotional components, leads toward the development of greater mutuality in the authority relations and practices of firms and other organizations. Power relations then become more horizontal than vertical, multiple voices are sought in the crafting of procedures and regulations, and responsibility becomes relational rather than individual.

BACKGROUNDS AND LOCATIONS OF THE PARENTS AND CHILDREN

This theoretical framework undergirds the remaining chapters in the book. Chapter 3 lays out the characteristics of the key parents that illustrate the confluence of old paradigm experiences and new paradigm needs. The parents contend with both personal and structural challenges and constraints to mobility, not the least of which is a vulnerability to symptoms of depression as they lose hard-won jobs and employer-paid health insurance during the economic downturn in 2001 and beyond. The parents utilize extant subsidies and work supports to augment inadequate wages and employ geographic strategies and community involvement to enhance their own and their children's well-being. These parents are found to be similar to millions of other low-income adults in the country today on a selection of demographic characteristics, extending the likelihood that their experiences and voices express widespread realities and sentiments. Chapter 3 also explores the role of "place" in economic mobility, concluding that although knowledge about place-based particularities is critical to the development of appropriate local policies and programs, state and national policies are the key to economic mobility writ large.

Chapter 4 leads us into the world of the children, illuminating the intersection of family history, developmental environments, violence and safety, and daily lives through the eyes and voices of the parents' preschool and school-age children and youth. Perhaps most important for intergenerational mobility, children of all ages cast a critical eye on the labor market based on how they experience their parents' work struggles. Although the children are grateful for the material benefits of their parents' new and better jobs, lessened family time, added family responsibilities, dangers and injuries to their mothers and fathers in the workplace, and mercurial job tenures seem to lead some children to express these concerns in the form of behavior and performance problems at school (details in Chapter 7) or through aggravated health conditions. Many children doubt that their merit will be rewarded with opportunity in the future as they see that trust, reciprocity, and mutuality are often lacking in the vital mobility spheres of firms and social policy.

The voices of the families and auxiliaries in the core analytical chapters of the book, Chapters 5 through 7, then show in depth how the institutions involved in economic mobility act and intersect.

WORKFORCE DEVELOPMENT PROGRAMS AND SYSTEMS

Chapter 5 takes us briefly through the history of federal education and job training legislation and programs, showing how they evolve from a human capital to a "work-first" focus. This evolution also entails a shift in nomenclature from "education and training" to "workforce development" which denotes a more systemic network orientation to employment and economic mobility.

Not fully successful yet in this goal at the federal level, local and regional workforce development networks, both in and external to the federal system, such as the one in which the key parents participate, are emerging. These new networks explicitly engage multiple organizations and institutions in a collaborative approach to both workforce and community economic development. Network partners often include but are not limited to workforce intermediaries, social and human service organizations, community colleges, vocational institutes, workforce policy boards, area businesses and firms, and state and local policymakers.

In effect, understanding that multiple institutions are integral to real opportunity for economic mobility leads toward the ways in which trust, power, reciprocity, and shared meanings can be used, horizontally and vertically, to craft and nurture dynamic and strategic partnerships among firms and other mobility-relevant social institutions. These partnerships aim to effectively span what Burt (1992, 2002) refers to in market relations as "structural holes," turning them into what we call *structured wholes* for the mobility of families and communities.

Countering earlier evaluation findings that education and job training programs "don't pay," conversion of workforce development networks into structured wholes constitutes the first bridge to economic opportunity for the families here. For sustained mobility, however, these networks need to be positioned to effect reciprocal changes in firms and public policy.

The Parents' Firms

Despite good initial jobs in a wide array of industry sectors that result from the parents' workforce development programs, system reforms, and the tight economy of the late 1990s, Chapter 6 reveals that yesterday's firms seldom sustain or forward the mobility efforts of today's families. For the most part, the seventy-four firms in which the key parents work between 1998 and mid-2003 take the form of "autocratic family," "disengaged family," "fair-weather friend," or "roommate" rather than the more reciprocal form of "firm as partner" per the new mobility paradigm.

Chapters 3 and 5 show that work supports and skill training are important but not sufficient for economic mobility. Chapter 6 shows that wages, the adequacy of the wages, and how firms are organized and run profoundly affect the economic mobility of low-income families. Reportedly, these factors increasingly affect the mobility of managers and white collar workers as well (Cappelli, 1999; Osterman, 2005). While some view wage inadequacy as expectable in a capitalist political economy (Braverman, 1974; Edwards, 1979; Lafer, 2002), this chapter suggests that wage inadequacy results from choices about organizational conditions and relations that workers, firms, educators, and policymakers make according to old paradigm assumptions and myths, as other scholars see it in part (Miller, 1999, 2003; Nee, 2003; Newman, 2002; Swedberg, 2003). Turbulent global, national, and local conditions affecting the production capacities and profitability of contemporary firms, together with old paradigm forms of wage distribution, organizational structure, and relations, intersect in firms' and workers' responses to these external and internal challenges.

Despite turbulence, two in five of the families make substantial progress toward family-sustaining incomes—at least for a time. Still, three in five families do not, many of whose progress is buffeted by firm, economic, family, and policy disconnects. Although many parents change firms two or three times over the five years we know them, in line with the old paradigm view of advancement, few find that their hard work or persistence ensures mobility. For all the families, sustained mobility requires an intersecting network that consists of their firms, the economy, public policy, and their children's schools.

The Children's Schools

Children's schools influence children's mobility vertically (intergenerationally) through human capital attainment, but they also influence family mobility horizontally (intragenerationally) through their impact on parents' work. Chapter 7 details the dangers, material inadequacies, and tensions that children confront in their daily "work" at school that are likely to influence their future mobility. At the same time parents and schools both confront stumbling blocks to their respective goals because labor market and educational institutions frequently do not recognize the other's value. This chapter details two sets of intersecting but misaligned actors: first, children's schools, families, and firms; and second, children's schools, families, and public and school policies.

Further, because the institutional actors are organized and funded as silos, the communication and creative strategizing that could emerge from trusted, reciprocal

relationships is philosophically and operationally absent. Parents make many sacrifices as they strive to meet their children's educational and developmental needs,
often in the form of lost wages or lost jobs as a result of this fundamental misalignment. Inter- and intragenerational mobility are then constrained in turn. Only
where multi-institutional alignments are created, fostered, and sustained can economic mobility for low-income families be widespread. What will it take to foster
such alignment?

ENGAGING THE "PUBLIC WILL" TOWARD AN AGENDA FOR FAMILY ECONOMIC MOBILITY

During the ethnographic research and writing of this book, we expected to present
a set of policy recommendations in Chapter 8. Instead we recognize that a wealth of
program and policy strategies to move low-income families forward through work
have been offered in recent years, yet most have not been funded or implemented,
leaving one to ponder, where is the "public will"?

Accordingly, Chapter 8 expands upon the premise introduced in Chapter 2
that we (the people) *can* and *do* make choices about our own and others' well-
being that keep low-income families relatively immobile but *could* help them
be economically mobile. We articulate in this chapter how the philosophical and
distributive principles that constitute a new view of mobility, such as trust and
reciprocity, equity and equality, and above all, social relatedness can move toward
institutional structure and form. We ultimately suggest reframing the notion of
individual (personal) responsibility as "responsibility for persons" or "relational
responsibility," an action that forces attention to the interdependence and mutuality
of purpose that can improve conditions for individuals, families and institutions
alike in today's world. We conclude with a series of recommendations for action
toward an agenda for family economic mobility.

Finally, we suggest that *Jobs Aren't Enough* can be read consecutively or se-
lectively, through either engaging with the "whole story" or through focusing on
chapters that amplify particular institutional and family characteristics and experiences. As with most stories however, we believe the coherence and richness of the
book are cumulative. To enhance accessibility, we put several detailed documents
in Appendices for those who wish to more deeply examine the research design and
data.

Ultimately we hope that the book as a whole, as well as individual chapters, will
be useful for educating students about the intersecting roles in economic mobility
of stratification, poverty, education, workforce development, urban environments,
gender, race and ethnicity, families, and institutions. We hope that policymakers
and professionals will become more informed about the scope of the problems
facing millions of American families that stem from an outdated view of mobility
and be moved to remedy these through collaborative action. We hope that scholars
in economic sociology and related fields will find this book a useful contribution
toward further development of mobility theory. And finally we hope that all readers
will find the families' stories compelling enough to consider new perspectives on
mobility that can forward the country's foundational principles of interdependence,
equity and real opportunity for all.

2 From the Old to the New Economic Mobility

EVERYONE HOLDS IDEAS about how things work, what causes events, and what the good life or good world is. For centuries scholars and others have theorized in particular about people, society, and work. For example, during the period of widespread industrialization and the development of advanced capitalism, sociologists put forth various explanations for economic differences in the population. In the late 1800s, Marx (1867/1978) attributed these differences to the exploitation of workers by the owners of the means of production. Holding that mobility is impossible under capitalism, Marx argues that only a socialist revolution can eliminate economic inequality. In the early 1900s, Weber (1922/1978) expands the explanation of economic differences to class, status, and political processes, positing multiple causes and origins of economic, social, and political inequality. At the same time Weber holds that bureaucratic forms of organization both create and mediate such inequalities.

Since the mid-1900s, scholars and policymakers have focused more intensively on inequality and differential attainment, spurred by Blau and Duncan's (1967) research on stratification and mobility in education and employment. Civil rights activism and legislation, and the growing recognition that, rhetoric to the contrary, opportunity for economic mobility is for some but not all in America, subsequently led to a bifurcated line of study. Accordingly, stratification research tends to focus on the effects of ascribed individual characteristics such as race, gender, or family background on attainment (Blau & Duncan, 1967; Kerckhoff, 1996), whereas poverty research tends to focus on attained individual characteristics such as education or work experience (Danziger & Haveman, 2001), although race, as a socially constructed rather than ascribed category, is a recent focus as well (O'Connor, Tilly, & Bobo, 2001). At the same time, studies of occupations and organizations tend to examine the mobility of those at the middle to upper end of the income scale relative to professions, occupations, firms, or gender (Baron et al., 2002; Gerson 1985; Newman, 1988; Padavic & Reskin, 2002). Recent volumes extend Marx's and Weber's earlier focus on how the interaction between worker characteristics and firm structure influences attainment (Holzer, 1996; Osterman, 1999). To our knowledge, none examine how the major social institutions of family, education, labor market, and the state *intersect* to affect mobility.

The latest round of welfare and workforce reforms in 1996 and 1998 underscores the intersections among poor people, society, and work. Although scholars and the public still focus on how individual characteristics affect attainment, the discourse increasingly includes the ways that changes in the organization of firms and the labor market affect families' economic paths. The confluence of these policy and scholarly trends slowly extends the focus of inquiry about economic mobility to a broader swath of low-income workers and families like the ones in this book.

At base, powerful myths about initiative and opportunity, meritocracy, and individual responsibility form the platform for the structure and actions of the major social institutions involved in economic mobility: family, education (workforce development and children's schools), labor market (firms), and the state (public policy). Regardless of their concordance with reality, the theories or views about people, society, and work underlying these myths have essentially coalesced into a *paradigm* (Kuhn, 1970) about economic mobility: what it is, what facilitates it, what hinders it, and what the relations are between people and institutions in it. Kuhn (1970; Conant & Haugeland, 2000) ultimately defines paradigm as shared belief in the particular nature and form of a phenomenon that helps to determine what are accepted as questions and explanations. We use the notion of paradigm here to signify the constellation of myths, beliefs, assumptions, and explanations that intersect in the phenomenon of economic mobility. Importantly, the notion of paradigm incorporates both micro- and macrolevels of social organization.

This chapter critically analyzes what we call the *old paradigm for economic mobility* that has prevailed in our society since the early part of the twentieth century. We base our argument on the ways that myths about economic mobility intersect with research and scholarship on stratification and mobility, including the theoretical origins of that intellectual production. We argue that research, education and job training, firm practices, popular belief systems, and public policy all reflect an old paradigm emphasis on individual and atomistic actors and institutions and on action that is rational, self-interested, gendered, and utilitarian. We further argue that this old view of mobility is theoretically and practically limited, inappropriate, and even detrimental to many of today's workers, families, schools, firms, and policies. Thus we call for a *new paradigm for economic mobility* that acknowledges multiple intersecting institutions, social relatedness, complex choice and decision processes, and dynamic variability.

We organize this chapter to show the way that we move toward the notion of a new paradigm for economic mobility. We start with three persistent myths about economic mobility that are built on assumptions about initiative and opportunity, merit, and atomistic actors despite research findings to the contrary. We show how these individualistic assumptions are embedded in the actions of social institutions that we argue are inherently interconnected: family, education, firms, and ultimately policy. We move then to identify the perspectives and constructs of the strand of economic sociology that form the bedrock for thinking about mobility in new ways. And finally we offer initial premises to be considered toward the construction of a new paradigm or guiding view about economic mobility.

MYTHS ABOUT ECONOMIC MOBILITY

MYTH #1: "INITIATIVE GETS YOU IN THE DOOR"

"Initiative gets you in the door" is an individualistic, old paradigm myth based on the assumption that education and work are available to all but attained only by those who seize the opportunity. In the United States, a person's education epitomizes his or her "initiative" and is considered the key to moving up economically. For example, standard human capital theory predicts that wages increase with experience and time on the job, largely as a function of accumulated education and training. Thus two educational institutions are centrally implicated in the relationship between initiative and economic mobility: mandatory public schools and the voluntary workforce development system of remedial, vocational, and job training programs. The organizations in both institutional domains presumably offer clear routes to work opportunity, depending on individual initiative. The structures and practices of these educational institutions are further based on an old paradigm assumption that the opportunity for attainment is not systematically differentiated according to race, gender, ethnicity, or other ascribed characteristic such that individual initiative can overcome any inequalities that might randomly exist.

The research literature, however, tells another story about human capital attainment, initiative, and mobility. This literature identifies the complex relationship between education and skills and the mobility of low-earning workers. A "skills gap" or "skills mismatch" between the education of entry-level workers and the needs of companies is posited and attributed to the technology revolution in twenty-first-century firms (Freeman & Gottschalk, 1998). Related, the practice of deskilling is charged with thwarting mobility (Braverman, 1974; Marx, 1867/1978). In deskilling, technological progress does not necessarily replace workers by machines but lowers the skill necessary to manage those machines, as suggested by the pattern of substituting semiskilled operatives for skilled craftsmen in assembly-line production that Blau and Duncan (1967) report. In both skills explanations, conclusions about the connections between technology and mobility are contested (Morris & Western, 1999). Further, although numerous education-related explanations are offered for growing wage differentials, many scholars conclude that the overall evidence for a general increase in the demand for cognitive over mechanical skills is weak (Appelbaum, Bernhardt, & Murnane, 2003; Harrison & Weiss, 1998; Holzer, 1996; Lafer, 2002). This leaves initiative, as defined by education and skill attainment, a limited explanation for mobility.

Moreover the notion of human capital itself, as developed in contemporary economics by Becker (1976, 1993), is critiqued by Bourdieu (2001) for failing to consider processes of education within the family. As Bourdieu (p. 99) holds, "The scholastic yield from educational action depends on the cultural capital previously invested by the family." Importantly, cultural capital is *not* the motivation or values of the family toward education, but the family's ability to provide educational enrichment for children in the form of computers, encyclopedias, visits to museums, and travel, on which academic accomplishment builds cumulatively. Insufficient resources thus inherently affect the capacity of both families and schools to provide such capital for their children.

Equally problematic for human capital theories of mobility is that even in the economy of the 1990s, roughly half the workforce never goes beyond high school and more than two-thirds never attains a college degree (Duncan, Boisjoly, & Smeeding, 1996). At the same time, high-school-educated workers earn about half (51 percent) the wages of college graduates (McCall, 2000). *If* skill and knowledge are mandatory for the twenty-first-century workforce (Lafer, 2002), millions of today's workers are already behind. Some suggest, however, that at the entry and low-wage ends of the labor market, particularly for urban African American males, the "signal" effect (Beck & Colclough, 1988; Ehrenberg & Smith, 2003) of an education or job training program, whereby a firm credits the job seeker with the positive characteristics of the sponsoring organization, or the "credential effect" of a vocational certificate that Bourdieu (2001) calls institutionalized cultural capital, may be as important to occupational attainment and economic mobility as the associated skill and learning competencies (Iversen, 2002; Parsons, 1947), although Becker (1993) argues otherwise. If signals are important for mobility, the impact of social and cultural capital in schools and job programs and workforce development systems may trump the impact of human capital-based initiative on attainment.

MYTH #2: "HARD WORK PAYS OFF"

"Hard work pays off" is a myth based on an old paradigm meritocratic view of the relationship between workers and firms. In effect, if workers proceed according to the initiative that gets them in the door, the firm will reciprocate in kind. Horatio Alger and his famous maxim, *"Strive and succeed,"* epitomize this myth.

The "hard work" or "strive" part of this myth is based on an old paradigm assumption about firm structure and organization. The myth presumes that firms are organized according to career ladders that enable workers to steadily move up in job responsibility and income. This system of career ladders, also called *firm* or *internal labor markets*, is intended to protect employees from volatile external market pressures via the decisions that firms make about wages, job mobility, and training (Morris & Western, 1999), although others argue that internal labor markets provide a way for firms to control labor (Edwards, 1979). Traditional career theory posits a system of regular wage progression through internal labor markets that Hunter (1999, p. 1) characterizes as "a job structure within a firm that includes ports of entry for new workers followed by promotion from within," and that Edwards (p. 180) characterizes as "a set of procedures contained within the firm for performing the functions of the external labor market, the allocation and pricing of labor." Typically an internal labor market is characterized by a lifetime job in which wages progress regularly such that one parent can support a family while the other parent stays home. Old paradigm assumptions about linear pathways, worker and firm loyalty, hierarchical relations, gender, and time are thus entrenched in firms' policies and procedures.

A large body of literature now refutes the accuracy of these historic normative assumptions. The importance of a worker's loyalty to a firm and the presence of internal mobility ladders are both contested in today's labor market (Cappelli, 2000). Globalization, downsizing, outsourcing, and flexible management are contemporary firm practices thought to lessen job security for workers. In effect, "flexibility" describes changing employment relationships from the perspective of employers, whereas "insecurity" describes such changes from the perspective of workers (McCall, 2000, p. 238). Although scholars disagree about the extent and nature of the decline in protected internal labor markets, most agree that secure, firm-based career pathways have eroded (Bernhardt et al., 2001), especially for low-earning workers (Osterman, 1999; Osterman et al., 2001). Others argue that career ladders are less one dimensional and automatic than internal labor market theory posits and that the notion of career-tree models with varied branches and portals to and from key positions is more descriptive of how firms are actually organized (Rosenbaum, 1990).

The "payoff" or "succeed" part of the meritocracy myth pertains to wage income. Wage growth is considered a fundamental measure of a successful career, which puts it at the core of economic mobility (Bernhardt et al., 2001). This myth also presumes that even people who grow up in poverty can incrementally accrue family-supporting wages if they work hard and play by the rules of the firm. Traditional career theory holds that the majority of lifetime wage growth occurs during the first ten to fifteen years in the labor market whereas steady but slower growth occurs thereafter (Blau & Duncan, 1967; Bernhardt et al.). On this view, remaining in the same firm is the typical route to wage advancement after an initial period of job hopping yields sizeable increases in income.

Recent research finds that wage mobility for low-earning workers is now predominantly lateral rather than vertical (Carnevale & Rose , 2001; Osterman, 1999). Wage growth for less educated workers may seem larger in job changes between than within firms (Duncan, Boisjoly, & Smeeding, 1996), but only because wage growth tends to be low when they work for the same employer, not because their wage returns to job change are high. Importantly, changing firm patterns and mobility outcomes pertain not only to low-income earners and men but also increasingly to women and middle-income earners (Cappelli, 1999; Hachen, 1990; Rank, 2004). Moreover, wage disadvantage is found to be cumulative over time: low returns to job changing early in the career accumulate to generate a persistent low-wage path (Bernhardt et al., 2001). Thus the expected pattern of substantial wage increase over time and tenure no longer pertains, especially for those less well educated. Gottschalk (2001) cautions further that there is considerable heterogeneity in wage growth both within and between firms. The bottom line is a marked deterioration in upward economic mobility that Bernhardt and colleagues characterize as "one that threatens the meaning of prosperity in postindustrial America" (p. 111). The authors conclude that the "structure of economic mobility has been fundamentally transformed, to the detriment of the majority of the workforce" (p. 126).

Other recent research shows that the payoff to hard work is affected by gender, race and type of work schedule. Morris and Western (1999) report that at the top of the income distribution men's wages hold in value from 1973 to 1996, but wages at the bottom decile drop by 20 percent. In contrast, the gains for the average woman worker are modest at about 5 percent but the gains for women in the top decile are nearly 30 percent. McCall's (2000) recent findings mirror this pattern, noting further that the real wage of low-skilled women has declined. At best, women's earnings per se remain only about three-fourths of men's (U.S. Census Bureau, 2004a).

Less commitment or attachment to work is a gendered old paradigm explanation for the wage differential between women and men. Women are thought to choose to work fewer hours than men or to prefer work at lower paying jobs in a tradeoff for other benefits such as flexible time or less stress. For these and similar reasons women are also thought to seek jobs in lower paying industries. In addition, the assumption still prevails that young women, unlike men, are only intermittently attached to the labor market (Keith & McWilliams, 1995). The explanation for wage inequality underlying Myth #2 is that women don't work hard enough for it to pay off.

In contrast, empirical studies find that women are more strongly attached to the labor force than are men. Bielby and Bielby (2002) suggest that net of other factors there is either no relationship between gender and work commitment or a slight tendency for women to exhibit higher levels of commitment than men. In reality, women have long constituted a significant part of the labor force. In 2003, women's labor force participation rate is 59.5 percent, and they comprise 47 percent of the total labor force (U.S. Department of Labor, 2004). Between 1950 and 2000 the number of women in the paid labor force increases by more than 250 percent (AFL-CIO, 2004). In contrast, the labor force participation rate of men declines from 80 percent in 1970 to 76 percent in 2003 (AFL-CIO). Other recent evidence suggests that each new cohort of women that enters the labor market exhibits higher overall participation rates, more continuous participation, and more education than the one before (Keith & McWilliams, 1995, p. 126).

Analyzing the payoff to meritorious hard work according to race shows a different story. As Morris and Western (1999, p. 627) report, "The decline in the race gap in income that began in the 1960s, ended in the early 1970s and reversed by the mid-1970s, leaves blacks in the early 1990s at about the same earnings levels as in the late 1970s." Corcoran's (1995) review finds that being born into a black rather than a white family dramatically reduces a child's adult economic prospects, a finding that replicates Blau and Duncan's (1967) report over three decades earlier. Moreover black men who find jobs will likely encounter discrimination in the labor market that constrains their economic futures (Moss & Tilly, 2001).

The payoff to hard work also depends on the type of work schedule a firm offers. The expectation of payoff is founded on the assumption of full-time year-round work. In 1993, twenty-one million workers (19 percent of the U.S. workforce) worked part time (Tilly, 1996, p. 13). Although in recent decades fewer women work part time and more work full time, women still comprise two-thirds of the part-time workforce (Tilly), often not by choice. Although gender explains almost half of the increase of the rate of part-time employment between 1969 and 1979 in Tilly's study, it explains none of the increase after 1979. Moreover, many part-time workers prefer to be employed full time, and workers with this preference are growing faster than the workforce as a whole (Albelda & Tilly, 1997, p. 50). Old paradigm assumptions about normative full-time work schedules may pertain to yesterday's firms but far less to today's, thus payoff depends on firms' structural practices as well as on individuals' hard work.

MYTH #3: "PULL YOURSELF UP BY YOUR BOOTSTRAPS"

The myth that it is possible to "pull yourself up by your bootstraps" is based on an old paradigm assumption about individual actors who exemplify normative demographic characteristics. In earlier decades the entry-level labor market is populated by young, single, white, physically fit men who are generally high school graduates. According to Blau and Duncan (1967), such men are assumed to be in preparatory stages of their careers. In reality, bootstraps were never enough to achieve mobility, even for these workers. Vocational guidance in schools, nepotism in firms' hiring practices and apprenticeships, and use of contacts, now viewed as social networks or social capital resources, have always been operative factors in mobility.

Today's entry-level workers at preparatory stages of their careers are often without such social resources. They are young school dropouts and parents or they are older parents with children and partners or other family members to support. They may be male, female, multiethnic, undereducated, or underskilled. They may be immigrants or political refugees or they may have spent time in prison or rehabilitation facilities. Moreover, as older parents they are firmly lodged in the child-rearing years that are normally among the poorest years of individuals' work lives (Gitterman, Howard, & Cotton, 2003). In most ways then, these workers are chronologically and substantively mismatched to the demands and the lessened reciprocity, loyalty, and wage sufficiency of today's entry-level jobs, what we call a *life-stage mismatch* (Iversen, 2002). This life-stage mismatch is reminiscent of what Grint (1991, p. 2) calls "the allegedly archetypal significance of the male factory worker isolated from his domestic world." In reality, the fact that the mobility of these new workers benefits from policy supports and new forms of intersecting organizations, such as workforce intermediaries and workforce development networks (Giloth, 2004b; Iversen, 2004; Osterman et al., 2001), rebuts the view of mobility as an atomistic bootstrap process in favor of the view that mobility is relationally embedded.

Choice and decision processes are also related to bootstrap notions. According to the old view of mobility, choices are made rationally, instrumentally, and individually based on a calculus of costs and benefits relative to job opportunities. In the old view, although decisions may be conceptualized as "contingent," the relevant contingencies are typically seen as individual characteristics. The structure and practices of most welfare and workforce programs exemplify this view. Related research focuses on which program aspects facilitate participants' optimal job choices (Clymer, Roder, & Roberts, 2005; Kauff, Derr, & Pavetti, 2004). In contrast, a new mobility perspective views choice and decision "preferences and actions as fundamentally connected to and affected by cognitive biases ... nonconscious and ambivalent feelings, role expectations, norms and cultural frames ... classifications and myths" (Guillen et al., 2002, p. 7). Importantly, recent views about decision making acknowledge that family members and social capital resources often represent critical aspects of choice processes. Major decisions are not made in isolation of persons and conditions that influence workers' family and economic lives. In effect, decision processes take the form of "intercontingencies" rather than simple contingencies (Becker, 1998).

March and Simon's (1958) notions of "bounded rationality" and "satisficing" also challenge the view of choice making and decision making held by institutions and programs that reflect the old view of mobility. Recognizing that choices and decisions are often made under conditions of considerable complexity, the authors posit that bounded rationality, or cognitive processes that are subjective and contextual, and satisficing, or concentrating on a few salient problem areas, are more descriptive of choice making and decision making than are the classical rational choice notions of ordered preferences, balancing gains and risks, and maximizing utility. Similarly informative, Kahneman and Tversky (Kahneman, 2003) hold that relative to current status, people are more likely to make decisions to avoid risk or loss than decisions that hold out the possibility of gain—the opposite of what rational choice theorists predict. In other words, when the properties of alternative options are evaluated as advantages or disadvantages relative to one's current situation, the disadvantages of the alternatives loom larger than the advantages. Kahneman and Tversky (Kahneman) also find that people's choices are influenced by their emotional responses to the way that choices are framed and ordered. This has long been recognized in survey and market research but less so in job training and career assessment practices. These perspectives on choice and decision processes thus have profound implications for the direction and content of welfare and workforce development programs.

In a related view, Granovetter (1978) amplifies Durkheim's (1933/1984) notion that most individual actions are influenced by a "collective consciousness" to posit what he called bandwagon or domino effects in group decision making. Granovetter finds that outcomes (choices or decisions) are driven by the distribution of thresholds at which each person in a group will act. Notably, thresholds are constructed through social interaction or observation of the behavior of others. However different from "social contagion" models, the decisive factor is each person's individual threshold for action in terms of the number of others in the group whose action thresholds are similar. We argue that the threshold process might also apply to decision making in contexts such as the family, school, workforce development program, or job in which choices and decisions may be influenced by relationships or network ties. Granovetter suggests, in fact, that the bandwagon model may also pertain to small-group settings. Implications of these challenges to the old paradigm view about choice and decision processes are particularly germane to the policy arena.

MOBILITY MYTHS AND PUBLIC POLICY

The three mobility myths and their accompanying old paradigm assumptions also intersect in the policy arena, especially as these assumptions are reflected in the design, formulation and implementation of welfare and workforce policy and programs (Bartik, 2001; Duncan & Chase-Lansdale, 2001; Edin & Lein, 1997; Friedlander & Burtless, 1995; Iversen, 2000; Lafer, 2002). Recent "welfare reform" legislation, the Personal Responsibility and Work Opportunity Reconciliation Act of 1996 and its Temporary Assistance to Needy Families (TANF) program, lends initiative to welfare leavers, which enables them to enter the door of economic mobility through work. Time limits and mandatory work requirements are designed to ensure the hard work it takes to get off welfare and stay off through steady employment. TANF's welfare-to-work programs prioritize "work first" over education and skill training accordingly. TANF programs reflect a bootstraps perspective in that limited postemployment follow-up and support are considered sufficient for families to become economically self-supporting. At that point presumably the normative old paradigm career pathway will be launched.

Similar to TANF, the core service of the "workforce development reform" legislation, the Workforce Investment Act of 1998 (WIA) and its One-Stop Career

Center system, is work attachment. Intensive services and job training through an Individual Training Account voucher system are available primarily when the prior service component does not result in employment. Although WIA requires twelve months of follow-up job search or postemployment support, which may be extended until an individual achieves "self-sufficiency" as defined by a local workforce development area, limited funding makes more than twelve months of follow-up rare. WIA's predominant "work first" orientation, despite the carrot of training for some, also reflects the old paradigm bootstraps perspective.

Policy-funding streams also reflect outdated old paradigm assumptions. Much as workers are viewed as atomistic actors rather than as families, funding is disseminated through siloed rather than integrated streams. As Eisenstadt (1963/1993) argues historically, silos ensure that a central administrative body provides resources to various interest groups—or "lower authorities" as Weber (1915/1946) calls them—such that resources from these groups are mobilized in return. Although Eisenstadt refers to the ways that institutionalized political systems develop out of autonomous regimes and empires, his framework may apply to the siloed structure and funding of contemporary institutions as well. Many modern bureaucracies function along lines that are similar to Eisenstadt's early "bureaucratic empires": independent groups vie for resources and power to protect their turf and a centralized administrative and fiscal structure allocates resources on the basis of political capital and expected resource reciprocity. Silos thus sustain the bureaucratic order.

So it is with the contemporary American political structure. The federal bureaucracy is organized into self-contained departments that vie for budget allocation, use the resources they receive reciprocally for their own resource production (i.e., the job they are charged to do), and thus ensure their survival. As Weber (1915/1946) acknowledges in his typology of a pure bureaucracy, a silo structure may be inefficient and less than ideally effective in a complex intersecting society. Metaphorically, the right hand may not know what the left hand is doing—each is invisible to the other. In the sphere of public policy then, the targeted beneficiaries may be the ones to suffer from this lack of integration, and because of the risk of turf and funding loss, potentially more fruitful collaborations seldom emerge. Although the federally funded workforce development system under WIA aims to consolidate departments and funding streams, few states have succeeded in this to date. Consolidation is not even a goal of TANF.

In sum, despite contradictory research and institutional explanations, individualistic myths and their underlying assumptions about human and organizational behavior underpin what we call the old paradigm for economic mobility. The experiences of the families and their associated auxiliaries in this book graphically illustrate how and where these myths and assumptions persist. The families' relative *lack* of economic mobility, despite initiative and hard work, and the ways they benefit from sustained policy and relational supports versus being relegated to bootstrap isolation, propel us toward the vision of a new economic mobility. Selected concepts from economic sociology further move us toward the construction of new theoretical components that, if applied across social institutions, might result in economic mobility for many more working families.

ECONOMIC SOCIOLOGY AND A NEW
ECONOMIC MOBILITY

Over the past couple of decades a strand of scholars in economic sociology has blended concepts from economics and sociology to more fully explore the ways in which labor market and individual processes intersect. For example, Swedberg (2003, p. xi) defines economic sociology as "the patterns of social interaction and the institutions that people create and use in their attempts to make a living and a profit." Patterns of particular relevance to economic mobility involve the notions of reciprocity, trust, context, power, structured institutional relations, family and social network relations, and norms, values and preferences.

Given economic sociologists' concern with processes *and* outcomes, as well as with equality *and* efficiency, pioneering work by Granovetter (1973, 1983, 1985, 1995) examines job search processes as socially and economically embedded phenomena. Granovetter argues that sociological processes such as social networks, coworker relations, and firm practices are critical factors in labor mobility, not simply market processes alone. Subsequent research refines knowledge about job search categories, career dynamics, and firms' recruitment procedures, but infrequently assesses the link among these phenomena and differential wage outcomes (Granovetter, 1988, 1995). Although neither his nor others' work in the area finds a systematic association between job search methods and wages, Granovetter (1995) suggests that methodological issues may influence this lack of association.

Despite the early attention to labor mobility, recent work in economic sociology seems puzzlingly muted about this area of study (a notable exception is Granovetter, 1988). For example, the topic of "mobility," "economic mobility," "stratification," or "inequality" each appears in the index of only one of four major volumes in the field (Guillen et al., 2002; Granovetter & Swedberg, 2001; Swedberg, 2003; Brinton & Nee, 1998), although one index (Swedberg, 2003) lists both poverty and stratification. At the same time these scholars and we heed Granovetter's (2002, p. 54) charge: "The challenge for the new century is to build theory for the more general case where contexts, structure, and individual actions interact and change together." As Swedberg (p. 289) adds, "it would be very strange if economic sociology was *not* concerned with the end result of the economic process—or who gets what and how." Moreover, Fligstein (2000, p. 63) holds that in economic sociology, "households, labor markets, firms and product markets are all legitimate objects of study."

Our ethnographic findings form a platform from which to use the relational, multi-institutional perspective of this strand of economic sociology to move toward a new paradigm for economic mobility. The use of ethnography for the exploration of economic mobility is in concert with what the authors of a major review of literature on mobility and income inequality suggest: "As the link between firm restructuring and wage inequality begins to be made, it is natural that we return to *individuals' work histories* to analyze whether wage growth has deteriorated, whether the rate of job changing has increased, and how the sequence unfolds over the life course" (Morris & Western, 1999, p. 652). Granovetter and Swedberg (2001, p. 15) urge "a generally social perspective that sets the interactions of real people at its center" (p. 1), in particular, "to take into account how and why the actors, *in their own view*, do as they do." Ethnographic methods and findings thus move the discourse about economic mobility from the solitary and proprietary perspective of the analyst to the multiple viewpoints of all involved actors. So doing, theory as well as knowledge develops inductively.

Granovetter (1985) argues similarly that it is important to embed both supply and demand factors in institutional contexts. Likewise, Morris and Western (1999) argue that systems of education and training, labor exchanges, social welfare, and the penal system all figure prominently as institutional sources of inequality in sociological research. These positions undergird our focus on multiple social institutions and their intersections in considering a new paradigm for economic mobility.

Finally, Bernhardt and colleagues (2001, p. 16) reinforce the importance of the topic of economic mobility: "Mobility is key to a definitive assessment of the emerging postindustrial economy, for mobility is where the link between labor market structure and individual life history is made, where we gain insight into the dynamic processes that actually generate inequality, and where we assess how well America is meeting its meritocratic ideal." We argue that the link needs to be made between labor market structure and the life histories of *whole families*. Understanding the lives of individual workers to be inextricably entwined with the lives of their family members leads us to the view that "workers are families, not individuals." We pose this as a contextual construct to emphasize that the idea of worker embeddedness in families is critical to a new paradigm, especially in relation to job choices and actions.

TOWARD A NEW ECONOMIC MOBILITY

We propose four premises toward a new paradigm for economic mobility. These premises suggest that multiple and multidirectional institutional influence, social relatedness, complex choice and decision processes, and dynamism are necessary components for thinking about and analyzing contemporary economic mobility. The premises are lodged briefly here in the theoretical and research literature and more deeply in subsequent chapters in the ethnographic findings.

PREMISE #1: MULTIPLE INSTITUTIONS ARE INTEGRAL TO ECONOMIC MOBILITY, AND THE DIRECTION OF INSTITUTIONAL INFLUENCE IS SIMULTANEOUSLY VERTICAL AND HORIZONTAL

Multiple institutions constitute society and its opportunity structure for economic mobility. As Polanyi (2001, p. 36) put it almost fifty years ago, "The human economy is embedded and enmeshed in institutions, economic and noneconomic." Although Polanyi's use of the term embeddedness is slightly different from current use, Granovetter (1985) subsequently argues that economic actions are embedded in concrete, ongoing systems of social relations and later suggests the opposite as well—that networks or social relationships exist in all market interactions (Granovetter, 2002). Swedberg (2003, p. 28) also argues that "an economic action is in principle always 'embedded' in some form or another of social structure."

Trust, power, reciprocity, and shared meanings thus become salient components (Fligstein, 2002).

We extend this direction to suggest that economic processes are embedded and enmeshed in *all* major social institutions, not just labor market institutions. The institutions of import here are the family, education, the labor market, and public policy. Grint (1991, p. 2) also argues that "The spheres of work, employment, and home are necessarily intertwined. To separate them as if they could exist independently is to misconceive the complex reality of work and misunderstand the significance of the relationships which it embodies." We argue that educational institutions and public policy need to be added to Grint's essential entwinement, as these institutions are also inseparably entwined with those of family and labor market.

Most important, these institutions intersect *simultaneously*, vertically and horizontally, to influence processes such as economic mobility. Historically, the influence of education on work and mobility has been conceptualized and examined individualistically and *vertically*, as a property of individuals and as a process between persons and institutions that may involve power and compliance. For example, a worker's level of education influences his or her job pathway and children's school performance influences their future attainment. Although the source of authority in each case is different, power may be a factor in both.

A new paradigm holds that children's educational institutions influence parents' and children's economic mobility through *horizontal* channels as well. Policies and practices in children's schools cumulatively influence not only parents' employability but also parents' choices about jobs and their ability to retain and advance in jobs. In like manner, policies and procedures in firms, as they intersect with those in children's schools, affect parents' ability to reinforce or ameliorate their children's school behavior and performance. A new economic mobility draws particular attention to these horizontal institutional intersections. Although horizontal relations may involve trust and cooperation, that is not always the case. Improved horizontal relations may, however, increase trust and cooperation and decrease the power imbalance and alienation that often inheres to vertical relations (Granovetter, 2002).

We caution, however, that to some extent the concept of "institution" ineluctably denotes a silo. If one thinks about the family as institution, its integrity is based on privacy and autonomy from the state and other "public" bodies. Education, labor market and policy institutions are constructed according to a similar atomistic conception. We may eventually have to generate new terms to signify intersection and interconnectedness. Perhaps the idea of *structured wholes* that we develop in Chapter 5, building on Burt's (1992) concept of structural holes, moves in this direction.

PREMISE #2: ECONOMIC MOBILITY IS A THOROUGHLY RELATIONAL PROCESS THAT REQUIRES SOCIAL AND CULTURAL CAPITAL IN ADDITION TO HUMAN CAPITAL

On the view of mobility as a relational process, explanations that give primacy to the attainment of human capital should be extended by explanations that incorporate the accumulation of social and cultural capital.

Many social scientists theorize about the concept of "capital," Marx, Weber, Simmel, Coleman, Becker, Bourdieu, and Lin among them. In most formulations, capital is both a thing and a set of relations. Coleman (1990, p. 304) defines human capital as what "is created by changing persons so as to give them skills and capabilities (thing) that make them able to act in new ways." Economic mobility then is commonly thought to be a function of the match between the human capital characteristics of the individual and the skill and education requirements of the firm. Educational and training institutions are the main purveyors of human capital, directly to individuals and thus indirectly to firms.

In recent decades more complex views about capital have been constructed—social capital and cultural capital, in particular—that emphasize the set of relations more than the thing. Arguably, contemporary ideas about social capital have roots in Weber's (1922/1978, p. 68) *Economy and Society*, in which he holds that "social relationships which are valued as a potential source of present or future disposal over utilities are, however, also objects of economic provisions." Although Adler and Kwon (2000) critique the concept of social capital as too inclusive, Woolcock (1998) characterizes it as over-explanatory, and Portes (1998) cautions that it can be used in exclusionary ways, Coleman (1990, p. 304) defines social capital as "what is created when the relations among persons change in ways that facilitate action." Similarly, Putnam (1995, p. 67) describes social capital as "features of social organization such as networks, norms, and social trust that facilitate co-ordination and cooperation for mutual benefit," and Lin (2001, p. 25) defines it as the "resources embedded in social networks accessed and used by actors for actions." Social capital is thus not embodied in an individual but in the *relations* among persons—generally persons in the social rather than immediate family environment. Social networks, social programs, and educational and workforce development institutions are considered sources of social capital, especially when the ties between person and source are "weak" and broad rather than "strong" and narrow (Granovetter, 1973, 1995).

Within the social capital concept, Zelizer (2002) expands on Granovetter's weak and strong ties with the notion of "differentiated ties" which recognizes that people differentiate among particular kinds of interpersonal relations and give these relations unique names and meaning that in turn form different practices, rights and obligations. Differentiated ties thus form in all spheres of social life, including schools, religious organizations, firms, and policy settings, and are often salient to choice and decision processes. The crucial point for economic mobility, as evidenced by the families and auxiliaries throughout this book, is that fundamental concepts like trust, power, norms, and meaning cannot be understood except in relational terms: their very definition relies on social relationships, they are produced in social networks (Granovetter, 2002), and they are dynamic (Woolcock, 1998).

Cultural capital, on the other hand, resides largely in the relations among family members, within the family as social institution. Whether embodied in the form of personal dispositions (i.e., culture and cultivation), objectified in the form of cultural goods (i.e., computers and art), or institutionalized in the form of educational certification (Bourdieu, 1998, 2001), different accumulation of cultural capital generally results in different attainment. The ways in which the horizontal intersections among low-income families, resource-poor children's schools, and low-wage firms foster or constrain the development of cultural capital are thus relevant to intra- and intergenerational economic mobility.

By the use of multiple formulations of capital, the concept of the "individual" can be replaced by the concept of overarching social and institutional relatedness. A relational view of persons and responsibility incorporates processes of social and cultural capital in addition to human capital, as all are necessary for economic mobility. A relational view of institutions opposes viewing them as isolated or free-standing silos, which is the way they are generally structured and funded, and understands them to be philosophically, structurally, and practically interconnected in ways that can potentially exert more leverage for economic mobility.

PREMISE #3: CHOICES AND DECISIONS INTEGRAL TO ECONOMIC MOBILITY INVOLVE COGNITIVE AND EMOTIONAL PROCESSES

Scholars report that individuals seek jobs that provide valued extrinsic and intrinsic characteristics (Johnson, 2001): in other words, pay and status *and* a work environment that may be social, enjoyable, or flexible. In the American employment opportunity structure, individuals must often make choices and tradeoffs between such characteristics (Dwyer, 2004), but the old view of mobility posits that such choices and actions occur through rational, intentional analysis. Job seekers are thought to calculate the gains and losses of possible job opportunities and choose the one that will maximize gains and minimize losses. In reality, both cognitive and emotional processes are used to resolve co-occurring and potentially conflicting goals such as income, family cohesion, stress reduction, and work pathways.

For example, men supposedly choose a job according to a two-way cost-benefit analysis of the job's intrinsic characteristics and their needs, viewing providing financially for self or family as the calculus for the decision. Decision making for women, on the other hand, is thought to involve the same two-way process *plus* a third one—that of balancing responsibility for children's emotional as well as financial subsistence. Women's decision process is thus exponentially more complicated and more emotionally fraught. It is also one that many contemporary fathers share. It seems then that the job choice calculus for both men and women in today's America, perhaps especially for low earners who contend simultaneously with the challenges of dangerous neighborhoods, insufficient incomes, inadequate housing, unaffordable or unavailable childcare, and other disadvantages of impoverished urban environments, involves incorporating work, family, *and* other institutional variables.

Thus the new view of economic mobility posits job choice as cognitive, value-laden, and influenced by social and institutional ties. The new view also holds that the notion of separate, gendered job decision processes no longer pertains. Information is always incomplete, thus interpretation and meaning become salient. In contrast to the pure instrumentalism of rational choice explanations of motivation and behavior, Granovetter (2002, p. 38, emphasis in the original) argues that "people typically pursue multiple purposes simultaneously in intersecting social formations" and that outcomes from these interactions *"cannot be accounted for by the incentives of individuals."* Sen (1977) amplifies Granovetter's point. Even though Sen holds a relatively instrumental view, he argues that actors may make choices that are contrary to their economic or other self-interest if they are propelled to this goal by value commitments. For example, although prioritizing children's immediate needs may limit a parent's economic mobility, this commitment may outweigh what rational choice-based programs and policymakers often view as the *irrational* job choices and actions that low-earning parents make. Such a perspective is useful for understanding why job seekers drop out of training programs, why low earners switch to an even lower paying job, and why parents may have little tolerance for discordant working conditions. Similarly, children's future decisions about work and mobility may be influenced by both cognitive and emotional responses to their parents' low-wage work. As Zelizer (2002, p. 296) cautions, "So long as analysts presume a sharp, consequential distinction between one world of instrumental rationality and another of sentimental solidarity, they will never adequately describe, explain, prescribe or intervene in sites where intimate ties and economic transactions collide."

When one considers further that the "benefit" aspect of the rational choice calculus in terms of work opportunity may be complexly influenced by experiences or perceptions of racism, the absence of internal advancement ladders, low wages, moderate or no nonwage benefits, and few on-the-job advancement opportunities, parents may choose immediate benefits to their children, such as sufficient time to oversee homework and other direct parenting tasks, over promising but risky benefits available in the workplace. The choice and decision processes of the families in this book repeatedly illustrate how the complexity or contingency of these processes influences economic mobility.

PREMISE #4: ECONOMIC MOBILITY PATHWAYS ARE INCREASINGLY DYNAMIC AND VARIABLE

In the new view of economic mobility, the old mobility concept of predictable, normative career paths is replaced by the view that career paths are increasingly dynamic and variable. This dynamism and variability results in part from the fact that increased numbers of older, familied, multiethnic workers are trying to forge career paths in firms that are changing at the same time; in other words, the lifestage mismatch. The reward structure of the new economy also contributes to the dynamism and variability of mobility, as industry shifts influence patterns of wage growth. For example, Bernhardt and colleagues (2001, p. 147, Table 6.7) report that the finance, insurance, and real estate industries, as well as professional services, now rank disproportionately in the top decile for wage growth, whereas construction, manufacturing, entertainment, public administration, and wholesale and retail trade have dropped relative to their earlier position. Organizational practices within individual firms, such as type of schedule, use of outsourcing, and skill requirements dynamically influence the variability in wage growth and mobility as well. In effect, wage growth is to a great extent an intersection of education and skill training, access to jobs, and the robustness of the opportunity structure in particular occupations and firms. As a result, the matching of persons and jobs must consider not only the wage distribution and mobility opportunities in an industry sector as a whole but also how a firm or occupation performs in terms of others in that industry.

New partnerships and organizational forms for helping low-income workers access, keep, and advance in jobs, such as workforce intermediaries (Giloth, 2004b; Iversen, 2004; Meléndez, 2004; Osterman et al., 2001), exemplify one response to the intersection of the new demography and the dynamism of today's firms. The view that mobility occurs through relationship and negotiated processes, rather than through atomized individual efforts, is at the core of local or regional workforce development networks in which workforce intermediaries form the nucleus. Perhaps most important, these processes are dynamic not static, as Granovetter and other scholars recently note (Krippner et al., 2004). Although workforce intermediaries may not be sufficient (Iversen, 2002; Lafer, 2002), they and other new forms of organization may comprise an increasingly necessary component of economic mobility (Iversen; Taylor & Rubin, 2005).

SUMMARY

The myths and assumptions underlying what we call the old paradigm for economic mobility no longer apply to many of today's workers, families, firms, or policies. Those moving toward a new paradigm might hold that economic mobility is lodged in a dynamic nexus of actors, social institutions, and social networks, not in individuals alone. Without the redistributive influence of broad social networks and public policies, structural aspects of contemporary institutions mired in outdated assumptions and myths block opportunity for millions of hard-working parents and children. The families in this book demonstrate grit, self-reliance, and perseverance, but their Alger-like big chance has not come, as Chapters 5 through 7 illustrate. Alger's message is too simple for today's complex world. As the voices throughout the chapters challenge the truth of opportunity, meritocracy, and individual responsibility, we argue that in all social institutions, trusted networks, reciprocal responsibility relations, and shared beliefs (Iversen, Furstenberg, & Belzer, 1999; Nee, 2003) about social and economic phenomena are essential rungs on any ladder of real opportunity in contemporary America.

Above all, given the persistence of outdated explanations and assumptions about economic mobility and the equally persistent disregard of years of contrary evidence, a paradigm shift calls for significant change in the "public will" toward understanding the inadequacy of the "frontier individual" myth in contemporary society, toward accepting that a healthy, thriving United States *requires* reciprocity and cooperation among the social institutions of family, education, labor market, and state, and toward acting on these realities. Our explicit hope is that the family stories in this book will be informative and useful toward this end.

3   The Parents

Their Backgrounds, Lives, and Locations

"Never Give Up"

Never give up on your dreams.
Times are hard sometimes; I want to scream.
Just hang in there and tough it out.
You know, that is what it's all about.
Keep your faith and you will see,
You can be what you want to be.
Stay in school no matter what you do.
You are the prizewinner so keep your head cool.
Never give up, no matter how hard the ride seems.
Never give up on your dreams.
                    —*Written by Rachel Quinn, New Orleans*

WHO ARE THE PARENTS IN THIS BOOK?

The section under "The Story," which opens Chapter 1, provides a broad brush of who the parents are in this book. More detailed information about them in this chapter sets the stage for learning how their intersections with other social institutions forward or constrain their goal of economic mobility. We first ask: are the parents in this book unique or are they similar to other low-income working parents in the United States today? In fact we find that on selected characteristics that are believed to influence economic mobility, the twenty-five key parents seem very similar to millions of other low-income working parents across the country. The chapter then looks more intensively at these characteristics at the time the parents enter a job training program[1]: specifically, their age, gender, racial or ethnic background, family composition, education, public assistance, work supports, work history, assets, and health. We also examine how these characteristics change over our years of contact with the families.

The second part of the chapter looks at economic mobility in terms of prevailing economic and labor market conditions and the housing environment of the families in each of the five cities: Milwaukee, New Orleans, Philadelphia, St. Louis, and Seattle. Does "place" matter to the families' experiences and outcomes? Is place determinative? We find that place plays a role in the *particular* ways a family experiences poverty and mobility, which in turn has implications for the design and implementation of policies and programs at the local level. We ultimately conclude that family mobility outcomes are affected more deeply and pervasively by national economic trends and characteristics of the low-wage labor market.

Table 3.1 gives an overview of the twenty-five key parents and how they compare on selected characteristics to three groups: (1) all adults placed in or locating

TABLE 3.1. Key Parents Compared to All Training Program Participants Placed in or Locating Jobs, UI Recipients, and TANF Recipients: Selected Characteristics

Characteristics	Key parents $n = 25$ (%)	All adults placed in or locating jobs in the five cities[a] $n = 3999$ (%)	UI recipients in 1998[b] $n = 3907$ (%)	TANF participants in 2001[c] $n = 268{,}575$ (%)
Age				
Age 18 to 35	52	64	34 (16–34)	74 (20–39)
< 18, > 35	48	36		7 (Teens)
Gender				
Male	36	50	56	10
Female	64	50	44	90
Ethnicity				
White, non-Hispanic	4	11	66	30
Black	72	70	13	39
Hispanic	20	6	13	26
American Indian or Alaskan Native	0	2	9.3 (All other)	1
Asian, Pacific Islander, or Filipino	4	7		2
Other	0	3		1
Difficulty with English				
Yes	12	11		
No	88	89		
Marital Status[d]				
Single	72	77		67
Married	28	23		12
School/Highest Grade Completed				
< 8	0	2		6 (0–6 years)
8	0	2		12 (7–9 years)
9	8	4		
10	8	9		30 (10–11 years)
11	20	15		
12	44	41		49 (12 years)
13	12	12		3 (13+ years)
14	0	8		
15	4	2		
16	4	4		
17 or over	0	1		
School Certification				
No Certification	16	12	18	
High School Diploma	60	46	54 (Dipl. + GED)	
GED	20	14		
Technical Certificate	12	8	16 (Tech +	
Vocational/Occup. Skills	28	13	Voc/Occup. + Assoc.)	
Associates Degree	0	3		
B.A.	4	3	9	
Other		3	3	

TABLE 3.1. (*continued*)

Characteristics	Key parents $n = 25$ (%)	All adults placed in or locating jobs in the five cities[a] $n = 3999$ (%)	UI recipients in 1998[b] $n = 3907$ (%)	TANF participants in 2001[c] $n = 268,575$ (%)
Family Income at Training Program Enrollment				
< $3,000	16	25		
$3,000–$5,999	28	19		
$6,000–$8,999	12	14		
$9,000–$11,999	8	11		
$12,000–$14,999	12	10		
$15,000–$19,999	12	8		
$20,000–$24,999	4	5		
> $25,000	8	7		
Public Assistance at Training Program Enrollment				
TANF + Other	84	56		100
No	16	44		

[a] Hebert et al. (2002).
[b] Needels, Corson, & Nicholson (2001).
[c] U.S. Department of Health and Human Services (2001).
[d] Total TANF does not equal 100% because some states switch two-parent families to other assistance programs.

jobs after participating in demonstration-affiliated training programs in the five cities, (2) unemployment insurance (UI) recipients, and (3) Temporary Assistance to Needy Families (TANF) recipients. TANF is the implementation program of the "welfare reform" legislation of 1996 that requires work in exchange for public assistance and imposes a lifetime limit of sixty months of assistance.

We compare the key parents with other adults locating jobs after training programs affiliated with the demonstration to assess whether they are representative of this broader universe of program completers. We compare the key parents to UI and TANF recipients because UI is increasingly the "safety net" for low-wage workers after implementation of welfare reform (Rangarajan & Razafindrakoto, 2004), and because at least one parent in most of the families draws upon TANF assistance (formerly Aid to Families with Dependent Children [AFDC]) at some point in their adult lives. In addition, although some parents who are eligible for UI draw upon it during our contact with them, those who are not eligible—or those who don't know whether they're eligible—may utilize TANF assistance for short periods between jobs (Vroman, 2002). We use chi-square analysis to test for similarities and differences between the key parents and adults in the other three groups. Although organization and administrative records are often inadequate sources of data (Becker, 1998), we know of no systematic deficiency in record-keeping across sites that would bias the findings in Table 3.1.

How typical are these low-earning parents? First, we find no significant differences between the key parents and the almost four thousand other adults who attain jobs after attending demonstration-affiliated job training programs in the five cities. Second, given the size of the UI and TANF samples, some comparisons between those groups and the key parent group are statistically but not substantively significant, as we discuss later. Overall the key parents are more similar to than different from the recipients of UI and TANF. These comparisons thus suggest that at least on one set of characteristics salient to economic mobility, the twenty-five key parents are *not* unique and that their experiences may be generally shared by millions of other working parents and their families across the United States.

AGE, GENDER, RACE, AND ETHNIC IDENTIFICATION

Although the key parents range in age from eighteen to forty-five years, they are in their early thirties (average thirty-two) at our first contact with them. They are similar in age to UI recipients and slightly older than TANF recipients ($\chi^2 = 13.7, p = .0002$).

Nine key parents are male and sixteen parents are female. Recipients of UI tend to be slightly more male ($\chi^2 = 4.0, p = 0.04$); and recipients of TANF more female ($\chi^2 = 18.8, p < .0001$) than the key parents, but the real differences are small.

The key parents are multiracial and multiethnic by study design (see Appendix A, Research Design). Sixteen are African American, one is a non-Hispanic white, three are Hispanic American, two are of Hispanic origin, one is an Asian refugee, and two emigrated from Africa, one an immigrant and one a refugee. UI recipients show a higher proportion of whites and a lower proportion of African Americans than the key parent group ($\chi^2 = 81.6, p < .0001$) and TANF recipients show a higher proportion of whites and a lower proportion of African Americans but the same proportion of Hispanics and Asians compared to the key parents ($\chi^2 = 12.8, p = .01$).

English is the primary language for most of the key parents (twenty-one, or 88 percent), but the second language for some (four, or 12 percent) at rates that are similar across the five cities.

MARITAL STATUS

The classification of marital status in social science research tends to be inexact. Many mothers technically classified as "single" have resident or near-resident partners who contribute instrumental as well as emotional support (Cancian & Reed, 2001). Program and subsidy eligibility criteria often discourage formal marriage, rewarding low-income individuals for remaining "technically" single. In addition, some state TANF records do not include married recipients because they are reallocated to other assistance programs. Thus we regard TANF figures on marital status as approximate at best. We also find that the ethnographic reports on "marital status" differ from program administrative data. Because of these inconsistencies across programs we make "eyeball" but not statistical comparisons of this characteristic.

For example, nearly three-fourths (eighteen, or 72 percent) of the key parents are reported as single and seven (28 percent) as married in program data, but when we first meet them we find that half (thirteen, or 52 percent) are "partnered," either married or unmarried and residing with a partner. The remaining half (twelve, or 48 percent) live alone with their children, having never been married or divorced. Comparing on program data alone, the key parents are similar to their five-city counterparts. Both groups are classified as "single" at similar rates to TANF parents, but "married" at about double the rate of TANF parents, likely an artifact of the program reallocation noted earlier.

In addition, the key parents' marital status fluctuates over time, as is typical across America where 1996 calculations show that approximately 20 percent of men and women have ever divorced and between 23 percent and 30 percent have never married (Kreider & Fields, 2002). Over half of the key parents (thirteen, or 52 percent) change marital status over the five-year research period. At last contact in mid-2003, fourteen (56 percent) are "partnered," and eleven (44 percent) are not. The importance of the spouses and partners of the key parents to family economic mobility is evident in the family stories in subsequent chapters. In all, the research team has regular contact with forty parents over the study period.

NUMBER AND AGES OF CHILDREN

When we first meet the parents, fifty-nine children live with them, ranging in age from infancy to twenty-one years (data shown in Table 4.1). The families bear seven more children over our years of contact for a total of sixty-six. Only one family has children over the age of eighteen in residence. Given the parents' average age of thirty-two, it is not surprising that the average age of the oldest child in the family is eight years and that two-thirds of the children are under the age of thirteen. Eighteen additional children of the key parents or their spouse or partner reside elsewhere—with another biological parent, grandparents, or friends, in another country, or as emancipated young adults over the age of eighteen. Thus a total of eighty-four children are involved with and affected by the twenty-five families here. The families average 1.7 adults in residence (median = 2). Two parents live with their own parents for a period which slightly increases the overall ratio of adults to children.

EDUCATION

Two of the key parents complete only nine years of school and one parent completes sixteen years of education. Roughly one-third (36 percent) of the parents complete fewer than twelve years of school, two in five (44 percent) complete twelve years, and one in five (20 percent) completes more than twelve years of education. The mean number of years of completed schooling is 11.8 and the median is 12. The median educational attainment of TANF recipients is similar to that of the key parents, but a higher proportion of TANF than key parents drops out of school before ninth grade and a lower proportion completes schooling beyond twelfth grade ($\chi^2 = 27.1$, $p < .0001$).

We know, however, that years of education do not translate directly into degrees received. Fifteen key parents (60 percent) receive a high school diploma and one earns a bachelor's degree in his native country. Over the research period, five of the nine parents who drop out of school before twelfth grade complete the General Educational Development (GED) credential. At last contact, four parents (16 percent) still hold no educational degree. These levels of educational certification are similar to those of UI recipients. In terms of economic mobility, however, the *quality* of the parents' education is generally poor, as most attended schools that are similar to those their children attend (see Chapter 7).

Family Income

Although the focus in this book is on key parent rather than on family income, Table 3.1 shows that the key parents report extremely low annual family incomes at the time they enter a job training program. Moreover, as we discuss in Chapter 6, the income metric does not assess how adequate the income is for a family. The annual family income of the key parents is similar to that of their five-city counterparts.

Public Assistance

Considering the family income figures in Table 3.1, it is not surprising that one or more parents in twenty-one of the twenty-five families (84 percent) uses some form of public assistance in the late 1990s before they begin their mobility efforts. About half of the families hold an adult that collected TANF cash assistance (twelve, or 48 percent). Key parents show higher usage of public assistance than their counterparts in the five cities ($\chi^2 = 7.63$, $p = 0.006$). Although this is not a large difference it suggests that the key parents are slightly more economically disadvantaged than their five-city counterparts and, further, that they are not a sample selected for their economic "success." Comparison of the key parents with the TANF sample is significant but meaningless, as eligibility for public assistance is a selection criterion of TANF.

Work Supports

Over time, the families' utilization of work support programs far outstrips their participation in the TANF program (Table 3.2), and by the end of the research only one parent is enrolled in TANF. Work support programs supplement the wages of low-income working families with children through services rather than cash, and typically include food stamps, nutritional assistance (WIC), children's medical assistance (Medicaid or the State Children's Health Insurance Plan—S-CHIP), the Earned Income Tax Credit (EITC), and child-care and housing subsidies. Although the EITC provides direct income support, it is commonly included under the broad rubric of work support programs (Zedlewski, 2005). When eligible, the parents also use Unemployment Insurance (UI). By the "type of assistance" metric then, the families are moving forward economically. Three families never use public assistance or work support. Three critical work support programs deserve further discussion here: the EITC, Medicaid/S-CHIP, and the Child Tax Credit (CTC).

TABLE 3.2. Utilization of Public Assistance and Work Supports: 2000 to Mid-2003

TANF cash	Medicaid or S-CHIP	Housing	Child care	WIC[a]	Food stamps	Unemp.Ins	EITC
Blessed	Delvalle	Jeremy	McDonalds	Delvalle	Gomez	Lopez	Blessed
Lopez	Faithful	Quinn	Lopez	Jeremy	Lopez	Miracle	Delvalle
Raca	Gomez (+ self)	Raca	Smith	Jenkins	Quinn	Quinn	Jeremy
	Jeremy	Russell	Tracy		Shanks	Raca	Lopez
	Jones (+ self)	Seabrook	Tucker		Tracy (mother's food stamps)	Vanderhand	Muhammad
	Lopez (+ self)	Smith	Walker		Tucker	Walker	Quinn
	McDonalds	Tucker (elig).			Walker		Russell
	Quinn	Stewart			Winters (mother's food stamps)		Seabrook
	Raca	Walker					Shanks
	Russell (suppl.)	Winters (mother's Sec. 8)					Smith
	Seabrook						Stewart
	Shanks (+ self)						Tucker
	Smith						Walker
	Stewart (suppl.)						
	Tracy (+ self)						
	Tucker						
	Vanderhand						
	Walker						
	Winters						
$n = 3$ (12%)	$n = 19$ (76%)	$n = 9$ (36%)	$n = 6$ (24%)	$n = 3$ (12%)	$n = 8$ (32%)	$n = 6$ (24%)	$n = 13$ (52%)

[a] Special Supplemental Nutrition Program for Women, Infants, and Children.

EITC

The EITC is central to the mobility efforts of the key parents and other low earners across the nation (Table 3.2). The 52 percent utilization rate of EITC among the key parents is over twice the average national rate of 20.4 percent among tax filers in large cities in 2001 (Berube & Tiffany, 2004). The parents' higher rates seem to result from the fact that they are generally informed about such work supports by case managers in their job training program—a service that welfare caseworkers offer less consistently (Joyce Foundation, 2002). Berube and Tiffany also find that 15 percent to 20 percent of tax filers who are eligible for the EITC fail to claim the credit, which is mirrored by the parents here (20 percent). Seven parents (28 percent) are not eligible for reasons ranging from too much income, no income, or under-the-table income. The parents who access the EITC report using the refund for necessities such as paying off debt, buying children food and clothing, and paying tuition or rent.

A further aspect of the EITC should be recalled when reading about the families and their firms in Chapter 6. The refund for ten of the thirteen families who use the EITC while we are in contact with them ranges from a low of $341 to a high of $3,888, the latter figure being the maximum credit allowable for the 2000 tax year (Berube & Forman, 2001). Although the EITC is rightly credited with improving the financial well-being of families with household incomes under $35,000, it is far from a panacea, largely because the base wages of the key parents are relatively low. In terms of wage adequacy (see Chapter 6), the EITC refund does not raise any of the families' incomes to 200 percent of the poverty level (data not shown). Although the EITC refund increases the adequacy of the parents' incomes between 12 percent and 23 percent, the federal poverty calculations are based on *potential* rather than on actual annual incomes, and are thus overestimates in some cases, as Chapter 6 details.

Precipitous phase-out rates for income supports such as the EITC also limit their utility for family economic well-being. The EITC phases out rapidly as family income increases, regardless of the fact that the income of one or other parent is often not constant (see Chapter 6). Families are no longer eligible for the credit when their income reaches $33,692 (or $34,692 filing jointly; Internal Revenue Service, 2004) or just short of 200 percent of the federal poverty line, which leaves them still in the range of "low income" (Waldron, Roberts, & Reamer, 2004). That said, the EITC is a vital support for the mobility efforts of the families here (Berube, 2006). Guidance for its access and utilization needs to be presented consistently in workforce and welfare programs.

Medicaid/S-CHIP

Despite increasing numbers of persons without health insurance coverage since 2000, allocations for and enrollment in Medicaid and S-CHIP have compensated for the sustained economic downturn and its associated reduction in employer-sponsored insurance coverage, particularly among low-income families (Ku, Broaddus, & Wachino, 2005). Three-fourths of the families here (nineteen, or 76 percent) use Medicaid or S-CHIP for their children for at least some of the research period (Table 3.2), in two cases only as a supplement to employer-based insurance.

Fifteen use Medicaid or S-CHIP for the entire research period and four alternate between employer insurance and Medicaid. Where available, such as Wisconsin, Louisiana, and Pennsylvania, five parents use Medicaid or S-CHIP during periods of unemployment. Nine families (36 percent) use employer-based insurance for their children for all ($n = 5$) or part ($n = 4$) of the research period. A few parents choose to remain on S-CHIP or Medicaid rather than utilize their employer's health insurance plan, largely for financial reasons (see Chapter 6).

CTC

Finally, the CTC does not appear in Table 3.2 because only one of the twenty-five key parents accesses it at any point during our contact with them. Given that the CTC eligibility threshold in 2002 is an income level of $10,350 or higher (Gitterman, Howard, & Cotton, 2003), most of the parents here are eligible for as much as $600 per child toward their tax liability or as a refund (increased to up to $1,000 per child in 2003). However, work support policies are only valuable if parents receive information about them. According to one report (Center on Budget and Policy Priorities [CBPP], 2004, p. 11), "most low-income families got little or no benefit from the CTC before new rules providing for CTC refunds took effect in 2002." An additional disincentive may result from the credit's administrative complexity. Despite apparent similarity to the EITC, CTC rules are different (Gitterman, Howard, & Cotton, 2003). With limited time, navigating the complexities of one more credit may contribute to low rates of access (CBPP, 2004). Equally likely, after a workforce or welfare program's postemployment support period has ended, parents have few avenues of information about such income-expanding aids. Given that the CTC is selectively available to immigrants, its administrative complexity and an "information gap" could discourage or preclude utilization by families that have few subsidy alternatives. Moreover, the CTC disproportionately benefits higher earning families. The proportion of income refunded by the CTC is less than 1 percent for a family with two children earning $11,000 in 2003 compared to 6 percent for a family with two children earning $25,000 (CBPP). Problems with access and utilization of the Child and Dependent Care Credit (CDCC), a nonrefundable tax credit to help families pay work-related childcare expenses, are similar to those of the CTC. None of the parents here know about or utilize this potential work support.

Use of the other subsidies in Table 3.2 is discussed in the context of the family stories in later chapters.

ADDITIONAL FAMILY BACKGROUND CHARACTERISTICS

WORK

The key parents have all worked at some point in their adult lives, although not necessarily immediately before they enter job training. Three parents were in prison in the years before training, a fourth participated in a residential drug treatment program, and a few alternated between TANF assistance and short-term jobs. Some worked in full-time year-round jobs that offered below or near minimum wage and others who earned $7 per hour or more worked only part time or part year. The parents' employment histories, wages, and the adequacy of their wages are discussed in full in Chapter 6.

ASSETS

Assessing economic well-being by income alone does not fully reflect a family's ability to navigate times of financial hardship. Among low-income families in particular, the presence of assets and savings may be critical to exiting poverty (Danziger & Haveman, 2001; Shapiro & Wolff, 2001; Sherraden, 1991). Four families here hold assets in the form of home ownership, although one loses her home during the 2001 economic recession (see Table 3.6 later in the chapter). High mortgage-to-income ratios render the long-term security of the parents' housing assets uncertain, especially when labor market turbulence threatens longevity in employment.

Owning a car may potentially be an asset, especially as it facilitates transportation to work or meeting children's needs, such as multiple child-care arrangements. According to 2000 Census data almost 90 percent of American households hold one or more vehicles; only 10.9 percent have no motor vehicle ("car") (Parker, 2002). Almost three-fourths of the families here (eighteen, or 72 percent) own or have regular use of a car, although most are of relatively old vintage and unpredictable performance. A number of families hold savings accounts for themselves or their children, but only two families avoid dipping into or depleting these accounts during the sustained recessionary period after February 2001. Several of the key parents participate in Individual Development Account (IDA) programs sponsored by their training site in which the program matches their savings toward post-secondary education, homeownership, or business ownership. Their IDA programs deliver financial and budgeting instruction as well. The families' IDA accounts were similarly depleted after the recession.

HEALTH

Health is another kind of asset or deficit for working families. Health problems are disproportionately severe nationally among families with low or below-poverty incomes compared to those with higher incomes (Mullahy & Wolfe, 2001). In person the key parents and their children seem generally healthy and energetic. On closer inquiry few are without health problems (Table 3.3), although not all problems curtail the parents' work efforts. Some of the parents' health problems are chronic and severe, some are chronic but tolerable, and some are relatively recent injuries suffered on the job. Exhaustion, fatigue, and depressive symptoms are among the most common health problems that impact economic mobility, either directly or indirectly though vulnerability to workplace injury. As Table 3.3 shows, parents' health problems often co-occur with children's health problems (see Chapter 4 for full discussion of children's health), increasing the likelihood that health issues will impact parents' work lives. The family stories in Chapters 5 through 7 reveal how parents' and children's health, work, and school intersect.

TABLE 3.3. Health Problems of Key Parents, Close Family Members, and Children

Key parent/close family member/child (age)	Health problems: workplace and general
H.W. Blessed (40)	Workplace: Two herniated disks; repeated flu; two bouts of pneumonia; material-related rash
	General: Recovered alcoholic; severe whiplash
Spouse (37)	Epileptic seizures; intermittent drug abuse; possible cervical cancer
W. Delvalle (32)	Workplace: Verbal harassment; chronic gastrointestinal condition (exacerbated by stress); headaches
Children: (14), (inf)	Son (14): ADHD
J. Faithful (23)	
Spouse (19)	Difficult pregnancies—bedrest
Children (1½), (inf)	Infant born premature
S. Gates (40)	
Children: (14), (11), (9)	Daughter (11): Chronic condition that causes language and learning impairment; developmentally delayed
	Son (9): Possible ADD
A. Gomez (26)	General: Abusive former partner; complications from tubal ligation surgery
Parents: (in 70s)	Child caretakers: Diabetes; suspected heart problems
Children:(8), (3), (inf)	Son (8): Possible ADD
R. Jackson (40)	
Spouse (28)	Insurance not pay for birth control shots
Children: (5½), (4½)	Sons had ringworm during period of no health insurance
M. Jeremy (42)	Workplace: Job-induced back problems
Children: (2), (inf)	General: Heart virus; chronic headaches
J. Jenkins (28)	General: Gall bladder attacks and surgery; tubal ligation surgery
Spouse (35)	Two-month period of disability (on-job back injury)
Parents:	Mother: Triple bypass surgery
Children: (11), (10), (1),	Son (11): Sickle-cell trait; accident-prone; hit by police car
(inf)	Son (10): Broken fingers; possible dyslexia
	Toddler (1): Surgery for undescended testicle
	Infant: Corrective ear surgery
T. Jones (24)	Workplace: Hand burns
	General: Toxemia; high blood pressure; asthma; repeated flu and bronchitis; pneumonia; ovarian cyst; pregnancy with forced bed rest
Children: (2), (1), (inf)	Daughter (2): Chronic breathing problem since birth; adenoid and tonsil surgery; reconstructive nasal surgery in future
L. Lopez (27)	General: Untreated depression; self-medication with marijuana; assaulted by child's father
Parent/Family:	Mother: History of alcoholism; massive, debilitating stroke; breast cancer
	Uncle: Disabled (in residence)
Children: (7), (3)	Daughter (3): Oral surgery as toddler; speech delay
K. McDonalds (29)	
Children: (6), (5), (3)	Son (3): Chronic asthma
L. Miracle (46)	Workplace: Job-aggravated allergies
	General: Arthritis
Spouse (41)	Prior on-job back injury; allergies; high blood pressure; appendix and cyst surgery
Children: (9), (4)	Daughter (9): allergies
	Son (4): Periodic seizures

(Continued)

TABLE 3.3. *(continued)*

Key parent/close family member/child (age)	Health problems: workplace and general
A. Muhammad (45)	Workplace: Life-threatening back and shoulder injury as CNA
	General: Past domestic abuse; migraines; anxiety attacks; heart malfunction; high blood pressure; clinical depression
Children: (21), (19), (12), (10), (10)	Daughter (19): Pregnancy; high blood pressure
	Twin sons (10): Premature births; (one twin) lead poisoning and subsequent developmental delays; ADHD; learning disability. Other twin: Special learning and behavioral services; ADHD
R. Quinn (42)	Workplace: Arm and knee injuries; ankle sprain
	General: Chronic arthritis; periods of depression
Children: (16), (15)	
A. Raca (18)	Workplace and General: Possible dyslexia (number reversals)
Children: (1), (4 mo), (inf)	Daughter (at 6 mo.): Severe burns from scalding bath water
T. Russell (43)	
Child: (10)	Son (10): Special education for reading
E. Seabrook (37)	
Parent (62)	Mother: Severe heart problems
Children: (4½), (2½)	Son (4½): Chronic asthma
	Daughter (2½): Chronic asthma and ear infections; periodic hospitalization; surgery in infancy for throat problem; subsequent speech lag
T. Shanks (33)	General: Cancer surgery; gout
Children: (15), (14), (11)	Daughter (15): Rheumatic fever as child; pregnant at age 18
I. Smith (31)	Workplace: Job-induced fish asthma
	General: Childhood abuse; rare and potentially fatal blood disorder; former heroin addiction; Hepatitis C; intermittent depression
Parent	Mother: Severe mental illness
Children: (4½), (2½)	Both sons born heroin-addicted; both in therapeutic development program
	Son (4½): Probable physical abuse in foster care; severe asthma
	Son (2½): In high-risk infant clinic: severe asthma; pneumonia; chronic ear infections
M. Stewart (24)	Workplace: Job-induced back injury
Parent/Family	Father: Alcoholic
	Brother (as child): Hepatitis C; two kidney transplants
Children: (6), (3)	Daughter (6): Asthma
	Daughter (3): Asthma; acute disorder of peripheral nervous system
T. Tracy (21)	
Parent: (36)	Mother: Low blood pressure (work disability)
Children: (2½), (inf)	Daughter (2½): Born with heart murmur; seizures
	Infant: Born 6 weeks premature
S. Tucker (37)	Workplace: Job-induced leg pain; chronic hernia problems
Sister (resident)	Repeated bouts of depression
Children: (13), (7), (3)	Daughter (13): Slight heart murmur
	Son (7): Severe stutter; speech therapy; special education for reading
M. Vanderhand (32)	Workplace: Job-induced tendinitis and possible carpal tunnel syndrome; two shoulder surgeries for Thoracic Outlet Obstruction syndrome (reason for hand problems)
Spouse (48)	On-job back injury; knee operation
Children: (13), (11), (8), (7)	

TABLE 3.3. (*continued*)

Key parent/close family member/child (age)	Health problems: workplace and general
L. Walker (36) Children: (13), (9), (5), (2)	General: Domestic abuse (father of children); cyst removal from eye Son (13): Severe asthma; medication since age 2; severely overweight; borderline diabetic Daughter (9): Severe asthma; severely overweight Daughter (5): Severe asthma
N. Winters (19) Partner (17) Children: (1½), (6 mo)	Workplace: Job-aggravated asthma General: Periods of depression Physical incident with partner Son (1½): Asthma; tooth decay Daughter (6 mo): Asthma

DEPRESSION

Having depressive symptoms or depression is a special health condition that warrants deeper attention in terms of economic mobility (Iversen & Armstrong, 2004). We administer the Center for Epidemiological Studies Depression Scale (CES-D) (Radloff, 1977; Radloff & Locke, 1986) to the key parents at multiple time points during the research period to examine the relationship between depressive symptoms and their employment status, wages, and child well-being (see details in Appendix A, Research Design). Although clinical depression and depressive symptoms are different in severity and impact, depressive symptoms are associated with the risk of clinical depression and with poor employment outcomes, particularly if mediating program or policy supports are limited or absent (Lennon, Blome, & English, 2001). According to Gotlib and Cane's (1989) broadly used scale, CES-D scores below 16 signify "not depressed;" scores from 16 to 20 signify "mild depression;" scores from 21 to 30 signify "moderate depression"; and scores 31 and over signify "severe depression" (Table 3.4).

We look at the parents' depression scores according to year of research contact (Table 3.4) to see if the scores are associated with national economic conditions. Overall the fathers' and mothers' scores are more similar than different. Mothers and fathers both score below the depression range from 2000 through 2002, although mothers' scores come close to the score signaling "mild depression" at the time of the recession in 2001. In 2003, however, the mothers' average score

TABLE 3.4. Depression Scores (CES-D) of Key Parents by Year

Year	Fathers' average depression score	Mothers' average depression score
2000	12	11
2001	8	14
2002	7	10
2003	21	18

jumps to the mild depression level and the fathers' average score jumps to the "moderate depression" level. The final administration of the CES-D in mid-2003 coincides not only with persistent unemployment in the five cities and significant reductions in already-low wages in many industries, but also with the fact that the parents' postemployment contact with staff and case managers at their job training programs has ended.

Although it is impossible to definitively ascertain the causal direction of situational and economic conditions and parental depression, the prospective administration of the CES-D is suggestive. The fact that the initial administration of the CES-D takes place in 2000 and 2001, yet scores do not move into the depression range until 2003, suggests that the training, employment, and year, or occasionally more, of postemployment services provided by the parents' job training programs help to mediate negative effects of the economic downturn on parents' stress levels, at least for a while.

Further interpreting these results in the context of the ethnographic data, the fathers' scores may rise to the depression range in 2003 because of the compounding factors of sustained job loss and volatility in the industries in which they are more likely to work, such as manufacturing and construction. Although the mothers are more likely to be employed in industries that fare better during the economic downturn, such as health care and finance and insurance, over time their scores rise as well. Moreover, the depression scores in 2003 of the mothers employed in construction and manufacturing resemble the higher scores of the fathers. Most important, the ethnographic and depression data reveal that during periods in which the parents' incomes reach or exceed 250 percent of the federal poverty line, mothers and fathers score in the "not depressed" range, irrespective of differences in educational attainment, family stress, job tenure, or job quality. Policy and family supports facilitate their reaching such incomes. Overall, however, such periods of adequate income are rare and often not sustained (see Chapter 6). The prevailing economic, labor market and housing conditions in a city, region, or state may intersect with the life experiences of these and millions of similar families to affect their economic mobility. Thus we turn now to the role of "place" in the families' lives.

"PLACE": CITY, REGION, AND STATE

The average visitor to a city sees its alluring "public" face. Visitors to Philadelphia see the Liberty Bell, Independence Hall, the Art Museum, center-city shops and the trendy South Street and Seaport areas. Visitors to New Orleans spend time in the famed French Quarter to view the historic cathedral and park on Jackson Square, drink in the jazz spots and Preservation Hall, buy multicolor beads and boas in the voodoo shops, choose among Cajun delicacies in the French Market, have *café au lait* and beignets at Café du Monde and stroll among Victorian homes with intricate wrought-iron railings. Visitors to Milwaukee see a refurbished downtown and revel in new riverfront shops, boat outings on Lake Michigan, and convention events. Visitors to St. Louis see the famous arch, attend major sporting events in a downtown arena and wonder at the mysteries of the mighty Mississippi as it wends its way downstream to New Orleans and beyond. Travelers to Seattle marvel at the confluence of mountains and sea and savor the outdoor Pike Place Market, gourmet eateries in upscale neighborhoods, ubiquitous parks, museums, and ferry rides on Puget Sound.

Each of these cities has a different and more "private" side that is the general environment of the families in this book. Their Philadelphia consists of neighborhoods struggling against the characterization of "most dangerous" in the city, with drug wars and shootouts on corners that were eased temporarily during the mayor's short-lived "Safe Streets" initiative. Their Philadelphia also consists of a local/federal "Anti-Blight" initiative, overburdened job-training and human-service organizations trying to counter the city's problems, and children's schools in receivership. Living less than one mile from the city center, the Philadelphia families are quite isolated from its free library services and cultural events. "Public" Philadelphia feels foreign and potentially discriminatory. Less than five miles from these neighborhoods in an adjacent suburb one family lives in contrasting safety and resource richness.

The families' New Orleans is far from the French Quarter in both miles and milieu. Their New Orleans consists of barren public housing projects because residents fear that trees and shrubbery will hide thieves and gunmen; far-flung apartment blocs that gouge renters because they cater to those displaced by public housing relocation; generally dilapidated inner-city free-market housing; and child-care centers in malls that seldom let children play outside. Modest areas of relief occur in local community colleges, at carefully selected magnet high schools, and in churches.

The families' St. Louis consists of a near-deserted downtown, empty of cars, shoppers, or business people even in midday. The city proper stretches for miles to affluent county townships but the route holds block after block of vacant lots, some menaced by packs of wild dogs; burnt-out homes and gunshot-pocked building facades; old, racially segregated gated communities for rich and poor; residents openly carrying firearms; streets full of unrepaired potholes; and little commercial activity. Their St. Louis is a city still reeling from violent race protests over discrimination in the construction trades in 1999; a city with gargantuan regional economic headaches that result from bi-state political divisions; and a city that has not recovered commercially from a clause in a charter agreement of the mid-1800s that prohibited expansion beyond the city–county boundary that was set at that time. Significantly, at morning rush hour on the largest expressway, three times as many cars travel from downtown St. Louis to the suburbs as vice versa. The reverse is of course true at evening rush hour. And for those families lodged in the city for work, residence, and underresourced public schools, although many family cultural activities are free, accessing them still means outlay for transportation and food.

The families' Milwaukee is relatively benign on the surface—broad streets, large old homes, sidewalk-lined neighborhoods, and grassy yards. Closer examination reveals that many of the homes are boarded up or overpopulated. Evangelical churches and church-fronts abound—over a dozen in one particular two-block square area—but the same area offers no commercial establishments: no banks, stores, or community centers—nowhere for children or parents to even shop for a soda without a car. The only commercial signs advertise rat poison and

extermination services. And although Milwaukee's downtown has been significantly revitalized, sales help and shoppers are predominantly white in contrast to a
local population that is 37 percent African American and 12 percent Hispanic. The
vital downtown convention center that generally draws out-of-town businesspeople
only exacerbates the economic divide.

And finally, the families' Seattle is a city of more subtle but strong contrasts.
City buses broadly advertised job opportunities until the technology bust in 2001;
at that point job ads were replaced by ads for tourist restaurants and sights. The
families live in neighborhoods far from the compact city center that are ringed
by noisy expressways and nearly inaccessible by public transportation. A portable
Section 8 housing voucher enables one immigrant family to live amid grocery
stores, an elementary school, community associations, child-care centers, and a
neighborhood "block watch" sponsored by the city police crime prevention department. This residence is mere blocks from a trendy mini-downtown area full
of restaurants, shops, and Birkenstocked young people driving SUVs. The poor
underside of this upscale community is starkly illuminated by the sign posted on
a utility pole outside one of the chic new restaurants:

NO
Sitting or Lying Down on Public Sidewalks
7am to 9pm
Neighborhood Commercial Zone

In sum, we wonder how these environments and their many contrasts matter
to the mobility efforts of the families. Does geographic location or place matter
to economic mobility? If so, how does place matter? In the face of welfare and
workforce policy devolution across the nation, place may or may not be increasingly
salient. We look first at how place is examined in related research, comparing
those views and methods with those of our study. We then look at city and state
specifics through the lenses of metropolitan-level data and the lived experience of
the families.

MULTICITY RESEARCH: DOES "PLACE" MATTER?

Metropolitan-level analyses are increasingly common as urban scholars try to
deepen knowledge about national and local experiences and trends. According to
the Census Bureau, "A metropolitan area usually consists of one or more population centers or central cities and the nearby counties that have close economic and
community ties to the central cities" (Jargowsky, 2003, p. 3). Although valuable
for providing a comparative context, census data yield limited information about
families' daily lives and work. In response, several recent studies have been conducted in more than one city to deepen understanding of lives as they are lived
locally and to explore the similarities and differences across cities under policy
devolution.

The Three-City Study (Winston, 1999) examines how parents and children in
Boston, Chicago, and San Antonio adapt to local implementation of welfare reform. The cities are selected opportunistically and strategically as locales that
exhibit ethnic, regional, and policy diversity. The sample is representative of

families (single mothers and their children) from designated neighborhoods making welfare and employment transitions over time. Discussion papers and policy briefs report findings about TANF sanctions, child outcomes and labor market opportunities (see www.jhu.edu/~welfare). Evidence from this study that contradicts other research findings about child and adolescent outcomes under welfare reform demonstrates the value as well as the difficulty of comparing findings from varied research designs and locales (Cherlin, 2004; Moffitt & Winder, 2002; Moffitt, Chase-Lansdale, & Cherlin, 2004). Little has been reported to date about whether or how place matters to the focal issues in the Three-City Study.

The Multi-City Study of Urban Inequality (Holzer, 1996; O'Connor, Tilly, & Bobo, 2001) focuses on low-income families, racial divisions and the labor market. The study sites include a rust-belt city (Detroit), a northeastern city (Boston), a "new South" city (Atlanta), and a multiracial west coast city (Los Angeles; p. 9) in parallel with the four census regions. In each city, men and women heads of households and a selection of employers are surveyed by telephone, and a smaller group of employers is interviewed in person. Although the researchers report local differences in how race and urban inequality intersect, they also find broad similarities across metro areas. Across the four cities aspects of race and social structure, such as the skills mismatch between inner-city residents and types of available jobs, the spatial mismatch between inner-city residents and location of jobs, patterns of residential segregation, and the types of social networks available to different urban populations, seem to explain more about urban inequality than place does.

MDRC's Project on Devolution and Urban Change is another multicity study that examines the early impact of welfare reform on urban welfare recipients, their communities and the institutions that assist them (Buck et al., 1999; Michalopoulos et al., 2003). Four counties are selected to represent a mix of older industrial cities and younger cities, all of which experience a disproportionate share of the TANF recipients in their respective states as do most of the cities in the one hundred largest metropolitan areas. Valuable early information about the effects of TANF policy implementation on welfare agency staff members and recipients in the four cities has been reported and in-depth reports from two of the four cities have been issued. To date, these reports find both differences in implementation and cross-cutting similarities in agency and family responses to the new welfare policy mandates.

In comparison with these multi-city studies, the Annie E. Casey Foundation's Jobs Initiative, which is the national workforce demonstration[1] from which we select the families in this book (see Appendix A, Research Design), is explicitly lodged in "place" (Giloth, 1995, 2004a). However, in contrast to place-based initiatives that target economic activity in high-poverty neighborhoods, the demonstration views the notion of place in a broader metropolitan and regional context as the systemic intersection of characteristics of neighborhoods, residents, city and regional economies, area labor markets, human service organizations, and local and national policies. The five demonstration cities (Philadelphia, New Orleans, St. Louis, Milwaukee, and Seattle) provide a fertile field for our ethnographic examination of these intersecting characteristics. These five sites, or what Marcus (1998) calls "multiple connected local determinations," also provide a base to discuss the structure or macrosystem through "multilocale ethnography" (p. 44).

Multilocale ethnography is "an ethnography that while it encompasses local conditions, is aimed at representing a system or pieces of a system" (p. 51). Burawoy (2003, p. 674) concurs with the position that "the spatially bounded site, unconnected to other sites, is a fiction of the past that is no longer sustainable." In other words, do cities or places illustrate "environing conditions" for families and other social institutions, or do cities and places have characteristics and experiences in common from which policymakers and program designers can learn? Becker (1998) suggests the latter view that processes, whether of economic mobility for low-earning families or other cultural phenomena, are similar no matter where they occur even though variations in locales create variations in local results.

After spending eighteen months with ten families in two cities (Iversen, 2002), the initial analyses suggested that having persistently insufficient wage income, even when parents work full time year round, overrides geographic particularities. The comparisons in Table 3.1 underscore this conclusion as do the families' experiences across cities. Even so, we arrive at a more nuanced position in our final analysis. The variables of interest and import to mobility *do* vary by locale. For example, cost of living, wages, job opportunities, subsidy regulations, housing, food, transportation, and child care differ considerably in the five cities. But they do not differ systematically. Place matters then through the ways in which particular state and local characteristics intersect with particular family characteristics. The discussion of neighborhood housing and residential mobility later in this section and the family stories in subsequent chapters illustrate these particularities. Such particularities thus require locally tailored program and policy efforts. But although place matters to *how* families experience unemployment, insufficient wages and incomes, persistent personal challenges, and local economic and social conditions, the larger issue is that low-earning families across the country *do* experience these problems, independent of their particular configuration. This issue raises serious questions about the role of the federal government and the character of the "public will" that we address in the final chapter.

Before we get to that larger discussion, however, we look more deeply into how place affects mobility. Notably, place is multiple, varied, and contextual in people's everyday lives. Each person or family is embedded in a number of different places or contexts that elicit and receive partial but not entire aspects of their persons. Place also includes the beliefs and practices that people carry with them into varied contexts (Lin, 2000), how the context may respond, and how beliefs and practices may change as a result. Part of what influences family mobility is the dynamic, changing nature of a city over time: its population, its racial and ethnic composition, its economy and its local labor market, as we examine next.

METROPOLITAN AREAS AND CENTRAL CITIES: MILWAUKEE, NEW ORLEANS, PHILADELPHIA, SEATTLE, AND ST. LOUIS

City population

The cities in this book are not only five of the one hundred largest metropolitan areas in the United States, defined by Census 2000 as those with at least 519,000 residents (Gottlieb, 2004) but also among the sixty-one metro areas with populations greater

TABLE 3.5. City Population Demographics: Census 2000 Compared to Census 1990

City	Population Gain/Loss 2000 vs. 1990 Census	Proportion Hispanic 2000 vs. 1990 Census	Proportion African American 2000 vs. 1990 Census	Proportion Asian 2000 vs. 1990 Census
Milwaukee	5% Loss	Higher	Higher	Higher
Philadelphia	4.3% Loss	Higher	Higher	Higher
New Orleans	2.5% Loss	Same	Higher	Lower
St. Louis	12.2% Loss	Higher	Higher	Higher
Seattle	9.1% Gain	Higher	Lower	Higher

Source: U.S. Census Bureau; 1990 Census; Census 2000; Summary File 1, P1 (SF1_P1); generated by authors using American Factfinder, http://Factfinder.census.gov/>; 2-25-04.

than one million persons (Jargowsky, 2003). The cities also reflect the four primary census regions of Midwest, Northeast, South, and West, as well as five of the eight census regions used in research conducted by the National Governors Association and the National Association of State Budget Officers (2002, 2003).

In 2000 the one hundred largest metro areas contained about two-thirds (63 percent) of the nation's total population, three-fourths (78 percent) of its metropolitan population (Gottlieb, 2004), and two-thirds (67 percent) of all jobs in the United States (Katz, 2004). Even so, population changes over time may affect family mobility more than city size per se.

Between 1990 and 2000, four of the five cities lose between 2.5 percent and 12.2 percent of their population, whereas the population of one city increases by 9.1 percent (Table 3.5). Over the same period all five cities became more densely populated by people of color. Seattle sees the largest proportionate increase in immigrant population, this in the context of a huge national increase. According to one report about 44 percent of the nation's 30.5 million foreign-born residents, or 13.3 million people, arrive in the United States in the 1990s (Schmitt, 2001). By 2001, immigrants make up 11 percent of the U.S. population—the largest share since the 1930s. Similarly, immigrants make up 12 percent of our study population. Although the relationship is complex, downward population shifts, if accompanied by migration of firms to suburbs, and being foreign-born, if English-language proficiency limits employment opportunity, may both negatively influence economic mobility. Given this complexity, we explore the larger economic environment in which the families and shifting populations are embedded, looking first at state economic conditions.

State economic conditions

Labor market indicators of the national economic condition, such as rates of unemployment, job loss, job creation, and wages relative to inflation, indicate that the sluggish economy following the 2001 recession persists into 2005 (Fronczek, 2005; Von Bergen, 2005). Sustained national economic downturn led to reduced state revenues and increased spending pressures, particularly on Medicaid, other health care and education, and created massive budget shortfalls despite states' curtailment of spending and creative reallocation of budget lines (National Governor's Association and National Association of State Budget Officers, 2002; Wallin, 2005). A national survey of state fiscal conditions in late 2002 reports that "nearly every state is in fiscal crisis" (National Governor's Association and National Association of State Budget Officers, p. viii).

State budget cuts thus take place at the same time that low-wage workers lose jobs and remain unemployed for longer periods. Thirty-eight states cut more than $13.6 billion from their fiscal 2002 budgets *after* the budget was passed (National Governor's Association and National Association of State Budget Officers, 2002). Louisiana did not report figures for FY2002 but cut its FY2003 budget by $100 million (6 percent). In FY2002, Missouri's budget was cut $750 million (4.4 percent), Pennsylvania's was cut $310 million (7 percent), Washington's was cut $112 million (4.6 percent), and Wisconsin's budget from a biennial calculation was cut $324 million (10 percent). In budget year 2003, twenty-six states planned to cut their budgets further by more than $8.3 billion (National Governor's Association and National Association of State Budget Officers, 2002). In fact, these cuts totaled $11.8 billion (National Governor's Association and National Association of State Budget Officers, 2003), affecting all study states except Washington.

About half of state budget cuts affect city governments through both actual decreases and select changes in funding (National Governor's Association and National Association of State Budget Officers, 2002; Wallin, 2005). Across-the-board percentage cuts and dipping into Rainy Day funds are the predominant strategies to reduce or eliminate budget gaps in the five study states as in most other states. Such cuts affect family economic mobility as they limit the availability of critical state-funded supports, such as health insurance and work subsidies that, when coupled with inadequate wages and economic decline at the local level, leave many families economically stranded. State budget cuts may also affect families more directly through local labor markets, as we examine next.

Local labor markets

Conditions in local labor markets may parallel or differ from state conditions. Although a broadly similar set of processes underpins the operation of every local labor market, the local market reflects particular intersections between families and those processes. Common processes include rates and patterns of local employment/unemployment; balance between labor supply and demand, including educational requirements (demand) and performance (supply); job creation rates; discrimination (gender, race, and ethnicity); dominant industry sectors (whether growth or not, wage levels and earnings, advancement opportunity, location, and differences in individual firms within sectors); active labor market programs (skill development programs, intermediaries, or employment services); passive labor market policies (UI, EITC, and safety); overall growth of jobs in a regional economy; and the mix of low-wage, near low-wage, and higher wage jobs.

For example, Milwaukee loses 21 percent of its manufacturing jobs during the decade of the 1990s (Levine, 2003), experiences a severe and persistent labor market crisis, sees a switch in its industry base from manufacturing to tourism, and increasingly locates jobs outside the central city in the suburbs. These local conditions are reflected in high rates of layoff in the Milwaukee families.

In Seattle, technology and information services, such as the dot-coms, and the demand for computerized numerical control (CNC) skills in manufacturing dramatically declined in 2001. Three years after the recession local job creation remains sluggish (Nyhan, 2004). The CNC bust prevents two parents from find-ing technology-based manufacturing positions and the dot-com bust halts another parent's notable mobility progress.

Racism persists in the St. Louis construction industry, disadvantaging one of the families, and transportation systems challenge other families trying to access jobs in distant county suburbs. Adequate housing is a serious issue as well, as neither subsidized housing nor accommodations in homeless shelters keep up with demand, which causes one homeless parent to move her family to another city.

In New Orleans, a weak industrial infrastructure flows from low levels of edu-cational attainment in the workforce, but the sectors of construction, services, and durable goods manufacturing grow during the economic expansion of the 1990s (Fogg & Harrington, 2001). Poor-quality education limits the mobility of two of the New Orleans families and three other families find the manufacturing and construction sectors less robust than state figures suggest.

In Philadelphia, manufacturing trends down during the economic expansion (Crone, 2000), but because productivity rises, the families with manufacturing jobs remain in the mobility queue. At the same time the mobility of other Philadelphia families is thwarted by the expanding spatial mismatch (Kasarda, 1995) between urban residents and suburban jobs that results in long, arduous commutes, even though the city is only moderately affected by the 2001 recession because of its generally flat economy.

The unique ways the families engage these processes and experience particular outcomes are described in full in Chapter 6. Here we simply identify that the notion of place is germane to local labor markets as Holzer, Stoll, and Wissoker (2004) find as well, although they caution as we do that other influences may be stronger than place.

Nevertheless, the families' education, work, and personal histories intersect with the kind of jobs a training program prepares them for and helps them find, with whether their industry sector can withstand the slings and arrows of economic turbulence, and with state economic conditions. To conclude this examination of place, we look at how the more proximal places of neighborhoods and communities intersect with broader economic conditions to influence family economic mobility.

NEIGHBORHOODS AND COMMUNITIES

In neighborhood-level research, census tracts are common proxies for neighbor-hoods (Jargowsky, 2003), but tracts often differ in size and climate from resident-defined boundaries. Real-life neighborhoods are multidimensional. They are "spa-tial units, associational networks, and perceived environments" (Brooks-Gunn, Duncan, & Aber, 1997, p. 9). Housing, neighborhood stability and geographic mobility, and community involvement, each of which we explore below, are thus salient factors for the families' economic mobility.

Housing

Table 3.6 shows the type of housing the families live in over our years of contact and what proportion of their income they pay for that housing, whether their housing

TABLE 3.6. Income Spent on Housing and Type of Housing, Housing Status, and Reason for Change in Proportion of Income to Housing: 2000 to Mid-2003

Key parent City	Proportion of income to market rate housing Year Percent	Proportion of income to subsidized housing Year Percent	Housing status: same or change	Reason for increase or decrease in proportion of income to housing
Vanderhand Seattle	'00 – 44% (rent) '01 – 36% (rent) '03 – 34% (rent)		Same	Decrease: Variable work hours—self and husband
Russell Seattle		'00 – 27% (Sec. 8) '01–03 – 18% (Sec. 8)	Same	Decrease: Wages increased
Jeremy Seattle		'00 – 29% (Sec. 8) '01 – 22% (Sec. 8) '03 – 35% (Sec. 8)	Same	Increase: Held lower-paying job; got larger apt. when second child born
Smith Seattle	'02 – 37% (rent)	'00 – 23% (Sec. 8) '01 – 25% (Sec. 8) '02 – 68% (Sec. 8)	Change	Increase: Fluctuating employment; lost job
Miracle Seattle	'00 – 60% (1 job; mortgage) '02– 27% (2 jobs; mortgage) '03 – 49% (2 jobs; new house and mortgage)		Same	Decrease: Took two full-time jobs; bought more expensive house/still two jobs
Jones Milwaukee	'00 – 21% to 30% to 15% (rent)		Same	Increase/Decrease: Fluctuating work attendance
McDonalds Milwaukee	'00 – 21% (rent) '01 – 15% (rent)		Same	Decrease: Wages increased (until unemployed/ self-employed 2001)
Jackson Milwaukee	'00 – 16% (rent) '02 – 12% (rent)		Same	Decrease: Wages increased
Shanks Milwaukee	'00 – 40% (mort) '01 – 26% (mort) '03 – 29% (rent)		Change	Decrease: Wage income dropped; lost house
Blessed Milwaukee	'00 – 21% (rent) '02–03 – 27% to 101% to 34% (rent)		Same	Increase: Fluctuating employment
Jenkins St. Louis	House was a gift; no mortgage		Same	Not relevant: House too small for # of residents
Tucker St. Louis	'01 – 22% (rent) '03 – 17% (rent)		Same	Decrease: Elig. for Section 8, but didn't find adequate house
Walker St. Louis/ Second City of Residence	'01 – 0% (mother's house)	'01 – 16% (pub.hsg) '02 – 14% (pub.hsg)	Change	Increase: Homeless between mother's house and public housing

TABLE 3.6. (*continued*)

Key parent City	Proportion of income to market rate housing Year Percent	Proportion of income to subsidized housing Year Percent	Housing status: same or change	Reason for increase or decrease in proportion of income to housing
Lopez St. Louis	'01 – 22% (rent) '02 – 0% (parents' house)		Change	Decrease: Fluctuating employment; overcrowded housing; family stress
Raca St. Louis		'01 – 7% (Sec. 8) '02 – 4% (Sec. 8)	Same	Decrease: Job fluctuation; third child born
Gomez Philadelphia	'01 – 12% (parents' house) '02 – 25% (rent)		Change	Increase: Moved from parents' to own house
Gates Philadelphia	'01 – 0% (parents' house) '02–03 – 10% (rent)		Change	Increase: Affordable because of good wage
Muhammad Philadelphia	'01 – 29% (rent) '02–03 – 23% (rent)		Same	Decrease: Wages increased
Delvalle Philadelphia	'01 – 11% (mort) '03 – 8% (mort)		Same	Decrease: Slight wage increase
Stewart Philadelphia		'01 – 26% (pub.hsg) '02–03 – 8% (relative's pub.hsg)	Change	Decrease: Move to relative's public housing
Seabrook New Orleans	'02 – 18% (rent)	'02–03 – 14% (Sec. 8)	Change	Decrease: Section 8; multiple jobs
Winters New Orleans	'02 – 25% (rent)	'02–03 – 0% (mother's Sec. 8)	Change	Decrease: Couple separated; moved to mother's Section 8 house
Tracy New Orleans	'02 – 0% (parents' house) 03 – 0% (parents' house)	'02 – $129 (no inc.) (Sec. 8 Mississippi)	Change	Fluctuates: On Section 8 list—expects two-year wait
Faithful New Orleans	'02 – 28% (rent) '02 – 27% (rent)		Same	Decrease: Slight wage increase (before fired and self-emp)
Quinn New Orleans		'02–'03 – 5% to 15%	Same	Fluctuates: Work hours inconsistent
Overall – 5 Cities	Average: 26%*	Average: 20%**	Same = 15 Change = 10	

* Average proportion of income to market rate housing (rent or mortgage), excluding 0% (live with family)

** Average proportion of income to subsidized housing (Section 8 or public housing development) status stays the same or changes, whether the amount of income they need for housing increases or decreases over time, and reasons for those changes. At some point during the research, sixteen families live in market housing; ten live in federally subsidized housing—seven of the ten use Section 8 vouchers and three live in public housing developments; and four own a home. Parents living in market rate dwellings pay 26 percent of their income for housing on average, whereas parents living in subsidized dwellings pay 20 percent on average. However, some parents experience periods in which housing costs them much more than the 30 percent of income that is considered the federal affordability standard (National Low Income Housing Coalition, 2004; Waldron, Roberts, & Reamer, 2004). Moreover the annual incomes on which these percentages are based *assume* consistent wage income, which is often not the reality as Chapter 6 describes fully.

Changes in housing status even more than the particular type of housing itself illustrate the precariousness of the families' housing conditions. Two in five parents (ten, or 40 percent) change the type of housing they live in over the research period, which affects the proportion of income they pay for housing. Increases in the proportion of income needed for housing result primarily from fluctuating employment and unemployment, but also to lower paying jobs after the 2001 recession, variable job attendance, not enough hours of work, or higher wages that reduce the housing subsidy allotment. Decreases in the proportion of income needed for housing result largely from wage increases, adding a second or third job, moving to a parent's home from a rental property, or accessing a Section 8 voucher.

Although a decrease in the proportion of income spent on housing is the predominant mode, that does not necessarily signify greater economic security. For example, one parent was forced to sell her house and move to a market rental and another moved into a relative's public housing apartment. Moreover, a partner's or spouse's income does not always lower the proportionate cost of housing as that income is generally as variable as the key parent's and not all relationships last over time. Even so, at times a spouse's or partner's income makes housing costs more reasonable, enabling the key parent to devote more energy to work or to upgrade education or training such as GED pursuit, apprenticeships, or community college study. Conversely, inconsistent performance in these upgrade venues often results from housing problems, which doubly jeopardizes future mobility. To understand these housing changes more broadly, we look now at residential stability, mobility, and poverty.

Residential stability, mobility, and poverty

Some hold that residential stability fosters long-standing and productive connections between families and other adults in the community (McLanahan & Sandefur, 1994). In other words, stability increases social capital through sustained community ties (Portes, 1998). Among low-earning families, however, residential mobility is often a proxy for changes in community resources such as schools, transportation, and community activities for children that can be positive or negative (McLanahan & Sandefur). Families may move to improve housing, to access better quality schools, or to live amid greater ethnic homogeneity. Alternatively, families may move because they lose their housing due to unemployment, eviction or changes in family status.

Neighborhood research tries to track the characteristics and outcomes of residential stability and change through analysis of tract-level census data. Zip code–level analysis is increasingly considered equally or more robust.[2] Still, because both levels of data are based on administrative records neither provides deep understanding about life in residential neighborhoods or what Coleman calls functional communities (Gephart, 1997). Zip code and ethnographic analyses together may partially fill that gap.

Neighborhood-level poverty research finds consistently that the presence of professional, managerial, or relatively affluent neighbors increases school attainment and decreases school dropout rates, largely through the higher level of community resources that are available (Gephart, 1997; Petit, 2004). Such resources include but are not limited to quality schools, playgrounds, supervised youth activities, libraries, adult role models in the labor market, and shared values among families (Gephart). Changing neighborhoods within cities as a strategy to attain such resources is not uncommon among low-earning families and the families here are no exception. Almost three-fourths of the families (eighteen, or 72 percent) change neighborhoods during the study period: six move once, eight move twice, and four move three times. Thirteen of the eighteen end up in a different zip code from where they start, and these relocations occur at similar rates across the five cities (see Figure 3.1).

This raises a salient question: when the families move, do they "move up"? According to census population data they do not (Figure 3.1). First, all but one of the moves is from a neighborhood that increases its population or remains the same to a neighborhood that loses population between 1990 and 2000, as we see earlier in Table 3.5. By itself this does not automatically signify downward economic mobility, but it is suggestive, as population loss may reflect area job loss. Second, all five cities see a decline over the same period in "high-poverty neighborhoods," defined as 40 percent or more residents with incomes below the federal poverty level by Jargowsky (2003) and 30 percent or more residents by Kingsley and Pettit (2003). However, poverty *increases* in neighborhoods with middle-range poverty levels, defined as 11 percent to 30 percent of such residents (Kingsley & Pettit). Nationally the share of all poor people in census tracts with poverty rates in the 20 percent to 30 percent range increases from 18 percent to 21 percent, and the share in the 10 percent to 20 percent range increases from 27 percent to 29 percent between 1990 and 2000 (Kingsley & Pettit, p. 1). These neighborhoods account for more poor persons than do "high" or "extreme" poverty neighborhoods: 31 million people compared to 6.7 million people. What are the families' neighborhoods like on this metric?

In 2000, eighteen families live in middle-range poverty neighborhoods (Table 3.7). One family lives in a neighborhood with a poverty level below 10 percent, and six live in neighborhoods that exceed 30 percent in poverty. By mid-2003, fourteen families live in middle-range poverty neighborhoods, two live in low-poverty neighborhoods, and nine live in neighborhoods in which the poverty level exceeds 30 percent of residents.

A closer look (Table 3.7) shows that over the three and a half years, twenty families live in neighborhoods where the poverty level remains the same. One family moves from a high-poverty to a low-poverty neighborhood and four move

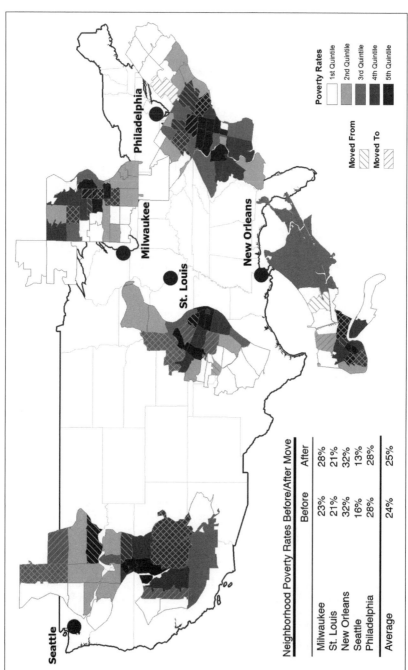

Poverty Rates	
	1st Quintile
	2nd Quintile
	3rd Quintile
	4th Quintile
	5th Quintile

Moved From

Moved To

Neighborhood Poverty Rates Before/After Move

	Before	After
Milwaukee	23%	28%
St. Louis	21%	21%
New Orleans	32%	32%
Seattle	16%	13%
Philadelphia	28%	28%
Average	24%	25%

FIGURE 3.1. Residency, stability, mobility, and poverty: 1998 to mid-2003

Source: Key Parent Address; U.S. Census Bureau (2000); Summary File 3, P87 (SF3-P87); generated by authors using American Factfinder: www.Factfinder.census.gov/home/saff/main.html?_lang_en. 2-11-05.

TABLE 3.7. Family Residence and Neighborhood Poverty by Zip Code: 2000 to Mid-2003

Mid-2003 zip code area	Zip in 2000: percentage in poverty	Zip in mid-2003: percentage in poverty	Change in level of neighborhood poverty	Change in percentage of poverty *within* same level	Percentage of residents in poverty in mid-2003 zip code
Milwaukee					
53206	25%	39%	Middle to High Level		31%–40%
53215	20%	20%	Same Level	No Change	11%–20%
53233	47%	47%	Same Level	No Change	41%–50%
53205	20%	45%	Middle to High Level		41%–50%
53218	25%	20%	Same Level	Decrease	11%–20%
New Orleans					
70122	18%	24%	Same Level	Increase	21%–30%
70115	29%	29%	Same Level	No Change	21%–30%
70117	38%	38%	Same Level	No Change	31%–40%
70117	35%	38%	Same Level	Increase	31%–40%
70125	39%	39%	Same Level	No Change	31%–40%
Philadelphia					
19140	24%	39%	Middle to High Level		31%–40%
19111	4%	10%	Same Level	Increase	0%–10%
19140	24%	39%	Middle to High Level		31%–40%
19134	39%	39%	Same Level	No Change	31%–40%
19144	25%	25%	Same Level	No Change	21%–30%
St. Louis					
63121	17%	17%	Same Level	No Change	11%–20%
63110	14%	24%	Same Level	Increase	21%–30%
65109	39%	7%	High to Low Level		0%–10%
63115	19%	26%	Same Level	Increase	21%–30%
63136	19%	19%	Same Level	No Change	11%–20%
Seattle					
98125	20%	12%	Same Level	Decrease	11%–20%
98108	15%	15%	Same Level	No Change	11%–20%
98118	14%	14%	Same Level	No Change	11%–20%
98126	21%	13%	Same Level	Decrease	11%–20%
98133	11%	11%	Same Level	No Change	11%–20%
Total	Low = 1 Middle = 18 High = 6	Low = 2 Middle = 14 High = 9	Middle to High Level = 4 High to Low Level = 1 Same = 20	Increased % in Poverty = 5 Decreased % in Poverty = 3 No Change in Poverty = 12	

Source: Key Parent Address; U.S. Census Bureau (2000); Summary File 3, P87 (SF3-P87); generated by authors using American Factfinder: www.Factfinder.census.gov/home/saff/main.html?_lang_en. 2-11-05.

from neighborhoods with middle-range poverty levels to neighborhoods with high poverty levels. An even closer look at neighborhoods where the poverty level appears to remain the same shows changes in the percentage of residents in poverty *within* the broader level. In other words, the concentration or density of poverty either increases or decreases. For example, among the twenty families whose neighborhoods remain at the same poverty level between 2000 and mid-2003, the percentage of residents in poverty actually increases in five of the families' neighborhoods, decreases in three, and does not change in ten. Overall, combining these five families with the four who move from middle- to high-poverty neighborhoods, over one-third of the families (nine, or 36 percent) encounter worsened neighborhood economic conditions over the period, poverty conditions remain the same for nearly half the families (twelve, or 48 percent), and only four families (16 percent) "move up," either through moving from a middle to a low-poverty neighborhood or through living in a neighborhood where the proportion in poverty decreases within the broader level.

At the same time, despite census poverty figures and the view in social disruption theory that residential mobility is counterproductive to cohesive community life (Petit, 2004), many of the families here feel allegiance to their neighborhoods and communities and act on this allegiance when they can, as the next section shows.

Community involvement

Ten families are active participants in Catholic churches, Islamic mosques, Buddhist temples, and churches of varied Protestant and Pentacostal denominations in either former or current neighborhoods. Seven more attend services periodically or conduct formal Bible study at home. Several of the families' religious facilities also offer ethnic-based community activities and one sponsors an active program of economic development. All serve as potential forms of cultural and social capital and suggest further that meaning-centered or associational networks may mediate spatial shifts.

In addition to religious involvement, eighteen families find bits of time to participate in other neighborhood or community activities, most of which are also associational rather than geographic or spatial. Some of the parents' activities also involve their children. Teresa Russell volunteers to teach adult evening classes in auto skills and basic mechanics at a school-based enrichment program, donates her catering services to civic events, and chaperones her son's group at a community-sponsored overnight camp. Randy Jackson establishes an ethnic cultural dance troupe in which he and his children perform at fairs and in the children's school. Isabell Smith's family is featured in a school newsletter. Hard Working Blessed is a volunteer mentor at his former rehabilitation facility. The Miracles participate in language lessons for their children at an Asian cultural center. Kevin McDonalds engages with his family in sports activities at a local community center. Tisha Shanks is a community mediation and advocacy volunteer and recipient of an award for inspirational speeches to children about women's nontraditional employment, and she and Randy Jackson deliver similar speeches to manufacturing and construction program trainees. Teresa Russell and Kevin McDonalds participate in national research conferences. Lynn Walker volunteers at a domestic abuse center. Loretta Lopez is involved with her son's scout program. Ayesha Muhammad is active politically in her city's mayoral campaign. Joseph Faithful contributes construction expertise to his church-based community economic development projects. Rachel Quinn conducts informal tutoring of children in her public housing project. In turn, her teenaged son Miguel mentors neighborhood youths.

Many parents want to serve others to reciprocate for the help they receive toward economic mobility, either from their job training program or from another service venue. For example, while homeless, Lynn Walker campaigns for affordable housing on the steps of the state capitol. Featured on the news, her story benefits others and results in her family finding housing. Maya Vanderhand serves on the Board of a nonprofit organization that donates interview clothing to job seekers. As she sees it, the program helped her and now she extends the same hand to others. In community building as a means to involve citizens with a vested interest in neighborhood-strengthening efforts, reciprocity may be an important factor. Shanquitta Tucker becomes a mentor to her extremely vulnerable sister through a community advocacy program. In return for her participation in the program she receives resources and referrals from a trained community advocate. This partnership benefits the community advocate's program and both sisters.

Time is of course the crucial variable in parents' ability to be involved in their communities. For many parents, extra hours beyond full-time work and full-time parenting are consumed by a second or third job, overtime, overnight shifts, off-the-job upgrade training, long daily commutes, efforts to reconsolidate their family, economical shopping in far-flung parts of the city, warding off neighborhood dangers, navigating and negotiating with children's schools, overseeing homework, resolving debt and bankruptcy, fighting depression, tending to chronically ill children or family members, ferrying children to enrichment activities, seeing to family needs in foreign lands, repairing old-model cars, bearing an additional child, and tending to aging parents. Thus despite the parents' desire to participate and generate what seem to be positive spillover effects on the children, community involvement may exact too high a price. Loretta Lopez wants to remain active with her seven-year-old son's scout troop, but it requires more parent involvement than her already-stretched schedule allows. Mike Jeremy's ethnic cultural group offers social solidarity for him, his refugee wife, and children. At the same time such strong ties (Granovetter, 1973) limit his adaptive learning about the American health insurance system and children's preschool programs such as Head Start.

A final price of community involvement is exposing one's children to neighborhood violence. Parents' concern about letting children play outdoors, exacerbated by inconsistent or lack of transportation to and from facilities, limits children's community participation, as Chapter 4 describes in greater detail.

SUMMARY

The twenty-five parents and their families at the heart of this book are trying to move up economically through work. They want what millions of other parents in the United States want—a good job—or what Lafer (2002) calls a "decent job"—with family-supporting wages; health insurance and other workplace benefits; decent and safe housing; good schools for their children; enough food; assets and savings; and a little money left over to enrich their children's development. Over time some parents make significant progress toward economically sufficient futures, at least for a period, as we see in Chapter 6. But two challenges constrain sustained mobility, no matter how hard the parents work or try to move forward.

First, past mistakes or persistent life challenges limit parents' mobility efforts. Some do not have enough education or the education they receive is poor quality. Past education then limits becoming more skilled, getting a job and keeping a job (see Chapters 5 and 6). Some flee war-ravaged countries but face knowledge and policy obstructions in the United States. Some have felony histories, which means that jobs and civic rights are limited, even though the parents have paid their debt to society and feel successfully rehabilitated. Others still suffer from histories of physical and mental abuse and the often-associated alternation of welfare and work. Many also face continuing health hazards and other life stresses, such as depressive symptoms, that together with ongoing family needs complicate attendance and performance at work. Despite these challenges, the parents labor to overcome their pasts and move into the future. They subscribe to the old mobility myth that hard work will pay off if they strive to improve their own and their children's futures.

The parents and their families face a second, larger set of mobility constraints in terms of both national and geographic "place." Conditions in local labor markets, as well as in the national and local economy after 2001, thwart financial gains the workers make during the upturn of the late 1990s and early 2000s. Lacking flextime and other supportive workplace policies, and vulnerable to changes in firm structure and organization, many parents' wages remain too low and their incomes are inconsistent and precarious, especially after the economic downturn (see Chapter 6). The parents use work supports that they learn about in their job training program to make their incomes more elastic, although subsidies such as childcare or Section 8 housing assistance often phase out before their incomes are steady. They then pay too much of their income for housing or they are forced to replace center-based child care with in-home care (see Chapter 4). They move to more affordable housing or to better their children's school environments, but few are able to escape impoverished neighborhoods. They engage in community activities, but the need to take two or even three jobs limits the time available for extensive social capital building involvement.

We conclude with three points about "place" from this research. First, certain aspects of economic mobility related to urban poverty, such as racial and housing segregation and inadequate public schools, transcend place, falling under the domain of federal and state public policy. Second, aspects of both place and job seekers at metropolitan and city levels intersect to require local program and policy solutions. Third, and overall, all aspects optimally require federal and state government investment and locally driven solutions.

Looking forward, excerpts from the families' stories in the next chapters document the persistence of the old mobility myths discussed in Chapter 2. Good workforce development programs and networks and work supports lay the groundwork for economic mobility, but outcomes are often eroded by the intersection of personal and structural challenges and underdeveloped networks (see Chapter 5). Good jobs lay further groundwork for economic mobility, but that soil is often eroded by labor market conditions, inadequate wages, and insufficient policy supports (see Chapter 6). Good public schools for the parents' children are few, which threatens present and future mobility for parents and children alike (see Chapter 7). First in Chapter 4 we examine economic mobility from the perspective of the children of the study parents.

4 The Children
Their Lives and Worlds

> I hope they are well brought up. Not disrespectful. Okay, that's not in the street. Like getting locked up, because that's what happens most of the time here. What I want for my kids is that they grow up, get an honest job, and have a family. It doesn't have to be a job that they make a lot of money. I do tell them, you like to have that, you want this, you want that, so for that, you have to work you know you have to study. —*Aida Gomez, Philadelphia*

WHO ARE THE CHILDREN HERE?

Accompanying the sixty-six resident children in this book to school, church, and family outings we see their lives from many vantage points. Talking to principals, teachers, family members, pastors, caregivers, and others we experience the children's challenges and successes. We hear their dreams about the future, aware that for some the distance between the two is lengthened by participation in underfunded schools and lack of access to affordable quality child care and after-school programs. We marvel at the children who stay afloat amidst environmental turmoil that could topple even the most seaworthy adult.

The children span a broad age spectrum, although many are very young. We see infants and preschool children adjust to busy days, waking early so that their parents can get to work, sometimes receiving care that does little to stretch their imaginations, minds, or worlds. We visit the elementary schools children attend, a few excellent but many with too few books and overburdened teachers, seeing firsthand what happens when children need far more than they receive. We see middle school children deal with normal albeit difficult transitions, some increasingly aware of things they want that parents cannot get. We see secondary school children shepherd young siblings, some managing both jobs and school. We see too many children with too few carefree moments, much of their lives witness to their families' struggles to secure the most basic of material resources. We see children of all ages, though proud of their parent's achievements, developing a view of work as something over which one prevails rather than as something to which one aspires. We see that celebrating the resilience of children, though inspirational, poses a false security and comes at a cost.

As we considered how to examine children's well-being in the context of ethnography, we found that prosocial indicators were limited in large surveys of children, especially those conducted among adolescents (Hauser, Brown, & Prosser, 1997). We also found formal measures of child well-being too clinical for the purposes of our study, as have other researchers (West, Hauser, & Scanlan, 1998). As a result, we look at aspects of child well-being used commonly in child development and poverty research (Child Trends, 1999; Furstenberg & Hughes, 1997; Furstenberg et al., 1999; Magura & Moses, 1986; Parcel & Menaghan, 1994; Scheuren & Wang, 1999). These aspects include family composition and size, health, child care, family background, home, neighborhood and community environment, family and community resources, and responses to parents' work. We present school-related aspects in Chapter 7.

We focus on the resident children in this chapter, although we describe the eighteen nonresident children in the developmental environment section. The chapter first describes the children's age, family size, and health. We look next at the children's developmental environments. Who are their primary child-care providers and what is the larger child-care context for such families? Closer to home, what are the characteristics of the children's family environments? We then look more broadly at the children's neighborhoods and communities. Are children safe or does violence predominate? Given their context, we then examine where families turn for help, presenting the policy and program factors that influence how and whether they have access to the child care, after-school and educational support, and child support that their children need. Finally we explore children's views and opinions about their parents' work and about their own work futures.

FAMILY SIZE AND CHILDREN'S AGE

Recalling that the average age of the key parents is thirty-two, it is not surprising that many of their sixty-six children are young (Table 4.1). Half (51 percent) are age five or under, one-fourth (24 percent) are between age six and eleven, and one-fourth (24 percent) are age twelve to eighteen. The families have from one to five children, averaging 2.6 children. The average number of children per family is thus slightly larger than the national average of 1.9 children in families that have children (Smith 2004; U.S. Census Bureau, 2003). Even so, half of the families (48 percent) have two children, consistent with national and state averages. Thirty-six (55 percent) of the children are male and thirty (45 percent) are female. The average family size, including adults and children, is 4.2 persons.

CHILDREN'S HEALTH

As Table 3.3 (Chapter 3) shows in detail, the children contend with numerous and varied health conditions that we also discuss here. When more than one child experiences the condition the number is noted in parentheses.

Learning conditions include: diagnosed attention deficit hyperactivity disorder (ADHD) (3); suspected attention deficit disorder (ADD); language and learning impairment (2); developmental delays (2); suspected dyslexia; special education for reading (2); and speech. Surgical conditions include toddler surgery for an undescended testicle, infant corrective ear surgery, chronic breathing problems involving adenoid and tonsil surgery, and oral surgery as a toddler. Pregnancy-related conditions include two teenage pregnancies (plus one pregnancy in a study child's girlfriend) and pregnancy-induced high blood pressure. Asthma-related illnesses include: periodic asthma (4), chronic asthma (2), and severe asthma (5). Accident-related conditions include one child with broken fingers, an accident-prone youth

TABLE 4.1. Number and Age[a] of Resident Children and Size of Family

Family name	Number of resident children	Age 0–2	Age 3–5	Age 6–11	Age 12–18	Age >18	Total size of resident family
Blessed	3	1			2		5
Devalle	2	1			1		4
Faithful	2	2					4
Gates	3			1	2		4
Gomez	3	1	1	1			5
Jackson	2		2				4
Jenkins	4	2		2			6
Jeremy	2	2					4
Jones	3	2	1				5
Lopez	2		1	1			3
McDonalds	3		2	1			5
Miracle	2		1	1			4
Muhammad	5			2	1	2	6
Quinn	2				2		3
Raca	3	2	1				5
Russell	1			1			2
Seabrook	2	1	1				3
Shanks	3			1	2		4
Smith	2	1	1				4
Stewart	2		1	1			3
Tracy	2	1	1				3
Tucker	3	1		1	1		4
Vanderhand	4			2	2		6
Walker	4	1	1	1	1		5
Winters	2	2					3
Total (Percent)	66	20 (30%)	14 (21%)	16 (24%)	14 (21%)	2 (3%)	Average = 4.2 Persons

[a] Age group during most of the study period.

who is hit by a police car, and an infant scalded in hot bath water as a result of malfunctioning public housing plumbing. Environmental illnesses include lead poisoning (2) and two children born addicted to heroin. One of the heroin-addicted children is suspected of having been abused in foster care while his mother was in a treatment program. Other conditions or illnesses include ringworm (2), pneumonia, chronic ear infections, heart murmur (2), acute disorder of the peripheral nervous system, tooth decay, possible sickle cell trait, and allergies. Any one condition on its own may not be life threatening, or even "serious," but when it intersects with school attendance, energy for learning, parents' health concerns, and parents' work, a child's health problem can be the proverbial straw that breaks the family's mobility path.

Among this list of children's health disorders, asthma is arguably the most life threatening. In Canada and the United States, five children die from asthma every week (Childhood Asthma Foundation, 2005). Although most children have mild to moderate cases, asthma is the "third largest cause of hospitalization among children under the age of fifteen and is the leading cause of chronic illness among children" (American Lung Association, 2004, p. 1). Similarly, among the children here, asthma is the main cause for school absence, hospital visits, and hospital stays. Eleven children suffer from childhood asthma, and one-third of them experience asthma-related hospitalizations during the research period.

Isabell Smith's experience exemplifies how work and training policies do not facilitate caring for sick children. Two-year-old Pedro Smith's asthma outbreaks result in frequent trips to the doctor, and one outbreak results in a five-day hospitalization that coincides with Isabell's enrollment in advanced computer training. Forced to drop out of the class because of variable attendance, Isabell misses upgrade training that could raise her skills sufficiently to land a higher paying job.

Like most parents here, Isabell does not have a reliable "sick child" backup plan. In hers and at least six other families the backup plan consists of relying on the generosity of relatives. These extended family arrangements are tenuous, especially when they depend on elderly caregivers who are often in fragile health themselves. Another sick child-related complication that influences parents' mobility efforts is that some child-care providers refuse to administer medication to children who need it for routine follow-up of problems such as ear infections. The policy at three-year-old Abigail Seabrook's child-care center states that "Staff cannot administer medication of any kind." This means that Elizabeth, Abigail's mother, has to take time off work or leave her medical technology training class to drive a half-hour to the facility (and back) to personally give Abigail her medicine. Although the policy is a child safety precaution to be sure, it also exacts loss of time, wages, and human capital development that the Seabrook family can ill afford. Such policies reflect that schools and other organizations often do not understand the constraints that many firms place on the actions of low-income parents (see Chapters 6 and 7).

Children's health insurance can be a complex system for families to negotiate (Wysen, Pernice, & Riley, 2003). When Lynn Walker is laid off, homeless, and relocates to an available shelter in another city, the disruption in her children's heath insurance penalizes child and parent alike:

> My plan changed and in the beginning I didn't have it (children's insurance) fully in order. When Kelly got sick (asthma attack) I had to take her to the emergency room at the hospital. Then we got a good private doctor, but she didn't take the medical group. We had to pay over $200 for that visit. That ate up all my emergency money. I also had to get Waldo Aloysius a physical so he could play football. *Lynn Walker, St. Louis*

As all the families experience, the systems that are intended to serve them, such as shelters and job training, seldom focus on the essential needs of the children in the families—an oversight that can have serious financial, emotional, or physical repercussions as family stories in this and subsequent chapters show.

Additional child health data are presented in Chapter 3 and data about children's learning disabilities and influence on school performance are presented in Chapter 7.

THE CHILDREN'S CHILD CARE ENVIRONMENTS

The thirty-four children who are not yet in preschool or K–12 school are involved in different types of care-giving environments as Table 4.2 shows. About two-thirds

TABLE 4.2. Primary Child-Care Status of Children

Primary type of child care	Number (%) of children over the research period
Parent care	8 (24%)
In-home care provided by relative	12 (35%)
In-home care provided by neighbor	2 (6%)
Center-based care: state-funded therapeutic child care (provided in a facility)	2 (6%)
Center-based care: Head Start	1 (3%)
Center-based care: Head Start/Special Education	1 (3%)
Center-based care: licensed child-care center	8 (24%)
Total	34 (52%)

are involved in in-home care, and about one-third in center-based care. The children in center care experience a variety of providers, including therapeutic child care, Head Start, and licensed child-care centers.

The most common child-care provider is a relative, either in a grandparent's or in another relative's home, and a smaller number of children are cared for by a neighbor, either in the child's or neighbor's home. Only a few of these in-home providers are licensed or eligible for child-care subsidy payments. A few parents are the primary child-care provider for their children.

In addition, more than three-fourths of the thirty-four pre-kindergarten-age children (twenty-six, or 81 percent) are in the secondary care of relatives either before or after going to their primary child-care setting, which includes sporadic care on sick days or when parents are between jobs (data not shown). In all, one out of three families with children under age thirteen contend with multiple care arrangements—up to three different care settings at a time—which requires parents to fine-tune their schedules and time commitments to stay in contact with their children's child-care and learning institutions.

As the literature and ethnographic data both reveal, choosing, accessing, affording, and arranging child care are persistent challenges for today's working families, especially for those with low incomes (Schulman, 2000). Each challenge in itself can result in lower quality care than the parent or child desires. Most often these challenges come in twos, threes, or all four, multiplying the likelihood that the child's care will be less than optimal, as the exemplars illustrate next. The status and experiences of school-age children are described in Chapter 7.

Affordability and quality of child care

The average cost of unsubsidized child care in the five cities of this research ranges from a low of $311 per month in New Orleans to $740 per month in Philadelphia (Runzheimer International, 2004). Either figure is too high for most families here. Child-care subsidy payments differ from city to city, as numerous federal- and state-funding streams and state-determined eligibility criteria are implicated in subsidy allocation. Complex co-payment rules are often based on such factors as the number of hours the parent works, the family size, and household income. One study reports that nationally only 6 percent of children ages zero to six, not yet in kindergarten, receive child-care subsidies, although utilization is higher at

10 percent for those designated "near poverty" (100 percent to 150 percent of the federal poverty level) (Kinukawa, Guzman, & Lippman, 2004), which is the income status of most of the families here. Another report estimates that states served about 14 percent of federally eligible children (about one out of seven) in fiscal year 2000 (Mezey, Greenberg, & Schumacher, 2002).

Despite low utilization rates nationally, ten families here (40 percent) apply for and receive child-care subsidies at one time or another during our years of contact. These families pay from $0 to $420 a month. For example, Seattle resident Isabell Smith pays $75 instead of $650 per month to a licensed child-care center for each of her two children. Given the average unsubsidized costs noted earlier, the income benefits of receiving a subsidy are substantial. Even so, the parents' low incomes, especially after the 2001 recession, make the monthly cost difficult—increasingly so as the income eligibility cutoff was lowered in each of the five research cities between 2001 and 2004, making assistance less rather than more available (Schulman & Blank, 2004).

Furthermore, child-care affordability and quality are frequently intertwined. For example, Hard Working Blessed's family is put in turmoil as he strives to get a better job. Suffering from depression and what he experiences as racial jokes at his Printing Company job, Mr. Blessed often brings home the stress of his work. Though glad to leave these troubles behind when he changes jobs, his lateral wage move is not enough to ease the family's serious financial problems:

> During the transition from the Printing Company to the Metal Company, things got a little hard financially. The bills backed up, but we're getting there. There were two weeks in between where I only got one check. *Hard Working Blessed, Milwaukee*

During the period that Mr. Blessed was unemployed and on probation in a new job, the family's child-care subsidy phased out. In response, the parents moved their daughter from a certified, developmental child-care center that cost $185 a week to what they characterize as less adequate in-home child care that cost $75 a week. Thus although Mr. Blessed seizes opportunities that may help his family financially, two-year-old Baby Miracle's short-term developmental needs are sacrificed, as Mrs. Blessed reports:

> Baby Miracle's in daycare now through someone we got through my aunt. I don't like it. It's not set up well enough. The house isn't neat. It's home daycare. The woman has teenage daughters. Baby Miracle is so dirty when I pick her up, even though I've sent along a change of clothes. She's had diaper rash. But it's $75 a week, which is affordable. A really good facility would be $185. That's what the last one cost. I want one where someone will spend time with her; someone who will cultivate her mind. She understands nearly everything. I want a daycare with developmental instruction. *Mrs. Hard Working Blessed, Milwaukee*

In another example, although many parents appreciate the ease of access, affordability, and general quality of relative or neighbor care, they are also concerned about the amount of learning that takes place in such environments (Coley, Chase-Lansdale, & Li-Grining, 2001). For example, single-mother Aida Gomez struggles with the competing issues of family culture, parent pressure, access, quality, and affordability. Aida's immigrant mother cares for her children, eight-year-old Juan before and after school and three-year-old Luis all day. The grandmother's [trans-lated] comments display her preference for in-home over center-based care:

> I don't see how the children will be raised, or she'll have to stop working to care for them. Because who's going to take care of them [after I am gone]? You can't leave just anyone in charge of them. It has to be the mother, or like me, the grandmother.
> *Grandmother of Eight-Year-Old Juan Gomez, Philadelphia*

Although quality of child care is positively associated with children's later school performance (Barnett, 2003), the parents here, like Aida, cannot afford a high-quality facility. They are not alone: in fourteen states child care costs more than double the tuition at a state university (Ewen & Hart, 2003). Aida wants to put Luis in a faith-based child-care center to augment the cultural capital available in her parents' home with the social and developmental enrichment available at the neighborhood facility, but its $100 per week cost is prohibitive. At a $10 per hour wage that puts her family of three at 133 percent of the federal poverty level, Aida is eligible for a child-care subsidy, but Pennsylvania is one of twenty states in which child-care waiting lists are increasing (Schulman & Blank, 2004). Pennsylvania is also one of only nine states that does not budget support for school readiness, pre-K, or Head Start programs (Philadelphia Citizens for Children and Youth, 2001). Aida is particularly aware of the need to help her three-year-old son start school ready, as her older son Juan has just been retained in second grade.

With these examples we see that child care choice, access, affordability and quality are not only intertwined with each other, but also with the policy environment. Micarla Stewart's story further illustrates this entwinement, highlighting the developmental implications of child-care choices that may affect future school success.

Comparing Center-Based and In-Home Child Care: Micarla Stewart's Family Story (Philadelphia)

In twenty-four-year-old Micarla Stewart's family, a child-care subsidy helps her chronically ill child begin to compensate for the human capital and social development she lost because of a severe childhood illness. Preschooler Latice Stewart has suffered from an acute disorder of the peripheral nervous system since she was two years old, one that required repeated hospitalizations and therapeutic treatments. Finally resuming a relatively normal life at age three and a half, Latice's mother enrolled her in a nearby licensed child-care center that cost $137 per week. A child-care subsidy reduced Micarla's portion of the payment to $35 per week.

Six months later Micarla worried that the child-care center did not provide Latice with a stimulating environment and also noticed high staff turnover:

> Latice really wasn't learning anything at the child-care center, and the teachers they would change every time I went in there, so she always had a new teacher and that is not good for kids. And then I saw some of them hollering at the kids; the way they would talk to them (was unacceptable). All the money you have to pay and you are not getting anything. *Micarla Stewart*

As a result Micarla withdraw Latice from the center and put her in the care of her cousin, Karen, who already took care of her developmentally disabled three-year-old son at home during the day. The research team spent a day with Latice and Micarla's cousin in the informal in-home child care. Now almost four years old, Latice knew all her colors, even the color gray. She sang the alphabet perfectly, although she could not yet recognize the letters by sight. She made several astute associations however. For example, she noticed that the capital letter "A" looked like a picture of a triangle. She loved to identify objects and proudly showed these skills by pointing at things around the house:

> This is the boat, and this is the truck, and this is the TV, and this is the ball, and this is the swing, and this is music, a yo-yo, and this is a clock, and this is a block, and this is a glove! *Four-Year-Old Latice Stewart*

Latice's comments also illustrated that reading was an integral part of the family's routine:

> This one is the *Little Mermaid*, and this is *Aladdin*, and *Snow White* and *Beauty and the Beast*. I read this book . . . My uncle helped me read this book, and my mom helped me read this book, and Shalon read the Pinocchio book. *Four-Year-Old Latice Stewart*

Karen explained the daily routine in her care setting. The children begin the morning by watching TV, typically educational shows like *Barney* and *Sesame Street*, then bathe and have breakfast. When the weather is good they are allowed to play outdoors. Karen judged it safe for them to be outdoors on their own, believing that they know the boundaries within which they could roam. In bad weather the children play in the living room, which serves as a communal family space and entertainment center with a TV, a play area, and a computer. It is also a multigenerational space where members of the extended family come in and out throughout the day.

Although comfortable, it was not certain that the in-home child-care arrangement met Latice's educational needs. Karen said that she often reads to the children and tries to introduce educational games and activities, but admits that she does not do this every day. Karen also feels that her son might restrict Latice's development:

> Latice is very smart. I think she needs to go to school to be challenged and to be with other kids, because my son is kind of slow when it comes to certain things, so he might hold her back a little bit. *Karen, In-Home Child-Care Provider of Four-Year-Old Latice Stewart*

Ongoing supervision was a further question, as it seemed that these three- and four-year-old children roamed freely, both inside and outside of the house. Although this allowed for discovery, the absence of trained adults with energy and the necessary skills to simulate learning opportunities may not have been optimal. In the Stewart family as in others, the options for affordable quality child care are limited (Barnett, 2003).

Therapeutic child care

In addition to the usual challenges of child-care access, affordability, and quality, Seattle parent Isabell Smith needs high-level therapeutic developmental child care for her children. The road for four-year-old Pedro and two-year-old Carlos and their mother Isabell, preceding the children's entry into the therapeutic care program, is a rough one. Isabell's first son, Pedro was born addicted to heroin, placed in the custody of Children's Protective Services (CPS), and eventually placed with her partner Domingo's relatives. Two years later and eight months pregnant with Domingo's son Carlos, Isabell entered a rehabilitation facility in order to prevent the foster placement of Carlos who was born with methadone and heroin in his system. Isabell kept custody of him on condition that she remain in the residential facility. Within one month of exiting the intensive eighteen-month treatment program Isabell finally unites with Domingo and her two sons. As Isabell said, "I barely knew how to feed my own face and I ended up with these two little munchkins."

The therapeutic development program is able to help Isabell improve her parenting expertise and assist Pedro to overcome abuse suffered in foster care during the time his mother was in the recovery program. Over the next couple of years, both children progress and ultimately enter "regular" preschool and school classes. These gains were fostered by the therapeutic program's one-to-four staff-to-child ratio, its staff expertise, and its comprehensive model that includes a blend of "nurturing, education, nutrition, and treatment" focused on the assessed needs of the family as a whole (Armstrong, 1997). In fact, this program, coupled with Isabell's job after participating in a business skills training program, enables the parents to form and sustain an intact family for the first time.

THE CHILDREN'S HOMES

The home environments of the children in this book are generally developmentally sound in spite of family disruption and parents' employment that is inconsistent or insufficiently compensated (Chapter 6). Children's substance use or sexual activity is not reported or detected until the end of the research period when three of the teenagers become pregnant (two study children and a girlfriend of the third). All children are expected to wear seatbelts or sit in safety seats although a few families enforce these rules irregularly. All homes have smoke detectors and most, although not all, of the homes meet the requirement of one room per person that housing researchers define as adequate space (Weicher, 1999).

On the more nuanced indicators of child well-being, however, those that commonly involve the intersection of parents' backgrounds, work environments, and children's school policies and practices, the developmental environments of the children look more challenged (Table 4.3). We address the environmental influences on children's school performance and behavior in Chapter 7.

LIVING WITH A PARENT WHO WAS A TEEN PARENT OR DROPPED OUT OF SCHOOL

Some of the children live in families where parents begin their families at a young age. One-fourth of the children (sixteen, or 24 percent) are born into a family with

TABLE 4.3. Parent Background Characteristics Influencing Children's Development

Parent background characteristic	Number (%) of children experiencing the characteristic n = 66
Children who had at least one teen parent	16 (24%)
Children whose parent dropped out of school	24 (36%)
Children who live with a single parent during most of the research period	47 (66%)
Children whose parent receives little or no child support[a]	27 (84%)
Children who have a parent and/or sibling that is or was recently in prison	21 (32%)

[a] The n of children with a noncustodial father from whom child support is indicated is 32.

at least one teen parent, and one-third of the children (twenty-four, or 36 percent) have at least one parent who dropped out of high school (Table 4.3). As Chapter 3 tells us, five of the nine parents who dropped out later attain GEDs but four still lack a high school credential.

The vast body of literature about teenage childbearing over recent decades presents varied and contested perspectives on the developmental, educational, and occupational outcomes for children of teen parents (Annie E. Casey Foundation, 1998; Dash, 1989; Farber, 2003; Farber & Iversen, 1996, 1998; Freeman & Rickels, 1993; Furstenberg, 1976; Furstenberg, Brooks-Gunn, & Morgan, 1987; Hayes, 1987; Iversen, 1995; Iversen & Farber, 2000; Musick, 1993; Parcel & Menaghan, 1994). Although outcomes seem less dire in recent scholarship than predicted during the decades of crisis rhetoric when teen pregnancy was declared an "epidemic," the "problem that hasn't gone away," and was "risking the future," most agree that beginning a family before completing one's education or becoming established in the labor market may result in financial and mobility challenges for parents and children alike. Such challenges include the higher likelihood of low birth weight, inadequate health care, truncated schooling, and eventual poverty (Annie E. Casey Foundation). To date, the children of teen parents here suffer few of these outcomes, although arguably the jury is still out on the children's later schooling, poverty, or mobility. Moreover, most of this literature, and even current attention to adolescent childbearing under welfare reform, pertains only to the children of teen mothers. Increasingly, as we find in our research, fathers—including teen fathers—are identified as key players in their children's developmental environments.

For example, nineteen-year-old Nasir Winters and his seventeen-year-old partner are the parents of a one-and-a-half-year-old and six-month-old when we first meet them. Arguably still a youth himself, Nasir embraces the responsibilities of a parent, tending to his children's immediate as well as neighborhood safety:

> I have to watch Damarius [at age two] carefully because he knows how to open a door now . . . I'm scared to even let my children go over that way [to the nearby park]. There's too much killing around where we stayed. *Nasir Winters, New Orleans*

At the same time, Nasir struggles with the dual tension of being both a young father and a person who wants to complete a GED. His mother points out that fatherhood interferes with Nasir's attendance at GED classes, but he feels that the need to support his children takes precedence over school, as he tells his mother:

> I can't get there right now. I need a job ... I put in so many applications places and nobody called me. I prayed and prayed that I would get a job. This was my last try. I was ready to give up and stand on the corner. I had to do something for my kids. *Nasir Winters, New Orleans*

LIVING WITH A SINGLE PARENT

Many books and articles have also been written about the disadvantages of growing up in a single-parent versus a two-parent household. Some highlight that the disadvantages of single-parenthood overlap with or compound the disadvantages of teen parenthood. One of the seminal books on single parenthood (McLanahan & Sandefur, 1994) reports that whether through divorce or unmarried parenthood, over half of all children in the generation of the 1980s and 1990s will live in a single-parent family at some point in their lives. The authors attribute elevated risks to family structure, similar to those reported for teen parents, but they acknowledge significant heterogeneity of outcomes at the same time. More recent research finds that when poverty status and parents' unemployment are controlled, the negative effects of family structure on child outcomes lessen or disappear (Rainwater & Smeeding, 2003). Still, logic tells us that it's harder to attend fully to children's demands when there's no partner to take a turn.

On the other hand, true single parenthood may be rarer than statistics suggest. Almost three-fourths of the sixty-six children (forty-seven, or 71 percent) live with parents that are classified as single in training program administrative data (Table 4.3). We learn though in Chapter 3 that, in fact, many fewer are actually single (or divorced) in the sense that no adult partner shares parenting. Rainwater and Smeeding (2003) find similarly that almost one-third of children in single-mother families in the United States have another adult present. Still, when we add income to the equation, the poverty rate of children in single-earner families in the United States is 35 percent compared to 11 percent in two-earner families. The "earner" category, however, may reflect labor market conditions rather than marital or partner status (see also Chapter 6). That said, Micarla Stewart's comments exemplify the stress of being the sole financial support of her children:

> I need to save money to move out [of dilapidated public housing]. I was trying to find a easier way but can't find no easier way out, it is just like me and the kids doing everything. *Micarla Stewart, Philadelphia*

CHILD SUPPORT

Almost half of the sixty-six children (thirty-two, or 48 percent) have noncustodial fathers, but only five (16 percent) of these thirty-two children receive child support (Table 4.3), which leaves twenty-seven children (84 percent) without such support. The proportion receiving support is thus lower than the U.S. average of one-fourth of the children in single-mother families (Rainwater & Smeeding, 2003). From the vantage point of the parent, only one in five noncustodial fathers (five of twenty-three, or 22 percent) provides support. Most of the fathers' monthly payments are low ($21, $50, $62, $174, and $260); only the top payment equals the national median annual support figure of $3,400 per year (Grall, 2005). The fathers' payments are also irregular for various reasons. Some of the fathers work in low-wage jobs, others are cultivating next families, forgoing obligations to the former, and the whereabouts of some fathers are unknown. In one case, the father of four children pays regular support for only one of them. Given that this father was at one time imprisoned for domestic violence against the mother, it is possible that holding out child support is a strategy to win back the mother's interest. If so, to date this strategy has failed.

The Tucker children's mother's efforts to obtain child support are typical. Uncomfortable about contacting a lawyer, Shanquitta cannot access the child support system. When she is aided by a professional community outreach worker, the child support process seems less forbidding and gets off the ground. Later when Shanquitta is again without regular child support, the support worker's earlier guidance seems to give her the confidence to contact an attorney:

> I don't know what's going on now. But he has gone back to work. I was going to talk to my lawyer yesterday (but) I haven't talked to him yet. Chris' (father is out of) work, but he doesn't send a thing. *Shanquitta Tucker, St. Louis*

Six of the key parents or their partners or spouses also pay child support. Kevin McDonalds has money taken out of his check for child support debt. Hard Working Blessed's accumulated debt of $20,000 includes child support for his minor nonresident children. Three immigrant parents (Tasha Jones's fiancé, Randy Jackson, and Maya Vanderhand's husband) send money on a regular basis to nonresident children who live in other countries.

Sam Gates's experiences shed light on the life of a noncustodial parent who is very involved in the lives of his children but makes mobility-related choices in order to pay child support:

> After taxes and 401(k) and child support is deducted, I get $150 a week, so moving out of my parent's house is basically out of the question right now. In terms of the demographic, I would like that to be heard. I mean, I have no problem with supporting my kids, okay. But at the same time, I really have to make some tough choices and one of them has been not having the kids here three nights a week because I know that I have to make more money. Now $150 a week isn't going to cut it, so how do I do that? I have to take the night courses or work a second shift at another job. That is where the professional versus the family side of things are clashing at this point, and it makes for some tough decisions. But when you look at a paycheck that says $150 a week, it kind of makes the decision for you to a certain extent. *Sam Gates, Philadelphia*

To earn enough to pay child support, Sam gives up time with his children—a trade he accepts but regrets.

What does not receiving child support mean to children? In addition to the obvious monetary problems, this research suggests that lack of child support affects some children's views about gender roles, as all of the "nonpayers" are men. It also affects the contact children have with noncustodial fathers. In one of many examples, Ayesha Muhammad reports her children's views about the centrality of her role:

> They [the kids] say, "She is my mother and father," and if they have any problems, they come to me. They don't go to their fathers because I'm there 24-7-365. *Ayesha Muhammad, Philadelphia*

Confirming her assertion, when the boys were asked who they see as a role model, ten-year-old Tom answered, "My mom." Tom's nineteen-year-old sister Fatimah expressed stronger disdain for her absent father:

> He tried to beat me but I told him I was going to kill him . . . We see them [our fathers] but they don't help. We know he don't love us. He was in jail; he was on drugs. He used to steal our clothes and stuff. I love my dad because he's my dad, but other than that I don't care about him. *Nineteen-Year-Old Fatimah Muhammad, Philadelphia*

Ayesha's goal for her daughters reflects similar disdain for the children's nonpaying, nonactive fathers, especially the one Fatimah refers to who used to beat Ayesha as well: "I want them to grow up to be self sufficient and realize they don't need a man to make it."

Often but not always no money from fathers means no contact too. Only eight of the twenty-three noncustodial fathers are in regular contact with their children. Consistent with research that positively associates child support payment and contact with children (Seltzer, McLanahan, & Hanson, 1997), the five fathers who pay child support are included in the eight who regularly contact their children. The remaining three fathers do not pay child support but engage with their children in nonfinancial ways and purchase occasional gifts or clothes for them.

Overall, the complex bureaucracy of the child support system and the limited time available to working parents to navigate this confusing system are obstacles to many parents who seek child support. The still-insufficient incomes of many of the families (see Chapter 6) underscore the need to create strategies to help parents hold their counterparts accountable.

CONTACT WITH NONRESIDENT CHILDREN

Seven families have a total of eighteen nonresident children living in other cities, families, or countries (data not shown). Some of these children are under age eighteen; others are over age eighteen and live independently. Many have regular contact with their nonresident parent and his or her new family; some do not. Overall the key parents with nonresident children give considerably more attention and support to them than do the nonresident fathers discussed earlier.

For example, the three children of Maya Vanderhand's husband, Jesus, live in another country but visit occasionally. Although generally congenial, these visits put a considerable strain on the Vanderhand's already cramped two-bedroom apartment, which normally houses four children and already exceeds the one-person and one-room formula for adequate housing (Weicher, 1999). Tasha Jones's husband helps to support his three children (ages ten, seven, and three) from a previous marriage who also live in another country. Although admirable, supporting Tasha's two children and an infant that he and Tasha bear together further strains his income production because his immigration status precludes open-market employment.

Mr. and Mrs. Blessed have a total of six nonresident children from prior marriages. The previously unaffordable orthodontic needs of Mr. Blessed's thirteen-year-old nonresident daughter Jasmine are an important factor in one of his job changes, as he notes:

> I can get braces for Jasmine under Printing Company health coverage. When I found that out, I said, "When can I start?" *Hard Working Blessed, Milwaukee*

During our time with the family, Jasmine and Mrs. Blessed's eighteen-year-old nonresident daughter, Blessed Daughter, join the family in Milwaukee for the summer months. Although it means more mouths to feed, the daughters help to care for Baby Miracle while both parents work, which results in helpful economizing as Mr. Blessed's job change at that time resulted in only a lateral wage move.

Randy Jackson sends money to his twelve- and fourteen-year-old daughters in Africa and to other family members there as well. His wife Shawn hopes that Randy's daughters will come to America for their education because she is "tired of all this sending money back and forth."

Finally, Aida Gomez's fiancé, Marcos, has two young children from a previous marriage whom he still supports. Marcos's devotion to Aida's two children, as well as to his own two and the child that he and Aida eventually bear, is endearing to Aida. It does not, however, fully make up for the fact that Marcos's lack of educational certification results in barely minimum-wage employment. Still, as the literature suggests, emotional attention is critical for children's development even if financial assistance is minimal or lacking. On this metric, the study parents are doing well by their nonresident as well as their resident children.

INCARCERATION

Nearly one-third of the children (twenty-one, or 32 percent) are growing up in families where a parent or sibling is or was recently incarcerated (Table 4.3). Over ten million children in the United States are estimated to experience the imprisonment of a parent. In 2001 alone, approximately four hundred thousand parents are released from prison and jail sentences (Hirsch et al., 2002). The children here who live in such families experience heartaches and what we call "developmental imprisonment," as they reflect the trauma of separation and legacy of incarceration. In one stark but not atypical example, the Shanks children view their mother's arrest, as their mother Tisha recalls:

> They put me on the floor and when I looked out my bedroom door, I looked straight into the dining room and living room and they had guns. One of them had Lita pinned to the couch in the living room with a gun to her head. The look on her face, I can't describe it. It was awful. *Tisha Shanks, Milwaukee*

Even years later after Tisha's rehabilitation, job training, successful manufacturing employment, home purchase "with legal funds this time," and location of superior magnet schools for her children's education, her by now twelve-year-old daughter

Maria responds in terror when police apprehend her mother for a minor driving infraction, as Tisha reports:

> So I got pulled over and then I got a ticket for driving without a license because I don't have a license until that morning. So what affected me was my younger daughter [Maria] was in the car with me, she was in the back seat sleeping, and the officer when he ran my name came up and said I was driving without headlights. He asked me to step out of the car and he asked me if my daughter was a minor and I said "yeah" and so he searched me and he asked me if I had any weapons on me, can I search the car? This was just maybe a month ago and he searched the car and my daughter is looking at me and my daughter has a mind that that is over with, it is no more fear, it is supposed to be done, and because she had so much experience with my past she just started crying, and I said, "He is just doing it, just don't panic." "You sure you are not going to jail mommy?" [Maria queried] and I said "No we are going home." After he gave me the ticket then we got back in the car and she was like "My mom ain't going to jail." *Tisha Shanks, Milwaukee*

Similarly, Hard Working Blessed's rendezvous with his then thirteen-year-old son Tank depicts the wrenching absence and dislocation that can result from a parent's incarceration, for child and parent alike:

> I was away for 5 years. I didn't see Tank from the time he was 7 or 8 until he was about 13. After I got myself together I went back to Chicago to see Tank. I met him outside the house. I said "Are you Tank?" He said, "Yes, who are you?" I said "Your father." He said, "What's your name?" I told him—and asked if he wanted to see my ID. He started shaking and tears were rolling out his eyes. He hugged me and tears were coming out of my eyes too. We've been inseparable since that day. I thought my leaving would be better for the whole family. I shouldn't have cut the contact. Not a day went by that I didn't think about them, worry about them. It was goofy—I thought they'd be better off not knowing where I was, what was happening to me. But I know now that they'd have been much better off knowing I was alive and that I still loved them. *Hard Working Blessed, Milwaukee*

Nineteen-year-old Fatimah Muhammad conveys a complex array of emotions when recalling her abuse by an incarcerated parent, as her earlier comment shows (Child Support section). Further reactions to incarceration ripple through the Muhammad family when Fatimah's twenty-one-year-old brother is jailed for eighteen months for a street robbery during the research period. Although Fatimah's ten-year-old twin siblings look up to their older brother, Tom's comments shed doubt on the brother's ability to be a role model:

> I want to be like my mom and a little bit like my brother but I'm not going to jail. *Ten-year-old Tom Muhammad*

THE CHILDREN'S NEIGHBORHOODS AND COMMUNITIES

VIOLENCE AND CHILD SAFETY

Many children here confront violence in one or more spheres of their life that may or does affect their developmental pathways. Domestic violence, neighborhood violence, and school violence confront the children both directly and indirectly.

Domestic violence and safety

Almost one in three of the sixty-six children has experienced domestic violence. Notably the children are safe from violence in their homes during the research years, largely because the mothers no longer reside with their violent partners. At the same time scholars alert us to the children's continuing vulnerability. Rates of lifetime incidence of domestic violence among welfare recipients, as one-third of the parents (eight, or 32 percent) were earlier, range from 34 percent to 65 percent (Kalil et al., 1998; Lawrence, 2002), with most in the 50 percent to 60 percent range. These figures compare to 22 percent women in the general population who experience domestic violence in their adult lives. Despite such incidence, disclosure of domestic violence to welfare caseworkers remains low (Lawrence), a finding that may pertain to workforce program case managers as well. The quality of the assessment and case management practices in workforce development programs is particularly important for the identification of domestic violence, as we illustrate below and discuss further in Chapter 5.

Illustrating the far reach of domestic violence, when Lynn Walker is laid off from her new job as a computer-assisted interviewer for a research firm and loses her housing at the same time, she leaves St. Louis rather than risk living with the abusive father of her four children. Between 15 percent and 30 percent of welfare recipients, such as Lynn Walker was before her research interviewer job, have been *recent* victims of domestic violence (Fremstad & Primus, 2002).

One year earlier the father of Lynn's children had been jailed for thirty days for assaulting her. Opting now to extricate herself from this relationship, Lynn and her family end up living in a shelter for survivors of domestic violence in a smaller city two hours from St. Louis. Ever resilient, Lynn uses the family detour to earn her GED at the shelter and secure a satisfying job at a library. However, despite Lynn's resilience, the move thrusts her two teenage children into a challenging new landscape. They enroll in a new middle school where 60 percent of the children are Caucasian, compared to their St. Louis school that was predominantly African American. Compared to living in their grandmother's home in St. Louis, they now live in public housing, which Lynn believes stigmatizes them by virtue of their address and the population distribution in the city that clusters persons living in poverty near the housing project. Despite these changes, her children attend a better school in the new city than they attended in St. Louis. From the children's perspectives, however, they have been taken from what they know, miss the family they left behind, and feel under pressure because the school is much harder. Their school performance is below grade because their peers had higher quality elementary educations. Although the Walker children eventually settle into a new routine, make friends, and improve some of their grades, the adjustment comes with difficulties that include a school suspension for fifteen-year-old Waldo Aloysius.

Neighborhood violence and safety

The development of children and youth is often tied to their neighborhood context (Anderson, 1990; Furstenberg et al., 1999; Wilson, 1987, 1996). These researchers connect opportunity with geography, describing how children in impoverished inner-city neighborhoods have the least access to human and social capital resources and often live in areas with high rates of crime, few employed role models, deteriorating buildings, and apparent lack of city funds to address these issues. Similarly, the schools in these neighborhoods are portrayed as having fewer financial and material resources and as providing more-limited services because neighborhood problems are mirrored in the school community (Entwisle, Alexander, & Olson, 1997).

Most children and parents here perceive their immediate streets and physical neighborhoods to be dangerous; thus they seek meaning-centered rather than spatial networks for resources and social contacts. In fact, thirty-nine of the sixty-six children (59 percent) regularly speak of the violence they face in their neighborhoods. The children's and parents' perceptions are underscored by FBI Uniform Crime Report data for 2001 (www.bestplaces.net/crime). Rates of violent crime (murder, rape, robbery, and assault) and property crime (burglary, larceny, and theft) in the five research cities are up to four times higher than national rates. Although Aida Gomez's and other parents' responses to unsafe neighborhoods are protective, they restrict the social capital available for their children's eventual mobility:

> I don't let [my eight-year-old son] play outside because it's too dangerous, especially for him to play outside by himself. There's a lot of crime, a lot of traffic, and things happen here. The other day there was a shoot-out. They were driving. I wasn't here. In the summer the only time he goes outside is when I'm outside. *Aida Gomez and Her Seventy-Year-Old Mother, Philadelphia*

Aida's son Juan concurs with his mother's and grandmother's assessment, explaining that he doesn't like to go outside "because the street is too bad," adding:

> They fight [in the street] when they drink a lot of beer. Usually at a party a guy got drunk and left, and his shirt was off and everything and he was fighting. *Eight-Year-Old Juan Gomez, Philadelphia*

Another parent feels that removing his teenage son from an even more dangerous neighborhood in Chicago is worth the extra cost of locating a semisuburban home:

> It costs a lot to live here in the suburbs, but I'm glad to pay. The kids can go outside and they don't have to worry about gunshots. *Hard Working Blessed, Milwaukee*

In a St. Louis neighborhood, where Loretta Lopez's rented house was spacious and carefully tended, open-air drug activity was evident. During several visits the research team was solicited for drug sales and observed drug arrests at the house next door. Loretta's concern for her children's safety means that her seven-year-old son is not allowed to play outside:

> You don't know what could happen—there could be a shooting, someone could drive over the curve, they could snatch and run and I can't have that. *Loretta Lopez, St. Louis*

A local member of the research team confirms Loretta's view about neighborhood danger:

> Things are getting pretty volatile and desperate in north St. Louis and I think it [Loretta's neighborhood] has become a hotbed as well. *Research Field Notes, St. Louis*

Moving from a home that was "roach and rat infested" and its roof was "caving in" to one in a neighborhood that showed above average increases in income and property values between the 1990 and 2000 censuses did not eliminate the dangers of the street for Ayesha Muhammad's family. Ayesha's strategy to protect her three middle- and high-school-age sons is to forbid outdoor activity:

> It's better than where we were before. But it's a drug area. I can't seem to get away from that. I keep the kids close and in the house. *Ayesha Muhammad, Philadelphia*

According to Ayesha and her children, "shooting" remains a problem. The children report that gunshots and other activity begin "around one in the morning" around the bar and take-out restaurant on the corner. Playing in the streets is likewise forbidden, as eleven-year-old James confirms: "You can't bike in the street or nothing."

Even what Isabell Smith perceives as a relatively safe Seattle neighborhood is subject to violence and consequent restriction of children to the indoors, despite easy access to a well-appointed neighborhood park: "Yes . . . the kids stay in the house a lot because there are a lot of crimes here." The field researcher's observations confirm Isabell's perceptions: "On at least four of my visits to Isabell's house I have seen at least one drug deal within a 4-block radius of her home or people looking fearfully at their neighbors. But this is not the predominant feature of the neighborhood; it is a background feature."

School violence and safety

Violence is omnipresent in schools as well as neighborhoods, as Chapter 7 presents more fully. In just one example, Ayesha Muhammad reported that "A little boy the same age as Tom and Don [age ten], no younger, put a gun to their head [at school] and threatened to kill them." When Tom told the boy, "Instead of me letting you kill me, I'm going to kill myself," school officials panicked. The school sent Tom home, took no action against the perpetrator, and sent Ayesha a demanding procedural letter that forced her to take extra time off work to find an alternative school for them:

> I was so mad I tore it up. [The letter said] "If you feel as though your children's rights are being violated or whatever, you can get in contact with the school board and press charges." I'm not going through that. I'll just take them out. *Ayesha Muhammad, Philadelphia*

A number of children (eleven, or 17 percent) encounter or engage in fighting and violent incidents in their schools. In terms of the ripple effects of violence in the home noted earlier, children in the families who have experienced domestic violence are not the only ones who receive suspensions and disciplinary actions from the school violence we report in Chapter 7, but they are represented in this group.

WHERE DO FAMILIES TURN FOR HELP?

Most families look first within or on the fringes of their own borders for help. With varied levels of information, competence, and trust, they also turn to community sources. For some researchers, turning the public's attention to the need for extended after-school services for older children is a priority (Kurz, 2002).

FAMILIES TURN TO OLDER YOUTH

Welfare reform evaluations are inconclusive about the effects of mothers' employment and welfare transitions on adolescent outcomes. One study finds a few positive effects for young adolescents whose mothers move from no employment to employment, but increased behavior problems for adolescents whose mother goes from employment to unemployment (Chase-Lansdale et al., 2003). Our research suggests that older youths' need for additional support is high regardless of parent work status, in part because the family income remains low even when the parent is employed. As a result, some older youth are expected to mitigate and accommodate the needs of the family. At least ten families here have two or more children under age five, which often puts a logistical and financial burden on single heads of households and on two-parent households when both parents work. As a result, nine older youth (ages twelve to eighteen) in the families bear considerable levels of responsibility, largely through the provision of regular backup parenting support.

For example, fifteen-year-old Lita Shanks exhibits an acute sense of responsibility for her siblings, well honed when her mother was in jail. Receiving a sobering introduction to adulthood at age eleven as she watched her mother's arrest, Lita tries to relieve her mother's pressure and make her own way. She works weekends at a fast-food restaurant and uses her earnings to pay for her phone line, buy a prom dress, and contribute $55 a month to her car insurance. Lita's willingness to help her mother is both admirable and necessary, as she notes: "I want the things my mother can't give us." Although her mother is demonstrably proud that Lita has opened a bank account to save some of her earnings for college, the extra time that Lita spends earning money and taking care of her siblings while her single mother works may cut down on the college preparation she needs to make up for having been retained in grade some years earlier.

As with other families here, Shanquitta Tucker's work schedule has a significant effect on the children. Thirteen-year-old Iesha Tucker provides care for her seven-year-old and two-year-old siblings on weekends and often after school. Iesha explains that her mother's weekend work schedule leaves her confined at home to watch her brother and sister. When asked what she would be doing otherwise, Iesha protectively responds "probably nothing." In fact, her responsibilities at home curtail the after-school activities, such as basketball and cheerleading, that Iesha earlier reported enjoying. When Shanquitta's work schedule changes to allow her to spend a full weekend a month at home, she is glad to relieve Iesha from her babysitting duties.

Thirteen-year-old Waldo Aloysious Walker bears considerable pressure with concern and maturity. About his impending homelessness, pondering what life in a shelter will be like he says:

> I feel bad having to be in at a certain time, and all those people. But that's what we have to do for a while, at least it's something. *Thirteen-Year-Old Waldo Aloysious Walker, St. Louis*

Later re-housed, Waldo makes it possible for his mother to work and know that her four children are safe. As his mother Lynn says, "His presence in the family really took a load off me." Offering a description of the children's after-school life Lynn adds:

> They don't do a lot because by me working the swing shift, once I get off at three and come home and get them situated as far as dinner and schooling and homework and stuff, I have to leave and be back by five fifteen. So by me not having a car, I am going to have to walk to work so I might have to leave early to get there on time. So they [older kids] normally watch the little kids while I am at work. *Lynn Walker, St. Louis*

Still, the pressures on Waldo, a morbidly obese youth with asthma, seem substantial. Recognizing that he may need backup support, Lynn asks a neighbor to stop in and check on the children at night. Reflecting on life's worries after one of many discussions of family finances, Waldo says wistfully, "I wish we were little kids. It was simpler then." Just entering adolescence, Waldo longs for a childhood long past.

Fifteen-year-old Bill Gates also cares for younger siblings. Life after his parents' divorce results in new challenges for Bill that his father reports with regret and pride:

> When Joyce first moved out, I think he had a lot of responsibility put on him when I wasn't around. He's been thrust into some difficult situations, I think, in terms of having to watch his brother and sister at an early age. But Bill has always come home to an empty house. When Rich and Jill were young they went into the after-school program (but Bill didn't). He's always been fairly responsible in that area. *Sam Gates, Philadelphia*

Ayesha Muhammad's primary helper is her nineteen-year-old daughter Fatimah whom she calls her "rock:"

> If it weren't for her, I don't know how I would be able to make it because she is here. She gets the boys out in the morning. [She makes sure] they are dressed the right way and everything so she's here just in case they have to call for somebody to come pick them up from school because they are sick or whatever. *Ayesha Muhammad, Philadelphia*

As a full-time working parent whose commute takes up to one and a half hours each way, Ayesha relies heavily on Fatimah's parenting help. However, it seems that this pressure may have had a derailing effect on Fatimah's efforts to pass the GED or pursue a high school diploma. Fatimah's efforts to pursue a building trade apprenticeship are similarly not successful. Ayesha describes her as "bobbing around" but likely to settle on a career path soon. Eventually Fatimah attends classes at a local college to obtain a high school degree, still providing child-care support during the day for her younger brothers. Pregnant at the end of the research period, Fatimah's future seems both promising and perilous. The responsibilities of impending parenthood, coupled with ever-changing career goals and lack of marketable skills, loom as stumbling blocks to her future mobility.

FAMILIES TURN TO EXTENDED FAMILY

The historic expectation of scholars, programs, and policymakers is that extended family members are the primary source of material and in-kind support for the day-to-day lives of low-income families (Stack, 1974, 1996). Our research also reveals that many families rely deeply on members of their extended family. At the same time, the families' experiences illuminate *both* up- and downsides of such reliance, which raises the question of whether it is reasonable to expect that extended family can or should be the first line of defense against poverty. Although there are compelling examples of how family members step in to provide invaluable support, equally provocative examples point to the need to take a more circumspect and nuanced look at the costs of extended family support.

On the upside, a few families offer vital assistance. Sam Gates's parents let him move back to their home after his marriage ended, which enables him to pursue upgrade training and simultaneously provide a stable environment for his three children, who regularly spend nights and weekends with him. Similarly, Lucky Miracle's extended family provides financial assistance that qualifies his family for a home loan, and their child care and tutoring allow Lucky to work two jobs while his wife pursues upgrade training. Mr. and Mrs. Blessed's extended families play a critical role when Mr. Blessed is between jobs that enables both parents and children to retain the gains they made through rehabilitation, work, and school, as Mrs. Blessed explains:

> He was not able to pay the rent, the light, the gas, the phone, buy the food, and take care of three kids and me. My mother said, "Send the bills that have to be paid and I'll do that." My uncle and aunt helped. We phoned Hard Working's ex-wife and drove to Chicago to get food from them. Hard Working's ex-wife and her husband get food stamps for the kids so they had food. [If people didn't help, if Hard Working hadn't gotten this new job, what would you have done?] We would have separated and gone back to our respective families. Me to my mother and him to his mother. We'd lose this apartment. We'd have real problems with the utility budget that we have to pay on. Some days, I don't know where we're going to get the next meal. God, he comes through with something. *Mrs. Blessed, Milwaukee*

To varying extents, at least thirteen families receive some kind of help from extended family members. For many families, though, the help may be tenuous. For instance, Elizabeth Seabrook calls her mother her "number one support system," recognizing that despite frail health, her mother provides invaluable child care and encouragement:

> The hardest part with my children is when they are sick—when they're sick I'm sick. If it weren't for my mom I'd be up the creek without a paddle. With my daughter sick the way she was, we all just stayed over here [mother's apartment]. She had such a fever. I'd give her medicine but the fever would just pop right back up, so I said "Mom I'm staying here" and that way she'll give me some release. I'll have to get up (sometimes when they are sick) but my mom will say "Go lay down I've got her," and I feel comfortable with that. If it were someone else I'd be like, "No I've got her." That's the best thing, my mom, it really is. *Elizabeth Seabrook, New Orleans*

Extremely grateful for this help, Elizabeth notes the tenuous nature of relative-provided child care:

> When my mom gets sick it really puts a damper on things. I was this close to not being able to work this weekend and I needed to work to pay my rent. *Elizabeth Seabrook, New Orleans*

An almost equal number of families are essentially on their own. Separated either by geography, ideology, or reasonable hope of assistance because their family members endure similar financial struggles, Shanquitta Tucker's experiences exemplify the downside of reliance on extended family.

New to St. Louis, Shanquitta and her children share a house with her sister as a means to cut expenses. This choice represents a costly tradeoff. When Shanquitta's sister becomes depressed and unable to pay her share of the rent, Shanquitta's phone is turned off and both families are evicted. The subsequent living arrangement in adjacent inner-city apartments stretches Shanquitta's financial reserves to their limit, as her sister's persistent health difficulties and consequent unemployment mean that Shanquitta often supports *two* sets of children:

> When I took Iesha and Chris for new backpacks for school this year, (my sister's) children wanted to know why they didn't have backpacks too. So I had to buy them some. That happens all the time. *Shanquitta Tucker, St. Louis*

These and many similar examples identify that expecting extended families to provide a "safety net," haven, or solution to work, life, and neighborhood challenges may leave low-income parents and their children in complex, vulnerable situations. The existence or absence of alternative and potentially more stable community interventions and resources is also important to weigh and consider.

FAMILIES TURN TO COMMUNITY RESOURCES

Parents sacrifice and go to great lengths to provide for their children, yet despite these efforts children often do without. Nearly half (44 percent) of the children participate to only a limited extent in enrichment activities after school, in their neighborhoods, or even in the summer. Lack of information, rigid medical and subsidy policies, and a scarcity of options contribute to the inability of many parents to fully meet their children's needs.

For instance, Mr. Blessed lacked knowledge about between-job health coverage for his children which means they went without medical care for several months. The McDonalds family often ends the month short of food despite the fact that both parents work full time. The family does not qualify for food stamps because the subsidy eligibility criteria count Kevin's irregular overtime income as regular.

School policies may also not be designed with the needs of children in mind. When living in Mississippi, Shanquitta Tucker's son receives speech therapy for a serious stuttering problem. Unfortunately her son's eligibility to receive speech therapy does not automatically transfer from Mississippi and months pass before he gets assistance. Sometimes the resources are simply missing as Maria Shanks's middle school counselor reports:

> I'd really like to have a mentoring program in place for some of the kids in this school
> like Maria. . . . But with the budget cuts, we only have one counselor—me. All of the
> teachers and staff are overworked and we don't have the extra-curricular activities
> that we once did, before the funding cuts. *Middle School Counselor, Milwaukee*

These and other examples show that children's needs for social support—in
particular what Briggs (1998, p. 178) calls "social leverage" that gives youth an
opportunity to get ahead by helping them, for example, to access scholarships
or get into specialized programs, are seldom met by the children's underfinanced
schools or impoverished communities.

We also see how children's lives stall in tandem with their parents. The Rock
Blessed complains that he can not have things like clothes and games because his
mother is unemployed:

> I don't go anyplace. They don't have gas money because my mother hasn't worked
> for a month. *Fourteen-Year-Old The Rock Blessed, Milwaukee*

Fourteen-year-old Miguel Quinn's experiences are similar to those of The
Rock's. Miguel's mother, who works in construction, often endures months without
work. Miguel acknowledges that mobility-enhancing enrichment is thus limited
for him:

> I can't go on the field trips now because I didn't have the money. I have to depend on
> mom's job. If she doesn't have work I can't go. *Fourteen-Year-Old Miguel Quinn,*
> *New Orleans*

Feeling pressured to fit in with his peers, Miguel applies for an early school release
program so he can get a job and earn the money he needs to attend the class picnic
and buy a class shirt and yearbook. For Miguel, the symbols and events tied to the
basic rites of passage in a child's school life are a privilege, not a right.

Parents often spend scarce income and time trying to secure community resources for their children's mobility. Hard-Working Blessed pushes successfully
to get fifteen-year-old The Rock into summer school. Rachel Quinn paves the way
for fourteen-year-old Sadé to get into a better school where her counselor helps
her to do what is necessary to be eligible for Louisiana's Tuition Opportunity Program for Students (TOPS) program. This program would offer Sadé free college
tuition as well as money for books and housing that her mother cannot afford. The
McDonalds family researches child-care programs and finds a good one for their
three-year-old son. They also discover that their eligibility for free and reduced
lunch makes it possible for their son to enroll in after-school activities. Theresa
Russell finds a quality summer program for ten-year-old Tom at a school-based
community and family enrichment initiative and also locates scholarship funding
for summer camp.

In contrast, some families need help to conduct this kind of research for their
children—immigrant families in particular. Despite the fact that Seattle parent
Mike Jeremy, an African refugee, makes many phone calls, he does not understand
the procedure to enroll his son in Head Start. Mike is also not able to identify nearby
classes in English as a Second Language that would help him and his wife with
job search and with the ability to communicate with the children's future schools.

One of the obstacles for the children of one in four parents is the lack of any or reliable transportation. Parents' time at home with their children is reduced by long bus rides to and from work. One mother walks three miles to and from work. Lack of transportation also deters some children from attending after-school and evening activities and often increases the isolation of all family members. Most schools do not provide transportation to and from extra-curricular events, which presents an additional obstacle to children's participation in tutoring, recreation, and enrichment activities. In response to these challenges that welfare leavers and other low-income workers frequently experience (Strawn & Martinson, 2000), a financial literacy-infused transportation program called Working Wheels, created by Seattle-based Port Jobs, assists Teresa Russell by helping her to secure a low interest loan to purchase a reliable car. This program also teaches her about insurance and budgeting. Her ability to get to work on time and to transport ten-year-old Tom to activities improves. She also establishes a credit history and learns skills that help her allocate her income more effectively.

CHILDREN'S VIEWS ABOUT PARENTS' WORK

One of the guiding assumptions of the recent welfare and workforce reforms is that a parent's employment provides children with an essential role model of the American work ethic. Reformers believe that without such models children will not develop positive values about labor market attachment. Our research, as does DeParle's (2004), suggests that exposing children to their parents' work evokes positive *and* negative responses. Importantly, the new economic mobility premise that both cognition and emotion are involved in parents' job choices (Chapters 2 and 6) also applies to the way that children evaluate their parents' work, as the following examples illustrate. In effect, children "know" that a parent's work provides them with necessary material goods, but they "feel" conflicted about the dangers, abuse, discrimination, and strain their parents contend with in low-wage jobs. Only the future will tell whether "knowing" or "feeling" decisions will guide the children's mobility efforts.

Children here develop a realistic idea of what happens when parents don't work, what happens when they do, and what their parents need to do to get ahead in their jobs. Children's impressions are formulated via a front seat to the trauma of joblessness and a lived follow-up, in many families, of both the downside of working hard in low-wage jobs and the upside of having a parent be more financially secure and fulfilled. Many children watch their parent go to work tired and return home tired, wearing the look of a "dead" person as Hard Working Blessed puts it:

> At Printing Company [because of the twelve-hour shifts] I'd go to work, come home, eat, and pass out. Then I'd get up, go to work, and do the same thing. I'm much happier now—all the way around. Especially with Mrs. Blessed. She sleeps a lot better if I'm in the house. Like when there was lightening. I missed being here at night when I worked at Steel Mill & Foundry and at Printing Company. I can breathe now. I'm not so tired when I come in; I have a pleasant look on my face. I'm not dead. I have time with my wife and children and my responsibilities. *Hard Working Blessed, Milwaukee*

Children like Tank Blessed know that parents' jobs are physically demanding and dangerous:

> They both come home tired and my mom is sore when she comes home. The place where my father works is very hot. You can see sparks flying from outside the building . . . I really don't like the type of job he has; he has to carry very hot stuff around. *Fifteen-Year-Old Tank Blessed, Milwaukee*

Although this knowledge does not deter Tank from applauding what his parents are trying to do, "They are for a better future," it seems to staunch the initial academic gains he makes after he and his father were reunited. During the period that his father experiences racial discrimination, multiple injuries, and demotion in wage and position at work, Tank's grades and behavior in school fall. Tank told us finally that he was very worried about his father's health. Like most teenagers, Tank does not express this concern openly to his family or teachers. Instead, teachers describe him as "preoccupied" at school and he makes little academic progress beyond his initial burst. Tank's problems at school mean that Mr. Blessed is summoned to school regularly to consult about his son's performance, and each time that he or his wife goes to school they lose wages. As Duncan and colleagues (1998, p. 409) report, "Economic pressure . . . is particularly detrimental to the self-confidence and achievement of [adolescent] boys." Similarly, when Mr. and Mrs. Blessed separate for a period, Tank returned to Chicago, which he describes as "a messed up place." Tank's choice to drop out of high school in eleventh grade may have been less a calculated decision than an emotional response to his parents' separation, as his father describes: "Tank lay down on the kitchen floor and sobbed when he heard we were separating and moving."

In contrast, some children develop an aware and optimistic perspective about what it takes for a parent to get ahead. Fifteen-year-old Bill Gates exhibits a wise but cautious take on what his father goes through in order to advance his career:

> *Interviewer*: Do you have an understanding of what is going on now with (your dad taking) classes rather than just working?
> *Bill*: I guess just so he can get better at it and get promoted or something, gain more skills so then he'll have a wider choice of things.
> *Interviewer*: Do you have any feelings about that?
> *Bill*: I think it's a good idea, but if it's too much for him I think he should stop. I mean there's always room for getting better at things; it's just if you can handle it. If he thinks he can handle it I think he should try it.

Still, many children watch parents try to move ahead only to have their plans go awry. Some take these lessons to heart. When we ask Waldo Aloysious what he wants to be when he grows up he says, "I still want to be a computer technician. But if it doesn't work out, you always have to have a back-up plan."

It seems that many children, including the youngest, get a view of the work world that conveys the image of employers as tough, relentless and uncaring of families, and as yielding benefits that make it nearly impossible for families to earn enough to save money. "No matter how hard you worked," as five-year old Carlos Smith said, "your mother can't save you money for toys or pizza."

The Vanderhand children's insight about the up and down sides of work is typical:

Work is good to pay the bills, but if you don't like your work and can only just pay your bills work isn't so good. *Ten-Year-Old Max Vanderhand, Seattle*

Eleven-year-old Zimba Vanderhand finds his father's work hard and lacking fair rewards:

The hassles and thing about my dad's work it that it is physically hard and your back hurts and they don't let you rest and then even if you work hard and long you might be laid off like my dad. *Eleven-Year-Old Zimba Vanderhand, Seattle*

Despite their realistic view of the work world, both Max Zimba and Zimba have strong and persistent career goals. Max wants to become a surgeon and Zimba a fireman, although they are still young. In contrast, between ages thirteen and sixteen, their sister Iesha's career goal shifts downward from interior design to cosmetology.

Children understand the importance of working and what it means when a family loses income. When Maya Vanderhand's husband Jesus is out of work the financial strain of supporting a six-person family is particularly hard:

We pay all the bills first; we've cut down on extra stuff. We used to take the kids to McDonalds after church, sometimes rent movies, get extra snacks. We don't do any of that now. The kids they understand. *Maya Vanderhand, Seattle*

At age eleven, Maya's younger daughter understands the family's stringent finances. As she works on her homework assignment Sahari notes how she economizes:

If I put the marker upside-down it fills up again. *Eleven-Year-Old Sahari Vanderhand, Seattle*

One of the most pervasive threads in the children's accounts is that they are frustrated by the lack of time they have with their parents. Inheriting their parent's schedule, children often rise early to get to child care so their parent can get to training or work on time. Not surprisingly, when we visit four-year-old Abigail Seabrook in her preschool class, she is disengaged and listless, having been awakened at 5:45 A.M. to be transported to her grandmother's house. The daunting work schedules of many parents reduce the time they can spend with their children. Lucky Miracle, who works at two jobs and hopes for a promotion at one of them, says:

A promotion would depend on whether there was an opening. I could be Head Night Supervisor. I would like this. I have more responsibility now. I set the alarm at night. I walk back and forth making sure everyone is out of the building. Then I set it at 11 P.M. I come home and shower, eat, and go to bed at 12:30. At 6:45 A.M. I wake up, take the kids to grandma's house, and go to Food Company. I'm tired; really tired. *Lucky Miracle, Seattle*

Nine-year-old Special Miracle complains about her father's seven-day work week. After hearing him praise her singing ability and writing skills, she says to him and the researcher, "But you never check it after I write something. He's too busy."

Fatigue is a factor in many of the parents' jobs and also in their efforts to advance. Working in a high pressure Tech company that requires mandatory overtime and rapid-fire workdays, Isabell Smith regrets not having enough rest or time to be with her children. Her son Pedro, although acknowledging that he wants his mother to work so "she can buy me stuff and food," first and foremost wants his mother to be more available:

> Maybe you can read us the (bedtime) story when you're not tired. *Four-Year-Old Pedro Smith, Seattle*

Some parents, such as Tasha Jones, the mother of two pre-school-age children, choose to spend time with their children over efforts to advance:

> Some of the advancement could take more days and I don't think I would be able to do that because the more time I spend with my children is the best time I could spend with them. *Tasha Jones, Milwaukee*

Tasha's mother notes that fatigue also plays a role in Tasha's decision to leave the well-paying manufacturing job she went to training for:

> Sometimes she might come home from work and she is tired and the babies are crying, both of them are crying at the same time, and she has to hold both of them at the same time and sometimes she might scream at them or something, and sometimes you can see the sadness on her face or feel the hurtness in her voice that I am failing because I am tired. *Mother of Tasha Jones, Milwaukee*

Children in these families are keenly aware of the sacrifices families must make to survive. Many develop opinions about their future that lead them to alternately embrace and question the role of work, as Juan Shanks observes:

> You have to work. And you have to look for what you want. You should give up something to get what you want, but you shouldn't sacrifice too much. My mom's made a lot of sacrifices. She works hard and she likes her job. She gets interested in a lot of stuff. I think the job training is a good thing because it's helped her go on to stuff and she learns about a lot. She seems really interested in what she's doing. It's helped the family in general. *Fourteen-Year-Old Juan Shanks, Milwaukee*

In addition to being exposed to their parents' work, children often hear advice from their parents about the connection between school and work. Elroy Jenkins, though experiencing difficulty in school, exhibits artistic skills. His drawings frequently display highly detailed dragons and ninjas, as we observe and Elroy's mother reports:

> He's an excellent drawer. He can really draw and he loves to draw, but that got him in trouble. He wanted to be a cartoonist when he grows older, so I told him, "As long as you keep your grades up; you need to get your grades up. You have to have some kind of schooling." *Jane Jenkins, St Louis*

Children's exposure to their parent's workforce development program (see Chapter 5) may help them to regard people and/or institutions as beneficial. When thinking about his mother's manufacturing training program, Juan Shanks says he believes that success is achieved through balance and meeting the "right people." It is possible that watching parents struggle at work may have a less positive effect on children's future mobility efforts than does watching how parents prepare for and get jobs.

SUMMARY

Children are growing up in families where parents work long hours and are often exhausted. Parents are under particular stress when a child has a chronic illness such as asthma. The dangers in neighborhoods and schools are everyday circumstances that children and parents both confront. At least half of the sixty-six children here live in neighborhoods where drugs and violence are commonplace. Parents confine their youngest children within their homes and fear that their oldest will be lured by the street. School and community resources to counter this isolation or resist this lure are in short supply.

After attending training programs, the parents' jobs and subsequent increases in income help them to provide greater cultural capital for their children. At the same time, practical supports such as affordable child-care and after-school programs for children and youth are often absent or not accessed by parents. Although a few parents have the energy, networks, and information to connect their children with better child-care programs, most do not. Restrictive subsidy and work-support policies contribute to this disconnect. The few times that such social leverage (Briggs, 1998) is available, as with Miguel and Sadé Quinn's access to magnet schools and Tom Russell's involvement with a school-based community and family enrichment program, they prove valuable sources of human and cultural capital.

Children want their parents to work and earn money. Their appreciation and understanding of the importance of education and training, and sometimes work, is advanced by watching their parents. Older youth may apply the lessons of their parents' training and work engagement to the way they approach their own lives, as evidenced by Juan Shanks's observation that it is important to "know the right people." At the same time, seeing the daily struggles of parents renders these efforts suspect, leaving one to wonder what the ultimate cost of children's disillusionment may be to their mobility futures.

This chapter shows that families, communities, schools, firms, and social policies intersect to influence child and youth development and student achievement. The next three chapters elaborate further on these intersecting relationships.

5   Workforce Development

Systems and Networks

> Without a start, there is no finish.
> —*Kevin McDonalds, Milwaukee*

WORKFORCE DEVELOPMENT: PAST AND PRESENT

As the previous two chapters show, the parents and children in this book exhibit strengths and competencies. Like millions of families in the United States they also contend with personal and labor market challenges that constrain their ability to support their families through work. Based on the old mobility paradigm assumption that acquisition of human capital is the key to labor market success, job seekers like these parents often intersect with "workforce development systems," which are the focus of this chapter.

Three main routes are available to persons who seek to expand their pre- and postemployment knowledge and skills: four-year colleges; two-year community colleges; and a scatterplot of public, nonprofit, and for-profit programs for those not wishing or eligible for "college." Each of these routes can be accessed directly through the national system of One-Stop Career Centers or through a regional or local workforce development network. Actually, many community college programs overlap with public and private programs, serving some youth and adults who will transfer to a four-year college, other youth and adults who enroll for vocational credentials, and—again overlapping—still other youth and adults who need remedial and specialized programs to compensate for inadequate or incomplete secondary education before they can advance to higher education or skill training. General Educational Development (GED), English as a Second Language (ESL), and Adult Basic Education (ABE) are the most common compensatory programs. This complex array of employment-related programs constitutes the landscape for the parents and their families here as they pursue economic mobility through both preemployment and postemployment efforts. To the extent that these programs are interconnected through the national system of One-Stop Career Centers, they are known as the "workforce development system."

We ask several questions about this workforce development system in relation to its role in economic mobility. What is the history of the system and how does that history guide the present? How is the system configured under recent welfare and workforce legislation? At regional and local levels, what additional or alternative workforce development networks and programs are available to job seekers like these parents, and how do the parents experience them? Finally, how can workforce development systems and networks be further structured and positioned to improve family economic mobility?

FEDERAL WORKFORCE DEVELOPMENT SYSTEM

Over its seventy-year history, employment-related programs in the federal workforce development system (known earlier as the "education and training system") have been designed to help individuals with histories of educational and economic disadvantage bridge the labor market. This history begins in the 1930s when the Works Progress Administration (WPA) and the Civilian Conservation Corps (CCC) vigorously attacked adult and youth unemployment during the Great Depression. With nearly one-third of American workers out of work during the Depression years, national solutions, such as public job creation and national economic planning, eclipsed independent local efforts. After World War II, as the economy recovered and these programs dissolved, the G.I. Bill spurred enrollment in college and vocational education (National Center for Public Policy and Higher Education, 2002). Yet despite the prosperity of the postwar 1940s and 1950s, access and sustained attachment to the labor market remained a problem for many. Thus a new stream of job training initiatives emerged from the Department of Labor, separate from public education and from broader economic development. These initiatives prioritized the strategy of training individuals for employment in the private sector over the strategy of public job creation (Lafer, 2002).

The new stream begins with the Manpower Development and Training Act (MDTA) in 1962 which spawned an array of remedial education, vocational training, on-the-job training, subsidized work experience, and job search programs both for workers dislocated by technological advances and for economically disadvantaged job seekers. Job Corps, a specialized, primarily residential academic and job training program for youth, was added in 1964. The Comprehensive Employment and Training Act (CETA) was passed in 1973 in an effort to consolidate these various job training programs. At the same time CETA decentralized program responsibilities to local governments (Karger & Stoesz, 2002). During the recession of the 1970s, decentralization resulted in a revival of public sector job creation as well as a continued focus on training individuals with little or no work experience for private sector employment. The subsequent Job Training Partnership Act (JTPA) of 1982 kept training attention on those who are chronically unemployed, creating the system of Private Industry Councils (PICs) to synchronize training and job opportunities locally (Karger & Stoesz). Despite intentions to the contrary, programs emanating from these legislative acts were plagued by fragmentation, antiquated pedagogy, and inadequate funding. Evaluations found that these programs were of limited effectiveness in increasing employment and earnings (Bloom et al., 1993).

At the same time another strand of federal work programs, commonly called "welfare-to-work," emerged through the public assistance system and targeted welfare recipients. The Work Incentive Program (WIN) created by the Economic Opportunity Act of 1967 and the Job Opportunities and Basic Skills (JOBS) program of the Family Support Act of 1988 are perhaps the best known of these. Both programs served recipients of Aid to Families with Dependent Children (AFDC), the cash assistance ("welfare") program before TANF. Evaluations of these welfare-to-work programs similarly reported modest if any increase in employment and earnings (Friedlander & Burtless, 1995; Gueron & Pauly, 1991).

Although these earlier welfare-to-work programs incrementally emphasized work attachment over training, the shift becomes fully articulated through passage of the Personal Responsibility and Work Opportunity Reconciliation Act of 1996 (PRWORA) and its Temporary Assistance for Needy Families (TANF) program, commonly known as "welfare reform." The reform legislation mandates a lifetime limit of sixty months' receipt of public assistance and makes receipt of assistance contingent upon participation in work activity. PRWORA devolved major responsibility for funding decisions to states through block grants and major control to states over implementation.

This scatterplot of federal programs also includes specialized pre- and postemployment programs that are aimed at persons who want or need to upgrade existing skills or learn a new field. These programs are available to economically disadvantaged individuals, but they also target current workers and persons who are temporarily unemployed, whether from layoff or from another form of dislocation. Such programs receive funding from multiple sources: commonly, the federal departments of Housing and Urban Development, Health and Human Services, Education and Labor, and a variety of state-level departments.

Responding to tepid evaluation results from what is less a "system" than an array of atomistic, un- or loosely connected education and training programs, the Workforce Investment Act of 1998 (WIA) attempts to integrate public and private programs into a more unified network, now called the "workforce development system" (America's Workforce Network, 2002). Devolution of funding and implementation to states is a feature of WIA as of PRWORA. Partnerships among multiple community and institutional actors toward this end are a key goal of this newly configured system at the local level. Workforce Investment Boards (WIBs) led by local businesses replace PICs, and programs in adult education and literacy, vocational rehabilitation, and vocational and technical education are to be integrated into a national system of One-Stop Career Centers to be used by individuals seeking employment and by businesses seeking skilled workers. The One-Stops also provide access to training services for economically disadvantaged job seekers and dislocated workers who have a demonstrated need for training and give them a choice of training providers. Another key system aim is active demand-side engagement with employers toward sustained labor market attachment and retention for job seekers. To date, the workforce development system has had only limited success in consolidating programs and funding streams (Buck, 2002; Employment and Training Administration, 2005), and statutory adjustment of WIA-related programs remains stalled in reauthorization (Workforce Alliance, 2005). Similarly, WIA hasn't yet had broad success in its aim to engage local businesses as partners in design and hiring (Van Kleunen & Spence, 2003).

Despite the attempts at integration and broader configuration, federal employment efforts share three characteristics. First, they are funded from separate, often disparate federal streams and rely heavily on state resources to supplement federally funded training. As such, most are structured and evaluated as self-contained, siloed programs, without acknowledgment of the roles that other social institutions play in economic mobility.

Second, these initiatives have never been funded adequately to meet demand or outcomes, especially during the post-2001 recession period of sustained joblessness. As O'Leary, Straits, and Wandner (2004, p. 13) report, "Federal expenditures on job training in 2000, at 0.4 percent of gross domestic product (GDP), position the United States in the bottom 20% of OECD nations in terms of government spending on job training." Lafer (2002, p. 43) reports similarly that "The entire federal training budget is only sufficient to serve 5% of the eligible population." Inadequate funding is partly due to the fact that employment-related programs are conceptualized and funded outside the system of "regular" (i.e., public) education (Grubb, 1996) and outside national economic development (Giloth, 2004c).

Third, the effectiveness of these initiatives has seldom been assessed over a long enough period of time. The few studies that assess program outcomes over the long term, up to nine years after program completion, report better results than do the short-term evaluations (King, 2004; Krueger, 2003). Nevertheless, and stemming largely from these three characteristics, reports of limited outcomes of employment-related programs in the 1980s and early 1990s led the press, public, and policymakers to the conclusion that "job training does not pay" (Friedlander & Burtless, 1995; Gueron & Pauly, 1991). This conclusion then paved the way for the antitraining, "work-first" reforms in the 1996 welfare legislation and the 1998 workforce legislation.

Recent research challenges the conclusion that job training doesn't pay. In the early evaluation designs, success or failure was measured primarily by employment, annual earnings, and reductions in welfare payments (Grubb, 1996), rather than in longer term measures such as job retention and career advancement. Labor market variables were rarely included. One might ask whether the weak condition of labor markets for modestly skilled work could explain the pervasively mediocre results of workforce development programs (Grubb, 1996, p. 100), but evaluations do not ask this question. In contrast, evaluation of outcomes over a longer period of time finds what most workforce providers know: that education and skills training "do pay" (Acs, Phillips, & McKenzie, 2001; Fleischer, 2001; Hebert, St. George, & Epstein, 2003), even for job seekers whose educational and work backgrounds are most disadvantaged (Grubb, 1996; Carnevale & Desrochers, 1999; Krueger, 2003; Mathur, 2002; Smith et al., 2002). Regardless, a work-first philosophy and its accompanying reductions in allowable education and job training prevail in the federally funded workforce development system.

In response, local and regional workforce development initiatives have emerged to better help economically disadvantaged residents get jobs, keep jobs, and move toward family-supporting wages. To the extent that initiating organizations cooperate and collaborate with one another, these initiatives form regional and local workforce development networks that are characterized by structured partnerships among a broad range of community and institutional actors and by the multipronged goal of poverty reduction, employment and earnings increases, and area economic development (Harrison & Weiss 1998). Similar workforce development networks that are structured to some extent outside of the federally funded workforce development system form the landscape for the parents here.

WORKFORCE DEVELOPMENT NETWORKS

DEFINING WORKFORCE DEVELOPMENT

What exactly is "workforce development"? Although there is no single definition, Meléndez (2002, p. 2) describes workforce development as "a synthesis of the fields of employment and training, social services, economic development, and corporate human resources." More broadly, workforce development "encompasses the traditional social and supportive services necessary for job seekers to succeed in the labor market, as well as employer services and employer-intermediary relationships that influence successful recruitment and incorporation of workers into the workplace, career advancement, and increased productivity" (Meléndez, 2004, p. 29). In short, multiple community organizations, institutions, and entities partner to form a workforce development system utilizing the One-Stop Career Centers as a backbone, whereas the same or different array of actors forms regional and local networks toward simultaneous development of the workforce and local economies.

FROM STRUCTURAL HOLES TO STRUCTURED WHOLES

Contributions from economic sociology frame the notion of this network structure and function. On the job seeker side, Granovetter (1973, 1983, 1995) argues that weak ties, those characterized by distance and infrequent interaction, are more likely than strong ties to be sources of novel information about job possibilities. Interactions among the institutional actors in a workforce development network and between training program case managers and job seekers are examples of relational but nonfamilial weak ties. Strong ties reflect connection with others who are close to a job seeker and are thus less likely to transmit new information or provide new connections. Family or ethnic networks are examples of strong ties.

On the side of corporate actors—here we would substitute workforce development actors that include but are not limited to corporate actors—Burt (1992, p. 2) holds that "structural holes," or the "network of relations that intersect in a player," can be bridged for "entrepreneurial opportunities for information access, timing, referrals, and control." Further, "structural holes are an opportunity to broker the flow of *information* between people and *control* the projects that bring together people from opposite sides of the hole" (Burt, 2002, p. 155). Granovetter (2002, p. 52) similarly posits the importance of cross-cutting ties that are a "level of coupling between discrete networks or institutions that provide channels through which a strategic actor may leverage weak attachments across segments so as to assemble resources into a larger social entity." Again, the actors comprising a workforce development system or network, such as training providers, intermediaries, policymakers, human and social service organizations, businesses and K–12 schools, are examples of discrete institutions. In effect, trusted relationships and reciprocal partnerships among these actors toward the goal of economic mobility and economic development (Blair, 2005; Giloth, 1995) form what we amend Burt's (1992) concept to call *structured wholes* to benefit job seekers, workers, firms, and communities alike.

WORKFORCE INTERMEDIARIES

These structured regional and local networks are often initiated and coordinated by a new form of workforce organization called a "workforce intermediary" (Giloth, 2004b). A workforce intermediary, which holds no single definition, is broadly conceptualized as a local or regional coordinator of job seekers and workers, workforce development programs, business, and community-based organizations (CBOs). More than simply employment brokers, workforce intermediaries initiate development strategies, coordinate funding streams and services, and navigate "on the-ground partnerships" aimed at career advancement (not just "a job") and business development (Giloth; Poppe, Strawn, & Martinson, 2004). In effect, workforce development intermediaries structure intersecting public and private programs and organizations into a systematic whole to address employment-related and economic development concerns. In the federally funded workforce development system under WIA, local WIBs are charged with fulfilling these workforce intermediary functions. In local and regional workforce development networks, both public and private entities serve as workforce intermediaries: for example, city government offices, CBOs, nonprofits, business associations, and others. Families, firms, education, job training programs, and policymakers are among the essential actors that must intersect if a workforce development system or network is to be broadly effective. Given the myriad policies, program missions, beliefs, bureaucracies, unions, organizations, and political allegiances involved in local workforce development networks, it is not surprising that job seekers experience them in varying ways, as the family stories show next.

STRUCTURE OF THE PARENTS' WORKFORCE DEVELOPMENT PROGRAMS AND NETWORKS

Broadly, the workforce development programs that the families experiences are flexibly affiliated with a national demonstration whose goal is systemic workforce development reform (see Appendix A, Research Design). The structural core of the reform effort is a workforce intermediary in each of the five research cities (Philadelphia, New Orleans, Milwaukee, St. Louis, and Seattle) that develops strategic partnerships with an array of education and workforce development programs and other community organizations and institutions to create a regional or local workforce development network. The array of workforce development programs for the parents here includes welfare-to-work or "rapid attachment" programs; short-term job readiness ("soft skill") and basic computer skill programs; soft-skill programs that feed into vocational training at unions, technical institutes, and community colleges; and programs that offer extended skill training for specific trades, industries, or occupations. These programs receive time-limited funding from the intermediary, direct funds from federal and state sources such as TANF and WIA, and occasional supplemental funding from private sources such as local foundations and business consortia. Although a few programs were created by the local intermediary, all but one job readiness program are structurally and programmatically autonomous and serve job seekers beyond the demonstration.

The parents' workforce development and job training programs offer services on site or in conjunction with their network partners. Program components generally include orientation, assessment, employment or career planning, preemployment training, job placement or job search guidance, case management, and follow-up or postemployment services. The extent and delivery of these components, however, as they intersect with the parents' histories, interests, and characteristics, variably influence mobility. As context for understanding the effects of these variations, we briefly describe the typical menu of program components.

Eligibility and orientation

The parents' workforce development programs are generally guided by the income eligibility criteria of federally funded programs: in all cases below 200 percent of the federal poverty level. Some programs explicitly target youth and young parents (age eighteen to thirty-five) and all target residents of impoverished inner-city communities and African American men. The parents generally learn about the program through marketing efforts, referral from another organization, or word of mouth. When they contact a program they receive a general orientation to its structure and scope of services. Information and referral services are generally provided to those who are not interested in the program's menu of offerings.

Assessment

An initial assessment generally explores what the parent wants from the program, her or his strengths and challenges in terms of getting and keeping jobs, and the programs or services for which she or he may be eligible or appropriately matched. Assessments typically examine educational skill levels, occupational skills, prior work experience, employability, interests, aptitudes, and supportive service needs. Ideally assessment includes evaluation of the parent's eligibility and need for work supports such as housing, medical and food assistance, and the Earned Income Tax Credit (EITC). These inquiries may be conducted by a case manager or another staff member. Variations in intensity and efficacy depend on both program structure and assessor expertise.

Preemployment training

In the current "work first" environment, preemployment training is not universally available to job seekers. Where it is available it includes job readiness training that may offer elementary computer training but primarily emphasizes "soft skills" such as workplace behavior, job search techniques, résumé construction, and English and math. Preemployment training programs in local workforce development networks may also include "hard skill" training content that is (or is not) aligned with a job seeker's assessment results and is keyed to an industry sector or occupation. Soft- and hard-skill training may be offered sequentially or concurrently through an integrated approach.

Case management, follow-up, and career advancement

In these and most other workforce development programs, case management covers a broad terrain. When programs have no official "case manager" role, the parents often informally seek out a staff member for career guidance, emotional support, and policy information about work supports and subsidies. Other programs structure intensive and extended relationships between case managers and trainees and program graduates. Although most of the parents' programs offer some form of follow-up or postemployment (retention) service and support, as is increasingly expected under TANF and WIA, these services and supports vary in intensity and relevance. Programs in workforce development networks that are articulated with registered apprenticeships offer postemployment upgrade training for career advancement, but most programs are funded and designed to help job seekers get and keep rather than advance in jobs.

Employer involvement

Increasingly workforce development programs try to engage employers as network partners for program design, implementation, and job placement. In some cases, firms guarantee jobs to successful program graduates. In other cases partnerships between programs and employers are as yet underdeveloped.

Given the complexity of the network formation task, the structuring of regional or local workforce development networks, within or external to the federally funded system, takes place to greater and lesser degrees. As such, the workforce development programs that the key parents experience are generally typical of the landscape of relatively independent job training enterprises focused on specific purposes and service niches. Accordingly, the families/job seekers contend with issues that cut across workforce programs and networks to affect economic mobility.

The remainder of the chapter draws on family stories and the views of family members, instructors, work supervisors and others who are vested in the parents' success to elaborate upon five such cross-cutting issues: (1) assessment, (2) preemployment training, (3) case management, (4) the "signal" effect or reflected credibility of the program or system partners on employers (Ehrenberg & Smith, 2003), and (5) postemployment training and services. Some stories show that local networks of employers, intermediaries, and workforce training organizations form structured wholes that help job seekers develop knowledge about careers and career paths (Osterman et al., 2001) and make fruitful contacts to this end. Other stories show that more isolated programs or underdeveloped networks may constrain new workers' economic mobility, particularly if postemployment training and services are limited or nonexistent. Most stories identify that policy actors are necessary but generally absent actors in workforce development networks.

CROSS-CUTTING ISSUES IN WORKFORCE DEVELOPMENT

CROSS-CUTTING ISSUE # 1: ASSESSMENT

Workforce development programs commonly conduct initial assessments of job seekers' strengths, challenges, and career goals. In their landmark evaluation of welfare-to-work programs, Gueron and Pauly (1991, p. 242) describe the typical process as "a structured, intensive upfront assessment, followed by the development of an individualized employability plan and referral to services deemed appropriate by the case manager and/or welfare recipient."

Focus of assessment—individual or family?

Commonly, however, program assessments focus on the "individual," which means that the family context in which the job seeker is embedded is addressed tangentially if at all. The families here illustrate how the experiences of partners, spouses, children, and grandparents affect the key parents' mobility efforts, for good and ill.

For example, because Mike Jeremy is a recent refugee, comprehensive assessment of the family's financial status might have resulted in a way to help Mike negotiate the complex and confusing world of American medical payment (Armstrong, Lord, & Zelter, 2000). Before Mike entered training, his wife Christine needed medical care for a broken collar bone that resulted from a car accident in which Mike's friend was the driver. The bill remained unpaid for several years until a judgment was rendered against Mike's friend. The lengthy challenge of dealing with the world of medical insurance required Mike to take unpaid days away from work that had a debilitating effect on his family's income and credit.

Another important but generally underexamined aspect of workforce development assessment is the employment status of the job seeker's partner or spouse. Although case managers or other staff assessors may ask generally whether a partner or spouse is employed, few pursue this critical element of family well-being in depth or at later points in the program. The partners and spouses of the key parents exhibit equally if not more tenuous holds on employment and wage earning, which markedly influence how the key parent navigates job training and, as we see in Chapter 6, makes choices about promotion and retention at work. For example, Maya Vanderhand's decision to not pursue an advancement opportunity at work rests largely on her husband's intermittent income production.

A few parents persuade their training program to help their partner find a job in its network of firms, but more often workforce development networks are not yet deep enough to address the "other half" of the mobility equation. For example, Lucky Miracle's case manager learns from the research team that Lucky did not locate a job through the manufacturing training program's network and thus remains stuck in a job he's held for ten years without promotion or advancement:

> We did career assessment when he first came. The program was just starting. Sometimes there was not enough time to go into his history, how he got here. I rely on what clients tell me. I guess I need to question them. *Case Manager of Lucky Miracle, Seattle*

When program staff members were unable to find employment for Lucky because of an industry slowdown, a comprehensive family assessment could have revealed that Lucky's wife would soon lose her job, which would then mean the loss of family health insurance coverage, and that a recent move put Lucky's family in debt. These circumstances led Lucky to abandon his search for a manufacturing position—and career—and take a second job as a school custodian instead, thus sidetracking his economic mobility progress. When his wife lost her job, she was misguided into a computer training program that surpassed her language ability, which further stalled the family's progress.

Mike's and Lucky's are two of many parents' experiences here that suggest how comprehensive family rather than individual assessment can better inform partners in workforce development networks, such as training institutions and firms, about job seekers' or new workers' needs.

Assessing the match between job seeker and training program

The subject of assessment raises the critical issue of "matching" for economic mobility, identifying that mobility may be slowed when the training choices available in a workforce development network are underdeveloped. In related research, Batt, Hunter, and Wilk (1998) identify that the worker–firm match significantly influences retention. Our findings suggest that the ability of a workforce program to match a job seeker to appropriate training similarly influences mobility. Appropriate matching may be aided by comprehensive family assessment and a broad network of skill training and employer partners, as Tasha Tracy's somewhat opposite experience suggests.

Job Seeker Training Network Match/Mismatch:
Tasha Tracy's Family Story (New Orleans)

Tasha Tracy does not lack determination. Her rallying cry is, "If I say I'm going to do something, I'm going to do it." When Tasha entered the job readiness portion of her training program at age twenty, she was in her words, "going all kinds of ways." Health care training advisors in the program encouraged Tasha to hone her "soft skills" so that she might one day fulfill her goal of becoming a pediatric nurse. Tasha valued the guidance the job readiness program provided toward her goal of establishing her own household. At the same time, underdeveloped assessment of her goals and abilities in the context of her family needs, coupled with underdeveloped articulation between the job readiness program, health care training partners and state policy, slowed her forward movement.

Mother of two-and-a-half-year-old Rachel, Tasha is a high school graduate who received business technology training in the Job Corps but left before she received certification. When it was time to fulfill the community service component of the training, Tasha's mother became ill and Tasha felt obligated to help care for her younger brother. Although her mother recovered, Tasha did not return to training. Instead she used six months of TANF assistance while she devised her next plan.

Having expressed an interest in nursing, Tasha's TANF caseworker referred her to a job readiness program that partnered with a Licensed Practical Nurse (LPN) program at a local community college. The readiness program planned for graduates to enter the college immediately after program completion, but this proved a difficult transition for most because New Orleans secondary schools did not prepare them academically for the community college's challenging and competitive environment. A readiness program administrator reported that the program learned about the community college entry problems over time: "We severely underestimated the need [our readiness graduates had] for academic remediation."

In response, the readiness program next attempted to partner with a for-profit institute for a medical coding program under development and with a vocational institute for its existing LPN program. According to the readiness program administrator, the vocational institute's eighteen-month LPN program was less demanding, but it was also unaccredited, which meant that credits Tasha earned would not transfer to an accredited LPN or RN program. Conversely, the community college program would be longer, more challenging, and accredited, but Tasha was not referred to it. Speaking generally, the administrator acknowledged that assessment was very important for a good training placement match:

> We need to do a better assessment to decide who needs to go to the community college, who to the vocational college, and who to a coding class. *Health Care Administrator at Tasha Tracy's Job Readiness Program*

Given Tasha's interests and academic record from a public high school considered "academically above the state average" (Louisiana Department of Education, 2001), it was unclear why the readiness program did not steer Tasha to the community college's LPN program. Her entry into the readiness program before its training network developed beyond a single partnership, and the fact that her program application did not show that she held a high school diploma (she had marked "no degree" because "I have no college degree"), may have interfered with a comprehensive assessment of her academic potential. Although Tasha scored at the high school level (between grades 10 and 12) on the math and spelling sections of her Wide Range Achievement Test (WRAT), she scored at grade 5 on reading. Even though the reading result was not consistent with her academic record, she was steered away from the college LPN program without further assessment of these discrepancies.

While Tasha waited for the readiness program to more fully develop its partnerships with the noncollege health care programs, the readiness program placed her in a dietary service position at Hospital-LA at a wage of $5.58 per hour. This full-time wage resulted in an annual income of $11,606, approximately $350 below the federal poverty level (FPL) for a family of two in 2002. Complicating matters, subsidy policies in Louisiana were not generous, according to Tasha: "I had to go four weeks, a whole month, just to get the money for child care." Although the cost of child care was partially subsidized by the state for the first two months of employment, by the third month, regardless of income, parents must shoulder the cost alone:

> I was on the program Child Care Assistance that pays child care for you. But once you get a job or anything that consists of income it automatically cuts everything off. . . . Once you get any kind of income it ends. *Tasha Tracy*

The readiness program did not seem aware of the effect that child-care policy had on the emancipation goals of its graduates. Subsidy assessment and information were considered the domain of the program's peer mentors who generally based their knowledge on their own experience. Although valuable, personal experience is rarely adequate in a rapidly changing, complex policy environment. Many families here, including Tasha's, have difficulty interpreting and negotiating housing, food, and child-care subsidies, often spending countless hours on such efforts.

Over the next year Tasha took several below-poverty wage jobs while she waited to be matched with health care training. Tasha's job readiness program sought permission from the state to certify the vocational institute's LPN program, but certification was not approved during our time with Tasha. The onset of the medical coding program was also postponed—a common occurrence in the articulation of new policies and programs that disadvantages trainees (Iversen, 2000). Although Tasha had little interest in the field of medical coding, she viewed it as a step closer to her goal of nursing: "If that's just the start, it would probably help me to get where I want to go." Further driving Tasha in this direction, the readiness program's tuition benefit for the community college LPN program had expired. As she waited, Tasha lost traction toward a health care career and bore the opportunity cost of not being able to increase her wage from minimum to skilled level.

By our last contact with Tasha, eighteen months after she completed the job readiness program in preparation for health care training, neither program had materialized. Although she located a security service position that paid more than her earlier jobs had, her career and emancipation goals are thwarted by continued program delay. For Tasha to reach the level of career advancement she is capable of reaching, her tenacity needs to be matched by a workforce development program that offers comprehensive family assessment and an effective network of training partners.

Assessing debt and financial literacy

Some but not all workforce development programs here offer debt assessment and financial literacy instruction. Given the experiences of the families across the five cities, this direction seems both sound and essential. Almost half the parents (twelve, or 48 percent) hold debt that ranges from $700 to $20,000, commonly stemming from unpaid medical bills, car accidents and court costs, household bills, and for-profit education or training programs. Some debt results from predatory telephone and utility practices. Upwards of one in five of the key parents has declared personal bankruptcy—an action that may help in the short run but limits mobility in the long run (see Sam Gates's story in Chapter 6).

Debt can cause particular problems for families who have spent time in prison, as several illustrate here. In Milwaukee, Tisha Shanks accumulates $5,700 from cosmetology school loans and $3,000 in utility bills for lights left on in her home as an antitheft precaution while she was incarcerated. Hard Working Blessed sustains a postprison debt of $20,000 for school loans, medical treatment, and child support that limits his ability to move ahead:

> Financially, it's hard to get back on my feet. I have a lot of creditors calling. Most people in my situation are in financial trouble or need to know how to file bankruptcy. I should have done it two years ago, but I didn't know about it. That would be a good thing for a job training program to teach about—how to file for bankruptcy. *Hard Working Blessed, Milwaukee*

Kevin McDonalds works overtime to pay a pretraining program tax debt that accrued while he was in prison. He had unknowingly filed his income tax statement incorrectly and this mistake compounded to $9,000 during and after incarceration. The Internal Revenue Service did not inform him about this debt until five years after he was released. Staff members at Kevin's printing program, who are not officially case managers but who acknowledge that they "act like case managers," help him understand the tax system and draw on legal advice to advocate for debt relief. The program's debt assessment and the presence of legal partners in its workforce development network result in the reduction of Kevin's debt to a more manageable amount.

More generally, in Philadelphia Sam Gates experiences the bankruptcy of his newspaper business and Ayesha Muhammad has $1,500 debt. Although Sam's manufacturing training program includes a debt management component, neither it nor Ayesha's welfare-to-work program thoroughly assesses debt status or helps them strategize about mobility-enhancing ways to address their debt. Debt constrains the ability of both parents to pursue off-the-job upgrade training for career advancement. Similarly, Lynn Walker owes $1,200 in pretraining utility and rent debt, but her customer service training program does not yet provide financial literacy instruction. In contrast, Loretta Lopez receives advice from one of her program's partners about debt reduction. The program suggests that Loretta apply her anticipated tax refund to an Individual Development Account (IDA) program. IDA programs are a type of asset-building strategy that offers matching contributions to low-income job seekers and workers to help them save for postsecondary education, home purchase, retirement, and microenterprise (Sherraden, 1991; Zhan & Schreiner, 2004). Loretta also follows the IDA program's advice about how to set a goal to eliminate her debt.

Seattle parent Isabell Smith makes efforts to streamline credit cards and manage debt. These efforts fall apart as her debt piles up between jobs and as she opens more credit cards to pay essential bills. Nevertheless, over time she reduces her $7,000 debt to $3,000 and eventually to $1,000. As Isabell explains, debt assessment and the financial "lessons in the [business training] program stuck with me."

African political refugee Mike Jeremy in Seattle faces ongoing debt related to financial support of family members in his home country, as does African émigré Randy Jackson in Milwaukee. When immigrants support relatives in other countries, as many do, family obligations can lead to unmanageable debt and obstruct economic mobility efforts as Mike's experience illustrates:

> When I went home [in 1996], I took money out to help my family. I tried to pay it when I came back, but I got behind so I declared bankruptcy. I got bankruptcy clearance, but that stays with me. *Mike Jeremy, Seattle*

For-profit job or vocational training programs are a common source of lasting debt. In St. Louis, Jane Jenkins completed an earlier veterinary assistance program that resulted in $5,000 debt and no job prospects. Ten years later the Internal Revenue Service notified Jane that she still owed the entire sum and was in "default status," which threatened her family's already precarious finances and prohibited her from future student loans. This latter obstacle postpones Jane's long-term goal of becoming "a family crisis counselor."

In New Orleans, Elizabeth Seabrook incurred $3,000 in debt from a for-profit nursing assistance program she attended. For years afterward she forfeited her tax refund, extra income that might have reduced her current three-job regimen to two jobs or fewer and given her more time and energy for her current upgrade training program. She also owes $2,000 for medical and telephone expenses, the latter incurred as a result of a predatory telephone sales package.

Ahree Raca's young St. Louis family confronts a related financial problem—no credit. Although the family is debt free, the lack of credit history stands in the way of their purchasing a reliable car for Ahryal's access to and Ahree's punctuality at work. Lack of credit also hinders the family's ability to move out of public housing. In the quest to establish credit, Ahree values the fact that his construction training program partners with a union to offer financial literacy training:

> [Financial Institution] came to the seminar [and] talked about saving money and investing. Those were the main two things, saving and getting out of debt. I told them, "I don't have any debt. The only thing I owe is this computer." He was like, "That is so great. You're young and you can save money and invest in a lot of different things." He was like, "We can help you and guide you in setting up a financial goal." That's what I want, I'm saving my own money, and that's what I like. He can help me save my own money. He asked me questions like, "How much money do you want for your kids when you get older?" So we set a goal and just start saving that. *Ahree Raca, St. Louis*

The intersection of debt, lack of or poor credit, the need to work to support one's family, and participation in preemployment and postemployment training to attain or advance in jobs resonates in the family stories. Yet, although financial literacy services are integrated into some workforce development training programs, such instruction rarely continues into the workplace, despite the fact that many programs try to engage new workers and their network employers around such topics. Arguably, with new income *and* new expenses, this is precisely the time such information and knowledge are needed. Asset building strategies (Sherraden, Zhan, & Williams, 2003) are valuable, but to manage them some families need simultaneous advocacy and intervention for debt reduction, others need guidance about how to approach debt consolidation, and still others need advice about how to invest EITC payments, apply to IDAs, and build credit. The inclusion of financial assessment and information in workforce development programs and networks, including on site at their employer partners, might prevent families from being the victims of predatory practices that threaten their mobility progress and simultaneously foster the asset development component of economic mobility.

CROSS-CUTTING ISSUE #2: PREEMPLOYMENT TRAINING

Mobility outcomes depend not only on the comprehensiveness of assessment practices but also on the policies and programs that constitute the landscape of workforce development training. Access, length, type of training, and the span of a workforce development network are aspects of preemployment training that may significantly influence family economic mobility.

Access to training

As noted earlier, skill training opportunities in the federally funded workforce development system under TANF and WIA policies are limited by legislative design. Training is primarily available to job seekers who are not able to find a job otherwise. At the same time, by means of demonstration programs or state waivers from federal regulations, some local or regional workforce development networks are able to circumvent the training restrictions of TANF and WIA. Even so, accessing training is particularly difficult now that financial assistance during training, commonly in the form of TANF for public assistance recipients or unemployment compensation for unemployed individuals, is of limited duration. Few workforce development programs are funded to provide stipends during the training period, which affects program completion, as families here and elsewhere seldom have savings or sufficient non-job income to survive long weeks without income production. Still, given the paucity of skill training available in the federally funded system, the promise of an advancement-focused training program, especially one that is free even if not compensated, helps the families here to put previous unproductive training experiences behind them and reenter the world of workforce development.

Length and type of training

How long does training need to be to move an economically disadvantaged job seeker into a mobility path? According to Carnevale and Desrochers (1999), two hundred hours of education or training—the equivalent of a full semester courseload—may result in $10,000 more annual income for job seekers who have some postsecondary education or are high school graduates. However, job seekers whose skills are similar to those of high school dropouts need at least nine hundred hours—four and a half semesters—of education and training to boost their skills to a basic level (Carnevale & Desrochers, 1999). What length and type of workforce development training do the families here get?

One-third of the parents (nine, or 36 percent) attend workforce development programs that last from zero weeks (that parent is immediately placed in a job) to four weeks (Table 5.1). For the most part these are job readiness programs as described earlier in the chapter. In effect, most are typical "work first" programs. Two-thirds of the parents (sixteen, or 64 percent) attend longer programs that augment the soft skill component with general "hard skill" training for selected industries or occupations. Thirteen of the programs last between five and twelve weeks. Area employers often help to design the curricula for these programs and in a few cases guarantee a job to program graduates. One parent is in a sixteen-week Certified Nursing Assistant (CNA) program that consists of job readiness plus in-class and clinical training and two attend a sixty-week manufacturing skills program. The latter program partners with a local community college toward associate's and bachelor's degrees in manufacturing as well as with area firms for curriculum design, instruction, and hiring of graduates. In one of the research cities all job seekers attend a four-week job readiness program en route to enrollment in a community or technical college skills program. As we see in Tasha's story above, the skill training sequel to the readiness program has been problematic procedurally and financially.

Although the connection between length of training program and wage outcomes can only be suggestive, longer, predominantly hard skill training is roughly associated with higher wages, both at the six-month point of the parents' work pathways ($F = 2.19$, $p = .09$) and after they have worked for more than one year ($F = 2.48$, $p = .11$; data not shown). This association is also reflected in a comparison of the parents' base hourly wage in their pretraining job to the base hourly

TABLE 5.1. Parents' Preemployment Training: Length and Type

Length of training	Four weeks or fewer	Five to twelve weeks (skill based)	Thirteen to twenty-five weeks (skill based)	Over twenty-six weeks (skill based)
Type of Training	Welfare-to-work Job readiness Job search Basic computer or Short skill-based	Manufacturing Construction Business/Office Automotive Customer Service Printing	Healthcare	Manufacturing Construction
Parent Enrollment	Blessed Gomez Jackson Jones Muhammad Raca Seabrook Shanks Tracy	Delvalle Faithful Jenkins Jeremy Lopez McDonalds Miracle Quinn Russell Smith Vanderhand Walker Winters	Tucker	Gates Stewart
Total (Percent)	9 (36%)	13 (52%)	1 (4%)	2 (8%)

wage at their initial post-training job. The median base wage after programs that last four weeks or less and consist primarily of job readiness training increases 30 percent on average. The median base wage after programs that last one to three months and are predominantly hard-skill based increases 44 percent on average. However, as Chapter 6 presents in detail, such increases may be artificially inflated by low wages or less than full-time year-round work in prior jobs.

Parents' responses to preemployment training

What helps? What's missing? When parents talk about what helps and what's missing from their preemployment training, it's often in the same breath. Most appreciate both instrumental and expressive aspects of the workforce development process in the form of skills that facilitate attainment and supportive personal relationships that facilitate action. For some parents, even a four-week or shorter program results in job-site preparation, feelings of accomplishment, and basic skills that are transferable to the job site, as these short excerpts typify.

Hard Working Blessed's two-week manufacturing training program prepared him mentally for subsequent foundry work, which he believes helped him to stay employed:

> Its key is that it lets you know what you're getting into. If I wasn't mentally prepared for Steel Mill & Foundry, I would have quit right away. It helps you to know how to conduct yourself. How you can handle it. I can tell you I was mentally prepared for the foundry. If I wasn't, I wouldn't have come back the second day. *Hard Working Blessed, Milwaukee*

Aida Gomez valued the personalized support that her four-week welfare-to-work program offered and noted with particular satisfaction that the program enabled her to get her GED:

> I needed that, trying to do better for myself. They really opened my eyes there and taught me what I know now. Not everything I know, but when I was with his [three-year old son, Luis's] father I was going to GED classes. He didn't let me go to my classes so he wouldn't let me finish. The welfare-to-work program, they made the appointment for the test because I told them 'I'm ready. I didn't finish [classes] but I can try to take the test.' That month, during that month and a half, I got my GED test and passed. I was ready to work, and I was more confident. I got a job right away. *Aida Gomez, Philadelphia*

Aida also appreciated the program's instruction in debt management as well as its no-nonsense approach that one instructor described as a softer version of a "boot camp" orientation. Aware of the program's approach, Aida wrote on her application, "In my opinion, I think it is good that you make it hard on the student because you make sure we know what's out there in the real world and how to work with pressure or stress, in other words with a rude boss."

As a recent refugee from a war-torn African nation, Mike Jeremy felt he benefited from the pretraining job readiness portion of his manufacturing training program:

> I learned a lot of things that I use now—how to communicate with people; management. For one week they gave a good class—how to be friendly with people; customer service. *Mike Jeremy, Seattle*

Mike also valued the ensuing eleven weeks of training in Computerized Numerical Control (CNC) for the manufacturing industry, new friends that carried over into a supportive cadre at the jobsite, and took pride in the high marks he earned: "I was the first student in the class that had a lot of A's." At the same time Mike regretted that he did not learn broader skills, "math rather than assembly," and that the training period was only three months long: "It should be two years." He believed a longer period was needed to develop more skills and become eligible for a higher salary. Mike's case manager concurred with the need for longer training as well as longer support:

> They need more training because they need to make more money. They still need support. The program managers say support services are the last resort. This needs rethinking. *Workforce Program Case Manager of Mike Jeremy, Seattle*

Similarly, Wendy Delvalle specified how preemployment training both helps and constrains her. She valued certain aspects of the sixteen-week customer service training program curriculum:

> Basically what we were learning was how to treat customers, like the steps you would take in trying to solve a customer's problem, and how not to take things personally when a member is angry. They also had math and grammar—that I liked, because you forget everything after not being in school for so long. It was like a refresher course learning all of that stuff over again. I enjoyed that a lot, that to me was the like best part. *Wendy Delvalle, Philadelphia*

In the same breath, Wendy lamented that the program was not long or specific enough. Both critiques are reflected in the challenges she reports facing in her post-training job as a health insurance representative:

> It was not enough, not enough at all. They have four departments where you can do customer service—banking, hospitality, insurance, and retail. When they test you they tell you where you will best fit in those four categories and they ask you where you would want to be in that category. I think, and this is my opinion, that they need to train you (more specifically), so that like in banking you know the terms that they are going to use and the how all the procedures work, (same) as for health insurance. They should know a little bit more about how HMOs work, I think that would be much better. They don't give you any kind of training on what health insurance is going to be all about. The health insurance companies come in and talk and they tell you what they want and what they are looking for and stuff like that but they are not educating you on what the terms are going to be or what the health insurance industry is all about. With a little more education it (would be) much better. I think what they should do is hire people who come from (a specific) background who can educate (trainees). We never got phone practice. You go out there and you think you are ready and oh my god there is so much you don't know. *Wendy Delvalle, Philadelphia*

We heard the "too short" lament from trainees, instructors, and employers in every city about every type of program except those longer than a year. A computer instructor in Ayesha Muhammad's four-week welfare-to-work program echoed Ayesha's assessment that the computer training was not sufficient for a job seeker to secure a position in an office environment:

> The early computer training was too basic. We spent a lot of time on soft skills. They might only have learned how to save a file on the desktop, delete a file, and edit a document. *Computer Instructor, Welfare-to-Work Program, Philadelphia*

Insufficient training was also mentioned by Ayesha's workplace supervisor after she became employed, as Ayesha reports:

> When you get on the job site, you do get lost. You really and truly do get lost. It just so happened, my supervisor, she is the type of person (who says), "If you don't know call me and I will come over and help you. I will take you step by step to take you through it and help you get where you got to get." *Ayesha Muhammad, Philadelphia*

Finally, training program outcomes also may be influenced by the span of the workforce development network in which the program is embedded, as Elizabeth Seabrook's experience exemplifies.

Span of the Workforce Development Network:
Elizabeth Seabrook's Family Story (New Orleans)

Elizabeth Seabrook, the thirty-seven-year-old single mother of four-year-old Joseph and two-year-old Abigail, viewed skill training as the route to improve her family's economic future. She enrolled in a four-week job readiness program that promised to link her with its community college partner's medical technology certificate program, expecting that human capital development will lead to a better wage and career than her earlier CNA positions in nursing homes did.

Elizabeth's job readiness program prepared participants for the transition to college through self-esteem and confidence-building exercises, training on financial aid applications, help on the numerous placement examinations, and discussions about what to expect from "college life." Even so, Elizabeth was overwhelmed by the college environment, to some extent because of the level of remediation the college program required. She understood that initial coursework consisted of "prerequired" hurdles, as these courses were predetermined by her scores on the Test of Adult Basic Education (TABE) that she took at the end of her job readiness program. As an eleventh-grade high school dropout from an under-resourced, low-performing New Orleans school, although Elizabeth scored at the college mean on the reading section of the TABE, her scores of sixth-grade level in English and eighth-grade level in Math placed her at the remedial level for those subjects.

For two years, Elizabeth struggled with remedial English and math courses, not yet in the position of official entry into the medical certificate program. Summer courses were out of reach because she had exhausted her Pell Grant during the academic year and thus had no money for summer tuition. Worse yet, she had to take a full course load to qualify for the Pell Grant, which meant she was in school full time, worked three-fourths of the time at her main job, and often worked seven days a week at a second or third job.

The details of Elizabeth's average week bring home the multi-institutional reality of the new mobility that, in Elizabeth's case, includes both her own and her children's schools:

So on Mondays I get up like maybe five thirty, quarter to six and get them together. Then I get the children out of the house and drop them off to school. I don't give them breakfast, I have little snacks and stuff, you know, but the school feeds them breakfast. Sometimes after I drop them off in the morning I'll stop by my mom's to say hi to her. I have my math class at twelve, so I use that time between eight thirty and noon to study, and then I get ready for my twelve o'clock class. I leave that class and I also have a one o'clock class and it lets out at one fifty.

OK, Wednesdays and Fridays, now this is hectic. This is very hard, but I do it. I get up at four thirty and I take care of myself first. I take my shower, get my clothes, I set the clothes out the night before. So I make sure I'm together, and then I wake them up because if we're not out of here by quarter to six or twenty minutes to six, I could really hang it up because I have to be on the Interstate by no later than ten after six to beat traffic. We usually hit traffic anyway because that time of morning the traffic is hectic. Then I take them to my mom's house (half hour from her house) because that's too early for them to be in school, so I take everything, uniform, tennis shoes, hair accessories and drop them off and then I'm headed right out the door on the Interstate to go out to my 7 A.M. class (the other direction, back to downtown New Orleans). Now to get from my mom's to school on a good day takes maybe twenty to twenty-five minutes, but on a bad day it takes about thirty to forty-five minutes, and then I'm late for school.

The traffic going back to my mom's is actually not that bad because the traffic is going into the CBD (Central Business District) and nothing is coming, you know from the CBD at the time so it's like smooth sailing, but I also bring home a classmate that lives on my way to my mother's house and I drop her off, so I think (it still takes) maybe fifteen to twenty minutes. Then I get the children ready for school. Like I said, my mom, she can't really do much (she has chronic heart disease). Sometimes she would have on their shoes and socks but not much more. So I get them ready and get them out to school, and then I go home and study or I might take little cat naps, and then I go to math and sociology between 12 and 2 P.M., followed by work again from 2 to 5 P.M. Some days I go pick up the children after work around five, then take them to my mother's, and then drive back for a 7 P.M. class.

Sometimes they go to bed around ten thirty or eleven, and then sometimes it will be a normal night, but then it's not always you know. I think the (children) should have like eight hours or more of sleep. My mom says on Saturdays they take naps and in school they take naps, but they get up in the morning, I guess because they're used to it. You know, when I call them, they're up, and they don't show no signs of like sleeping in the car or whatever. I mean they're bright and they ready to roll once I get them up, so I guess they're used to it. Like I said, I am doing this seven days a week. *Elizabeth Seabrook*

Despite Elizabeth's efforts to work, attend medical training, and forge a better future for her children, Joseph's preschool teacher complained that Elizabeth did not help Joseph with homework. She said that in another month she would "just stop sending it home if there's no response because I'd rather not waste my time preparing it and waste the materials." Although the teacher knew that Elizabeth recently moved, she did not seem to know about Elizabeth's demanding school and work schedule. Nevertheless, Elizabeth heeded the teacher's comments and introduced homework time into the household's already stressed daily schedule:

I know the homework has to be done, so we now have homework time. It's to help them and it gives us that bond, you know, to help make up for the time we don't spend together. So we get to do the homework thing. Four-year old Joseph has homework due every Tuesday, but it's for every day of the week. Sometimes I don't get a chance to do it with him but like tonight, we gonna do homework from Tuesday, Wednesday, Thursday, Friday, you know, to catch up, and then when Tuesday comes, he'll have it, then they'll load me up again with more homework. For two-year old Abigail, her homework is due every Friday, and then Joseph will help with that too. He'll cut out, naming her colors, repeating certain words to her in Spanish that she needs to know for the class, letting her do creative little things like with construction paper, making the letter E, you know. I would say for each of them it's like an hour a night. For Abigail too, her little homework is quite simple, but it still takes time because you have to supervise it and watch what they're doing. But it gets hectic because while I'm spending time with Joseph, Abigail is cutting up or she wants to write also, but we don't have room on the little table in their room for her to write so I have to bribe her to look at TV until I'm finished. I can't do both of their homework at the same time, and I am always late with one of them, but we get through it. *Elizabeth Seabrook*

To complete her own homework in the face of the preschool's demand for homework, Elizabeth dons earphones to listen to study tapes at night while she sleeps. If Elizabeth is able to maintain this grueling pace, and if she is eventually granted official entry, the eighteen-month medical technology certificate program will have taken at least forty-eight months to complete—at considerable opportunity cost in lost wages and at considerable emotional cost, as she describes above. Still, if she survives the multiyear regimen of school, family and work, and obtains a full-time medical technology position, the income she gets now from three jobs will double in a single job and her earnings will exceed 200 percent of the poverty level.

As related research suggests (Armstrong, 2002; Mathur et al., 2004) for Elizabeth and others here, if program assessments are comprehensive and family-focused, and if local workforce development networks are comprised of a broad range of institutional partners, economic mobility may be better fostered. We look at case management next, as that process may help to knit job seeker assessment and training program opportunities into structured rather than underdeveloped network wholes.

CROSS-CUTTING ISSUE #3: CASE MANAGEMENT

There may be as many definitions of "case management" and "case manager" as there are welfare, workforce development, and social and human service programs. Predictably this variation is replicated in the workforce development programs here. At a minimum, the person in this role assesses, assists, motivates, monitors, and brokers services for program participants (Gueron & Pauly, 1991). Case managers also vary along another dimension that is crucial for economic mobility—their expertise (Iversen, 1998, 2001). As a rule case managers in human and social service organizations are expert at assessing emotional and contextual concerns but have far less knowledge about how characteristics of the labor market impact the job seeker's or worker's ability to maintain or advance in employment. In contrast, case managers (or job coaches, employment guides, or retention counselors as they are often called) in workforce development organizations are experts on the labor market but may have far less knowledge about how situational and emotional concerns of job seekers impact their getting, keeping, and advancing in jobs. This disconnect is partially mediated by workforce development networks in which human service and job training organizations form structured partnerships to provide comprehensive workforce development services.

Although Gueron and Pauly (1991) report that universal case management is of mixed importance to the job outcomes of welfare recipients, later work (Rangarajan, Schochet, & Chu, 1998) and the research here suggest that targeted services may facilitate positive outcomes. Some but not all workers need the kind of workplace mentoring that is crafted by the training program–employer network that Tisha Shanks experiences, the reemployment information and guidance that Kevin McDonalds's printing network provides, the help accessing subsidies that Shanquitta Tucker gets from multiple community support organizations, and the navigational support for emergencies that Maya Vanderhand gets from her case manager when her husband loses his job. Parents' ability to remain steadily employed often hangs on such network connections, which in turn impact their future mobility and the well-being of their children. The mobility potential of broad-based case management across the actors in a local workforce development network is seen through Isabell Smith's story.

Case Management across a Workforce Development Network:
Isabell Smith's Family Story (Seattle)

Thirty-one-year-old Isabell Smith's ability to seek and utilize supports was a critical feature of her success in a twelve-week business skills training program and in the job she landed afterward. Lacking family help, Isabell created a network of service providers and select friends to counter the ravages of former abuse and heroin use and dramatically improve her children's well-being. Her workforce development program was part of a similarly well-articulated network. These two networks ultimately form a structured whole that forwards the mobility efforts of Isabell's family.

Isabell left home at age eighteen, after years of physical and sexual abuse and obtained a series of low-wage or low-level managerial positions because of her "reliable" reputation. Isabell connected her work ethic with the nonabusive part of her past: "I come from a family that always worked very hard. They do a lot and you don't complain about being tired, you just keep going." In her early twenties Isabell was diagnosed with a rare and often fatal blood disorder that she interpreted as certain death:

> I felt like somebody had just stamped an expiration date on my forehead. They told me I was going to die within ten years. *Isabell Smith*

As a result Isabell "started living my life as if I was going to die. I just went off the deep end for a while." This meant showing up at work sporadically and often "high." Isabell eventually took a seasonal position for about five years in a fishing company in Alaska where she discovered her desire and ability to work hard, a pattern that she repeated in her post-training job: "I got to be a trailblazer." Before that time however she also discovered her "sea of self-hatred," which she connected with her vulnerability to street drugs and eventually heroin.

As noted in Chapter 3, when Isabell's first son Pedro was born addicted to heroin, Children's Protective Services (CPS) took custody and eventually placed him with relatives of her partner Domingo. Later pregnant with Domingo's son Carlos, Isabell entered a rehabilitation facility to prevent foster placement of her second child. Despite being born with methadone and heroin in his system, Carlos was allowed to remain with Isabell because she was in a residential treatment facility. During this period Isabell arranged for Carlos's acceptance into a therapeutic child development agency for at-risk children with special needs. Isabell's observations about eleven-month-old Carlos, that "He was far behind other one year olds; he couldn't walk, he could not talk at all, not even a word," were echoed by child development agency staff:

> Carlos was like many floppy drug-affected babies; we wondered if he would walk. *Therapeutic Child Development Agency Social Worker*

After eighteen months of rehabilitation—Isabell's first experience of sustained support—she moved to an apartment that was affordable because of a Section 8 rental subsidy. At the same time Isabell and CPS staff advocated successfully for Pedro's return to her. For various reasons, Isabell saw Pedro only sporadically during his years in foster care and so his "return" to her care at age three and a half was more aptly their introduction to one another. Pedro's entrance into the family was the biggest adjustment for all four family members during Isabell's transition to work. This challenge was exacerbated by the therapeutic agency's assessment that Pedro had been abused while in kinship care, as his initial responses to maternal discipline suggested:

> When he first moved into the house and the first time he had ever got in trouble he says "Are you going to lock me in the bathroom?" "We don't lock people in the bathroom in this house," I said. He said "Are you going to hit me then?" and I said "We don't hit people either." *Isabell Smith*

Recognizing his needs as she had Carlos's, Isabell had also negotiated Pedro's enrollment in the therapeutic agency. With their help, Isabell understood that Pedro's behavior resulted from his experience: he rarely cuddled with her, was often confused about her parenting role, tested limits, refused the help he needed (e.g., to tie his shoes), protested leaving child care and engaged in long crying spells before Isabell left for work in the morning. Pedro's behavior commanded capacities for time and patience that rarely exist in the best of circumstances. For Isabell, struggling with a demanding new job, it was often overwhelming:

> I get so frustrated because I talk to the child development agency and I talk to a therapist and I talked to this lady who taught my parenting classes and Pedro is really a difficult child. *Isabell Smith*

With the help of her network of supports, Isabell was able to parent less reactively, even under stress. Isabell consulted with the therapeutic agency's teachers and counselors at will: several times daily during times of greatest need. Recognizing the vulnerability that stemmed from her abusive background, Isabell and the agency staff viewed these contacts as critical to preventing a further generation of abuse.

Supportive relationships were as critical to Isabell's training and employment as they were to her children's development. One month into her new home and family of four, Isabell enrolled in a business skills training program where her case manager helped her cope with multiple, concurrent transitions:

> "L" was my original case manager. She was so awesome. I was trying to do everything and I was moving, getting my son back for the first time, supposed to start school at the same time and I called her up freaking out. She was great, and she told me, "Girl, you are nervous, but don't worry about it. School will still be there; you can do the one in June." *Isabell Smith*

The case manager's validation calmed Isabell's escalating sense of failure and allowed her to prioritize her commitments. As a result Isabell postponed training for several months, a decision that fostered her eventual success at both training and work.

As part of the twelve-week business training Isabell worked for five weeks as an intern with Tech Company, an Internet-based product-oriented company. Isabell credited the skills she gained in training with her ability to get a job there as a customer service representative:

> I haven't worked in many, many years [since 1996]. I never would have gotten a job like I have today if I hadn't had the opportunity to go to school. I'd still be stuck at 7–11 or McDonald's. *Isabell Smith*

Getting the job was only the first hurdle. Isabell described her early days at Tech Company as "so scary, especially when you are now talking to real people." Although transitions are stressful in the best circumstances, Isabell's job became more intense as the company prepared for the holiday retail season. The fact that Isabell survived her first few months of work, when demands were highest and her preparedness and confidence lowest, was testament to her resilience and network of supports. At home the children competed for her attention and threw tantrums that she had little energy to resolve. The tumult of this period was confirmed by therapeutic agency staff who observed that the children were more aggressive in the classroom and Isabell had less time to talk with them about the children.

Just as Tech Company and Isabell regained balance after the stressful holiday period, Isabell received a call at work from the Child Support Enforcement Office that set her apart from her coworkers and challenged her ability to keep work, family and history separate. She learned that she was being held responsible for the financial support of Pedro for the years he spent in foster care. Having to address this call at work, in a public forum comprised of few workers with families, increased her burden:

> This guy calls me at work and he said I owe fourteen thousand dollars and he wanted to garnish me. He kept wanting me to say at work that the reason why I didn't have my kid is because I was a heroin, he wanted me to say "junky" on the phone and I was like "I am not going to say it because I am at work." *Isabell Smith*

Once again Isabell marshaled the partners in her personal and workforce development networks: a new caseworker at the protective service agency, a counselor at Carlos's high-risk health clinic, and for the first time her training program's postemployment case manager. After a laborious documentation process that also engaged the expertise of a legal partner in the workforce network, these support persons had helped Isabell demonstrate poverty status during the time Pedro was in care and reduced the amount she owed from $14,000 to $900. Isabell emphasized that her case manager's particularly attentive listening helped her to remain stable on the job during such tumultuous times:

> The more I talk about it the less power it has because [until] I outlet it, I don't see the good stuff. I sometimes just see all the bad things that are happening and the more I talk about it, it is like "You know, things are pretty darn good." *Isabell Smith*

She also needed her workplace to listen, as the continuation of Isabell's story in Chapter 6 reveals. To conclude the discussion of case management here, however, the breadth of the support network available to Isabell is evident in her employment progress and in her children's well-being. By the time Isabell sustained nineteen months' employment at Tech Company, she had been promoted once and her wages increased from $11 per hour to $13 per hour. At age four and a half, Pedro "graduated" from the therapeutic agency after fifteen months of treatment, and his carefully chosen, subsidized child-care facility confirmed and reinforced his gains in ways that translated into more positive behavior at home:

> He acted out a couple of times, but after that we talked about it and he has been pretty good since at school [child care]. His getting in trouble [at home] has toned down a lot too. He used to get in trouble daily and it has gotten a lot better. *Isabell Smith*

At age two and a half, Carlos had progressed from an initial diagnosis of "Developmentally Disabled" to "Developmentally Immature," and the therapeutic agency professionals predicted that he would eventually be able to enroll in a mainstream kindergarten class, which he did by the time of our last contact with the family.

Illustrating the intersection of family mobility and policy, Carlos's gains were consolidated by the fact that although he was past his state-allotted fifteen months of treatment, Isabell's workforce development network partners negotiated extended services at the agency. Isabell's postemployment case management was also informally extended beyond the two-year mark, which further consolidated family gains. Isabell's family's economic mobility will likely depend on periodic access to network partners that can help her navigate looming challenges, such as permanent layoff, threatened withdrawal of her child-care subsidy, and accessing postemployment upgrade training.

In sum, Isabell Smith's family story suggests that a structured whole comprised of networked partners that provide comprehensive assessment, active outreach, individualized attention, community services, effective preemployment training, postemployment support, and knowledgeable case management can help new workers negotiate jobsite and family responsibilities and stay employed. Connecting families to community supports and fostering existing personal networks are especially important, as programs' case management services are rarely funded or implemented for more than a few months postemployment. In short, Isabell's story shows that local or regional workforce development systems can forward economic mobility through both support and access to jobs. We look at the cross-cutting issue of job access next.

CROSS-CUTTING ISSUE #4: THE WORKFORCE DEVELOPMENT SYSTEM OR NETWORK AS A "SIGNAL" TO EMPLOYERS

To date the federally funded workforce development system and many local workforce development networks have limited credibility with the business community. This is problematic for the mobility efforts of job seekers like the parents here because, in addition to its training function, the credibility that a system, network, or program reflects on its participants can affect employment outcomes. This reflected credibility is often referred to as the "signal" effect (Ehrenberg & Smith, 2003) or "brand halo" effect (Laufer & Winship, 2004). Given employers' increasing desire for employees with good "work ethics," "work habits," and "attitudes toward work" (Lafer, 2002), the signal effect may be equal to or even greater than the skill effect for job access, especially among economically disadvantaged or stigmatized job seekers. Workforce development systems or networks that successfully engage employers in sustained partnerships may increase the reach of the signal effect.

The signal or brand halo effect may be particularly critical to the mobility of parents who return home after completing a prison sentence. An ex-offender commonly has great difficulty entering or reentering the labor market because of employer stereotypes, lack of education and skills, and legal status, yet employment may be essential to avoiding recidivism (Hirsch et al., 2002; Mukamel, 2001). As Western (2002, p. 528) notes, "a criminal record signals to employers that a potential employee may be untrustworthy." In contrast, a credible workforce development system, program or network can signal legitimacy. Such signals may be particularly important for African American males who are incarcerated at disproportionate rates (Western). For example, in contrast to the outcome of a previous independent training program, a network comprised of a skill-training program, union, and firms in the printing industry forms a structured whole that enables Kevin McDonalds, a twenty-nine-year-old African American male who had been incarcerated twice, to get a job with the potential to support his family:

> I was in a plumbing course before the printing program. It was different from this one. You had to go to look for a job yourself. If there had been more help job searching— like this program (printing), it would have been a nice program. At the time I didn't know what I was looking for. I didn't have my driver's license. I was a felon and that was looked at negatively. I was into the program, the classes, and figured they'd help me find a job. We were a team. I was thrown for a loop when they didn't. I never went for the final aptitude test at the local union. We were supposed to take it together (everyone in the class). But the teacher left. If people would have cut the yellow tape, sent us to meet Bob, Joe, Lou it would have helped. Like the printing program (did).
> *Kevin McDonalds, Milwaukee*

Similarly, a respected manufacturing training program, union, and firm network bridges employment for Hard Working Blessed as an ex-felon. Although Mr. Blessed believes that the skill component is the bridge, it seemed that the positive signals of his workforce development program and its firm partner that hired him extinguished the negative signal of Mr. Blessed's felony history for subsequent employers:

> I filled out an application at Metal Company just for the heck of it. My manufacturing training experience [and initial post-training job] at a foundry was the reason I got the job. I know about the metal industry—know about metal. I got my forklift certification there; my license. *Hard Working Blessed, Milwaukee*

The signal effect can also bridge employment for job seekers without education credentials, or institutionalized cultural capital in Bourdieu's (2001) terms. For example, thirty-two-year-old Hispanic mother of four, Maya Vanderhand, dropped out of school after tenth grade, had not yet passed the GED test, and thus had a history of minimum-wage jobs. After completing a twelve-week business skills training program that was part of a local workforce development network, she was hired as a personal lines operator by an insurance company, despite no secondary degree.

Maya's experience, however, shows that in some venues the signal or brand halo effect may be limited in its reach. Although the credibility of her skill training program and its network compensated for the lack of GED in obtaining the insurance job, the signal may not extend to her future aspirations:

> I want my GED. Not having it is not holding me back at Insurance Company, but there was a time when I did need a GED to get a job. But now there isn't time to study for the GED after work. This job offers more than what I was offered before, particularly without the GED. I was going to the X College for the GED but I didn't like the way the teachers treated me. They treated adults like kids. So I stopped going . . . Because of the GED I can't really go forward, not with the company because I know I can, but outside the company because I would like to get a job [in immigration]; they do require a GED. *Maya Vanderhand, Seattle*

Moreover, although Maya's company would reimburse GED pursuit, she anticipated a several-year delay in this advancement step because family responsibilities absorb the time she needs to prepare successfully for the test:

> That could be maybe next year's goal to get my GED, to really focus on that because I can't really do two things at a time. It is hard and then with the four kids, no I am not going to even try to do that because I might even fail. So even I found out that through the job that they might even pay for it. [Time off to do it too?] No, they won't give me time off but I am going to have to work my schedule so that I can go to school and then work at the same time. *Maya Vanderhand, Seattle*

It might help parents like Maya if workforce policy and programs ensure the completion of a secondary education credential before job seekers enter or reenter the world of work. Alternatively, partners in workforce development networks could negotiate with firms for GED pursuit on company time. In contrast to old paradigm expectations, postemployment training is often out of reach for hard working parents, as we discuss next.

CROSS-CUTTING ISSUE #5: POSTEMPLOYMENT TRAINING AND SUPPORT

The remaining challenge arising at the intersection of workforce development and economic mobility is the availability and accessibility of postemployment upgrade training and services to support the advancement efforts of new workers. Now that firms provide less upgrade training (Cappelli, 1999), particularly to low-skilled, low-educated compared to higher skilled, higher educated workers (King, 2004; O'Leary, Straits, & Wandner, 2004), postemployment training devolves for the most part to the workforce development system. Compounding matters, funding is disproportionately larger for preemployment than for postemployment skill training programs (King). For example, few workforce development programs are funded to educate job seekers or new workers, after they are employed, about the process of career development, transferable skills, or orderly advancement steps. Other actors have not taken up this role either, even in well-developed workforce development networks (Osterman et al., 2001).

Working and going to school is hard in the best of circumstances. For families with children, debt, insufficient incomes, limited or lapsed postemployment case management, and inadequate policy support, old paradigm expectations about mobility through human capital attainment are misplaced. For upgrade as for preemployment training, structured partnerships between firms and workforce development programs facilitate but do not assure utilization. Policies and practices in firms, children's schools, and subsidies can derail parents' advancement efforts as detailed in Chapters 6 and 7. In the new view of mobility this multi-institutional reality involves choices about upgrade training that are both cognitive and emotional. Most simply, interests, time, competing values and availability of support are part of the decision calculus, as Shanquitta Tucker's story typifies.

Trying to Pursue Postemployment Upgrade Training:
Shanquitta Tucker's Family Story (St. Louis)

Thirty-seven-year-old Shanquitta Tucker was always a working mother. Her long history of nursing education and employment experience in the South was interspersed with a series of unskilled but occasionally managerial positions. Before having children Shanquitta completed high school, took two years of community college classes in preparation for a "nursing major," and earned a Certified Nursing Assistant (CNA) certificate.

Many years later when she separated from her husband, Shanquitta and her three children moved to St. Louis for a fresh start. They initially lived with Shanquitta's sister and two daughters, ages nine and three, in the sister's two-bedroom rented house in a St. Louis County community. Shanquitta enrolled thirteen-year-old Iesha and seven-year old Chris in the district school and located a childcare center for two-year-old Kenyetta so that she could look for work. Soon after the move Shanquitta was contacted by a community outreach worker who was working on a grant-funded child abuse prevention project that aimed to increase social service utilization among low-income mothers. Although Shanquitta's sister was the initial target for the project, Shanquitta was enrolled instead, an "exchange" that project administrators viewed as a kind of "protection" for her sister's family. The community outreach worker described her role as "helping out with housing, employment, childcare, clothing, and other issues related to the transition from welfare to work." Accordingly, she helped Shanquitta apply for food stamps and a housing subsidy. At this point Shanquitta's children were already covered by Medicaid health insurance and Shanquitta remained under her ex-husband's health insurance policy.

To make ends meet, Shanquitta took a job in the deli section of a grocery store at $7.00 per hour, working twenty to twenty-eight hours a week without benefits. Shanquitta did not qualify for TANF assistance, despite the fact that at twenty-eight hours per week, her potential annual income of $10,192 was almost $7,000 below the federal poverty line (FPL) for a family of four. Demonstrating the strength of weak ties (Granovetter, 1973, 1983), the community outreach worker informed Shanquitta about the healthcare training program in which she enrolled less than one month after arriving in St. Louis.

Shanquitta's health care training began with a six-week work readiness component that was followed by ten weeks of Certified Nursing Assistant skills training that entailed a rigorous program of classroom instruction and hospital internship. A health care program administrator explained that CNA training requires considerable commitment but near-certain employment: "If participants complete training and pass the State Board Examination, permanent employment is 99.9% guaranteed." He added that full benefits including vacation time, sick days, dental, and vision would begin at the point of hire and most jobs would offer tuition reimbursement for upgrade education. At the end of the course Shanquitta passed her certification exam and obtained a CNA position at the hospital that partnered with the training program for her internship. Shanquitta began work on a 6:45 A.M. to 3:15 P.M. shift, earning $10.20 per hour with full benefits—over $1 more per hour than she anticipated and $3 more per hour than any previous job in her long work history. For the preemployment portion of Shanquitta's mobility efforts then, her training program–employer network constituted a structured whole.

Shanquitta's tenure at Hospital-MO proceeded smoothly for a few months until a change in Chris's school necessitated a burdensome commute each morning. Shanquitta informed her supervisors that she would be late for work and contacted her health care program's postemployment retention counselor (i.e., case manager) for advice. Going "above and beyond," the counselor volunteered to take Chris to school in the morning so that Shanquitta would not be late for work. Shanquitta noted that the counselor's mere mention of this prospect revived her forward progress. For a time, Shanquitta and the counselor spoke frequently to strategize about the issue and ultimately Shanquitta rearranged her morning routine to reach work on time.

After several more months on the job, Shanquitta considered enrolling at the local community college for Registered Nurse (RN) training, adding that tuition reimbursement offered by the hospital was an incentive: "They want us to go back to school and they will pay for it." However, Shanquitta did not enroll in the next set of RN courses, despite the fact that her supervisor encouraged her to take "at least one class." Shanquitta's sister had been evicted from her house because she could not pay the $600 monthly rent, thus Shanquitta and her children had to move again just as she began stable employment.

Finding a new apartment was a challenge because of Shanquitta's busy work schedule, myriad tasks as a single parent, and unfamiliarity with the region. The transportation route to her job and the children's schools was also a consideration in her decision about location. With the help of the community outreach worker— perhaps more aptly the role of a training program postemployment counselor— Shanquitta had become eligible for Section 8 housing, but none of these prospects materialized as the family prepared for the coming school year. Perhaps worse, Shanquitta felt that her income, even though demonstrably insufficient for her family's needs, would soon disqualify her for Section 8 assistance, especially if she worked overtime:

> I wanted to use [Section 8], but once I got my job, I was like right at the mark money-wise, and if I worked over or something like that, I would have got cut off. *Shanquitta Tucker*

Shanquitta's housing subsidy dilemma is shared by many families. As soon as families earn a little more money, although not enough to cover their needs, vital subsidies are withdrawn, which leaves them even further from self-sufficiency (Iversen, 2002). In this regard, as in others, policymakers are essential actors in broadly effective workforce development networks.

Eventually, Shanquitta and her sister moved into adjacent apartments in the inner city, which meant leaving a tranquil and relatively safe county community for a neighborhood known for drug trafficking and a relatively high crime rate. Shanquitta's sister was relieved to continue the joint living situation as she valued having Shanquitta to "go to about my problems . . . she's the only one I can talk to about anything." Shanquitta's sister struggled with depression and relied heavily on Shanquitta for financial and emotional support.

At the time the next set of RN courses began, Shanquitta was still adjusting to the housing move and her children were adjusting to their third change of schools in a year. Shanquitta also noted that the need to pay $600 up front to take a course presented an obstacle, even though the healthcare training program would reimburse the $600 down payment and Hospital-MO would reimburse course tuition. Program and employer subsidy at the front end rather than reimbursement at the back end might have facilitated Shanquitta's enrollment.

Over the following year, Shanquitta remained unable to enroll in upgrade education. While obtaining an RN position would increase her income and career fulfillment, the intersecting demands of institutions outside her network rendered this prospect daunting. For example, hard-fought test results that identify Chris's learning disability did not get transferred to his new city school, so Shanquitta spent time navigating this transfer while her own and Chris's educational goals suffered. Yet without upgrade training Shanquitta's wage progression will be minimal.

It would be helpful to consider some type of strategy, perhaps through postemployment case management or retention services, in addition to employer release time for upgrade education, to make the RN track a more obtainable goal for Shanquitta. Although the community outreach worker modeled how intensive case management can guide new workers to resources like housing subsidies and quality summer programs that sustain them and enrich their children, if the network of the health care program, hospital, and college RN program were more of a structured whole Shanquitta might access mobility-enhancing postemployment training more rapidly.

SUMMARY AND CONCLUSIONS

Despite earlier research findings to the contrary, workforce development programs can contribute to the mobility of low-income families. In Kevin McDonalds's words, they are "a start." However there is growing recognition that these programs cannot by themselves ensure economic mobility and a strong workforce (Iversen, 2002; Lafer, 2002). Sole reliance on the human capital-based "initiative" of the old paradigm does not account for institutional complexity in contemporary lives. For the new mobility, workforce development strategies need to be systemic, collaborative, and reciprocal.

The families and organizations in this chapter identify that workforce intermediaries may bridge structural holes (Burt, 1992, 2002) in both federally funded workforce development systems and regional and local workforce development networks such that partner institutions form *structured wholes* for low-income families to access skill training and jobs. To be effective for career navigation and advancement, the workforce development system and related local networks will require construction of sustainable networks of training institutions, community-based health and human service organizations, firms, policymakers, and children's schools. Although current federal employment-related legislation envisions such collaboration, rigid "work first" policies, siloed funding streams, and the lack of allocated funds constrict the formation of fully effective workforce development partnerships (Roberts, 2002). The information in this chapter points to the need for such an investment as well as for it to take place across the actors in a work-force development system. As we discuss in Chapter 8, such policy choices are not predetermined; they rest soundly on the public will.

In well-networked workforce development systems, the actors would discontinue practices that are based on the old mobility paradigm of individualism and its associated structure of siloed funding. For example, programs would replace assessment of individuals with comprehensive assessment of families, understanding that mobility is embedded in family and social networks not in atomistic job seekers. Interviews with intermediary and training program staff in the five research cities reveal that early efforts in this direction are taking place. Different assessment models and partnerships are being explored and in some cases used. Comprehensive family assessments, however, require sufficient program capacity and staff expertise to identify and respond to the needs that arise when firms pay inadequate wages, children's schools take parents away from work and training, and subsidy allotments are insufficient.

Similarly, well-networked workforce development systems would create, coordinate, and fund more systemic strategies for retention and advancement. One of the harder things is getting people interested in apprenticeships, an intermediary staff person said, because "They're getting okay wages" and they are "scared of school." The stories here show that accessing postemployment upgrade education is more complex than that, involving multiple intersecting institutions that require coordination and navigational guidance. Moreover, firms are critical actors in the workforce development network equation in terms of both pre- and postemployment education and skill training and wages. Workforce intermediaries might demonstrate to firms through workforce program and labor market data that investing in the skills and education of low- as well as high-earning employees yields lower turnover, higher productivity, and increased investment in communities. Government policy might foster this direction through tax credits to firms for active engagement in preemployment training and for expanding onsite upgrade instruction during the work day and offering release time for off-site training. These efforts could benefit all players. To ensure family economic mobility and community development, well-networked workforce development systems need to actively position firms (Chapter 6), children's schools (Chapter 7), and public policy (Chapter 8) in central roles toward such goals.

6   Yesterday's Firms and Today's Families

Connects and Disconnects

WITH MICHELE BELLIVEAU

> As old as I am, I've worked in just about every shop on the east coast so I know
> how everybody else works. This plant and mind thinking is a completely
> different setup than most places. Here you can try and do, and nobody's going to
> come down on you if you do something wrong, didn't do that right. That kind of
> atmosphere builds you to try to do even more things. It all works together to
> boost everybody's thinking. At this plant it's 100% support, and it shows in the
> things everyone does.—*Tool and Die Maker, Coworker of Sam Gates at
> Technology Management Company—Electronics Division, Philadelphia*

> People like me who go back to work later in life—companies hire younger
> people at lower wages and expect them to stay in the company for a long time.
> Eventually they make better wages, in time for their family's needs. Me, I'm
> older and I'll be less long in the workforce. And my family has needs right
> now.—*Hard Working Blessed, Milwaukee*

CONTEXT

Day shifts, overnight shifts, factories, offices, hospitals, tech companies, corporations, independent pharmacies, and more. The matched sets of workers and
firms in this chapter help to identify the ways in which families and firms intersect to influence inter- and intragenerational economic mobility. We begin with
a brief discussion of the national economic context in which the firms and families are lodged and then describe the seventy-four firms in which the key parents work during our years of contact with them. We see how firms' wage structures, economic recession, and what we call a *life-stage mismatch* between today's
workers and yesterday's firms (Iversen, 2002) intersect to keep these full-time
year-round working parents from earning a family-sustaining income. The family stories then take us deeply into advancement opportunity in contemporary
firms. We focus on wage returns to job changes, workers' job choice processes,
and advancement structures in firms—three phenomena that illustrate the persistence of the old paradigm of economic mobility (Chapter 2). We then look
at how other structural and ground-level aspects of firm organization and authority relations converge to impact mobility. We conclude the chapter by examining industry, job, and wage projections for the coming decade, describing
what "firm as partner" to the families' goals of economic mobility could look
like.

THE NATIONAL ECONOMIC CONTEXT

The economy of the 1990s and early 2000s sets the immediate context for this look at the parents' firms, job pathways, and economic mobility prospects and actions. In the mid-to-late 1990s when the key parents begin their mobility efforts by enrolling in a job training program that is part of a local or regional workforce development network (Chapter 5), the labor market is tight and jobs are plentiful. The confluence of a growth economy, an aging workforce in some industries, and entry-level opportunities in new industries means that many firms desperately sought workers (Osterman et al., 2001). Such firms were thus willing to partner with job training programs in workforce development networks to employ persons they previously excluded from their hiring queues, such as welfare recipients, immigrants and refugees, ex-felons, racial and ethnic minorities, and those without high school degrees. By the early 2000s, economic recession and firm and labor market restructuring intersected to thwart the economic mobility of these new workers.

First, the economic recession that technically began in March 2001 ends what many economists describe as the longest period of economic expansion in U.S. history: 120 months from March 1991 to March 2001 (Crutsinger, 2004). Whereas the recession *officially* ended in late 2001, rates of unemployment rose from about 4 percent in March 2001, a figure generally considered to be "full employment" (Appelbaum, Bernhardt, & Murnane, 2003), to 5.8 percent in March 2003, two years after the recession officially began (Associated Press, 2003), en route to a peak of 6.3 percent in September 2003. Between February 2001 and October 2003 between 2.3 and 3 million jobs were lost (Mishel, 2004), depending on the measure used, which left three unemployed workers for every job vacancy. Nearly 90 percent of the job loss occurred in manufacturing, continuing thirty years of job reduction in that industry (The new protectionism, 2004). Some describe this period as the largest sustained loss of jobs since the Great Depression (Mishel), using such terms as "jobless recovery," "job loss" recovery (Minehan, 2004), and "anemic economy." Employment and wage growth remain slow in 2005 and, according to Shapiro, Kogan, and Aron-Dine (2005, p. 1), job creation has not only "underperformed the historical average, but *every* comparable period since the end of World War II."

The five states in this book are among thirty others that show a net loss in jobs between March 2001 and June 2004 (Hakim, 2004). Moreover official unemployment rates do not include "discouraged workers" who have dropped out of the labor force temporarily or permanently, as a few parents here do. In March 2003 more than 74.5 million adults were considered outside of the labor force, up more than four million since March 2001—almost twice the two million jobless in the jobless recovery (Davey & Leonhardt, 2003). If labor market dropouts were included in the "unemployment" calculation, the real rate of unemployment in September 2003 would be 7.1 percent (Price & Fungard, 2004). Compounding matters, the working age population that includes several of the book's younger parents grew by 3.7 percent over the same period (Price & Fungard). The state of the national economy, then, is not conducive to economic mobility for many U.S. workers, including those here.

Second, widespread restructuring and reorganization of the labor market and firms over the last several decades—some say over the past century (DiPrete, 1993)—further constrains the efforts of low-income parents to move up through work. Patterns of job mobility have shifted from predictable upward pathways (Blau & Duncan, 1967) to lateral or downward paths (Osterman, 1999), altering the traditional mechanism for advancement (Kalleberg & Mastekaasa, 2001). Although Lafer (2002) argues otherwise, Holzer (1996) predicts that "even the high rates of future job growth predicted for some low-skill occupational categories do not necessarily imply an abundance of jobs without major (cognitive and interpersonal) skill requirements" (p. 64), such as "dealing with customers, reading and writing paragraphs, doing arithmetic calculations, and using computers" (p. 47). Additionally problematic, persons in jobs with low starting wages or slow wage growth are most likely to find similar jobs in the process of job change (Connolly & Gottschalk, 2001).

Aspects of restructuring for the economic mobility experiences of the parents here, as across the United States, include globalization, or the worldwide spread of modern capitalism and increased transnational competition (Swedberg, 2003); offshoring, or sending American jobs overseas (DiMaggio, 2001); mergers and acquisitions (DiPrete, 1993); and downsizing, or reducing the workforce (Baumol, Blinder, & Wolff, 2003). Downsizing may be accomplished through outsourcing or contracting out units or job responsibilities formerly handled within firms (Cappelli, 2000) or utilizing a greater share of nonstandard work arrangements, especially temporary and part-time workers (DiPrete, 1993; Tilly, 1996), which Kalleberg and Marsden (2005) call "externalization" strategies. Purported results of this restructuring that affect mobility include the reduction or elimination of internal career ladders (Osterman, 1999), or what Kalleberg and Marsden (2005) call "internalization" strategies; the loosening of firm responsibility to employee and employee loyalty to firm (Ansberry, 2003; Cappelli, 2000; Kalleberg & Mastekaasa, 2001); the emergence of a customer model of management (DuGay & Salaman, 2000); the expansion of labor market segmentation by function, product, or customer, in which intrafirm departments are replaced by geographically diffuse ones (Lane et al., 2003); the replacement of hierarchical by flatter, more individualized yet less reciprocal authority relations (Garsten 1999); and the reallocation of risk from employer to employee, especially in the area of health and other nonwage benefits (Jacoby, 2004).

The extent to which these and other economic and organizational developments are new, universal, permanent, or influential is much discussed and hotly contested (Burawoy et al., 2000; Jacoby, 2004; Katz, 2001; Minehan, 2004; National Research Council, 1999; Osterman, 1999; Osterman et al., 2001; Swedberg, 2003). For example, although most rhetoric links globalization with losses to U.S. workers, a comparative institutional advantage perspective on political economy (Belussi & Garibaldo, 2000; Hall & Soskice, 2001) cautions that globalization pertains to work and workers leaving *and* coming to the United States.

Many scholars note, however, that service and blue-collar workers such as the parents here are especially vulnerable to organizational restructuring and reorganization, whatever its extent (Bernhardt et al., 2001; DiPrete & Nonnemaker, 1997). Others report that middle management is increasingly vulnerable to labor market changes as well (Bell, 1996; Cappelli, 1999; Jacoby, 2004; Putnam, 2000). In addition, the nature of what Baron (1984) calls "subordinate primary" jobs, such as semiskilled factory work, low-level administration, and clerical positions, varies across firms, which suggests that organizational context influences the ways that specific job characteristics affect mobility. Althauser and Kalleberg (1990) note further that the relationship between specific job characteristics and career outcomes also varies across firms. DiPrete and Nonnemaker (1997) add that mobility responses to restructuring vary sharply by industry group as well.

This chapter contributes to the debate by illuminating the organization and structure of the firms in which the parents work, the parents' experiences at work, the actions and views of supervisors and coworkers, and the contemporary policy responses to economic conditions in firms and families. In effect, the economic context is viewed through the lens of the lived and intersecting experiences of workers, families, firms, and policies.

THE PARENTS' FIRMS

The research team spends hundreds of hours at the parents' firms.[1] We observe, interview and audiotape supervisors, managers, CEOs, union representatives, and coworkers, accompanying parents as they fulfill their tasks and duties. We also gather current and retrospective data about firms from parent reports, promotional materials, company or corporate Web sites, public documents, and the press. Together these sources yield five years of data about the intersections between parents and the seventy-four firms in which they work between 1998 and mid-2003. These data support Granovetter's (2002, p. 38) argument that labor market and other social institutions intersect in ways that "*cannot be accounted for by the incentives of individuals*" (italics in original). As Bielby and Bielby (2002, p. 197) note, "structural features of the workplace that promote long job tenures, embedded social relationships among workers and between workers and employers, and perceptions of fairness are likely to lead to a workplace culture that can sustain the implicit contract." Structure here refers to the type of organization and authority relations in firms, and thus the relationship between workers and firms. As reflected in the new mobility paradigm (Chapter 2), a dynamic view of intersecting structures, institutions, firms, workers, and families emerges from the longitudinal ethnographic findings.

Analytical Typology of the Firms

A central concern in classical social theory is the impact of organizational hierarchies on individuals and society. Marx holds a deterministic view about the inherent exploitation and alienation of workers by firms under capitalism (Marx, 1867/1978). Weber posits a more dynamic view that social actions oriented to one another constitute social relationships that over time may turn into a so-called order, such as a firm (Weber, 1922/1978). Recent abstraction of the attainment process from its organizational and institutional context results in an emphasis on the personal determinants of success or failure rather than on how the distribution of labor market relationships and outcomes intersect with individuals, firms, and society (Baron, 1984, p. 60).

More in line with Weber's view, we find that firms vary considerably in how they organize and manage production. We thus discuss the parents' mobility processes here in relation to a broadly used, albeit idealized typology of organization and relations in firms: Fordism, Neo-Fordism, Post-Fordism (Grint, 1991; Hirst & Zeitlin, 1997), and the customer model (DuGay & Salaman, 2000).

Fordism is characterized by organization and management practices traditional to manufacturing firms, such as well-defined authority structures, closed systems of control, and centralized decision making. Fordist firms also often implement a version of the "scientific management" techniques that Taylor promoted in the early 1900s (Grint, 1991, 2000) with their emphasis on task fragmentation, monitoring of task completion time, and deskilling, all toward greater efficiency and cost reduction. In effect, Fordist firms replace the personal bonds between workers and bosses, typical of early industrial establishments, with the impersonal force of company rules or company policy as the basis of control (Edwards, 1979). Workers in a typical Fordist mass production system hold limited and firm-specific skills, are differentiated through clear division of labor, and are thought to be isolated and alienated from management and firm profits. Customer satisfaction results from the structure and mode of production within the firm. We append Osterman's (1999) notion of "firm as family" to "firm as autocratic family" here to describe the patriarchal management, hierarchical control, and supposed reciprocal loyalty characteristic of such firms. When Fordist firms function according to bureaucratic control procedures, "we" comes to mean "we the firm" rather than "we the workers" (Edwards).

Neo-Fordist organization and management resemble the Fordist pattern in terms of mass production and supervisory control, but also move in the direction of flexibility, an expanded range of products, quality, and a workforce that is engaged in multiple tasks using multiple skills. Extending Osterman's (1999) "firm as...." metaphor, we suggest that "firm as disengaged family," a family form in which relationships are strained and communication is lacking, characterizes firms evidencing these traditional but also changing roles and relations and lessened firm loyalty to employee.

Post-Fordism is characterized by even more flexible organization and management, product specialization, customization and niche markets, elimination of the assembly line, lessened division of labor, teamwork, and flatter authority relations. It is also characterized by a weaker relationship between job tenure and rewards among *both* low- and high-skilled workers (DiPrete, Goux, & Maurin, 2001). Increased differentiation of demand and customization leads to production and management techniques such as total quality management and just-in-time production. The metaphor of "firm as fair-weather friend" is descriptive of post-Fordist organization, wherein loyalty is temporal and conditional.

The customer model is one of the newest forms of firm organization and relations (DuGay & Salaman, 2000). In this model the firm's primary goal is to meet customer needs; in turn the customer evaluates and defines work performance and work relations. Relationship, innovation, flexibility in all domains, choice, variety, vision, meaning, and the "dual customers" of consumer and workforce are part of customer model discourse. Rather than the personal, face-to-face ties between bosses and workers typical of early entrepreneurial establishments in the 1800s (Edwards, 1979), face-to-face in the customer model takes place horizontally from worker to worker. As such, relationships may reflect norms of reciprocity, trust and shared values (Fukuyama, 2003) or tentativeness, competition, and uncertainty. The metaphor of "firm as roommate" might apply here. Peers supplant family relations, firm loyalty to employee is contingent or may be false, and change rather than stability is the rule.

Firms functioning according to the new view of mobility might be described metaphorically as "firm as partner." Family-supporting wages, employer-paid benefits, release time for on- or off-site postemployment upgrade training, clear and supported career ladders, flextime, and mentor programs are a few characteristics of partner firms. A full complement of characteristics exists in only nascent form in a few firms. We ultimately argue that "firm as partner" signifies the full partnership and real, reciprocal relationships between employees and firms that can pave the way to the new mobility goal of *household and profit*, as we discuss more fully at the end of this chapter.

Our analysis of firm Web sites (sixty-five of the seventy-four firms) and other promotional and interview material according to the key words or key characteristics listed above in the four firm categories yields thirty-five examples of predominantly Fordist rhetoric, twenty-eight examples of neo-Fordist, thirty-nine examples of post-Fordist, and seventy-seven examples of customer model rhetoric (examples in family stories in this chapter). We also find that although the rhetoric may be new (predominantly post-Fordist or customer model), most firms' policies and practices remain old (predominantly neo-Fordist or Fordist). The use of multiple rhetoric in the promotional materials of firms underscores others' findings that although one form of organization may be dominant, varied forms generally coexist within any one firm (DiMaggio, 2001; DiPrete, Goux, & Maurin, 2001; Hirst & Zeitlin, 1997; Hollingsworth & Boyer, 1997; National Research Council, 1999). Most of the seventy-four firms evidence characteristics of at least two of the modes of organization and relations and some show three or all four. In contrast to the old mobility assumption held by many dual labor market theorists that some industries provide good jobs with stable employment and high wages whereas other industries provide bad jobs with low wages and no mobility, Morris and Western (1999) find as we do that these employment strategies are now utilized *together* within industries and within firms. Most notably, observations, interviews, family experiences, and the press highlight contradictions between the rhetoric and practices of firms and the workers' experiences on the ground. Although some firms make informal efforts to partner with their workforce, explicit policies enable only two of the seventy-four firms here (Ayesha Muhammad's and Sam Gates's) to approach this goal.

CHARACTERISTICS OF THE PARENTS' FIRMS AND JOBS

As context for the ensuing discussion of how firms and families intersect to influence economic mobility, we briefly describe the main characteristics of the seventy-four firms in which the key parents are employed between January 1998 and June 2003 (see Table B.1 in Appendix B). Industry classification, occupation, nonwage benefits, type and size of firm, safety record, union presence, and a category we call "firm issues" are discussed first. The parents' wages and wage adequacy (see Table B.1 in Appendix B) are discussed in a subsequent section because of their centrality to economic mobility. The final sections of the chapter focus on advancement through microscopic examination of the families' decisions and patterns of job change, the advancement structure and organizational relations in their firms, and future projections for their industries, occupations and wages.

INDUSTRY CLASSIFICATION

Table B.1 in Appendix B shows that the seventy-four firms represent fifteen of the twenty categories in the North American Industry Classification System (NAICS 2002) (U.S. Census Bureau, 2004b). NAICS does not include self-employment. Although the key parents' initial post-training jobs[2] are located in eight of the fifteen industry categories, the range of industry environments in which they work nearly doubles over the five-and-a-half-year period (January 1998 to June 2003).

Over half of the parents' initial firms (fourteen, or 56 percent) are located in the manufacturing, construction or automotive industry (one parent remains at a preprogram firm), while about two in five (eleven, or 44 percent) are in service industries. Over time this proportion reverses. Looking at the study period as a whole, two in five of the parents' seventy-four firms (thirty, or 41 percent) are located in manufacturing, construction or automotive industries, while three in five (forty-four, or 59 percent) are in service industries. This shift mirrors the general trend of postindustrialism as well as the recent economic downturn in the United States. In 1970, 25 percent of the American workforce worked in the manufacturing industry compared to 12 percent in 2004 (The new protectionism, 2004, p. 28). Equally relevant to the mobility of the parents here, the steep loss of manufacturing jobs in the recent recession disproportionately disadvantages African American workers. As of 2003, 10.1 percent of the twenty million manufacturing workers are African American. These workers lost 15 percent of the jobs they held before the recession compared to a 10 percent loss among white factory workers (Uchitelle, 2003).

OCCUPATION

Most of the parents' occupations, in both initial and subsequent firms, would be considered entry level or low skilled (Table B.1, Appendix B). These occupations include "operator," "assistant," "helper," "laborer," "apprentice," "clerk," "technician," and "guard." Two parents hold lower management positions: Lucky Miracle in a firm that precedes his involvement in the job training program and Hard Working Blessed who reaches that level five years after his initial post-training job. Isabell Smith is in training for an office manager position.

NONWAGE BENEFITS

One of the expectations of the workforce programs here is that a "good job" will offer nonwage benefits, especially health insurance, even though this expectation runs counter to the national decline in employer-provided benefits over the decade of the 1990s (Nafziger, 2000). This decline continues to the present, as Holahan and Cook (2005, p. 1) report: "Between 2000 and 2004, the number of uninsured Americans (adults) increased by six million, primarily because of a decline in employer-sponsored health insurance. Two-thirds of the growth was among Americans below two hundred percent of the federal poverty level."

In this study, as Table B.1 (Appendix B) shows, most of the initial twenty-five jobs (twenty-two, or 80 percent) offer health insurance to entering workers, yet only sixteen of the parents utilize these benefits for themselves or family. The other six parents elect to remain on Medicare, are covered by a spouse's insurance, or are uninsured. The parents tend to not utilize employer health benefits when their contribution to the premium costs more than $15 per month (Iversen, 2002). As Gerstel and Clawson's (2001) research underscores, affordability is key to taking advantages of benefits that are offered. Three parents are not eligible for employer-provided health benefits.

By mid-2003, fewer than half the jobs the parents hold (44 percent) offer health insurance, about the same rate as reported nationally (Kalleberg Reskin, & Hudson, 2000). Eight parents (32 percent) are uninsured for some or all of the research period, almost double the 18 percent of Americans who have no health insurance at some point during 2000 (Appelbaum et al., 2003). Four families alternate between employer-based insurance and Medicaid. Thus, on the health insurance metric alone the parents get fewer "good" jobs over time and the description of nonwage benefits as "fringe" becomes increasingly apt.

Because workers in the United States obtain health insurance primarily through employment, family health coverage is further constrained during between-firm job changes. Loss of health insurance while job-hunting and during probation in a new job often lasts up to four months, hurting children's health as Randy Jackson's wife Shawn reports:

> We don't have any health insurance right now. It's tough on the kids. The kids have been sick a while. We only have money for over-the-counter medicine. We spend a lot of money on that. We used to take them to the private hospital, but now go to the county hospital. We still have bills coming. The kids got ringworm in school, but we couldn't afford to take them to the doctor. The drugstore medicines didn't work very well. It took a long time to go away. We had to take them to the hospital. *Shawn Jackson, Milwaukee*

Only one parent reports being told about bridge health insurance when making a job change, even though the 1985 Consolidated Omnibus Budget Reconciliation Act (COBRA) legally requires employers that offer health insurance to provide such information.

TYPE AND SIZE OF FIRM

Virtually all seventy-four firms are private rather than public companies (Table B.1, Appendix B). Although some argue that public and private firms are different (Swedberg, 2003), others hold that the "public/private" distinction is increasingly blurred by the spread of market forces (Grint, 1991). We find here that both types of firms are vulnerable to market turbulence and that differences are not systematic.

Using data from NAICS 2002 (U.S. Census Bureau, 2004b), firms' materials, and parent reports, we conclude that two-thirds of the firms (fifty, or 68 percent) contain more than one hundred employees and one-fourth of the firms (nineteen, or 26 percent) contain fewer than one hundred employees. Size data are missing on five firms. The predominance of larger firms here is thus counter to the general pattern of firm size in the United States. Over 90 percent of the more than six million business establishments in the United States employ fewer than fifty workers, even though larger firms still contain over half the American workforce (Osterman et al., 2001). Accordingly, a higher percentage of key parents (68 percent) than welfare leavers (50 percent; Holzer, Stoll, & Wissoker, 2004) work in large firms. This difference may be due partly to the fact that our data are longitudinal and most welfare data are cross-sectional, partly to the fact that workforce development programs are more likely than welfare-to-work programs to provide the skill training that large firms want, and partly to the fact that larger firms may be more likely than smaller firms to hire during economic recession, as vacancy theory predicts (Swedberg, 2003). Alternatively, the size of the industry may be a factor, as the job training programs here seek partnerships with firms in industries that are significantly represented in their urban region.

Firm size is considered a proxy for mobility opportunity as large firms are thought to better protect workers against labor market turbulence than smaller firms. Yet DiPrete (1993) finds that industry contraction in the 1980s results in high rates of unemployment for service and blue-collar workers, which suggests that large firms no longer buffer the effects of industry contraction on mobility. What buffering that exists pertains primarily to higher level, more experienced workers. Hollister (2004) suggests that this trend persists in the 2000s, largely due to corporate restructuring. Similarly, neither size nor industry protects the low-earning parents here from layoff or from the lessened likelihood of being offered employer health coverage (Holahan & Cook, 2005), even though larger firms are historically more likely to offer health benefits.

SAFETY RECORD

As Katz (2001, p. 204) reports, "Over 10,000 workers are killed and more than six million injured on the job each year." Safety is a problem in nearly one-third of the parents' firms (twenty-two, or 30 percent) according to inspection records from the Occupational Health and Safety Administration[3] (OSHA; U.S. Department of Labor, 2004; Table B.1, Appendix B). OSHA categorizes safety violations in descending order of seriousness as follows: (1) *Willful*, one committed with an intentional disregard of, or plain indifference to, the requirements of the Occupational Health and Safety Act and regulations; (2) *Repeat*, a citation is issued where OSHA has previously cited an employer for a substantially similar violation and that citation has become final; (3) *Serious*, a violation in which there is substantial probability that death or serious physical harm could result, and the average employer knew, or should have known, of the hazard; and (4) *Other-than-serious*, a condition which would probably not cause death or serious physical harm but would have a direct and immediate relationship to the safety and health of employees (U.S. Department of Labor, 2001, pp. 1–2). The twenty-two firms here cited by OSHA accumulate 2 willful, 121 serious, and 21 other-than-serious violations between 1998 and 2003. To the greater extent that safety conditions affect life and health, they intersect with parents' work efforts to affect mobility as well, as Hard Working Blessed's story illustrates later.

Union Presence

Wages and benefits are thought to be more generous in union than in nonunion positions (Mishel, Bernstein, & Boushey, 2003). This outcome pertains to some but not all union positions here, as Rachel Quinn's story highlights later. Others report that some union jobs, such as parking attendants (Jeremy) and janitorial services (Miracle), evidence wage stagnation in the current labor market (Shipler, 2004). Either way, the option of a union pathway as a route to economic mobility lessens over time for the parents. Seven parents hold unionized positions in their initial post-training jobs, and an eighth would have but left the firm too soon (eight of twenty-five, or 32 percent). If we include those parents who remain at their post-training job, nine of the twenty-five parents (36 percent) hold or can potentially hold union positions; thus over time the rate of unionization among the key parents appears to be four times higher than the 9 percent of employees reported in private sector union positions in 2000 (Ehrenberg & Smith, 2003). However, many of the parents' jobs are short term, and in some cases the parent does not join the union. The majority of the parents' firms (fifty-two, or 71 percent) are nonunion. Union information is missing for seven firms.

Firm Issues

In the final column of Table B.1 (Appendix B), information from the interviews, promotional material, and press yields issues in firms that can hinder or foster mobility. What we categorize as troublesome issues surface in more than nine out of ten firms for which we have data (fifty-six out of sixty-one, or 92 percent). Troublesome issues include no clear advancement path (absence of internal ladders); no provision of benefits; downsizing; layoffs; globalization; outsourcing; production decreases; plant, branch, and division closings; on-the-job injuries; demotion; perceived racism; acquisitions and mergers; unhealthy work environments; informal wage arrangements; insufficient work; mandatory overtime; bankruptcy; strike threats; massive organizational restructuring; state funding cutbacks; lawsuits; and takeovers. These issues in the parents' firms reflect the national and international debates about firm restructuring, contemporary production systems, and national economic troubles that we discuss earlier. In contrast, issues that may foster mobility, such as having a strong employee focus; receipt of quality awards; holding a corporate art collection, which suggests concern about employees' work environment although arguably could be a customer marketing strategy; implementing wage parity between contingent and permanent workers; and supporting minority business, are evident in a handful of firms. As constructive as these issues are, they do not counterbalance the panoply of troublesome issues that affect the parents' mobility efforts either directly or through their influence on other firm characteristics and practices, as the family stories show.

In sum, Table B.1 (Appendix B) shows that even after five or more years of full-time work, most of the parents remain in or just above entry-level positions that Ehrenberg and Smith (2003) characterize as "lowest paying." About one in four workers nationally holds such positions: 20.6 percent of men and 33.3 percent of women in 2000 (Ehrenberg & Smith, 2003, p. 477). The parents work increasingly in service industry firms that offer limited health insurance or on-the-job upgrade training. Despite the large size of these firms, union protection is scant, and safety and other establishment practices are troublesome. These characteristics alone endanger the parents' economic mobility. The parents' wage pathways and analysis of the adequacy of their wages further endanger mobility, as the next section describes.

WAGES, WAGE ADEQUACY, AND JOB PATHWAYS

WAGES

Wage and salary earnings are the primary source of family income (McCall, 2000), particularly for families at the low end of the wage scale who seldom hold major savings or assets. The analyses in the next sections of the chapter and in Table B.1 (Appendix B) explicitly pertain to wage income only, as the dominant concern in assessing economic mobility and family well-being over the long run is what a parent can earn. Although transitional subsidies and wage supports like food stamps, housing assistance, and the Earned Income Tax Credit (EITC) mediate low incomes in the short run (see also Chapter 3), earnings are ultimately the key to fostering intra- and intergenerational economic mobility. As Duncan and colleagues (1998) warn, family economic conditions during children's early years, particularly for low-income families, are critical influences on children's later school achievement.

Definitions of "low wage," "near low wage," and "chronic low wage" vary slightly from one source to another. Kalleberg and colleagues (2000) define a low-wage job as one in which the hourly wage is in the bottom quintile of workers age eighteen and over—below $6.00 per hour in 1995 dollars. Katz (2001, p. 352) characterizes low-wage work as full-time earnings that are less than two-thirds of the median pay. Bernhardt and colleagues (2001, p. 153) categorize a chronic low-wage worker as one whose "permanent hourly wage by age 34 is less than $11/hour in 1999 dollars." The workforce programs and networks here use $7 per hour in 1995 dollars as the wage floor for a "good job" (Fleischer, 2001), drawing on the old paradigm expectation that wages will increase regularly over time. All but two of the key parents' initial post-training wages exceed the floor figure. In fact, the average post-training wage across the programs as of 2000 is $9.13 per hour (Abt Associates & New School University, 2000). For perspective on the wage figures in Table B.1 (Appendix B), a $7 per hour wage in 1995 is the equivalent of $8.81 in 2005 (U.S. Department of Labor, 2005). Nationally 28.5 million of the 69.1 million hourly wage jobs (41 percent) are considered low wage (minimum wage) or near low wage (up to $7.50 per hour, or $8.96 in 2005 figures) per Smith and Woodbury's (2000) definition.

In all five cities the parents' post-training wages are significantly higher than wages they earn in prior employment (analysis not shown). Entering these jobs in the late 1990s for the most part, parents in Seattle, Milwaukee, New Orleans, St. Louis, and Philadelphia average wage increases of 42 percent, 39 percent, 45 percent, 55 percent, and 18 percent, respectively, over preprogram wages. These increases derive from several sources: a greater amount of full-time year-round work; entrée into higher-paying jobs and industries than the parents are able to access before training; and moving from welfare reliance or a mix of welfare and work income, incarceration, refugee histories, or insufficient skills and education to a full-time good job. The increases are not to be interpreted as indicative of better jobs in one city or another, as the preprogram wage floor differs by city and within cities by different jobs.

According to the wage metric, these parents fare a little better than other low earners across the country. As noted in Chapter 1, in 2003 about one in every four full-time year-round workers earns less than $9.04 an hour, which may not keep a family of four out of poverty (Mishel, Bernstein, & Allegretto, 2005). This finding alone alerts us to the fact that hourly wage is an important but not sufficient index of economic well-being. The adequacy of the wage in the context of family size, locale, debt, health, and the structures and characteristics of firms needs to be assessed alongside base wage data to fully understand a family's potential for economic mobility. The family stories below illustrate these intersections.

WAGE ADEQUACY

Whereas *low wage* refers to a worker's actual hourly wage, *low income* is a broader concept that uses hourly wage or annual income and an official measure to assess how adequately a parent's income meets family needs. The Federal Poverty Guideline, commonly called the Federal Poverty Level (FPL), is the most common measure. Most literature and many subsidy programs use 100 percent FPL, also called the "poverty line," as the cutoff between poor and not poor. In contrast 200 percent FPL—twice the poverty guideline—is frequently considered a *minimum* sustainable family income (Mishel, Bernstein, & Boushey, 2003). As mentioned in Chapter 1, median income in the United States is just under 300 percent of the federal poverty level (Gitterman, Howard, & Cotton, 2003), more than half again the income of most of the parents here. By any measure, the wages of nearly all the key parents do not adequately meet their families' needs (see Table B.1, Appendix B).

One reason for wage inadequacy is structural, as many policymakers and scholars consider the federal poverty level a poor measure of family economic status (Danziger & Haveman, 2001; Iversen, 2002; Mishel, Bernstein, & Boushey, 2003; Rainwater & Smeeding, 2003; Shipler, 2004). Means-tested programs for families with low incomes, such as food stamps, housing subsidies, and adult and children's health insurance, are currently indexed to the federal poverty level, whereby income relative to family size is the only criterion. Complicating matters, state, local, and federal government departments use different calculations and different multiples of the poverty guideline to determine program eligibility. In this respect "place" matters a great deal to economic mobility. Deciding on an improved federal measure is critical to the economic mobility of low-income families, as the adequacy of a parent's wage intersects with the policy environment in terms of eligibility for work supports and subsidies.

The debate for and against the federal poverty metric further revolves around whether the poverty line (100 percent FPL) should be set at "minimum subsistence" or higher than "subsistence" levels, whether it should be developed and updated in "absolute" or "relative" fashion (Fisher, 1995), whether a poverty line should be set nationally, globally, or according to "societal poverty lines" (Rainwater & Smeeding, 2003), or whether it should vary by region and locality. These debates have resulted in the development of alternative metrics for assessing income adequacy and subsidy eligibility (Short, 2001), one of which is the Self-Sufficiency Standard (SSS) that we use here (Pearce, 2000, 2001; Wider Opportunities for Women, 2001, 2004; Table B.1, Appendix B). The SSS assesses income adequacy according to the monthly local cost of basic needs such as housing, food, child care, transportation, health care, and taxes in addition to income. The SSS and other self-sufficiency standards also require differential assessment of family needs according to children's age. As our research also finds, calculating "how many" children a family has does not account for differences in the cost of certified child care or preschool compared to public school, differences in the cost of feeding an infant compared to a teenager, or differences in housing costs. Use of an absolute national formula based on "number in family" also does not account for significant geographic variation in these costs both within and between states. An income that reaches 100 percent of the Self-Sufficiency Standard is thought to adequately meet a family's basic needs.

Further evidence of the need to accurately measure wage adequacy is the fact that in 2000, earnings of 16.2 percent of all prime age workers (full time and part time) fall at or below 100 percent of the poverty line: 21.7 percent of these workers are women and 12.3 percent are men (Mishel, Bernstein, & Boushey, 2003, p. 351). As recently as 2002, more than one in four (27.4 percent) working parents with children in the United States earns less than 200 percent of the federal poverty threshold (Waldron, Roberts, & Reamer, 2004). Moreover wages per se have deteriorated in recent decades. Compared to youth who enter the labor market in the 1970s, the real median wages of those who enter in the 1980s and 1990s declines 21 percent by the time they are in their thirties, and this decline is concentrated among less educated workers such as some of the parents here (Bernhardt et al., 2001). Even more relevant, although real wages have fallen for men and advanced for women as a whole over the past two decades, the real wages of low-skilled women have actually declined (McCall, 2000).

In this research, few parents' annual incomes[4] reach sufficiency by either measure: 200 percent FPL or 100 percent SSS (Table B.1, Appendix B). Over time wage adequacy rises or falls depending on employment status, type of position, family composition, and emergency needs. *Even with* sizeable increases over prior job wages, the parents' annual incomes at their initial job after training average 122 percent of the federal poverty level (see Table B.2, Appendix B) and 69 percent of the Self-Sufficiency Standard—well short of the ability to support their families. Even work supports such as the EITC do not raise most of the families' incomes to 200 percent of the poverty level, as noted in Chapter 3.

Critically, more often than not, parents' incomes that appear sufficient are *potential* not actual incomes. They do not reveal income reductions that parents experience due to periodic layoffs; partner's unemployment; debt (as much as $20,000 in this research); prior bankruptcy; erratic overtime that inflates an annual income figure and results in ineligibility for or premature phase-out of housing, food, or child-care subsidies; medical emergencies during a job transition period before new insurance kicks in; and summonses from children's schools or doctors that require unpaid time off from work. Tasha Jones's family story is one of many that illustrates how this disconnect between potential and actual income intersects with firm characteristics and family demands to limit wage adequacy and economic mobility.

Disconnect Between Potential and Actual Income: Tasha Jones's Family Story (Milwaukee)

Tasha Jones is a twenty-four-year-old single mother of two preschool-age children. She held a series of low-wage jobs after graduating from high school and tried to boost her career path through a travel agency training program, but the program offered no placement help and few jobs were available. In her early twenties, Tasha enrolled in a manufacturing training program in hopes that it would result in a job with increased earning power. After seven weeks of unpaid training, Tasha was hired as a machine operator at Manufacturing Company, a firm that partners with her training program to find suitable replacements for its rapidly aging workforce. Tasha's starting hourly wage of $9.84 was *potentially* a $5,000 increase in annual income over her previous employment that would put her above 100 percent poverty level for the first time in her life. Still, her potential income only reaches 120 percent FPL and only 31 percent SSS, even without counting wage reductions from unpaid work days that result from her preschool children's severe and chronic healthproblems.

Tasha acknowledged reluctantly that even at full attendance her income is not enough to cover emergencies. A company union representative and Tasha's floor supervisor both underscore Tasha's assessment of the inadequacy of her wage:

> Wages are not adequate. In 1984 we took a two dollars an hour cut because of the threat of closure because our product wasn't selling. We used to have piecework and they took that away. *Manufacturing Company Bargaining Committee Member*

> We made the same hourly rate in 1980 as today. $10.36 in 1980 is $11 today. *Manufacturing Company Floor Leader, Tasha's Immediate Supervisor*

The department supervisor echoes his colleagues' concern about the adequacy of the company's wage scale for a person like Tasha:

> In my opinion, a husband and wife have to both work if they're making these wages— eleven or ten dollars an hour. That gives you roughly twenty thousand dollars a year. And a woman with two kids is not having an easy time on that. I think you need about $30,000 for one person to raise two kids. *Manufacturing Company Assembly Department Supervisor*

In contrast, the firm's plant superintendent believes that wages in Tasha's department are adequate: "They're not as high as in the skilled trades, but they can support a family."

Tasha's potential annual income in 2000, *if* she were able to work every day, would be $20,000. Median household income in the United States in 2000 was $42,148, but only $28,116 for female-headed families like Tasha's (DeNavas-Walt, Cleveland, & Roemer, 2001). Because Tasha's partner's immigration status forces him to settle for under-the-table wages, he does not earn enough to extend her income to either the national median or the level that her firm's managers consider sufficient. Moreover, the organizational control measures in Tasha's firm compound the wage problem, as the continuation of her story later in the chapter shows. Similarly, the EITC is of reduced help to a worker like Tasha whose actual annual income is decreased significantly by lost wages.

The mobility question then becomes: How do the parents' incomes and the adequacy of their incomes change over time?

CHANGE IN WAGE AND WAGE ADEQUACY OVER TIME

An expectation of most workforce development programs and of persons holding traditional meritocratic views about mobility is that workers' wages will progress upward over time. A further expectation, based on the assumed career path of the old mobility paradigm, is that wage gains will increasingly enable a parent to support his or her family. Recent research challenges these expectations and assumptions. Bernhardt and colleagues (2001) find that if a worker's permanent wage qualifies as low by the age of thirty-four, he [male sample] is stuck on a long-term, low-wage career trajectory. Carnevale and Rose (2001) find an even narrower window of mobility opportunity, reporting that those who remain in a low-earning niche in the labor market for five years seldom move higher. Osterman's (1999) analysis of men's earnings pathways finds similarly that virtually half (49.2 percent) of those that start at the bottom of the distribution in 1979 remain at the bottom in 1995. Only 2.6 percent of those that start at the bottom of the earnings distribution in 1979 end up at the top in 1995. In contrast, over half (54.3 percent) of those that start at the top of the earnings distribution in 1979 remain at the top in 1995. In the same study, the men's average hourly wage increases only 6 percent over the sixteen-year period: from $17.40 in 1979 to $18.17 in 1995. Given inflation, this is effectively a dramatic wage decrease. Some estimate that a 2 percent earnings gain per year is an index of "doing well" in the earnings pathway (Osterman, 1999). Related, Andersson, Holzer, and Lane (2005) find that the earnings increase for those who have persistently low earnings but stay at the same firm is about 2 percent per year.

Table B.2 in Appendix B shows the wage changes of the key parents from the starting wage at their initial post-training job until their last known wage during the research period. The period between the post-training job and last known wage ranges from five to fifty-eight months, with an average of 30 months. Over time, the parents' wage mobility ranges from minus 25 percent (downward wage change) to plus 61 percent (upward wage change), averaging an 18 percent wage increase for the group as a whole. An 18 percent wage increase over the five-year period is almost twice Osterman's (1999) estimate of 2 percent per year, or 10 percent over five years. Those parents whose wages rise experience increases between 3 percent and 61 percent, averaging a 27 percent increase. Those parents whose wages fall experience decreases between 15 percent and 25 percent, averaging a 21 percent decrease. The percent of wage change is not correlated with the length of time the parent works (analysis not shown).

We caution that the percentage of wage increase may distract from the parents' relatively low wages per se. Without critical examination of wage adequacy, the percentage increase may obscure how adequately the wage covers family needs, as the adequacy measure takes into account inflation and changes in family size. Thus we next examine how wage adequacy changes between the post-training and last known wage, according to the federal poverty metric (Table B.2, Appendix B).

The adequacy of the parents' wage in their post-training jobs averages 122 percent of the Federal Poverty Level (FPL) and increases to an average of 132 percent FPL at the time of the last known wage. The range of change for those whose wages become more adequate is plus 6 percent to plus 83 percent, with an average increase in adequacy of 33 percent. The range of change for those whose wages become less adequate is minus 2 percent to minus 126 percent, with an average decrease in adequacy of 54 percent. The average change in wage adequacy for the group as a whole is plus 9 percent, and, the changes, as for wages, are not due to length of time in the labor market. Notably, although none of the parents' wage incomes reach 200 percent FPL at their initial post-training job, three parents' incomes exceed 200 percent FPL at the time of their last known wage.

We draw three conclusions about wages and wage adequacy. First, the parents' wages *are* increasing at a higher-than-average rate relative to samples in recent research. This suggests that on average the parents' wages are moving forward, whether at the post-training firm or a subsequent firm, despite a turbulent economy. Second, some parents are moving upward substantially in wages and wage adequacy and others are moving dramatically downward. Third, when both wage and wage adequacy are considered, the progress toward economic sufficiency for the parents as a whole, after up to five years in the labor market, is quite modest; thus the old paradigm expectation of reaching economic sufficiency over time does not appear to hold here. Even if the parents' wage gains are regular, which many are, base wages remain too low for incremental increases to result in an adequate family wage. Contrary to the old mobility expectation, hard work and sustained labor market attachment *are not* enough to ensure mobility.

Numbers tell one part of the wage story. The family story excerpts that follow expand on the data in Tables B.1 and B.2 (both in Appendix B) to help us better understand the experiences of parents whose changes in wage adequacy are extreme, defined as one standard deviation from the mean. Four families fall into each of two categories—extreme *upward* or *downward* changes—that we illustrate here with exemplars. We further categorize these change pathways as either *apparent* or *real*. The pathways show how firms and other intersecting institutions affect the parents' movement and suggest whether the up or down movement might be sustained in the future. As the stories exemplify, vulnerability persists for families moving upward *or* downward because of insufficient wages, too few hours, competing advancement and family demands, uncertain or apparently racist industry conditions, and firms' intentional or unintentional disregard for immigrants. The mobility futures of the families' children are thus fragile as well. Highlighting the overall tenuousness of mobility, the other families here share these characteristics and experiences, even if in slightly different forms and proportions.

ECONOMIC MOBILITY PATHWAYS

Apparent Upward Economic Mobility: *Rachel Quinn's Family Story (New Orleans)*

Forty-two-year-old Rachel Quinn looks like a success story until we learn that her construction employer assigns her work very infrequently. Thus Rachel's wage figures and the adequacy of those wages are *potential* not actual.

Rachel Quinn came to a four-week job readiness program after two-plus years of college education, no degree, and a history of short-term jobs. Construction skill training following the readiness program launched her into a full-time position that she had held for three and a half years by summer 2003. After training Rachel was placed at Union, a local trade union that generally assigns her to jobs at Events Company where she constructs booths and display areas for trade shows held in the convention center or in large city hotels. The employment section of Events Company's website heralds its dual customer and employee focus:

> We are always looking for talented, enthusiastic people who will give our customers the best possible service. We know that our employees are our competitive advantage. So we *treat them like the stars that they are* [emphasis added] by offering an excellent employment package with competitive compensation, first-rate benefits and great employee programs; a culture that is one of excitement, energy and pride; a company that is committed to coaching, mentoring and continuous learning; a responsible management team; and a work/life flexibility program, recognizing that work and life are inextricably linked. *Events Company Promotional Material*

Observations, interviews, and Rachel's experience reveal that Events Company does not treat Rachel like a star. Rachel rarely works more than four hours per day and generally works only partial weeks. According to a union leader, "Only about one hundred of the two hundred fifty to three hundred union members at tradeshow sites work a full forty-hour week." All others work part time except during sporadic busy periods. During such periods Rachel works overtime "until two in the morning," but these periods are as unpredictable as are forty-hour weeks:

> You can't really count on if you're going to work that whole week. I might be out of work a whole month. It happened I was out of work a whole month, close to two months. *Rachel Quinn*

In fact, Rachel had at least one period of *four months* without work.

Event Company's "work/life flexibility program" illustrates that "firm flexibility" is often experienced by workers as "firm insecurity" (McCall, 2000). Without work to occupy and challenge her, Rachel becomes depressed as a depressive symptom inventory (CES-D) confirms: in her words, "You know what my problem is? When I don't work every day." Erratic work also impacts her family. When they do not have enough to eat Rachel resorts to purchasing what her son calls "boot-leg food." Further, without consistent hours Rachel remains ineligible for Union's health insurance plan, a serious problem for someone with chronic injuries, many of which are job related.

An administrator at Rachel's job readiness program understands the union's complicated health insurance plan as follows:

> Have to work six hundred hours within two quarters plus a two month sit-out period. Once on the plan, the employee can be out of work or not make full hours for up to six months, but then the worker must pay for the policy themselves. The contractor is paying for the insurance for each worker in the form of $3.96 an hour *off their pay* but the contractor doesn't necessarily insure everyone. *Job Readiness Program Administrator*

Thus according to the program administrator, the time a worker has been *out of work* for a sustained period is the time that the union expects him or her to pay for health insurance. A union official informed us that Rachel needs over 1,200 hours of work per year plus 160 hours of training to qualify for union-paid health insurance. The official acknowledged that the insurance system is designed with construction workers in mind. With irregular work schedules, trade show apprentices and journeymen cannot access the policy even though their wages are docked for it.

The readiness program administrator was shocked to learn how few hours Rachel was allotted after three years of apprenticeship, but was torn between the program's advocacy role and his meritocratic view about individual responsibility:

> The union offers a minimum of 1,260 hours per year. That's based on a 2,080-hour work year. Something's wrong there. Does she check every day—call them, versus be on call only? Nudging is a good thing. *Job Readiness Program Administrator*

As an African American woman in a predominantly male industry, Rachel's position in the hiring queue is low. Although the rule is supposedly first-come first-assigned, social networks play a large part in who is and is not called to work. According to her financial consultant's estimate, Rachel's *actual* annual income for 2001 was $6,000, not the $23,816 it would be if she were assigned full-time year-round work. The fact that she qualifies for the lowest level of contribution to her public housing apartment corroborates this estimate. The unemployment insurance she collects during down periods and during training amounts to $77 per week.

A job readiness program staff member describes the union program as "inden-tured apprenticeship." Acknowledging the sporadic nature of the work, a union representative cautions that workers need to "be prepared to budget their money to last through the slow times, and that's hard." At a real annual income of 87 percent FPL at best, budgeting for Rachel seems a thoroughly inadequate solution to an industry and local labor market problem.

A more subtle dimension of Rachel's inconsistent work situation is how it intersects with her adolescents' views about their own work futures. As Parcel and Menaghan (1994) underscore, the types of jobs that low-income parents hold can have an important effect on their children. Rachel's goal for her children is that they will both attend college and thus secure good jobs. To this end, Rachel carefully researched and selected high schools that were academically superior to the neighborhood school and where her teens would get college preparation and academic counseling. Likewise, Rachel does not let them visit the union hall or her worksite as she considers them negative influences:

> I want them to go to school and do something else with their life. I can't afford to let them do this kind of work. *Rachel Quinn*

The goal of Rachel's sixteen-year-old daughter, Sadé, is to get her mother and herself out of the projects. She frames her goal to attend college in terms of her own and her family's well-being:

> One day I'll be able to move [Rachel] out of this place. It's important that I go to college so I don't have to be [in the housing project] all my life. *Sadé Quinn*

Still, Sadé makes decisions that reflect the family's constrained mobility and its intergenerational reach. Because her career goal is to become either a pediatrician or a dentist, Sadé was accepted by the state university medical school for an eight-week summer program designed to give underrepresented minority students hands-on medical experience. However, Sadé ultimately opted to work in a grocery store to earn money for school activities and graduation expenses estimated at a thousand dollars that her mother cannot afford on a part-time income from her full-time job.

Unfortunately for Rachel and her children, the week in October 2002 that she worked forty hours was the *only* full workweek in three and a half years on the job, and she is still not eligible for union health insurance. Unless Rachel is allotted full-time work hours her economic mobility will remain apparent rather than real.

Real Upward Economic Mobility:
Sam Gates's Family Story (Philadelphia)

As a divorced father of three children who live with him half time, Sam Gates gave up a lucrative but enveloping newspaper service business for manufacturing training and employment. Technology Management Company-Electronics Division (TMC) offers Sam a laddered mobility path, even as it also implements contemporary production practices. Per our metaphors, Sam's firm is a mix of "autocratic family," "fair-weather friend," and "partner," as its promotional material, our observations and interviews, and Sam's perspective suggest:

> Technology Management Company embarked upon an aggressive program of quality improvement and product introduction using the *kaizen* philosophy … it is now considered a model of manufacturing excellence—nationally and internationally. *Technology Management Company Promotional Material*

Sam associates the firm's continuous improvement philosophy of *kaizen* and its just-in-time inventory/production and total preventive maintenance practices with mutual benefits to both employer and employee:

> Well, the goal is to make the product easier to make. That's in the operator's best interest. It's in the company's best interest because they're happy, they'll work faster, and they won't get hurt. And all of that makes the supervisor's job easier. . . . At my end it gets a little frustrating because I'll make something I think is fantastic. And you know what? It is. But it's only fantastic for six months until they decide to change it and make it better. Now that makes me a little nuts. . . . The word *kaizen* means . . . continuous improvement. I think that's what helps people want to stay. *Sam Gates*

Sam's supervisor also feels that the *kaizen* philosophy fosters low rates of employee turnover and collaborative employee relations:

> Usually people leave here because they've gotten an education and are able to move on to something else. Most of the people who are here, other than that, stay here . . . One woman left here because she wanted to work in an office environment. Another woman left here because she wanted to work on computers. She went to school for that. One woman retired, she was 66. Very few people walk in here one day and say, "You know what? I don't want to do this anymore." It's a clean factory. The management here is very concerned about the concerns the people have. . . . We have a program called CVR. I forget what it stands for, but basically what it is, people fill out a questionnaire: How do you like your job? How do you like your boss? Do you think there's favoritism? How do you like your benefits? Based on the answers we have scheduled meetings with the employees in which they get to air some of their concerns, make recommendations and suggestions. Some of those recommendations and suggestions can be handled at my level. Others need to go to the CEO. *Technology Management Company Supervisor*

Sam also believes that the firm's traditional internal career ladder offers him the possibility of further mobility either within the firm or through moving to another firm:

> I'm ahead of where I should be in terms of pay because I took on some supervisory positions when I was at TMC-Cable Division. So my hourly range was machinist plus supervisor so to speak. So I got a head start that way. . . . Whereas I got a sixty cent raise here, in my final year when I become a journeyman I might get $1.20 as a jump. It won't be huge just because I'm already on target, I'm already progressing. What that does is it also gives me mobility once I have a journeyman's papers. In a lot of trade jobs in order to make a significant increase in pay you've got to move on. So I would expect I'll have to find another job and shoot for a 10 percent or 15 percent pay raise. The papers are state and national. . . . Then I'll get something similar to this but it will say "Journeyman." And when I go apply for a job they'll say, "Do you have any papers?" "Yes". And right away that puts me at a certain pay scale. Then I'll say, "I'm making this much here. Make me want to come to you." *Sam Gates*

Despite the firm's promotion-enhancing environment, Sam's future mobility is constrained by the need to juggle decisions about furthering wage power through schooling or working overtime, meeting his growing children's immediate needs, and spending time with them. As a noncustodial parent with proscribed periods of time with his children, Sam Gates is forced to choose between these values in ways that most resident parents are not. For the next seven years Sam also confronts the fallout from a bankruptcy declaration in 2001 that resulted from the precipitous shut-down of his independent news dealership at the time of his divorce. He cannot buy a house so he must spend extra money for rent and he cannot establish credit. Essentially he cannot move forward to develop assets and savings. Forty-year old Sam Gates should remain economically mobile. However, without paid release time for schooling or financial advocacy, it will likely take him longer than it would take a single twenty-five- or thirty-year-old or even a married forty-year-old—an example of the kind of contemporary, *non*-normative mobility pathway that we call a life-stage mismatch (Iversen, 2002).

Apparent Downward Economic Mobility: Joseph Faithful's Family Story (New Orleans)

When twenty-one-year-old Joseph Faithful completed construction training after the readiness portion of his job program he was hired for a construction appren-ticeship at Union. After waiting weeks to be called in for work his sole assignment was to pick up garbage for an entire day:

> I did not go to all this training and take two months out of my life so that I could go pick up trash. *Joseph Faithful*

A former union member reported having to pay $87 dues up front, $20 for a workbook, and $300 worth of tools just to be placed on an "out of work" list. Because no other construction option was available at the time, urgent financial needs compelled Joseph to take a job outside of the construction sector:

> I graduated in March and I was ready to work, but for two weeks nothing happened, and in two weeks I decided to forget about it. They had so many people graduating that I was on a waiting list. There were some contractors that the workforce program worked with but they had all the people they needed, so I went and got another job. *Joseph Faithful*

According to one of Joseph's training program administrators, landing a con-struction job quickly is rare in New Orleans. Drawing on program statistics the administrator reported that by spring 2002, 263 candidates had completed both soft and hard skills training and about 165, or 63 percent, had been hired for construction jobs. Several factors accounted for what he considered a modest hir-ing rate. After September 11, 2001, contractors slowed their activities because their financial backers withdrew support. Projects were put on hold, in some cases permanently, which constrained the program's capacity to help its graduates find jobs. On top of market problems, the light rail system in the city is inadequate for construction workers because of a geographical mismatch between routes and job sites. Few candidates can afford a car. Moreover the entry end of the construction market was saturated in New Orleans, largely due to the program's prior referrals. A training program and industry partnership needs a strong and broad network to counter such factors.

In need of money to support his wife and new infant, Joseph took a service job in a hotel. A year later he moved to an informal construction "apprentice" position under the auspices of his church. His wage plummeted accordingly. The church pastor described two parts to the Church Construction Company. First, Joseph contributes unpaid work as part of his church stewardship. He works with other church members who are in construction, thus he learns while he works. Second, Joseph works independently for George, a fellow church member and self-employed contractor who holds state building construction and mechanical licenses. Joseph is a "crew lead" for George, which means that he works with and learns directly from George and that George also assigns him to certain jobs and sites on his own.

Joseph's driving goal is to permanently escape poverty:

> [And how are you managing financially?] I guess standard . . . you know, getting your bills paid. That's my mission anymore, just working to pay bills. I don't like that because to me that's like sharecropping. You're working just to give it right back, you know, and I was telling Lisa [his wife] that's what it takes to pay the bills. We need to start doing something to create an investment ourselves because just working paying bills is a circle and we're tired of this poverty. We've been living it so long being that our parents and seems like they didn't want to go no further than where they at and we're breaking that generation curse. I don't want my sons to just be working hard sweat and don't have no money because you got to pay this bill and you got to pay that bill. We got to do the things to enjoy life, so that's what I do now on Saturdays with the money that I make. I put it on the side. How can I use this to make more of it, I mean send it out [i.e., invest it]? *Joseph Faithful*

A potential obstacle to Joseph's goal is the possibility that he receives less adequate construction training from his informal church mentors and teachers than he might gain from a union apprenticeship program. Although Joseph and the pastor believe that the informal training is sufficient, even superior, a readiness program administrator disagrees, laying out the limits on what Joseph is allowed to do:

> He's not learning fully about carpentry, doing what he's doing. He's not getting the business side of it. . . . You can do remodeling without a contractor's license as long as the total cost of the job is under fifty thousand dollars. If it's over fifty thousand dollars, you need a license. You have to have a business license for construction. . . . The contractor license—it's no easy test. *Job Readiness Program Administrator*

Joseph maintains that he learns a lot through George and other church contractors. One listing of recently learned skills includes, "Install ceramic tile; Install vinyl floor; Install vinyl siding; Trim work; Add-ons; Pour concrete; Electricity." George also feels that the "match" is better between Joseph and church construction teachers than it would be with a union apprenticeship program. At the same time George pays Joseph "under the table," a potentially exploitive practice that George lodges in a career-building rationale:

> I know I didn't hire a skilled craftsman . . . [I pay him] two hundred fifty dollars a week. Then about three weeks ago, I brought him up to three hundred dollars. . . . This is a profitability thing and understanding that concept, I don't want to hear from my guys getting hung up on the mentality of, you know, working by the hour and working for a wage. I want you to be more geared toward the sharper you are, the

more you make.... See I'm not concerned with the time. I'm concerned with the product and the reason for that is to motivate you to understand that's how life is. Nobody can just talk about how much time you put in; I want results.... That's really the key here. To get him to the part where he's a contractor. *George, Joseph Faithful's Church Construction Company Boss*

George's compensation practice does not take into account the broader financial condition of Joseph's family, such as no health insurance coverage, inability to access federal work supports such as the EITC because his wages are not reported, and the erosive effects of uneven income on the family's mobility goals.

Still, Joseph may benefit more from working with George and others through the church than he would at the formal union program, which is why we characterize his downward mobility as "apparent" rather than "real." In addition to hard skills, Joseph receives friendship, guidance, sustained encouragement and mentoring. Given an adolescence of poverty and occasional misjudgment, as well as participation in after-school learning and urban nonviolence programs, Joseph needs all of these to succeed at a career. However, Joseph was laid off about six months after we talked with George. As Joseph explains, "Business slowed up for George. His money was too spread out—he had money for materials but not for labor."

At our last contact in summer 2003, Joseph had just started his own construction company. Classes on entrepreneurship and Individual Development Account (IDA) start-up that Joseph attended at the time will possibly smooth the family's transition to self-employment and reverse his downward wage trend. The family intends to use the same resource for home-ownership education and guidance. Evidencing continued optimism and grit as well as an old paradigm confidence in meritocracy, Joseph's final words to the research team were "This story is going to be a good ending."

However, the construction industry and economic infrastructure in New Orleans needs to be more robust to translate Joseph's mobility from an apparent downward to a real upward category.

Real Downward Economic Mobility:
Loretta Lopez's Family Story (St. Louis)

During one of twenty-seven-year-old Loretta Lopez's several periods of job training she was placed in a temporary telemarketing position for outbound calls at Business Company for $8.00 per hour. This was not the job Loretta wanted, but she had to "get some money coming in quick."

A hiring announcement from the parent corporation describes Business Company's orientation to Loretta's outbound call division, arguably the least desirable of call center/ telecommunications services, in neo- and post-Fordist terms:

[Parent corporation] values a good work ethic and makes every attempt to promote from within ... We're currently hiring Outbound Customer Care Representatives [for affiliates such as Business Company]. Day or evening positions are open. Salaries are hourly and not based upon quotas or commission. The parent corporation also offers health, life and dental benefits, vacations, paid holidays, and *will make arrangements for unpaid personal days off* [emphasis added]. *Business Company's Parent Corporation Promotional Material*

Loretta benefited from none of the corporate rhetoric or promises—especially an arrangement for unpaid personal days off. Business Company was not a "disengaged family" much less a "fair-weather friend." In five weeks at the firm, Loretta was not able to work a full forty-hour week due to reasons ranging from being sent home if she was not making money for the organization, to unapproved absences, to receiving inadequate hours. Loretta's final paycheck recorded only fifty-six hours for a two-week pay period compared to an expected eighty hours; as such her check only netted about $300.

Loretta also reported harsh working conditions at Business Company. When workers went on break they often found themselves without a desk to work at upon their return—a sort of musical chairs scenario. Obviously, being left without a place to work can translate into difficulty meeting stringent quotas and limited productivity:

> [How does that affect your productivity?] Yes ma'am, and your concentration, don't leave that out. It was just so odd because I have never experienced such chaos in my life at a workplace. *Loretta Lopez*

The work environment at this branch of Business Company has an especially negative reputation, as a staff member at Loretta's customer service training program reveals:

> There's a second-line supervisor there who is not so skilled. The atmosphere is like a *zoo*. *Training Program Staff Member*

In such low-end firms temporary positions are likely to be the rule. Encouraging strong social ties among employees to bind them to a firm is contraindicated for employees like Loretta who are likely to become less vital to a company over time (Cappelli, 2000).

Loretta's supervisor at Business Company eventually wrote her up for numerous infractions, most having to do with attendance and tardiness, but some having to do with a failure to "rebut rebuttals," which means trying to convince disinterested customers during actual sales calls. Loretta provided notes from her son's doctor to account for some of her absences, but others were due to a housing crisis for which no note was possible. When she was fired after five weeks, she was to some extent relieved to be freed from what she viewed as a chaotic and punitive workplace.

It remains hard for Loretta to keep a job. Although her wages drop by one-third in her last known job in spring 2003, the adequacy of her wages drops 79 percent, largely because the job at $6 per hour is only part time. Throughout Loretta's involvement with two different training programs and churning short-term jobs, Loretta was never given a thorough mental health assessment. Unless Loretta is assessed for cognitive and emotional symptoms that may be depression related, such as poor concentration, temper, discouragement, and use of marijuana to self-medicate, firms will likely not retain her. Loretta's sustained dedication to the emotional and educational lives of her children needs to be matched by workforce development networks that can offer expert assessment and partner with firms that are not "zoos."

ADVANCEMENT: THE PRESENT

Changing jobs, whether within or between firms, is the assumed labor market mechanism for economic mobility. The normative pattern of the old paradigm, based primarily on young white men, is several job changes within the first ten years or so of labor market activity followed by "settling" in to a stable career path, generally in one firm, that can buffer the career turbulence caused by family formation. As noted earlier in the chapter, families like those in this book travel far from the normative path. Instead of matching the old mobility pattern, their age, family status, firms' expectations, and wage pathways coalesce in a life-stage mismatch (Iversen, 2002). Considering the advancement part alone of the life-stage mismatch, scholars find that promotions rarely occur after age thirty-five in certain skilled occupations, even when strong internal job ladders are present (Rosenbaum, 1990). Jacobs (1993) finds similarly that career mobility from unskilled service occupations into managerial, professional, technical, clerical, and sales occupations is highest for workers ages sixteen to twenty-four and progressively lower for those in older age groups.

Promotion and advancement are complex issues for the parents here. First, advancement intersects with whether job changes are voluntary or involuntary or within or between firms, and how these changes affect wages. Second, advancement intersects with the ways that workers make decisions about changing jobs. Third, advancement structures in firms intersect with parents' responses to these different modes of organization in the form of reasons that they accept or refuse promotion, ways that firms offer "informal advancement," structural barriers such as seniority queues, and the role of values in advancement decisions. These dimensions intersect with each other and with policy and educational institutions to forward or stifle economic mobility, as Figure 6.1 and the family experiences in this section illustrate.

JOB PATHWAYS AND WAGE OUTCOMES

Figure 6.1 shows what kinds of job changes the key parents make between 1998 and mid-2003 and the wage results of these changes. Six parents (24 percent) remain in their post-training firm. Five of the six receive wage increases over time that average $2.65 per hour, and the wage of the sixth remains the same. Although it is normative in the old mobility paradigm to remain in a single firm, these parents' reasons for doing so are not always ones that foster economic advancement, as Maya Vanderhand's story illustrates later in the chapter. Three out of four parents (76 percent) change firms over the five-year period, and some make multiple changes. Most locate a new job within a month or so, but none secure a new job before they leave their current firm, in most cases because they leave suddenly or have no time to job search.

Seventeen of the twenty-two voluntary job changes result in reemployment in a new firm. These changes show an average increase of $1.61 per hour when wages increase and an average decrease of $3.11 per hour when wages decrease. The wage decreases are thus nearly twice as large as the increases for these voluntary changes. Two additional voluntary changes are to a different division or company

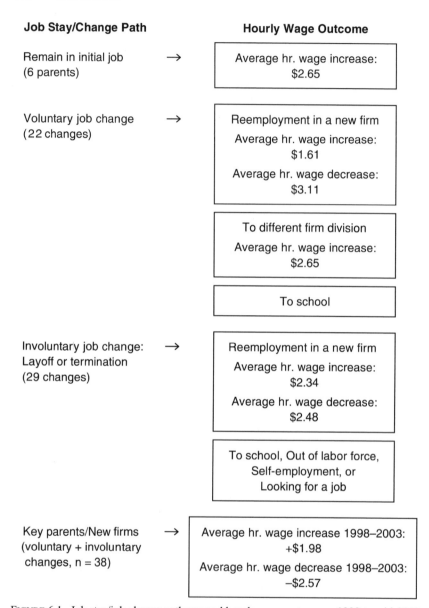

FIGURE 6.1. Job stay/job change pathway and hourly wage outcomes: 1998 to mid-2003

owned by the same firm and three result in return to school. We heed Dwyer's (2004) caution, however, about the classification of "voluntary" in the low-earner market, as voluntary exits may mask anticipated layoff or termination.

The twenty-nine involuntary[5] job changes are due to layoff, permanent layoff, or termination. Some workers lose multiple jobs over the period and some exit other jobs voluntarily over the period as well, underscoring Dwyer's (2004) definitional caution. Twenty-one of the twenty-nine involuntary job changes result in reemployment in a new firm. Eight involuntary changes result in return to school, self-employment, or job search. In one case, layoff begins a domino effect that results in homelessness and relocation to another city. Most, however, find new employment. The twenty-one involuntary changes to new firms result in an average increase of $2.34 per hour when wages increase, and an average decrease of $2.48 per hour when wages decrease.

However, given that many parents make *both* voluntary and involuntary changes to other firms over time, especially after the 2001 recession, the group average tells a more nuanced story about job and wage changes. For the parents as a whole who are reemployed in a new firm ($n = 38$), the average wage increase of $1.98 per hour is smaller than the average wage decrease of $2.57 per hour, and also smaller than the average $2.65 per hour increase experienced by those remaining in a single firm or those changing divisions within a firm.

These findings suggest that on the wage metric alone, the old mobility pattern of multiple job changes in the early years of employment is no longer a productive advancement pathway for today's low-wage workers. First, job change does not always result in significant wage gain or gain at all. Second, although these parents are at early stages of their careers, many are at later stages of life, as the life-stage mismatch denotes. They do not realize the expected returns to job change historically enjoyed by younger workers yet their need for income is considerably higher, which means that wage decreases exact a greater penalty. Consistent with findings on earlier cohorts (Bernhardt et al., 2001; Holzer, Stoll, & Wissoker, 2004), whether the exit is voluntary or involuntary, the average wage increase that results from changing firms is lower than the resultant wage decrease. Although this finding among today's workers and firms can only be suggestive, it bears serious consideration in the formulation of new theory about economic mobility and, practically, in the design of reemployment policies and services in welfare and workforce development programs and networks that serve low-income parents.

JOB CHOICES AND DECISION MAKING

Turning to why workers change firms, the parents' rationales illustrate the intersection of advancement, new knowledge about decision making (Chapter 2), organizational restructuring, and economic mobility (Granovetter, 2002; Sen, 1977). For the parents here, changing firms evidences both "getting away from" and "going to" rationales and emotional and cognitive decision processes. Some parents change firms to get away from transportation difficulties or distance from home; a poor match with a firm's environment, inconsistent or harsh supervision, dangerous working conditions, perceived racism, or no career path. Other parents change firms to pursue a field in which they are trained or interested, to increase wages, or to relocate. For the parents here, getting away from, or what Dwyer (2004) and Granovetter (1988) call a "push," is a more compelling reason to change jobs than is a going to or a "pull."

The push-pull notion moves us in the direction of how new decision theory intersects with economic mobility. As the previously cited reasons and scholars suggest (Granovetter, 1988; Johnson, 2001), job choice and job change actions are a result of many considerations and values in addition to or instead of a simple cost-benefit analysis of wage return. From the perspective of economic sociology, Swedberg's (2004) argument that actors often attempt to realize their interests with the help of social relations may pertain to choice making as well. From the perspective of the new institutionalism in sociology, North (1998) argues that "individuals typically act on incomplete information from subjectively derived models..." (p. 249).

The low-earning parents here make choices and take action according to emotional responses to firm culture and climate, especially when racism is perceived; to distance from home that prevents them from being available to help their children navigate dangerous neighborhoods; to ameliorate discomfort with the intensity and pace of work; to valuing time for community and church over promotion; and to work shifts that allow time to oversee children's homework and meet their developmental needs. These families illustrate Dwyer's (2004) observation that in the American opportunity structure individuals must often make choices and tradeoffs among characteristics. The choices and actions of these working parents also underscore that *both* men and women consider the overall needs and well-being of their children and family members in the decision calculus. Thus decision processes in the new view of mobility are emotional, nongendered, interest based and relational, with others rather than an atomistic self at the core of the calculus. Decision processes about advancement, in particular, are also strongly influenced by structural characteristics of firms.

ADVANCEMENT STRUCTURES IN FIRMS

Few parents are offered promotions at either their initial or subsequent firm, but a general and individualistic expectation of firms, particularly those organized according to internal career ladders, is that workers will seek or accept a promotion if offered. One of the surprising findings in the first wave of the ethnographic research (Iversen, 2002) is that parents such as Maya Vanderhand (next section) do not necessarily seek promotion or even accept an advancement opportunity when offered. In other cases such as Isabell Smith (see later), promotion is accepted after an initial refusal. The notion of "context-bound rationality" (Nee, 1998) helps to explain such actions and outcomes that *appear* irrational but have a coherent logic in their particular contexts. As Brinton and Nee (1998, p. 4) argue, "The actions of social actors are always in principle understandable, provided we are sufficiently informed about their situation." Importantly, the advancement structure in firms and worker characteristics intersect to influence opportunities and decisions (Holzer, Stoll, & Wissoker, 2004), as Maya Vanderhand's and Isabell Smith's experiences exemplify.

Refusing Promotion: Maya Vanderhand's Family Story (Seattle)

Maya Vanderhand obtained a personal lines operator position at Insurance Company because of skill acquisition and likely also the "signal" effect of her office training program. As mentioned in Chapter 5, the "signal" (Ehrenberg & Smith, 2003) or "brand halo" effect (Laufer & Winship, 2004) occurs when a firm credits the job seeker with the positive characteristics of the sponsoring organization, thereby reducing the risk potential of the hire. Accordingly, the signal or halo may help to counter stereotypes that an employer holds about a new worker with limited education or from a cultural minority group.

In the case of Maya, who holds both characteristics, this thirty-two-year-old mother of four knows that advancement opportunities, including on-the-job training, are available in her relatively Fordist-organized firm, as company material describes:

> New employees receive appropriate and necessary classroom and on-the-job training preparing them for their new assignment. Insurance Company also offers other learning benefits to qualified employees, including College Tuition Assistance, a sponsored program that provides up to $2500 annually for work-related courses and to obtain work-related degrees. Insurance Company also pays associated expenses for qualified employees to obtain vocationally related professional designations through our Professional Education Program. *Insurance Company Promotional Material*

However, the advancement structure at Insurance Company involves changing departments and likely even office locations, in line with the notion of labor market segmentation and geographic diversity described by Lane and colleagues (2003). Because Maya's husband is only intermittently employed, often leaving her the sole provider for their family of six, and because she lacks a high school diploma or GED, she hesitates to change departments or locations where she might feel less competent or fail and lose her job:

> I don't want to change departments any time; there is a lot going on. I have so much on my plate that I don't want to screw that up. I can go to another department but I want to get to know my job better where I am at. There is claims or underwriting or there is other things and they will train you, but I don't want to jump from one group to another.... Plus because my hands are not well, I would rather stay where I am at. *Maya Vanderhand*

The advancement strategy of changing firms does not pull Maya either, largely because an on-the-job injury resulted in a chronic hand problem that might affect her performance and attendance in a new firm. A new firm also might not offer her the ergonomic accommodations that Insurance Company did.

At the eighteen-month point at Insurance Company, Maya predicted that her supervisor would offer her a promotion, but her attitude about advancement remained framed by her desire to be competent within a known structure:

> I know I am very smart and capable and I do not like to work places where I am not sure I will succeed. *Maya Vanderhand*

Although Maya's definition of employment "success" cautiously includes advancement, the company's decentralized structure does not seem to support the continuity and familiarity she needs in order to advance her career in the context of family and physical challenges:

> To have the right job I guess, you are comfortable and you are happy with what you are doing and with the pay and there is room for advancement. It is not like you are going to be stuck in one spot and that is it. We have a lot of work. I like that pace,

there is work coming and you are always doing something. It is not where it is kind of slow and there is nothing for you to do. I am very comfortable. I am in my own cubicle. I manage my own desk, not even my manager manages my desk. This is what I am doing and I like it. *Maya Vanderhand*

If firms offer a more gradual advancement structure that includes on-site GED training and guidance, and if workforce development networks offer employment opportunity to participants' spouses, advancement for workers like Maya might proceed more rapidly.

Accepting Promotion: Isabell Smith's Family Story (Seattle)

Other workers like Isabell Smith accept a within-firm promotion, but not until six months after initially refusing it. Recently out of substance abuse rehabilitation and a business skills training program, Isabell Smith landed a customer service position at Tech Company. In her first months on the job, the thirty-one-year-old mother of two, whose continuing recovery from severe family violence in her teens illustrates another aspect of the life-stage mismatch, initially wavered in seeking or accepting an advancement offer.

In contrast to Maya Vanderhand's company, the relational structure of Isabell's customer model firm (DuGay & Salaman, 2000), whose promotional material emphasizes that it "offers employees the chance to work with great people," increased her confidence to move ahead. After a year on the job, having received the consistent supervisory support that company rhetoric promises, Isabell felt ready to consider the promotion she refused earlier. She moved up to a Tier 2 customer service position and her wage increased from $11 to $12 per hour. At Isabell's cutting-edge firm, the "new establishment effect" is in play wherein mobility opportunities are greatest when a firm is new and lessen incrementally as the firm ages (Lane et al., 2003).

In relation to further advancement, Isabell, like Maya, wants time to build confidence before plunging into another new set of skill demands. On-the-job training is available but because Isabell is new in the Tier 2 position she hesitates to participate, which is a response that employers often erroneously characterize as lack of motivation to move ahead rather than as a rational, context-bound decision:

> They are always offering training, but I don't feel that I am comfortable enough in my everyday job to go and learn something new. *Isabell Smith*

For workers like Isabell, undoing the ravages of past psychological and physical abuse and building confidence to move forward can be a lengthy process, as is found among welfare recipients whose journey to sustained employment takes many years (Herr & Halpern, 1994; Rangarajan, Meckstroth, & Novak, 1998; Wagner, Brooks, & Herr, 2004). In Isabell's case, the sustained instrumental and emotional help of her training program case manager together with help from multiple community providers in her workforce program's network enable her to navigate the simultaneous challenges of a new job and new family.

Even so, policy regulations can intersect problematically with the advancement efforts of working parents like Isabell, further challenging the old paradigm view of the atomistic worker. A state-subsidized postemployment Web training program for former TANF recipients that might enable Isabell to work from home and more closely supervise her two preschoolers, who have developmental problems of their own, is only available to unemployed persons. Accessing this program would require Isabell to quit her job. Alternatively, Isabell hopes that her former business training program's tentatively planned night classes in Web design will provide the skill advancement she seeks in a familiar and supportive atmosphere.

An additional array of challenges faces low-earning parents who actively seek advancement: practices that we call "informal advancement" and long seniority queues. These mobility challenges often emerge out of a disconnect between parent decision making and firm structure and organization.

Informal Advancement: Randy Jackson's Family Story (Milwaukee)

Parents frequently report a firm practice that we call "informal advancement," which takes the form of additional job duties, supervisory responsibility, or shifts from one type of position to another *without* wage increase, formal promotion, or higher positioning in the firm. Randy Jackson's story is one of many that illustrate this practice.

Randy Jackson's dependability at Construction Co-WI, his initial post-training job, distinguished him from other workers. On many occasions Randy said with pride that he had not missed a day of work. Early in Randy's tenure his construction company supervisor told the research team and a representative from Randy's training program, "He's great." Randy's tenacity is palpable as he describes his workday:

> But you know when you take a job you don't get to choose what you do. If you don't want to do something or if you don't know how to do it, you just figure it out. If you can't figure it out, you ask questions. Like today, I had to tear down this wall and a ceiling. I had to build a kind of bridge [a scaffold] to get the job done. I had to use a jackhammer to tear everything down. It was hard. I had to figure out how to do it. I had never done that before. Now I know how and the next time it will be easier. I don't understand why people get a job and think they are not supposed to work. Work is hard, but that is how it is supposed to be. *Randy Jackson*

After about six months on the job Randy's supervisor invited him to do office work instead of manual work, which Randy described as "daily logs and inventories and paperwork for all kinds of things." Neither his job title nor his wage changed as a result, as is typical in firms structured by post-Fordist flexibility and flatter authority (Garsten, 1999). As Randy reported, "Paperwork is a privilege. But I don't get extra money for it." This despite the fact that Randy holds a bachelor's degree from a university in his native African country.

If Randy tries to advance his career by changing firms, his new skills could translate into a higher level or higher paid job, but *only* if the new firm will acknowledge them without the signal of a U.S.-recognized academic credential or the signal of a prior promotion or wage increase. Moreover, if workforce programs are part of a broad network of partners, they might help job seekers like Randy locate scholarship funding for education-oriented mobility goals. As Randy says, "I want a career, not just a job. I want a career—like law." Although Randy earns good wages at construction, an attorney's income might secure his family's economic future.

Seniority Queues: Kevin McDonalds's Family Story (Milwaukee)

Other parents find that advancement opportunity is blocked by old mobility practices such as Fordist seniority queues. Dissatisfied by the absence of a career track at his initial post-training job at Bindery, the postemployment guidance at Kevin's printing training program enables him to move to Printing & Bindery six months later. Although his initial wage as a floor person was $9.76 per hour as it was at Bindery, Kevin did not view this as a lateral move. He viewed Printing & Bindery as a union position with room for advancement, including further education:

> At a bindery you can only do so much—there's a fixed number of machines. Now I also go to school through my worksite. I work on different machines. It pays about the same, but I can do a lot more. *Kevin McDonalds*

Twenty-nine-year-old Kevin actively sought the promotion and advancement opportunities offered by his firm. He attended three-hour printing classes for jogger and press operator at the firm's printing training affiliate one to two mornings a week after his shift, which meant working for twelve hours straight (11 P.M. to 11 A.M.). He paid for the classes up front, although his course grades of "A's and B's" qualify for full and near-full employer reimbursement. After completing the press operator classes, he planned to take computer classes for the press, viewing the transferable skills as critical to advancement in printing or elsewhere:

> There's room to move around. You're not stuck in tunnels. I could even move to an advertising agency to check colors, do desktop publishing. It's not a dead end.... You can really get ahead in this business. There is a lot of opportunity to do that. You can just keep moving up by taking classes. I don't know if I want to stay in it, but you learn a lot of things that will help. The classes are easy. Except going there after work. *Kevin McDonalds*

Despite his initiative, hard work, and merit, Kevin's ability to advance was contingent on open slots in his firm, thus it could be several years before he achieves a higher paying position such as pressman or foreman, as vacancy models suggest (Rosenbaum, 1990):

> I'm something like number twenty-seven now on the list for the next promotion. It will probably take three or four years until the next position, five at most. *Kevin McDonalds*

Already near the ceiling wage for his position, even three years is a long time to wait for an income large enough to compensate for a sizeable tax debt. Eight years earlier, Kevin filed income taxes incorrectly and learned only recently that he owes the IRS $9,000 because the small original penalty accrued interest while he was in prison. Kevin's wages are now garnished, which leaves him with very little to provide for his family, and demanding but compensatory overtime opportunity is limited by his firm's financial downturn:

> They garnish my wages fifteen percent; that leaves me with nothing. I got a hundred dollars last paycheck without overtime. To make up for this, I worked two twelve-hour shifts and Friday and Saturday last week. There I am, doing the right thing, and whoa!

Here I am trying to get it right and I'm in another hole that I've got to fill up. Before the tax problem, I was bringing home four hundred to five hundred dollars a week; twelve hundred to sixteen hundred dollars a month. They take child support out of my check too. How do they expect a person to make it without overtime? *Kevin McDonalds*

As firm practices such as varied levels of support for advancement, informal advancement, and seniority queues intersect with workers' family lives, a larger policy question arises: Who should provide upgrade training to workers? Firms benefit from an educated, skilled workforce through reduced turnover, higher productivity, and increased employee loyalty. Yet many firms today seem less interested in employee loyalty, preferring the vitality and creativity of a changing cast of workers to a stable but potentially stagnating cadre. Firms also seem less motivated to invest in worker training, leaving this domain to community colleges and other off-the-job, often for-profit sources. Reduced on-the-job training disproportionately disadvantages low earners who typically have neither time nor funds to upgrade their skills and credentials on their own time and dollars. Harder yet, federal and state funding allocations for upgrade training for low-income, as opposed to dislocated, workers under the Workforce Investment Act (WIA) are considered inadequate, making eligibility and access stringent, as Chapter 5 discusses more fully. We underscore the upgrade dilemma in this chapter because it centrally influences economic mobility in firms. Might firms be spurred to spend more dollars on in-firm training to draw and retain productive workers as a large portion of the workforce ages and retires in the decades ahead (Bingham, 2004)?

FIRM ORGANIZATION AND RELATIONS

In addition to a firm's wage and advancement structure, other aspects of its organization and relations influence how long a worker stays at a particular job and what his or her chances are for economic mobility. Salient aspects for the parents here range from the structural level of how employment relations are organized (part-time or full-time schedule) and how authority relations are implemented (firm rules) to the ground level of physical conditions (safety) and sociostructural environment (racial and ethnic discrimination). These aspects are often perceived and experienced differently by firm and parent/worker as the following disconnects between firms' public and management rhetoric, parents' and auxiliaries' reports, and our observations illustrate. As other chapters show, these aspects of firms are perceived and experienced differently by educational institutions and children as well.

ORGANIZATION OF EMPLOYMENT RELATIONS: TYPE OF WORK SCHEDULE

Economic mobility is influenced by the type of work schedule a firm offers its employees, particularly whether a firm hires predominantly full-time or part-time workers. Considerable hyperbole is expressed in the press and academic literature about the increase in part-time or "nonstandard" employment. According to one report, the share of total employment held by full-time workers has declined over the past decades: from 83.4 percent in 1973 to 81.2 percent in 1993 (Mishel & Bernstein, 1994). Others report that as recently as 1995 "the primary job of nearly 84 million (65 percent)" (Kalleberg, Reskin, & Hudson, 2000, p. 259) of the approximately 121 million employed Americans over age seventeen is a standard full-time job. They report further that "another 17 million (14 percent) work part time in standard jobs and the remaining 20 million (17 percent) work full time or part time in some nonstandard arrangement" (259), such as day labor and on-call work, temporary-help agency and contract-company employment, independent contracting, and other self-employment. Despite slightly different figures, most employment remains full time. Still, nonstandard work arrangements have increased in the United States over the decades of the 1980s and 1990s, particularly "*temporary employment* which has grown by about 11% per year since 1972" (Kalleberg, Reskin, & Hudson, p. 273). Bernhardt and colleagues (2001, p. 2) find similarly that "by 1996, 78% of firms report using at least one type of flexible staffing arrangement."

Few of the parents here work part time, as most seek and eventually attain full-time jobs. However, some parents use temporary employment agencies as a career entrée or are helped to find work in a temporary agency by their job training program in hopes that the position will become permanent after an initial probationary period. Lynn Walker's story is an exemplar of a neo/post-Fordist temporary position that does not materialize into permanency, and thus constrains mobility, and Ayesha Muhammad's story exemplifies a temporary position that leads to mobility-fostering permanency. The strength of the local workforce development network appears to influence both outcomes.

Temporary to Layoff: Lynn Walker's Family Story (St. Louis)

Thirty-six year-old Lynn Walker, single mother of four children ages two to thirteen, had six months left on her sixty months of lifetime eligibility for TANF assistance when she entered a customer service training program. Lynn characterized her employment history as "an up-and-down roller coaster," as wages were never sufficient to support her family, even with the addition of $3,380 annually in child support for *one* of her four children. All born of the same father, inexplicably the father supports only one. Lynn's last job before training, at $6 per hour as a customer service representative at a discount department store, ended when she was denied additional leave time to recuperate from surgery. Months later, Lynn described that she was ready for a change:

> I was sitting on the porch on welfare thinking that I'd like to work. I watched other people go to work and I knew that I didn't want to be at home all the time. I was watching other people's kids; I didn't want to do that. *Lynn Walker*

Lynn's words, although reminiscent of one of the stereotypes of welfare mothers as "sitting around," belie the reality that she had taken care of children since adolescence. Despite the fact that she was a "good student," Lynn dropped out of high school in the eleventh grade and went to work. Assuming the traditional role of only daughter, Lynn felt responsible for the support of her four brothers and five cousins, all of whom her single mother raised alone while working full time:

> There were family issues, a lot of life issues, period, to deal with.... I dropped out and went to work. My Mom had ten kids in the house at the time. The income I brought in was a "plus." Mom never said, "Go out to work." In fact, she said, "Go to school." But I felt bad about that too and wanted to help out. *Lynn Walker*

After customer service training Lynn located a job at Research Co. Temp Service that placed her as a Computer Assisted Telephone Interviewer (CATI) at Research Company. The Research Company director describes the firm as a "near-billion dollar national facility" and the company's promotional material highlights its dual attention to both market and employee customers:

> Quality of life is an important concern to Research Company. Our staff members are encouraged to *keep a balance in their lives* [emphasis added]. Research Company staff members are not only committed to their work, but also to their families and to community service. Research Company is committed to providing a work environment that enables staff members to maintain a healthy balance. Our programs and services are intended to help staff members meet their commitments both on the job and at home. *Research Company Promotional Materials*

Lynn's Research Company supervisor emphasized the company's flexible work hours, but also noted that the nature of the job—computer-assisted research inquiry—mandates nighttime coverage, which for working single mothers like Lynn may be antithetical to the company's public goal of keeping balance in its employees' lives:

> Daytime there are fewer interviewers. Some long-term interviewers are able to work in the daytime and a few people who do not want to take the bus late at night. The evening hours are busier; we need to keep the evening hours covered. *Research Company Supervisor*

Research Co. Temp Service's similar "dual customer" approach seems to prioritize the client over the temporary worker:

> We offer an array of standard support services that matter: 24 hours a day/7 days a week coverage, on-call standby staffing, custom reporting and employee management via our patented system, flexible billing and invoicing options, plus a full range of innovative staffing solutions. *Research Co. Temp Service Promotional Material*

Further evidence of this prioritization is that benefits at Research Co. Temp Service are only available to internal company employees. As a temporary employee Lynn was not eligible for health benefits at *either* establishment. Overall Lynn garnered few of Research Company's riches and most of its insecurity. When Lynn was laid off because the project she'd been hired for abruptly terminated, Research Company thought it would be able to rehire her in about a month when business improved, although it could not promise this.

Layoff began a downward cascade for Lynn and her children. She did not have enough savings to bridge a month without work, and because she'd worked for a temp service she was not eligible for Unemployment Insurance. At this same time Lynn's mother sold the home she lived in with Lynn and her four children, and Lynn and her children became homeless. Faced with two untenable choices, a St. Louis homeless shelter *if* she could find one that had space or living with the abusive father of her children, Lynn moved to a midsize city two hours from St. Louis in hopes of a better life there. Her family took refuge in a domestic violence shelter and eventually accessed an apartment in the city's only public housing development. Lynn's children went to stronger performing schools than they had attended in St. Louis, but also ones in which their middle school classmates tended toward pejorative racist and classist jibes. Lynn walked three miles daily from the shelter to the city to find a job, and after working several months for a cleaning service landed a more promising job at Library. The library job lasted for seven months until the state initiated layoffs.

Lynn's contingent employment at Research Company contributed measurably to her version of the downward mobility plunge discussed earlier. Despite the supervisor's laudatory comments about the quality of Lynn's work, the temp service made no effort to advocate that Lynn be "bumped" to alternative employment at Research Company while she waited for the research project to restart.

As Kalleberg, Reskin, and Hudson (2000, p. 274) note, temporary workers are not party to the incentive structures or loyalty responses that their *de facto* employer provides to its "real" employees and their *de jure* employer (the temp service) is not sufficiently apprised of the employee's performance or willing to advocate for him or her with the employer. Such workers thus have little hope of improving their position by working hard or performing well, despite the myths of meritocracy and opportunity. If temp agency partners in the workforce development network advocate to "bump" or locate alternative employment, job seekers like Lynn and her children might be spared months, if not years, of dislocation pain and limited mobility.

Temporary to Permanent:
Ayesha Muhammad's Family Story (Philadelphia)

After leaving a long nursing assistant career because of a life-threatening workplace injury, Ayesha Muhammad completed a welfare-to-work program but did not begin work until three months later. Her reason was simple: financial security. With three children under eighteen in the home plus two over eighteen, who after stormy adolescent years were trying to access vocational and GED training, Ayesha didn't just need a job—she needed a good job. Ayesha's program allowed her the time to look even though rapid job placement was a TANF funding requirement: in her words, "They stay with you until you find employment or until they find you employment." Although Ayesha was eligible for jobs the program recommended, such as restaurant waitress for which she was sorely overqualified, she held out for a job with mobility potential that she ultimately obtained through one of the program's network of partners, Temp Service-PA:

> I didn't settle for just anything. I wanted something where I was going to be able to
> grow and I wanted to be someplace where they had the benefits I needed, the security
> I wanted. Also I wanted to prepare for when I get older because I'm not a spring

chicken. I'm not one of those young girls who just started out there. When I get old enough, when I do retire and that little check comes, I want to have something else coming in also. *Ayesha Muhammad*

Several of the claims in Temp Service-PA's national promotional material that are matched by on-site observations pertain to forty-five-year-old Ayesha. One indicates that the life-stage mismatch is prevalent in the contemporary workforce:

> Increasingly today's 40- to 70-year olds are turning to Temp Service-PA for new opportunities. *Temp Service-PA Promotional Material*

Another claim indicates the importance of the job matching process. Although general knowledge, skills, and abilities were hiring requirements in yesterday's firms, firms now often expect that specific characteristics of workers will match the particular demands of the work (Batt, Hunter, & Wilk, 1998):

> At Temp Service-PA we pride ourselves on making the right "matches"—matching your job preferences and skill level with our clients' needs. *Temp Service-PA Promotional Material*

By way of a workforce development network of program, temp agency, and firm, Ayesha's welfare program engineered quality jobs for its graduates. After three months as a temp, Financial Services Company hired Ayesha full time and her wage increased from $8.25 per hour to $10.50 per hour. She and her large family also became eligible for a comprehensive benefits plan that includes on-the-job training and tuition reimbursement for off-site education.

Although Financial Services Company, as others in the industry, experienced tumultuous restructuring during the 1980s and 1990s when it decentralized operations and embarked on a series of buying and selling various businesses, by the time Ayesha Muhammad joined the firm the multinational corporation had settled into international, national, and retail divisions of life insurance. The company ranks among Fortune's top fifty companies for minorities, African Americans and Hispanics in particular, at both management and entry levels. The company is also ranked highly for working mothers. A parenting magazine reported that Financial Services Company "received special marks for raising the bar on family-friendly policies important to working mothers."

Ayesha's experience jibes with these accolades. Importantly, Ayesha's company manifests its goals through formal rather than informal policies. For example, Financial Services Company is the only firm out of the seventy-four in this research that offers an official *flexible time* policy. Hours taken away from work to attend to family needs are arranged in advance and made up later. In other firms, flextime is the province of individual supervisory discretion, which leaves the worker vulnerable as the continuation of Tasha's Jones's story illustrates below. Financial Services Company recognizes that flextime is critical to workers' ability to integrate work and family life and will result in satisfied employees. Ayesha's supervisor's longevity with the company is testament to this. After twenty years she stays there because of "the people and the benefits."

An indication that Financial Services Company formally recognizes the importance of family as well as worker enrichment is the company-sponsored "take your children to work day." Ayesha's three school-age sons joined her for this event and engaged in activities such as making posters for hospitalized children. Ayesha's supervisor even paid the youths fifty cents to work on the computer. The boys so thoroughly enjoyed their day they asked if Ayesha's supervisor would hire them for the summer. This company-sponsored day fostered the children's exposure to both work and their mother's multiple responsibilities. Their response parallels what Ayesha's supervisor interprets as their mother's experience in her new firm:

> [Ayesha] saw a piece of a world that she has never seen before in corporate America and that "I want to do something like that. I want to get in here somehow. I want to experience this. This is different than what I have ever seen before." *Financial Services Company Supervisor*

Ayesha's company offers several opportunities for growth and advancement. Classes in such subjects as computer skills and customer service are offered on company time. "Lunch and Learn" sessions offer information on women's health issues, joining a walking club, and other lifestyle topics. According to both Ayesha and her supervisor, Ayesha takes full advantage of these opportunities. Moreover, as a member of the Activity Committee, the supervisor noted, Ayesha "gets to say exactly what's going to be offered to employees in the future."

The company's tuition remission program and mentoring program are of even greater importance to Ayesha. The company pays 80 percent of the cost of college courses if they are relevant for present or future work. While this leaves a considerable 20 percent cost for the employee, it encouraged Ayesha to consider taking courses toward a career in underwriting and case management. Ayesha estimates that by taking the necessary courses and eventually moving up to a case manager position her income will increase from its present $22,000 per year to $35,000 to $45,000 per year.

Ayesha's impetus to take courses and advance her career is not the result of reimbursement policies alone. The company's mentorship program fosters Ayesha's motivation to take advantage of advancement opportunities at the firm:

> I was looking for a type of employment where I was able to grow that I wouldn't be stagnant and stay there too long. And by them offering this mentor program and them being able to reimburse me for any college classes that I take dealing with the type of work that I am trying to get into, I can advance. *Ayesha Muhammad*

Ayesha's supervisor thought her choice of mentor might be a good match for Ayesha, given their mutual interests, as she describes:

> You pick a mentor dealing with the type of work that you want to get into, and they pair you with a person that does exactly what you're looking for. She or he gives you the necessary encouragement that you need and lets you know exactly what you need to do for the position you want to be. *Financial Services Company Supervisor*

The mentor started Ayesha along the path to becoming an underwriter, meeting with Ayesha once a week or so to be, in Ayesha's supervisor's words, "a sounding board." A firm-sponsored program, mentorship takes place on company time: another example of this company's investment in employee advancement.

Ayesha faces tumultuous challenges ahead as she negotiates adequate schooling in a beleaguered district for her twin sons who are developmentally delayed. Because flextime and a clear, accessible, supported internal career ladder are essential to her future mobility, Ayesha's temp-to-perm story remains a model for the mobility that can result when workforce development networks are comprised of sustained partnerships among workforce intermediaries and agencies and agencies and firms, and when their partner firms are loyal to employees as well as to market customers. Many aspects of Financial Services Company illustrate the reciprocal mobility-enhancing employment relations that we characterize as "firm as partner." We discuss these characteristics and relations further at the end of the chapter.

AUTHORITY RELATIONS: FIRM RULES

In contrast to the mobility-enhancing relations evident in Ayesha Muhammad's firm, authority relations in many establishments are driven by the belief that employees will cheat or try to get away with things if not watched closely (Jacoby, 2004)—a position that is consistent with old paradigm and Fordist views of worker behavior (Bielby & Bielby, 2002). Depending on the prevalence of this perspective in a firm, different ways of setting and enforcing rules and regulations for employees result. The examples below illustrate how two seemingly opposite models of firm authority relations, traditional Fordism and the contemporary customer model, influence employee mobility.

Fordist Authority Relations: Tasha Jones's Family Story (Milwaukee)

Manufacturing Company, the employer of twenty-four-year-old single parent Tasha Jones whose story begins earlier in the chapter, illustrates traditional Fordist management through hierarchical authority and precisely written and posted rules. The company expects uniform supervisory enforcement of the control procedures, as the Plant Superintendent reports:

> We've had to make a stringent absentee program, but everybody is treated equal. [The supervisors] have to do it the same. There is no flexibility. *Manufacturing Company Plant Superintendent*

In truth, Tasha's firm evidences variable supervisory enforcement of the rules and regulations, or what Lipsky (1980) calls "street-level supervision"—an informal practice that did not enhance Tasha's mobility efforts. Tasha worried continuously about losing her job because of the conflict between her health problems, her children's health problems, and the regulatory system at her firm. In relation to her own health:

> I'm worried about losing my job. I had the flu a couple of times this winter and I got bronchitis. After I gave birth to Nami I almost died of pneumonia. I had toxemia and high blood pressure and I still have chest pains. They've given me EKGs [electrocardiograms] but can't find anything. If I turn left or a certain way, I have pain. I'm also short of breath. The doctor gave me an inhaler for when I'm short of breath.

One big problem is that even though it's forbidden, my co-workers smoke on the job. This makes me more sick. *Tasha Jones*

The children's health problems kept Tasha awake at night and increased her fatigue in the morning, affecting her attendance at work:

Nami [Tasha's two-year-old daughter] is sickly—she's going to be part of a sleep study. She was born with a flat nose. She may need surgery. She breathes really loud at nighttime—like she's trying to catch her breath. I need to stay close at night because she can die in her sleep. I sleep good, but wake up a couple of times a night to check on her. The hard part is in the morning time, well first of all at night. I go to bed at ten thirty and wake up at five thirty. I can't really go to sleep until they both fall asleep. I will check her in the middle of the night to make sure she is okay. I have to get up early in the morning, dress them both, carry them both downstairs, come back up the stairs just to lock the doors up. I mean it is hard for me and I be too tired to get up any earlier and so that is the hard part. *Tasha Jones*

Manufacturing Company developed detailed "Control Procedures" to deal with absenteeism like Tasha's, typical of those that mushroomed in firms in the early 1900s (Edwards, 1979). According to the company's twelve-point system, if an employee misses a day of work due to illness or childcare problems he or she receives one point (reduced to a half-point with a doctor's note).

Occurrence	Points
1. Tardy	$1/2$
2. Leave early	$1/2$
3. Absent 1 day with valid doctor's excuse	$1/2$
4. Absent	1
5. No call in or late call 30 minutes from start of shift	2
6. No call in for 2 consecutive days	2

Number of Points	Corrective Action
3	Verbal warning
6	Written warning
9	Final written warning
12	Termination

As one manager admitted, "You can use up a lot of points with kids." However, Tasha did not know how many points she accumulated. She had not received either a verbal three-month warning or a written six-month warning because her supervisor understood the difficulty of combining work and family responsibilities in today's world:

Well, the new people have more family problems because they're younger and they have young people's problems, like childcare. But they're different, more are divorced than the old workers were. There are more single parents and that makes things more difficult for them, and that affects work. Absenteeism is greater than it was in 1975. More time is missed today for family life. *Manufacturing Company Supervisor*

Tasha's supervisor's flexibility about the company's control procedures eventually boomeranged. The supervisor's boss decided to crack down on such flexibility, but Tasha did not know that. Tasha took personal leave after seven months of work because she had missed at least ten days because of Nami's health condition and over eighteen more for her own health problems, a car accident and court dates:

> I asked them if I could have a personal leave because I told them I didn't have a baby sitter. But that was just one of the reasons why I left. I felt that I needed to stay home with my kids. [My mother] She was able but she used to always say she was tired. [And they gave you leave?] Right but they didn't say when to return. *Tasha Jones*

Tasha's fiancé added: "They said they were going to call her when she should come back, but they never did and they just sent her a letter that she was terminated."

Perhaps because Tasha never fully understood how the point system was being applied to her or know how to negotiate personal leave, and perhaps because she also felt a sense of relief from family pressures, she took no further action when she received Manufacturing Company's official termination letter. Tasha's subsequent job entailed a sizeable wage decrease which stemmed her progress toward economic sufficiency.

Customer Model plus Fordist Authority Relations:
Isabell Smith's Family Story (Seattle)

In contrast, Isabell Smith's company seems organized according to mobility-enhancing authority relations. As we note above, Isabell Smith, thirty-one-year-old mother of two preschool children, took a customer service position at Tech Company after completing a twelve-week business skills training program—a job that training program staff considered a "plum." Tech Company epitomizes both the new form of identity marketing (DiMaggio, 2001) and the new model of customer relations organization (DuGay & Salaman, 2000). In effect, employers coordinate work by informal control through peers or the organizational culture (Baron et al., 2002). At the same time the company evidences vestiges of Fordist organization and management relations. Isabell seemed to experience both.

Companies have long marketed their identity, but in the past, such marketing aimed to build consumer loyalty to assure continued purchase of often-changing products. In the face of lessened job security in many contemporary firms, company identity marketing now aims to win the minds and hearts of its workforce as well as those of its customers through individualized promises that include new forms of organizing work relations and rules. Tech Company's promotional material illustrates this new marketing phenomenon:

> There are many things to consider when deciding on your next employer. At Tech Company we offer employees the chance to work with great people, on exciting projects, with a ton of opportunity for growth.... Working with smart people, on challenging projects, in an environment high on responsibility and low on politics makes most people look forward to the workday. Add the fact that the work we're doing is truly changing the way people find and discover products, and you begin to see that much of the root of our enthusiasm comes from our desire to do something that's never been done before. *Tech Company Promotional Material*

In particular, the employment opportunity section of the company webpage stresses its attention to what firms now often call "work/life balance":

> But we also recognize that Tech employees have a life outside of work and *need a break every once in a while* [emphasis added]. That's why we provide a full range of benefits for you and your eligible family members. Tech Company benefits are designed to meet your personal needs for financial protection—and match the pace of your life. *Tech Company Promotional Material*

Isabell definitely needs a break every once in a while if not more frequently. Both of her sons attend a therapeutic facility for developmentally delayed children: one delayed because of abuse in foster care and the other delayed because of Isabell's former heroin addiction, likely a delayed reaction to severe family abuse in her childhood.

Perhaps indicating Tech Company's tacit intention to hire young singles—in effect the old paradigm workforce in modern dress—Isabell found that supervisors and coworkers did not understand that her responsibilities as a parent often conflict with the demands of her job:

> I am the only one in the group who has children. No one understands what I go through—when a kid fell down the stairs or I tripped on the way to the car. It gets a little frustrating sometimes. I don't go home to my cat like they do. *Isabell Smith*

Within the first two months of employment Isabell's work schedule changed three times. Some months later Tech Company issued a new, arguably illegal policy mandating a forty-five-hour workweek for all employees and "strongly encouraging" fifty. One year after she began at Tech Company, Isabell worked fifty-five "mandatory" hours per week, over ten hours per day on the phones with mostly disgruntled customers:

> It is very high pressured job especially because I got hired on right before the holiday season and we ended up being on the phones ten hours a day, just phone call after phone call. It was just nuts and people were upset and they were screaming at us. *Isabell Smith*

Isabell's strain was compounded by her history of negative family "messages" about performance and multiple forms of abuse:

> I was raised that if you did anything wrong you deserve to die for it. I mean that is what was embedded into my brain so that whenever somebody tells me "You are not doing this right," I completely fall apart. I am working on it. *Isabell Smith*

She also perceived that her response to Tech Company's practices was not developmentally healthy for her children:

> I really took it too much to heart, being screamed at on a daily basis, all day long, and it affected everything. It affected my family, plus I was going to work at 6 A.M. and not coming home until 8 or 9 that night. So I would leave the house and the kids were sleeping and I would come home and they were on their way to bed or in bed . . . I feel like I don't have enough energy to do everything and feel like I should. We are

supposed to be the ones teaching them how to be and raising them to be good people and yet we are the ones that are not here. *Isabell Smith*

After seventeen months on the job Isabell learned that the company would close three months hence, eliminating the possibility of further advancement. The company cited higher costs at its local facility as the reason behind the job cuts. Isabell, expressing a mixture of shock and relief at the news, suspected her company of underhandedness:

> I didn't have the guts to quit this job but they asked so much from us. I've been unhappy for a while. I've had lots of issues with my boss. And then they raised the standards. I wasn't meeting them. I think it was a ploy to get people to quit. They were unreasonable. A lot of people quit over the holidays. I've been trying to leave stress at work but I've been exhausted all the time. *Isabell Smith*

Adding to Isabell's stress, she worked extra hours without pay, which likely provided significant savings for the company that was required to pay time and a half for overtime. The extra hours were encouraged by Isabell's supervisor who was concerned about meeting quotas for his department and instituted tight Fordist regulations in response. Isabell acquiesced for fear of being "written up."

More broadly, a national news article about a failed union drive (citation not included for confidentiality) confirms Isabell Smith's different reality from Tech Company's claim to value employees as well as customers:

> Many of the customer-service representatives complain that their wages, which usually run from $11 to $15 an hour, are too low for them to live well in high-cost Seattle. They also complain that they often receive little notice about schedule changes and having to work overtime. Several workers said that after working so much overtime they had tired of the CEO's mantra that it is Day 1 and Tech is a start-up in which workers need to work hard. "Our ownership feels hollow," said a 25-year-old customer service worker in Seattle. "They always say they are willing to hear our input, but there isn't follow-through. The inaction is the root of why we're organizing." *National Newspaper Article, 2000*

Consistent with the effect that reduced firm-to-employee loyalty can have on mobility, the job Isabell found next afforded only a lateral wage shift and was temporary, which constrains her forward progress.

PHYSICAL CONDITIONS: SAFETY

The physical environment is another aspect of a firm's organization and relations that influences employee mobility. Firms' public materials and management often express concern about safety policies, procedures, and training. Although this concern could be evidence of a new firm-to-worker loyalty, a more critical analysis suggests that it might pertain to liability protection. As one news article notes, "Twenty-five percent of the classes [in a new carpentry apprenticeship program in Wisconsin] focus on health and safety issues, which have become more important due to liability concerns" (Mader, 2002). Hard Working Blessed's experience, as others, reflects the more critical conclusion.

Workplace Safety: Hard Working Blessed's Family Story (Milwaukee)

After completing a manufacturing training program in Milwaukee, Steel Mill & Foundry hired thirty-eight-year-old Hard Working Blessed as a crane operator. He soon also drove a forklift truck, mixed sand, and worked as a grinder. Following the curricular advice of the union and employer partners in its workforce development network, the training program prepared Mr. Blessed mentally for the foundry work which helped him stay on the job. But even good mental preparation was eventually overwhelmed by physical aspects of the job. During his first twenty months at the firm, Hard Working Blessed suffered two herniated discs while lifting heavy metal jackets to put over metal molds, and the severe temperature changes in the foundry caused repeated bouts of flu and pneumonia. These injuries and illnesses plus a materials-connected allergic rash resulted in his being put on "light duty," which meant a demotion in job responsibility and a reduction in wages. Although he received worker's compensation, his total earnings were reduced from $600 to $400 a week. The workplace bulletin board posting at Steel Mill & Foundry underscores that such injuries are frequent:

> Suburb: Notice 3: Department First Aid Cases, Core = 22; Foundry-Indirect = 14; Office = 9.
> Milwaukee: 2 = Cumulative trauma and right wrist strain.
> Suburb: Notice 5 = Irritation OD, right groin strain, acute right shoulder strain, foreign body right eye, foreign body left eye infection. *Bulletin Board Posting at Steel Mill & Foundry*

Company personnel confirm that workplace injuries are common:

> *Interviewer* [to second shift foreman]: How often are people hurt at work?
> *Second shift foreman*: Oh, lots of accidents. And different kinds at different places. At Suburb it's eye injuries. Here in Milwaukee it's back injuries from lifting. You had that didn't you, Hard Working?
> *Mr. Blessed*: Oh, yeah. My back.
> *Interviewer* [to second shift foreman]: How often have you been injured?
> *Second shift foreman*: Mostly my eyes. I've been 5, 6 or maybe 7 times to the eye doctor for injuries.

A history of "serious" OSHA violations further confirms the firm's dangerous physical environment.

Hard Working Blessed not only endured physical hardship, but also his injuries rendered his future at Steel Mill & Foundry bleak. The second-shift foreman told us in Mr. Blessed's presence that he would be unlikely to recover his original position and wage after the demotion and wage reduction because of the firm's concern about liability:

> The company has to worry about your condition. I can't make that decision. Once you've got something they have to worry. The vice president of operations and the HR [human resource] manager will determine if you can return. I have to protect my employees and the company is liable if anything happens to you. And once you're transferred, even if you have a doctor's certificate saying that you can return, the position may be filled. *Steel Mill & Foundry, Second Shift Foreman*

Such hazardous conditions compound the lack of physical preparation given to older individuals for positions traditionally held by younger workers, or what we call the life-stage mismatch, as research field notes underscore:

> Being a grinder is exceptionally dangerous work. If you miss, the casting skids off the wheel and would cut you immediately down to the bone. When I was at the foundry, one of the workers just touched the selvage to the wheel and sparks flew. Being at work in a less-than-one-hundred-percent condition [e.g., Mr. Blessed's fatigue] is extremely hazardous. *Research Field Notes, Steel Mill & Foundry*

Mr. Blessed identified the life-stage mismatch in his own words:

> People like me who go back to work later in life—companies hire younger people at lower wages and expect them to stay in the company for a long time. Eventually they make better wages, in time for their family's needs. Me, I'm older and I'll be less long in the workforce. And my family has needs right now. *Hard Working Blessed*

A year later, staff at Hard Working Blessed's manufacturing training program reported that Steel Mill & Foundry had gone bankrupt, largely because it fared poorly in environmental studies. And although Hard Working Blessed found a new and more promising job as forklift operator in a printing company, his mobility was lateral rather than upward.

If training programs more fully assess job seekers' health and physical condition and partner with safety-focused firms, interrupted mobility such as Hard Working Blessed experiences might be avoided.

SOCIOSTRUCTURAL ENVIRONMENT: RACIAL AND ETHNIC DISCRIMINATION

The final aspect of a firm's organization and relations that influences mobility is its sociostructural environment, particularly in terms of practices of racial and ethnic discrimination (Annie E. Casey Foundation, 2001a, 2001b; Holzer, 1996; Moss & Tilly, 2001; Reskin, 2002; Wilson, 1987, 1996). Although the signal effect of the job-training programs in this research helped to bypass the discriminatory hiring practices many job seekers confront, that protection seldom extends to the workplace. Ahree Raca's story illuminates the power of a union-training program network to combat racism through the medium of an experienced mentor or case manager. The continuation of Tasha Jones's story then illustrates the racial tension that accompanies employers' need to hire from different sources during a tight labor market and focuses on antiracism strategies that her firm employs to counter such tension.

Antiracism Strategies of a Union-Training Program Partnership: Ahree Raca's Family Story (St. Louis)

Ahree Raca's experience illustrates that a union-training program partnership can protect vulnerable minority workers. After five months at Construction Co-MO, Ahree Raca, an eighteen-year-old African American father of two infants revealed that things had "always been a little rough on the job" but had gotten "real bad" lately. He said that his (white) supervisor had been "harassing" him and described how this occurred:

> He's racial, degrading to my religion (and) my family. He is hitting, punching me, throwing things at me. He said I was a mistake, my family a mistake. *Ahree Raca*

When the research team asked Ahree to clarify the events, he read the following information off his computer—a list of incidents illustrating the abuse of power that is possible under hierarchical Fordist authority relations:

- The supervisor told me that the only reason Black men are in construction is because of meeting quotas. The supervisor said this was due to the incident on the I-70 construction when Blacks blocked the highway due to no Blacks on the construction site.
- The supervisor asked me, "What do you bleed, because it can't be red." "Like I'm not a human?" I said.
- I was playing music at work when the supervisor came in and yelled," Turn off that nigger music!" The supervisor apologized later.
- The supervisor called me names, like "dummy, homie, home slice, and Muslim."
- The supervisor also said to me, "My daddy had slaves, now I have me one."
- The supervisor put his hands on me and smiled. When I asked him to stop, he said, "Get out and head for the house. Go to the union if you want."
- The supervisor kicked me in the rear. When I said, "Don't do that," he just laughed.
- The supervisor and another guy were throwing nails at me, just missing my head. They threw drywall and a knife at me (too). I know they were trying to not hit me, and they missed me (so far), but I was afraid they would (hit me) by mistake.
- Someone threw lit cigarette butts into my nail pouch and it started smoking. *Ahree Raca*

Ahree complained to his union and the union called Construction Company-MO. Ahree was told that it was possible that his supervisor would get fired. Construction Company-MO told the union that "they would take care of it."

The climate of racism and harassment had made it hard for Ahree to go work every day, but he continued to show up on time for every shift. Despite the abuse, Ahree felt a certain loyalty to his supervisor, which is perhaps why it took him so long to discuss the issue. For example, even after listing the supervisor's offenses he said, "I don't want him to get fired, he teaches me a lot. I just want him to stop."

During this period, Ahree also contacted George Wood, his mentor and case manager at the construction training program, who encouraged him to file a formal complaint with the union. Finally the "boss," the position above the accused supervisor, talked to Ahree and his supervisor together. The supervisor was not given the opportunity to deny Ahree's allegations as there was a record of previous charges against him filed by other workers. The boss reportedly told the supervisor that "times have changed" and that his behavior would not be tolerated. After this meeting, Ahree and the supervisor worked together for about a week without incident.

Ahree was then asked to help an African American supervisor finish a job. When the new supervisor asked to have Ahree transferred to him, Ahree quickly agreed. Ahree reported that the new supervisor was respectful and that the two of them got along very well. Moreover the work site with the new supervisor was close to his home, making his commute more convenient as well.

Ahree's willingness to pursue the formal challenges of grievance within the union served him well in resolving this highly problematic situation. His courage to address the issue propelled him safely back on the road of economic mobility, facilitated by the formal support of the union and the guidance and advocacy of his workforce program mentor. Without the union-training program network structure and Wood's detailed instruction about how to proceed with a grievance, Ahree might have remained mute about racism for fear of reprisal and would likely have become a retention casualty instead of an upward-moving construction worker.

Antiracism Strategies of Firm-Training Program Networks: Tasha Jones's Firm's Story (Milwaukee)

The partnership forged by Tasha Jones's training program and a suburban firm in its workforce development network lets us examine the sociostructural environment from the perspective of the firm. As we learn earlier in the chapter, Tasha Jones, a twenty-four-year-old African American woman, was an assembly operator at Manufacturing Company. Before she attended the manufacturing training program, she was a cashier at a household goods store that she described as openly racist. Notably Tasha did not feel that Manufacturing Company, a unionized facility in a Milwaukee suburb that employs about five hundred men and women, was racist. The research team talked with dozens of employees at Manufacturing Company at all levels to gather their views.

After a major industry downturn and organizational restructuring in the 1980s, Manufacturing Company's business was booming in the 1990s and early 2000s. The factory expanded, but the suburban community grew at the same time, bringing new businesses that competed for a smaller pool of local workers. Accordingly, the operations manager reported that the company needed to find a new pool of workers, noting that traditional hiring methods, such as word of mouth and using existing employees as a referral source (Granovetter, 1995) were now insufficient:

> I have been here thirty-two years. I've seen a lot of changes. We had a readily available workforce. People with skills and a work ethic. I think it was because of the kind of people around here, lots of Germans and Poles. There wasn't a lot of competition for workers. We got people in here with good wages and they told others about us so we didn't have to advertise to hire.... This is a traditional hiring network: like begets like, which often perpetuates racial discrimination, whether intended or not.
> *Operations Manager at Manufacturing Company*

The company partnered with a technical institute and Tasha's manufacturing training program as intermediaries to help them hire new, at least minimally trained workers:

> My company had to find what was out there if we were going to succeed. We found that as we were working with various agencies, educational institutions, and the

manufacturing training program, we were introduced into the state's workforce development program. This stuff all of a sudden was just snow balling and we said, "My gosh wake up, you might as well take advantage of this stuff here." All we were looking for is "How can we get a good worker?" If central city Milwaukee has got thirteen to fifteen percent unemployment why not go after them, and we learned. Like I said, I was the biggest critic. Hiring welfare people, give me a break. They all kid me a little bit of how I have been able to change my mentality on that and rightfully so, because we have been able to draw from this workforce through the training program, through working with the state, and it comes down to actually the partnering. *Operations Manager at Manufacturing Company*

In complex organizations, solution strategies often create new problems that require further strategizing. After Manufacturing Company and its inner-city partners solved the problem of finding workers, it then confronted the new problem of racial and ethnic strain among employees, as the operations manager related:

I think probably the biggest thing is to realize that there would be a culture change from white to black to Hispanic. You have to keep in mind the facility was 100 percent Caucasian. I mean it was just an environment, a culture, and now we were looking at bringing in minorities to the facilities. . . . First off, as you would expect, we don't discriminate, never have and never will discriminate with regards to race, color, I can rattle that all off for you. The most important thing is when you come from a hundred percent white to now adding a black population, obviously we had whites here that felt that we were giving them more attention than we were giving the white population. That was their first outcry, "Why are you treating them altogether different then they are?" Maybe the appearance was that way because we had customized training programs. They were getting trained, they were being trained on coming to work on time, work skills, how to fill out a time card. *Operations Manager at Manufacturing Company*

The firm's first solution to the new problem of racial and ethnic strain was to make program changes aimed at facilitating communication and trust throughout the workforce:

The employees at that time didn't realize why we were doing what we were doing, so we had total employee meetings to explain to them our need for a good strong work force. The majority of these people here in the blending of the culture think that the changes have been good, but we still have those folks out there that while I wouldn't say specifically, I wouldn't know them specifically, but I am sure there are racists out there simply by the comments I hear. I think the thing that helped us particularly was to go to the entire work force and explain to them why we were doing what we were doing. We were able to satisfy people that this wasn't a handout by the state, that if we were dealing with them a little differently than what they were exposed to, that was just a change in times. *Operations Manager at Manufacturing Company*

The next solution to the new problem of racial and ethnic strain was to establish a mentor program, which Manufacturing Company accomplished through its partnership with the network's manufacturing training program. Program staff wrote the mentor manual, trained employees together with the firm's human resource department and the union, and then provided the firm with continued oversight. As in all organizations, employees in different positions hold different opinions about how to solve entrenched workplace problems, such as racial and ethnic discrimination. These differences can either encourage or destroy mobility-enhancing antiracism strategies like a mentor program, as different employees report.

The operations manager thought the mentor program improved the workplace climate: "The feedback that we are getting is that it has been very beneficial to them. The jury is still out, but early indicators are that it is working. We have had feedback from other companies, saying, 'How can we get involved in it?'" In contrast, a company department leader reported intraorganizational challenges:

New employees. If we didn't have so many new employees, we wouldn't need a mentoring program. ... It took about a year for the union and company to put it together. There were problems between the union and company about it. [What kind of problems?] The union wanted more work time off for the mentors. We wanted mentor meetings and committee meetings [i.e., union and company] about twice a month. *Department Leader at Manufacturing Company*

A member of the Union Bargaining Committee outlined that the union's challenges with the mentor program revolved around joint "ownership" and implementation:

There really weren't any racial issues with supervisors. The Bargaining Committee talks with the supervisors. I have problems with the plant superintendent. I think we should tell people when they do a good job. You only hear when you do a bad job. We did the mentoring program and the orientation to help retain employees. We wanted incentives under absenteeism; that's a real big problem because of the new type of employee. They don't have a work ethic. These young people, all kinds, have a different work ethic. The inner core Milwaukee parents didn't work. Their kids didn't see that their parents worked. But you see changes after they're here awhile. Sometimes they don't learn fast enough or they're out of the door. The union's job is more difficult because of why they have to deal with new employees. Some whites think that blacks are treated better than whites. *Union Bargaining Committee Member at Manufacturing Company*

The management level produces yet another set of views on the efficacy of using a mentor program to solve workplace problems, as the plant superintendent reports:

Well, the training program employees are different. It takes more support to make them good workers. Preparation could include training centers where you duplicate the work site. And this generation of young people is not work oriented; this affects their work efforts. [How do the new employees get along with the older employees?] You're talking white and black? Well, for some it's hard to adjust. But it's not just white and black. There are some blacks who won't work with other blacks. One black woman wanted Spanish co-workers because she said they're hard workers just like her. I didn't expect that. We have the supervisors and management work with them on that. *Plant Superintendent at Manufacturing Company*

Line workers hold their own set of opinions about racial and ethnic discrimination, as Tasha's department supervisor reports, referring to the way the mentor program alleviated ground-level tensions:

> About two years ago there were some racial issues. Now people interact with each other. You hear comments that they didn't like someone and you could assume race. But now you can't always assume that. Communication is very important. I think that the program is a good idea because the mentor can point the person in a right direction. I think that the mentors help better communication. *Department Supervisor of Tasha Jones at Manufacturing Company*

Tasha's coworkers concurred with the department supervisor's assessment in a sentiment that we heard from many: "It is one of the best departments here. Communication is really good. We talk together. [Is there any prejudice?] No prejudice."

In sum, Tasha Jones's Manufacturing Company needed new workers. The company solved the new worker problem by partnering with a workforce development network to hire inner-city workers. The new workforce solved the staffing problem but caused the new problem of racial and ethnic strain. Solutions to the new problem—in particular, the collaborative establishment of a mentor program that potentially benefits the entire workforce—resulted in an improved workforce environment. Management and line workers agree that the company and its network partners will need to make conscious efforts to sustain these gains.

ADVANCEMENT: THE FUTURE

What are the future advancement prospects for these parents? The concluding section of the advancement story consists of two parts. First we look at employment and wage projections to 2012 by the parent's industry, occupation, and city to see if the future looks more economically robust than the present. A descriptive table for the first part of this section (Table B.3) is located in Appendix B. Table B.3 gives information about the forty-four firms, industry location and occupations that comprise the parents' initial post-training jobs and their last known jobs. Six parents remain in their initial post-training firm, and one parent was not reemployed after leaving her post-training job. Thus only one firm is listed for these parents, with the exception of Lucky Miracle, whose second full-time job, in addition to his initial full-time job, is included in Table B.3.

The second part of this section reviews the characteristics of two of the parents' firms and envisions what "firm as partner" might look like based on premises of the new mobility paradigm.

INDUSTRY, OCCUPATION, AND WAGE PROJECTIONS TO 2012

By 2012, total employment in the United States is projected to increase by 21.3 million jobs over 2002 figures (Berman, 2004). The labor force is also expected to grow, meaning that more persons will seek jobs. More than 80 percent of the jobs that will be created will require some postsecondary education, yet despite the popular description of the future labor market as the "knowledge economy," the number of positions for lower-skilled workers is expected to outpace the number of positions for highly skilled workers (Buehlmann, 2003, p. 3). Still, considering Holzer's (1996) description early in this chapter of the skills needed for low-skill jobs, many working parents across America, including quite a few here, will need help to satisfy these rudimentary cognitive and interpersonal requirements.

In the context of these national predictions and of the parents' up-and-down mobility pathways, this section raises the following questions: What might the parents' futures hold? What are the projections for jobs in the industries in which the first post-training jobs were located? Are these industries expected to grow or shrink over the next decade? If the parents remain in the initial post-training occupation, what can they expect to earn in the future? If they change firms or industries, what might they earn in the future? Overall, can they expect to be economically mobile in these occupations and industries over time?

Industry projections

Given the sustained loss of jobs in the manufacturing industry over recent decades, projections echo this pattern (Table B.3, Appendix B). Of the fifteen industries the parents work in at our last contact with them, manufacturing is the only industry expected to shrink in rates of employment between 2002 and 2012. At that, the projected annual rate of shrinkage is small at minus .1 percent. In the parents' particular manufacturing firms, growth and shrinkage are projected about equally, which underscores that firms vary *within* industries (DiPrete & Nonnemaker, 1997).

The other industry sectors that the key parents inhabit are expected to grow in employment. With the exception of Other Services and the Accommodation and Food Service industries, employment growth in service industries is projected to outpace growth in other industry sectors between 2002 and 2012 by about two to one (Berman, 2004). At the same time, when one looks at specific occupations within industries, patterns of projected growth and shrinkage in rates of employment exhibit considerable heterogeneity (Baron, 1984; Rosenbaum, 1990).

Occupation projections

Thirty-five of the forty-four occupations described in Table B.3 (Appendix B), are projected to grow in rates of employment between 2002 and 2012, and six are expected to shrink. The projection for three occupations is unknown. At the same time, the employment growth projected for particular occupations reflects a broad spectrum of potential employment. The jobs the parents initially hold after training reflect growth occupations for the most part. At a median annual rate of growth of 20.3 percent, these occupations are growing at a rate that is over five times greater than the shrinkage rate of the few occupations that are shrinking (3.6 percent). In some cases parents leave their initial post-training job in shrinking firms or shrinking occupations for similar or related jobs in more hearty firms in the same industry. In fact, the jobs the parents hold at our last contact, what we call their last known job, *all* reflect growing occupations. None move into jobs in which rates of employment are decreasing. Thus even when an initial position or firm falls on hard times, the parents are able to locate new jobs and firms with growth potential, even if their wage or wage adequacy does not reflect this (see Tables B.2 and B.3 in Appendix B).

Wage projections and mobility direction

If parents stay or had stayed in their initial post-training job, what would their hourly wages be in 2003 compared to their city's average wage for that occupation? What are or would wages be in their last known job? Although we are limited to wage projection data for 2003, even 2003 projections yield suggestions for future outcomes as the wage pathways of the parents in this study begin as early as 1998. For those parents without known 2003 wages, we use Osterman's (1999) formula of a 2 percent annual increase to calculate potential 2003 wage figures. In some cases these calculations may be underestimates, as the jobs could yield more than a 2 percent increase.

Comparing the parents' first- and last-known jobs (Table B.3, Appendix B), parents are more likely to experience downward than upward wage mobility, regardless of whether they remain in their initial firm or change firms. Wage mobility is or is projected to be downward in two-thirds of the jobs (twenty-nine, or 66 percent), upward in about one-quarter (twelve, or 27 percent), equivalent in two jobs, and one is unknown. Put another way, the wages of three out of five parents (61 percent) did or would have fallen an average of $2.79 per hour below the average hourly wage for their occupation in their particular city. Wages for two out of five parents (39 percent), however, did or would have exceeded the average hourly wage for that occupation in their city by $2.92 per hour.

Although the 2001 recession and its extended aftermath likely influence the predominance of downward over upward wage mobility, it is striking that wage projections move in the opposite direction of industry and occupational projections. As we discuss earlier, the employment rate in almost all the parents' industries and occupations is projected to increase annually, yet wages in these same occupations have or are projected to increase for only two in five parents. This means that although many jobs are projected to be plentiful over the next decade for low earners like these parents, not all will offer wages in the near future that will forward economic mobility.

Looking further out, given that two in five parents experience increased economic security after several years in the labor market, even if they are not fully or consistently able to support their families, might more reach greater financial security if firms become real partners in this effort?

SUMMARY AND CONCLUSIONS: TOWARD "FIRM AS PARTNER"

Nearly a century ago Weber (1922/1978, p. 200) held that "forms of establishment and of the firm must be 'invented' like technical products." Granovetter (2002, p. 54) posits a related viewpoint today: "Fundamental concepts like solidarity, power, norms, and identity cannot be understood except in relational terms; their very definition relies on social relationships, and they are produced in social networks." Similarly, in the study of firms and economic mobility in this chapter we avoid a sole focus on the activity of persons in favor of examining the relational and structural intersections among the working parents, their firms and their families. Policy and other social institutions are influential as well. We argue that economic mobility takes place at the nexus of these dynamic, contextual, and relational intersections.

The parents in this book begin strong upward movement through work, consistent with old paradigm myths. Through initiative they access workforce training programs that get them in the door of good jobs. For most, hard work pays off initially as their wages exceed those they had been able to earn before training. Many receive regular wage increases, either in the same or in a subsequent firm, and inch toward family-sustaining incomes. But history and the present collide to slow or reverse upward movement for many of the workers and their families. Wage levels in firms are too low to meet their needs; subsidies and work supports do not adequately boost wages to sufficiency; national and local economies fall into recession; and modes of organization and social relations in yesterday's firms intersect with the backgrounds, competencies, and decision processes of today's parents to constrain economic mobility.

As we conclude in Chapter 3, "place" matters in the details but not to the overarching realities of low-wage jobs in the parents' cities, industries, and firms. In most jobs across the five cities, wages are not set high enough for the needs of older workers with families; hierarchical or peer authority relations are untrustworthy; loyalty to firm is not reciprocated; employer-provided benefits are unaffordable or nonexistent; workplace policies do not accommodate children's developmental needs or the demands that other social institutions make on parents; and economic recession results in precipitous layoff, termination, and lower wages and amenities in subsequent jobs. Firm rhetoric and management assertion to the contrary, the parents in this book experience many of the seventy-four firms in which they work as contingent, untrustworthy, and unilateral: in short, as "fair-weather friends," "disengaged families," or "roommates." Although some firms incorporate practices designed to increase loyalty and trust, in only two cases—Ayesha Muhammad's primarily, and Sam Gates's secondarily—are these practices sufficient to approximate "firm as partner." What makes Ayesha's firm, Financial Services Company—FSC, and Sam's firm, Technology Management Company Electronics Division—TMC, stand out?

WAGE STRUCTURE

The wage structure makes Ayesha's and Sam's firms the exceptions. At his initial post-training job in 1999, Sam's wage was well below 200 percent FPL and 100 percent SSS, but after layoff and landing a new job at TMC, by mid-2003 Sam's wage income exceeds both adequacy metrics: 241 percent FPL and 110 percent SSS. Although challenges to his earning power remain, as his earlier story reveals, TMC offers "good"—even what some might call "decent"—wages (Lafer, 2002), which puts Sam and his family on a steady mobility path. Ayesha's firm also offers good wages, although her family needs are so great that her annual income still leaves her family of six below sufficiency. Still, over two years at FSC Ayesha's wages increased 26 percent to a respectable $13.25 per hour. If Ayesha can remain on the firm's well-supported upgrade track, she anticipates earning upwards of $45,000 per year. This would put her family at almost 200 percent FPL. Even now, her hourly wage would put her at 100 percent of the Self-Sufficiency Standard *if* the household contained a similar wage-earning partner.

Similarly important, although arguably only in the context of decent wages, Ayesha's and Sam's firms offer comprehensive nonwage benefits and richly structured routes to advancement—characteristics that the training programs and their workforce development networks identify as essential to good jobs. In addition, both firms are local divisions of larger corporations that offer "new," employee-as-customer practices that explicitly aim at *household and profit*, as the new mobility calls for. Such practices help to offset the problems of the life-stage mismatch for older, familied workers like Ayesha and Sam, as we describe briefly in the following cameos of the two firms.

Financial services company (FSC)

After considerable divestment and restructuring in the 1990s, Financial Services Company pared down its workforce and designed its organizational relations to satisfy both market and employee customer. To begin with, FSC instituted a voluntary mentor program, whereby the mentor is matched with the employee as a "career guide"—a role that Cappelli (1999) and Osterman and colleagues (2001) suggest is generally missing in the current labor market—to help craft the employee's career plans and skill upgrade opportunities, in and outside the firm. Importantly these mentor meetings take place *on company time*, helping Ayesha toward her goal to be certified as an underwriter, which will entail both underwriting and case management. Heralded publicly for the quality of the work environment for minorities and women, FSC offers tangible benefits to children, such as movie passes and "take your children to work" days. And as noted in Ayesha's temp-to-perm story earlier in the chapter, FSC is the only firm of the seventy-four in this research with an official flextime policy, which facilitates the ability of working parents like Ayesha to attend to their children's school, medical, and court needs. Toward advancement, FSC offers a menu of "lunch and learn" sessions, activity committees, and skill classes *on company time*—extending the career guidance role of not only the mentor but also the company as a whole. Moreover, employees are not just perfunctorily offered these classes. Management strongly encourages them to attend forty hours of classes per year on such topics as computer skills, customer service skills, and email—all potentially transferable as well as firm serving skills. In short, Financial Services Company has found a way to combine household and profit in its organizational structure and relations.

Technology management company—electronics division (TMC)

Technology Management Company is less family focused than Financial Services Company, but similarly dedicated to both production and its workforce. In response to global pressures in the 1990s, TMC instituted production practices based on the Japanese *kaizen* philosophy described in Sam Gates's story earlier in the chapter, that one of his coworkers calls "a business enterprise revolution."

Although TMC is essentially Fordist in its careful supervision of repetitive tasks, it also recognizes that autonomy and reasonable expectations increase a worker's ownership and pride in his or her work. As Sam's supervisor, the facilities manager at TMC reports, "We expect every operator here to build quality in what they do and inspect the work they do." The firm is also explicitly team oriented, as Sam's supervisor articulates:

> When Sam first came over from TMC-Cable Division we sat down and talked about what he did over there, and talked about what I was looking for here. The first thing out of Sam's mouth was, "Whatever you want me to do, I'll do it." You would think that any supervisor would love to hear that. Since then, though, Sam and I have an understanding. It's whatever "we" want to do that Sam will do. *Sam Gates's Supervisor at Technology Management Company—Electronics Division*

In subtle ways the company is wise about workers' needs. Operators and assemblers switch positions every couple of hours to prevent monotony and the mistakes that may accompany it, a practice that also fosters considerable, albeit informal training across competencies. And although a vestige of Taylorist efficiency guides both operation and assembly procedures, because just-in-time production is dependent on rapid completion of individual tasks, ergonomics guides the procedures both preventively and in response to identified needs. In relation to upgrading skills and encouraging education, TMC seems unconcerned about poaching or costly turnover of trained workers. Both informal and formal skill enhancement take place on site at TMC via a GED attainment program and an employee cadre of state-accredited apprenticeship trainers that provide on-the-job skill training and partner with an off-site community college for courses that the firm pays for in advance. The TMC promotion process—which a TMC assembler describes as "[supervisors, managers] keep bugging one of us"—is less formal than FSC's system of mentors, Web listings, official applications, and meetings, but effective nonetheless.

Consideration of the worker in the context of the whole family, rather than as an atomistic individual, in setting workplace regulations and procedures is less evident at TMC than it is at FSC, despite TMC's predominantly female (85 percent female; 15 percent male) and largely Hispanic and African American workforce. The senior apprentice trainer discusses the requirements for completing an apprenticeship in old paradigm terms: "If you were young enough or didn't have kids yet, you could probably swing it. It's a huge commitment." At the same time, the trainer's star apprentice is Sam—a 40-year-old noncustodial father of three whose family responsibilities conflict with the time demands of the apprenticeship.

The firm's somewhat excessive attention to attendance "presenteeism" and punctuality "on-timeism" potentially perpetuates Fordist and Taylorist impersonality. However, in a different way TMC is as concerned with the worker's voice as FSC is. Sam's company has instituted a formal program for workers and management to air problems, concerns, suggestions, and recommendations through both written and group discussion. These CVR meetings (no-one we encountered at the firm knows what "CVR" stands for) are led by firm management or the company president, and serve not only to give workers a voice in organizational procedures, but also, as Sam notes, "to build trust . . . it really is a 'we' thing." Finally, TMC pays its contingent workers, who may be welfare leavers, persons without a high school diploma, or individuals laid off from other firms, higher wages than the usual temp agency wage, explicitly to reduce disparity between the temporary and permanent workforce: in Sam's supervisor's words, "to level the playing field between them and a TMC employee." In addition, the company shows concern about its employees, and indirectly their families, through the policy of "performance payout," which is a quarterly check to employees across the board based on the firm's performance in production quality, daily planning, and worksite cleanliness—another example of attention to household and profit. In effect, the company tends carefully to reciprocity.

In conclusion, keeping Ayesha Muhammad's and Sam Gates's companies and workforce development networks in mind, we posit characteristics of firm organization and relations that are consistent with a new view of economic mobility. "Firm as partner" might include a family-supporting wage structure across the company; profit-sharing; affordable benefits; administrative advisory boards comprised of equal representation from management, workers, community partners and the public, with equal power; structured communication between management and workers; clear internal ladders with opportunity to upgrade skills on company time; and a family- and community-building orientation. A partner firm would no longer view or conduct itself as an autonomous institution but would articulate its organizational relations, policies and practices with those of related social institutions—an intersection that the next chapter shows is essential for family economic mobility. Finally, the firm as partner would seek consent over coercion, recognizing that institutions are constituted by workers who are persons (Burawoy, 2003), although we would also say they are families. What it would take from the government, the corporate community, and the public to maintain and foster more firms like Ayesha's and Sam's is a topic for the final chapter.

7   Children's Schools, Parents' Work and Policy

Alignment and Misalignment

> Education is so important and I will tell that to my children until I can't breathe anymore.—*Elizabeth Seabrook, New Orleans*

> [The teacher said,] "I need to see you before Friday." Now this is like on a Wednesday, and they call me and tell me, "Oh, I need to see you before Friday." You know, leave a message on my machine. So I will call them back and I'll get the person: "As you well know, I work. Just like you. I cannot just up and come into your office or into the school the next day or the day after. I have to give my supervisor ample time so she can find somebody to replace me, just like you would have to give your boss ample time."—*Ayesha Muhammad, Philadelphia*

DECADES OF RESEARCH have addressed the vertical and longitudinal intersections between school and home and between school and children's futures (Patchen, 2004). However, few scholars have looked at the horizontal and simultaneous intersections among children's schools, families, parents' work, and policy. Findings from this multiyear, multisite ethnography illustrate *that* and *how* these institutions are aligned or misaligned in relation to family economic mobility. In brief, children's "work" at school influences parents' work, home life, and ultimately the family's ability to move forward economically through employment. Reciprocally, parents' work influences family life and children's school success. School and public policies are continuous but little-acknowledged players in these intersections, and as the family stories illustrate in the following sections, frequently do not work in harmony. School policies are often not aligned with the policies of low-income parents' employers, and firms' policies are not always designed to provide low-income workers with the means to be actively involved in their child's school. Public policies are often misaligned with both schools and firms.

Examination of the intersections among children's schools, parents' work, family, and policy shows that reciprocity is lacking among these institutions. Interinstitutional trust relations are either absent or extinguished. In a downward spiral then, children's school behavior and performance worsen, parents are drawn in more frequently and more frantically, workplace mobility is thwarted, and families experience reduced economic security. In response, school policies and teacher practices tend to address the proximal or more immediate targets of child and family rather than the distal, or distant and thus harder to influence, target of parents' work environments.

The educational equivalents of the mobility myths in Chapter 2, such as "hard work is all it takes to succeed" and "pull yourself up by the bootstraps," are reflected daily in the assumptions made by teachers and administrators in inner-city schools that show little understanding of the rigors families face in the low-wage work world. Claims that "parents don't care about their kids' education" and "there isn't any discipline in the home" are leveled regularly, and thus become embedded in school policies and practices that are misaligned with parents' efforts to keep their families financially afloat. Simply put, home, school, work, and policy are viewed and treated as separate spheres (Gartrell, 1991).

The experiences and views of parents, children, teachers, school administrators, and field researchers, elicited from over 120 days spent in the children's eighteen preschools, twenty-two elementary schools, sixteen middle schools, and thirteen high schools, illustrate how the focus on proximal versus distal targets perpetuates unequal opportunity for the "next generation" of American workers—the children—and constrains family economic mobility at the same time.

In the first section of this chapter, parents' normative hopes and dreams for their children's education and their actions toward this mobility goal show that institutions and the populace alike are solidly lodged in the old paradigm myths of meritocracy, opportunity, and individual achievement, evidence at times to the contrary. The next sections of the chapter offer evidence for the need to move toward a new, intersectional view of economic mobility. These sections describe the multi-institutional intersections that horizontally and simultaneously influence intra- and intergenerational mobility, showing how children's schools, family well-being, and parents' work and policy are inextricably intertwined, for and against the economic mobility of low-income families.

PARENTS' VIEWS ABOUT EDUCATION

PARENTS' HOPES AND DREAMS FOR THEIR CHILDREN'S EDUCATION

No matter the age of their child, the parents here view their children's education as the first—if not primary—step to avoiding the life challenges they have experienced. Yet parents' views about education are often shaped by their own early schooling. Like many parents, thirty-seven-year-old Elizabeth Seabrook laments the poor quality of the education she received. Recognizing that her New Orleans public school background started her out "way behind," Elizabeth fiercely seeks better schools for her children: in her words, "Education is so important and I will tell that to my children until I can't breathe anymore." Philadelphia parent Ayesha Muhammad sums up her feelings and fears with the hope that her children "would not get to my age and still be struggling."

Sensing their own limitations and mindful of the effects of a poor education, some parents take a hard-line approach. Lynn Walker tells her children to buckle down and consider her struggles without a college degree. Laid off and homeless, Lynn moved her family to a smaller city two hours from St. Louis where she finally found what she considered a good school for her 13-year-old son Waldo Aloysious. As she tells him, "If you can't get an education here, you can't get an education anywhere. These teachers are willing to work with you; they are willing to help you. You have to be ready and willing to work with them." Aware of the consequences of having dropped out of high school in eleventh grade to care for four brothers and five orphaned cousins that her mother raised alone while working full time, Lynn said, "I'm here to help, but there is only so much I can teach you because I don't have a degree."

Such hopes and dreams suggest that these low-income parents hold normative values about education, as earlier research also finds (Farber & Iversen, 1996, 1998). Although the parents here may be positively biased toward schooling, given their willingness to enroll in a workforce development training program, they are demographically and experientially similar to other low-income research cohorts (Chapter 3). In contrast, scholars such as Murray (1984) suggest that low-income parents do not hold normative values about education. Similarly, through concepts such as "shadow values" and "value stretch," Liebow (1967) and Rodman (1971) suggest that low-income parents develop alternative values about schooling to adapt to their circumstances. These contrasting positions are not substantiated by the avowals and actions of the parents here, yet popular acceptance of "no values" or "different values" perspectives is evident in many aspects of public and school cultures, policies, and practices.

In contrast to value approaches, other scholars identify structural misalignment between families' educational goals for their children and the opportunity structure in impoverished urban communities. Although Lareau (2003) seems to find otherwise, the low-income parents here try to provide enrichment for their children at home, often limiting TV watching and buying "educational" toys and materials at discount. Despite these efforts, the families lag behind the computer and Internet explosion of the late 1990s. They cannot depend on their children's schools to provide adequate computer and Internet access either.

For example, in comparison to suburban and wealthier school districts with richly wired classrooms, most Philadelphia classrooms are limited to one computer for every thirty-three children (Reform Journal, 2003). To the extent that computers and other educational resources in the home are associated with higher test scores and academic achievement (Patchen, 2004; Wilhelm, Carmen, & Reynolds, 2002), the children here fall cumulatively further behind their more economically advantaged peers every year via limited opportunity to bring these forms of cultural capital to their subsequent education (Becker, 2002; Bourdieu, 2001).

PARENTS' ACTIONS TOWARD THEIR CHILDREN'S EDUCATION

As context for this discussion of how parents act on their hopes, dreams, and structural obstacles to forward their children's education, we first describe the children's grade status in four groups: Preschool, K–5, 6–8, and 9–12 (Table 7.1). Some children are represented in more than one group as we follow them through grade transitions. Over the research period, five children experience suspensions

TABLE 7.1. Children's Educational Status: 2000 to Mid-2003

Grade	Number (%) of children enrolled over the period
Preschool (center based or school based)	13 (41%)
Elementary K–5	21 (32%)
Middle 6–8	15 (23%)
High school 9–12	12 (18%)
College	1 (2%)
High school dropout	1 (2%)

from school, two are retained in grade, and three more are threatened with retention. One youth moves on to a four-year college program and one drops out of school in eleventh grade as a result of family disruption. Their stories are included among those interwoven in the balance of this chapter. Across the grades, parents regularly attend teacher-parent conferences and take pains to oversee their children's academic performance, praising them when they do well or encouraging (or punishing) them to do better.

PRESCHOOL: TRYING TO GIVE CHILDREN A GOOD START FOR FUTURE SCHOOLING

In recent decades policy and public emphasis is increasingly placed on a "head start" or "early start" for later school achievement, particularly for families with limited financial, social, and cultural capital. Thirteen children participate in eighteen preschool programs at one time or another over the research period. Parents universally voice the desire for quality developmental environments for their children as they near school age, understanding from media reports of academic research (Duncan et al., 1998; Rouse, Brooks-Gunn, & McLanahan, 2005) or simply presuming that early learning is important for children's later academic achievement, as the scenarios in the following sections illustrate. By the time they reach age three, two out of five children attend either a center- or school-based preschool program. To accomplish this, however, parents spend precious hours, lose wages, and risk unemployment to patch together such programs, in effect jeopardizing intragenerational economic mobility for the perceived promise of intergenerational mobility.

The families' preschool arrangements are stable for the most part, but perpetually subject to the ever-depleting stock of subsidies for which family members are eligible, as Loretta Lopez's experience illustrates. When Loretta's daughter Placeta was almost four, Loretta enrolled her in the preschool that her son attended years earlier because she liked its warm yet stimulating environment:

> Placeta is learning a lot there. She's sounding out letters, she's learning to color within the lines instead of all over the place like she used to. I've noticed a lot of things that Placeta has learned since she began school. *Loretta Lopez, St. Louis*

However, Placeta's progress was thwarted by the confluence of child care, welfare, and training program regulations. Loretta's job history was one of short-term, mostly temp agency assignments that she sought a customer service training program to rectify. At the same time she needed to earn income to support her family. Her biggest challenge was negotiating a balance between the work expectations of the welfare system and the attendance requirements of her new training program. She explained the tension between these worlds, and its likely byproduct for her daughter's preschool education, through her report of an incident with her welfare caseworker:

> [My caseworker was] talking about closing my childcare because she said I wasn't doing any work activities. Well, I explained to her that "I'm going to a customer service program from nine to two, but I work from one to five." She's like, "How

was you working and you being at [training?]" And I'm like, "Well, the organization honors the fact that I have a job, and if there's not a lot for me to do they'll let me go so that I can go to my job." [Caseworker:] "Well I don't believe that. I'm cutting your day care off. I don't care." *CLICK!* Oh … my daycare, that means Placeta's going to be out of school … So I went up there [to see her training program case manager] and I was like, "Could you please type me up some [papers]. I need verification of being in this organization because my caseworker is going to close my case." *Loretta Lopez, St. Louis*

Despite the intervention of training program staff, Loretta's child-care subsidy was terminated as was her daughter's learning start. Loretta eventually enrolled Placeta in a free Head Start program of undetermined quality in her neighborhood. Although Loretta's main criterion was that it "be free," she also said, "I want it to be curriculum based, or learning through play is good. I want her to be in a learning environment."

Many parents aggressively seek information about early learning resources for their preschool child. St. Louis mother Shanquitta Tucker researches magnet schools to get her three-year-old daughter Kenyetta into a more intensive learning environment. As Shanquitta puts it, "She's three now and she needs more school, so I want a magnet school because they have preschool."

Similarly, New Orleans mother Elizabeth Seabrook frets over her children's educational future. She calls her daughter's first preschool facility "just a babysitting service," noting that she went to the facility in the middle of the day to find the kids watching TV and, "I got the feeling that they do this a lot." Observations confirm Elizabeth's conclusion; children look bored and disengaged. For example, when told to color the toes of a lion and a child reached imaginatively for a red crayon, the teacher exclaimed, "Not red; he ain't got no red toes." After days of searching, Elizabeth located an affordable preschool for three-and-a-half-year-old Abigail that offers enriching resources such as a backyard garden, a science center, a math center, a reading center, an art center, and lessons in Spanish as well as in English. Elizabeth's choice to move her daughter is fortuitous, as the child's new teacher noted that Abigail is already behind others in the class. Elizabeth speaks about the new preschool with relief:

Learning Center is a good school. Abigail now knows all her colors; she never knew that at the other school because that was more like a babysitting service. But she knows all her colors, her alphabet, and she's starting to recognize letters, like the letter *s* that she will say *s* for you know, and *d*, duck, duck, duck. I am very impressed because she never did that at the other program. *Elizabeth Seabrook, Mother of Three-and-a-Half-Year-Old Abigail, New Orleans*

Elizabeth's efforts are rewarded. Having had surgery as an infant to correct a birth defect that limited tongue movement, Abigail's speech was not well developed. After eight months at the Learning Center, Elizabeth rejoices that "Abigail is conversing, understanding words, and putting them together in sentences." Abigail's teacher reported that Abigail had caught up academically and was ready to enter the pre-K class for four-year-olds with her peers the next fall.

ELEMENTARY SCHOOL: TRYING TO GIVE CHILDREN A SUSTAINABLE ACADEMIC BACKGROUND

Parents of the twenty-one children enrolled in twenty-two elementary schools over the research period hold firmly to the old mobility belief that their children can surmount school problems and get an education that will forward their futures, even though cumulative experience with educational institutions weakens their conviction in some cases.

Tom Russell, a fourth-grade Seattle student attended three different schools over a three and a half year period. Multiple visits to these schools reveal vast differences. The first school tends well to his personal and artistic needs but is not rigorous academically. The second school's classes are large, chaotic, and impersonal. Tom was frequently chastised for misbehaving, but his antics are mild compared to many others in his class of thirty. In the second school only 5.9 percent of the students passed state standards in math, 17.2 percent passed in reading, and 22 percent passed in writing (Seattle Public Schools, 2001). In this context, Tom's grades follow suit and plummet. Alarmed over her son's performance, his mother Teresa researches alternative schools and eventually moves Tom to a nearby private school. The private K–8 school immediately assesses Tom to be two years behind in reading. He is placed in a Title I reading class with elementary students and is simultaneously enrolled in middle school classes, a customized learning approach that was not available in his previous public school. Now enrolled in a class of seventeen, Tom can no longer get by on his natural charm or artistic skills or be bypassed because his teacher focuses more on managing than teaching. By the end of our contact with the family, Tom's academic skills, though still shaky, are slowly starting to improve.

Some elementary school parents feel isolated from their child's school. Aida Gomez, parent of eight-year-old Juan complains that the teacher "never sends home spelling tests" and that any knowledge of Juan's performance comes solely from a parent-teacher meeting about his report card. Over the year, Juan's behavior and academic performance become a growing concern. His teacher informed Aida that Juan had become "a behavior problem." Juan also copes with a weight problem, exacerbated by inactivity after school. Because school-based or after-school educational and activity programs are lacking, Aida tries to help Juan at home after exhausting days at work:

> I try to help him. I sat down with him, but the thing is he was getting me frustrated. I'm a busy person, you know, during the day. It is not like I am sitting at home doing nothing and I have all the patience in the world. At the end of the day when I pick him up and bring him [home], he would sit there and look somewhere else. I am like "I am telling you to read this word." *Aida Gomez, Philadelphia*

Aida feels she has no place to turn to get Juan the help he needs. Her parents, who provide his after-school care, do not speak English. The school's solution of retaining Juan in second grade renders his academic future precarious.

Other parents feel that the school does not recognize their interest in their children's education. Shalon Stewart attended first grade in a Philadelphia school where her science teacher said, "Parents don't seem to see school as necessary. The children so often don't do their homework." She lodged her conclusion in a global view of life in impoverished communities: "The neighborhood is rough and parents don't seem to care." The experiences of Shalon and the actions of her mother Micarla challenge this perception.

A first-grader who has read over three hundred books, Shalon is an honor-roll student performing at least one grade level and likely two above her current grade—a significant achievement given that she attends one of Philadelphia's "failing" schools. No steps, however, were taken to have Shalon tested for the gifted program even though her primary teacher said, "Shalon knows everything that I am teaching, and this is a difficult class." We asked her, since Shalon seemed to know everything that she is teaching, would she have her tested for the gifted program? The teacher responded that she could not decide whether Shalon should be tested, because although she reads at second grade level, she might be at the border of meeting the standard of the gifted child. When asked whether there would be harmful consequences if Shalon were to be tested for the gifted class and not pass the test, the teacher replied, "No, but I didn't request it." Because of the teacher's inaction the earliest that Shalon could be tested would be halfway through second grade, almost a year later. Over the course of the year Shalon became increasingly distracted and began to be labeled a "behavior problem."

In response, Micarla researched other public and private schools for Shalon. Despite having a well-paying manufacturing job, Micarla cannot afford private school tuition, and without documentation of her daughter's gifted status, scholarship funding is out of reach. After months of searching Micarla enrolled Shalon in a neighborhood "academic plus" school for the following school year. That school too, however, failed to arrange gifted testing for Shalon, despite her continued high performance. After Micarla was laid off, her hopes and actions toward improving Shalon's school environment are further constrained.

MIDDLE SCHOOL AND HIGH SCHOOL: TRYING TO PREPARE CHILDREN FOR FURTHER EDUCATION AND WORK

The parents of fifteen children in sixteen middle schools and twelve youth in thirteen high schools over the period also draw clear connections between their children's education and their futures. Wendy Delvalle, Philadelphia mother of fourteen-year-old Edwin, emphasizes the importance of human capital for future attainment, as we hear increasingly from parents of middle- and high-school-age children:

> I want him to have the best of everything. You love your children and you want them to have the best. I want him to get a good education; I want him to be able to go to college. I try to stress that a lot with him, because without an education it is hard to get a job. You are going to struggle; if you want to get a good job you have to work for it. You have to go to college and set your goals as of now, knowing what you want to do with your life. It is very important for you to get good grades so that you can work toward these goals and accomplish them. *Wendy Delvalle, Mother of Fourteen-Year-Old Edwin, Philadelphia*

At the same time, structural impediments to the children's human capital development are identified. Teachers at Tank Blessed's Milwaukee high school perceive that having insufficient equipment is a result of funding inadequacies that hurt the student:

> The problem is that there are so few books, and when they are taken home they don't come back. That's why books can't be taken home. *High School Teacher of Tank Blessed, Milwaukee*

Another teacher's ideas about what schools and families need to provide for student success are reminiscent of the benefits that are possible in well-developed workforce development networks (Chapter 5):

> I think that five outside entities could help. If we had a nurse, a clinic, a child-care center in school, if the parents had more money, and more time. *Another High School Teacher of Tank Blessed, Milwaukee*

Several parents identify and negotiate their youths' enrollment in magnet or higher performing high schools in neighborhoods far from their own in hopes that these schools will improve their children's life chances. For example, Tisha Shanks locates a Milwaukee public school for her son Juan that received accolades in a *Newsweek* article that ranks the top U.S. high schools. Juan's acceptance to a first-rate university for fall 2003 confirms the wisdom of Tisha's efforts.

Rounding out the children's educational status (Table 7.1), Tisha's elder daughter entered a four-year college in fall 2002, and Hard Working Blessed's son Tank dropped out of eleventh grade during a period of family turmoil. He had not reenrolled at the time of our final contact.

More commonly, when parents lose time at work and jeopardize their economic mobility to try to counter school-engendered limitations to their children's future mobility, they are forced to temper their dreams. In the midst of a difficult search for housing and decent schooling for her children, Philadelphia parent Micarla Stewart blends her hopes with her reality: "If I don't move to a nice apartment and find a nice school for the kids it doesn't mean their life is over or my life is over. They are going to get their education regardless of what school they go to, but I would like them to get a better school than what they get now." School performance data cast doubt on Micarla's conclusion.

SCHOOL PERFORMANCE

In contrast to the parents' old paradigm beliefs that their children's "initiative and hard work will pay off" in mobility-enhancing human capital attainment, school performance data paint a discouraging picture of the level of attainment that is generally possible. All five districts struggle to maintain their foothold, a daunting challenge given the quickly evolving landscape of educational reform that is exacerbated by the No Child Left Behind legislation's emphasis on testing, student, and teacher performance. Most of the children across the five states attend schools that are among 8,652 schools out of some 91,000 nationally that are designated as "failing for two years" in 2001 (National Center for Fair & Open Testing, 2002). As the children progress through the grades, most of their schools sequentially perform

TABLE 7.2. Reading Proficiency Scores: National Compared to State Tests

Fourth-Grade Reading Test: (Percent scoring at or above proficiency	Louisiana[b]	Missouri[c]	Pennsylvania[d]	Washington[e]	Wisconsin[f]
NAEP[a]	20	34	33	33	33
State test	61	34	58	67	82

Note: Author generated table from the following data sources:

[a]*Source:* National Center for Education Statistics: Information on Public Schools and School Districts in the United States. Retrieved December 22, 2004, from www.nces.ed.gov/ccd

[b]*Source:* Louisiana Department of Education. Retrieved January 3, 2005, from www.doe.state.la.us/lde/pair/1989.asp and www.doe.state.la.us/lde/ssa/773.html

[c]*Source:* Missouri Department of Elementary and Secondary Education. Retrieved January 3, 2005, from http://dese.mo.gov/schooldata/ftpdata.html and http://dese.mo.gov/divimprove/assess/stateresults/html

[d]*Source:* Pennsylvania Department of Education. Retrieved January 3, 2005, from www.pde.state.pa.us/a_and_t/cwp/view.asp?A=3&Q=83730 and www.pde.state.pa.us/a_and_t/cwp/view.asp?A=3&Q=103869

[e]*Source*: Washington State Office of the Superintendent of Public Instruction. Retrieved November 10, 2004, from http://reportcard.ospi.k12.wa.us/DataDownload.aspx and http://reportcard.ospi.k12.wa.us/Reports/WASLTrend.aspx?&schoolId=1&reportLevel=State

[f]*Source:* Wisconsin Department of Public Instruction. Retrieved January 3, 2005, from www.dpi.state.wi.us/oea/kcrawdat.html

worse than others in their state or local district[1] (analysis not shown). Moreover, the validity of state-level performance data may be questionable, as state-designed tests tend to produce higher performance results than nationally administered tests. In one comparison (Table 7.2), the percentage of fourth-graders scoring at or above proficiency in reading on the National Assessment of Educational Progress exam (NAEP) is much lower, other than in Missouri, than the percentage scoring at or above proficiency in reading on state tests (EdWeek, 2005).

Performance measures and the parents' and children's experiences with school suggest that all are influenced by the ways in which families and school systems intersect. The family stories in the next section provide an extended view of how additional actors in this landscape of families and schools are aligned or misaligned, affecting both inter- and intragenerational mobility. We first look at children's schools, families, and parents' firms. We then look at children's schools, families, and state and school policies.

CHILDREN'S SCHOOLS, FAMILIES, AND PARENTS' FIRMS: ALIGNMENT AND MISALIGNMENT

Children's Schools, Families, and Parents' Firms—Partially Aligned:
Ayesha Muhammad's Family Story (Philadelphia)

Ayesha Muhammad is a forty-year-old mother of six and grandmother of two. She is a high school graduate who got married, bore three children, and divorced after her husband became physically abusive. She later bore two more children, male twins, with a partner from whom she separated when he became unfaithful. In the early 1990s Ayesha earned certificates in phlebotomy technology and

Certified Nursing Assistance (CNA) and worked full time as a CNA until a workplace injury in 1999 threatened paralysis if she continued in that field. She took a year to recuperate and craft a new career direction, supporting her family with income from Unemployment Insurance and TANF assistance. When she regained her health, she sought office skills training at a four-week welfare-to-work program that was part of a local workforce development network. Although the program was "rapid attachment," its network included an established temporary employment agency through which Ayesha obtained a position at Financial Services Company (see also Chapter 6). After three months she was offered a permanent position there as an assistant associate in bill distribution at $10.50 per hour with full benefits.

Ayesha Muhammad's block was a one-way street of mostly lived-in houses with boarded-up buildings and vacant lots on the corners where "shooting" was a problem. She and her children were subject not only to unsafe neighborhood conditions but also to unsafe school environments. The incident mentioned in Chapter 4 where a classmate put a gun to ten-year-old Tom's head was not the only violent incident at the twins' elementary school. The children witnessed a child who came to school with a screwdriver and tried to stab his friends, as well as a fight outside the school that brought two police cars to avert future crises. Two years later, in spite of a new discipline code of "zero tolerance" for violence, two elementary school students were found with loaded guns inside Philadelphia public schools (Snyder, 2003).

In these challenging neighborhood and school environments, Ayesha's children struggled to have their educational needs met. Tom and Don were fraternal twins and in the fourth grade. Born prematurely at seven months, the twins spent several weeks in the intensive care unit. Don weighed considerably less than Tom and doctors were concerned "he would not make it." Although Don survived birth, as well as later hospitalization for an elevated lead level from exposure to lead-based paint, he experienced developmental delays. In December 2001, the aforementioned incidents of violence that were not adequately addressed prompted Ayesha to move the twins to another school.

Ayesha eventually settled on an elementary school within walking distance of her home where the twins had attended kindergarten. She had long tried to secure special education services for Don who had been diagnosed with Attention Deficit Hyperactivity Disorder (ADHD) and a learning disability that qualified him for such services. Ayesha also sought medical treatment for Don's ADHD with similarly little success. Absent professional support, Ayesha taught him how to avoid conflicts with other children that might bring him or others harm. She also tried to help him with reading and with "putting words together," something she admitted was difficult because of her own struggle to put words together. She took a day off work to facilitate the exchange of paperwork that would make her sons' school transfer possible, and delivered results of tests done to determine the extent of Don's learning disability into the hands of the new school's principal. These papers never reached the teacher or guidance counselor responsible for the development of Don's educational plan. For the rest of the year his education was guided by an outdated assessment.

At the new school, Don spent his school day divided between regular and special education. The teacher concluded that Don needed full-time special education classes or resources in his regular education classroom that did not exist in the underfinanced elementary school. The special education teacher expressed concern to the research team that Don was mentally delayed and that his problems were not the result of a learning disability like dyslexia, but of low IQ. When we asked if she had spoken about this with Don's mother, the teacher said she had been in touch with Ayesha, although Ayesha contradicted this report. The teacher's proposed solution to Don's delays was to promote him to middle school where special education resources were stronger, despite the fact that he *reads at first-grade level*.

Tom's teachers reported that Tom generally tried to do his work, completed homework assignments, and did not have any behavioral problems, but read two years behind grade level. The guidance counselor confirmed the school's concerns about Tom's learning as well as an absence of effort to contact Ayesha about it. The counselor said that Tom might not pass the exams needed for promotion to the next grade. She spoke with the researcher about putting a request in writing to have Tom tested for a learning disability, but never mentioned this to Ayesha, despite the fact that they had met recently. The school's limited efforts at communication left Ayesha uninformed about the extent of the twins' learning difficulties.

James, Ayesha's twelve-year-old son, was in the sixth grade in a Philadelphia middle school where he also experienced academic problems. James's teachers reported that James did not complete homework assignments, despite his ability to do the work. According to the math teacher, James's real problems stemmed from home: in her words, she "did not see any support for James at home." This view was disconfirmed by the structure and support the field researchers observed over many months in Ayesha's home, particularly in relation to the children's after-school life. The teacher cited Ayesha's absence from one parent–teacher conference and her belief that Ayesha did not read James's progress report as evidence for her assertion. Ayesha's interpretation was that teachers called her to come in for a meeting at the last minute, which was not possible based on her work schedule. She described an interchange with the teacher that illustrates this misalignment:

> [The teacher said,] "I need to see you before Friday." Now this is like on a Wednesday, and they call me and tell me, "Oh, I need to see you before Friday." You know, leave a message on my machine. So I will call them back and I'll get the person: "As you well know, I work. Just like you. I cannot just up and come into your office or into the school the next day or the day after. I have to give my supervisor ample time so she can find somebody to replace me, just like you would have to give your boss ample time." *Ayesha Muhammad, Philadelphia*

In the fall of the next academic year (2002–03), James, Tom, and Don were enrolled in the same middle school: James in seventh grade and Tom and Don in fifth grade. James was getting good grades and his homework completion had improved noticeably. He was scheduled for remedial help to begin in January. Tom received special services in addition to regular educational services, and Don was enrolled half time in the school's special education program where he was helped to manage the anger that was likely a behavioral result of an elevated blood lead level (FitzGerald, 2003). Tom's special education teacher was supportive, but she had only worked with him for two months.

Don faced greater challenges. During a January 2003 school visit, James and Don had been arrested and suspended from school. A school-based Philadelphia police officer had reprimanded James for having left the lunchroom without permission. According to the officer, James and Don then attacked her with kicks and blows and Don at one point jumped on her back. James and Don claimed that the officer laid her hands on them first.

Describing previous "run-ins" with James, the officer's view was that neither child had "respect for women in authority." Ayesha's contrasting view of the officer was that "she does not know how to handle children." Although the school did not pursue further disciplinary action against James, they chose to do so against Don, saying that Don would not be permitted to remain at Middle School but would instead be transferred to a district disciplinary school. Ayesha was frustrated and at a loss about how to advocate for her son. Concerned that Don's latest report card suggested that he needed a more specialized education environment than Middle School provided, Ayesha contacted a nonprofit legal program and asked the researcher to attend a meeting at the school with her later in the month. In the meantime, the researcher contacted the school's guidance counselor on Ayesha's behalf to inquire about resources for Don, lending legitimacy to Ayesha's efforts that could be supplied by a retention-focused workforce program case manager.

A spate of time-consuming meetings ensued between Ayesha and teachers, administrators, a psychiatrist, the school guidance counselor, the court, the legal advocacy center, an attorney, a school psychologist, and a hospital-based therapeutic program—all to ensure the best possible educational environment for Don. Critically, Ayesha's efforts were made possible by her firm's official flextime policy that allowed her to take the time she needed to address the needs of her children and make up the hours later. Official flextime meant that Ayesha did not lose wages for these hours spent in meetings, and time off was not contingent on the decision of an unofficial, "street level" supervisor's decision about the merits of her request (Lipsky, 1980).

Earning just 110 percent of the federal poverty level for her resident family of six, but on track for significant advancement through formal and informal training opportunities, retaining her job at Financial Services Company was essential to the family's economic future. The firm's flextime policy thus directly impacted Ayesha's ability to negotiate on her son's behalf in school, suggesting that when firms and children's schools are at least partially aligned, inter- and intragenerational mobility may be sustained.

Full alignment would require schools to reciprocate in kind, as Ayesha's firm could not counteract the deleterious effects of Don's school placement on the family and ultimately on Ayesha's upgrade training plans. Given the Philadelphia School District CEO's edict that "all violent students will be sent to disciplinary schools," Don's behavior was seen unidimensionally rather than possibly symptomatic of lead-related learning disabilities (FitzGerald, 2003). The for-profit disciplinary school environment that Don faced was experienced by another middle-schooler in this research as "more a prison than a school." Four hundred of the twelve hundred slots in this school—fully one-third—comprise "violent offenders" and "those returning from juvenile detention," and the school plans to enlarge its capacity to twenty-three hundred students (Snyder, 2002).

Although mobility challenges typically arise at the intersection of families, firms, and children's schools, Ayesha's firm's response is exemplary. At the same time, Ayesha's story reveals the plight of children enrolled in under-resourced urban schools that casts a critical lens on teacher-parent communication, especially in relation to the role of work in low-income parents' lives. In many other cases, such as Wendy Delvalle's, families, firms, and children's schools are misaligned.

Children's Schools, Families, and Parents' Firms—Misaligned:
Wendy Delvalle's Family Story (Philadelphia)

Families often view school bureaucracy as overwhelming and inefficient. Philadelphia mother Wendy Delvalle's experience is typical. When fourteen-year-old Edwin, who has ADHD, enters a one-year placement in a disciplinary school, his mother cannot confirm the reevaluation process for his return to regular school. Nor can his teachers. Not surprisingly, as time passes Edwin's placement seems more and more like a sentence. The rules and procedures of the disciplinary school are particularly ambiguous because of extensive reforms underway in the school district. These reforms appear to have a negative impact on meeting the needs of Edwin and other youth with serious learning and behavioral needs.

The children's school districts across the five states experience staff shortages, especially in the areas of special education, and funding shortages for "soft" positions for parent outreach and involvement. At the same time affordable community-based support such as tutoring and counseling are extremely hard to access and often require negotiating multiple bureaucracies. Wendy Delvalle's story underscores the frustration of a parent facing these obstacles. When it becomes clear to her that Edwin's school is not equipped to handle students with ADHD, despite claims that it specializes in special-needs students, she takes unpaid time off work, jeopardizing family economic mobility, to assess the school's range of services:

> I signed all the (admission) papers because they said this would be good for him and I believed it. When I went to the school the principal was like, "Children are going to learn, we promise this and that . . . " [but] I don't see the promises. I went to the school because I found out my son had ADHD and I wanted to know what they were going to offer, so I talked to the school psychologist who said that he was going to get him the help that he needed, [but] he only called me one time and I have never heard from this man again. *Wendy Delvalle, Mother of Fourteen-Year-Old Edwin, Philadelphia*

Because Edwin's school is insufficiently staffed, Wendy is forced to add the responsibilities of "behavior specialist" and "counselor" to her already full-time jobs of insurance company customer service agent and parent, despite having no formal training in the counseling specialties:

> Teachers call me constantly complaining about him. I say "He has ADHD you have to be patient with him. He needs to be seated in the front because the less distractions he has the better, and he needs a lot of individual attention one on one." I was like, "I don't know what else you want me to do." I talked to the psychologist and I spoke to everybody in the school. I really don't know, it is like in order to get things done you need to take all this time to go to these schools and again remind people what he has, and I don't have the time. It is hard; it is so hard. *Wendy Delvalle, Mother of Fourteen-Year-Old Edwin, Philadelphia*

The stress of Edwin's school situation intersects with Wendy's stressful new worksite that is organized according to Fordist, if not Taylorist, relations and control procedures (see Chapter 6). Wendy's solution is to return to a pharmacy technician job rather than remain in the customer service field for which she entered training and that pays 12 percent more than the pharmacy position does.

Seeing how the intersections among children's schools, families, and parents' firms are seldom in full alignment, we look next at how state and school policies align or misalign with children and families to affect economic mobility.

CHILDREN'S SCHOOLS, FAMILIES, AND POLICY: ALIGNMENT AND MISALIGNMENT

STATE BUDGETS AND FISCAL POLICY

With few exceptions, children are enrolled in inner-city school districts in which state budget crises and related fiscal policy decisions affect students and schools. The single variant from the urban landscape is one suburban district. Barely five miles from the rest of the schools in one of the research cities, the suburban school is a marked contrast to the inner-city school environments. Budget cutbacks are implicated in the more universal experiences of misalignment.

In Philadelphia, following the gun debacle at Don's former elementary school, as the Muhammad story describes earlier, Ayesha hopes that the new elementary school will better understand her son's needs and address them with the appropriate services. The budget at Don's new school was cut several times, each time reducing personnel. Although two staff members are literacy interns, there is no professional special education staff to help students like Don. In Philadelphia that year, over half the six hundred new teachers lacked full certification, and thousands of existing teachers held their positions under "emergency certification" (Mezzacappa, 2002). Ayesha laments the fallout on her son from budget-related teacher cutbacks:

> I just want Don to be able to deal with life when he gets older. With him having a learning disability that he has, he has ADHD, it's like a mild retardation, he's not getting reading. He's barely getting math. Nothing holds his attention very long. Nothing at all. *Ayesha Muhammad, Philadelphia*

Ayesha's twelve-year-old son, James encounters a similar problem in his middle school. His sixth-grade teacher believes that James needs "comprehensive support and testing for learning needs." James agrees with this assessment saying, "I think I have attention problems." But James's teacher tells Ayesha that in the current budget context such resources are reserved for the "extremes": "It's easier to get students into a special help class if they've missed lots of school or have been a behavioral problem." Thus the special education help promised to James for January 2003 was not forthcoming. Advocating for adequate services for her children in depleted schools limits the time Ayesha can spend on upgrade training to advance her family's economic security.

In Washington, state funding reductions include $300,000 from the governor's proposal to launch an initiative to reduce class size (Johnson, 2000) and a $1 million cut in flexible aid to school districts (Bach, 2003). Tom Russell's academic gains in a class of seventeen might be adversely affected by this, which could take even more of his mother's work hours to mediate.

The state education budget for Milwaukee is also cut. As a result schools plan to eliminate arts and reading programs and decrease counseling services. These particular cuts affect seventh-grader, The Rock Blessed's participation in extracurricular activities, such as being a tutor or playing basketball, because after-school transportation was cut as well: "I don't go because I ain't got no way to get back. They say they have an after-school bus but it doesn't go." Despite significant attempts at school reform, Milwaukee's funding cutbacks similarly reduce The Rock's academic enrichment supports, as a local newspaper columnist forewarned:

> The projected MPS [Milwaukee Public Schools] budget shortfall for 2001 will mean cuts in services for students with special education needs; the loss of music, art, physical education, library and reading specialist services; outdated textbooks; deferred maintenance; and less support for the most needy students from educational assistants, social workers, psychologists, and other staff (Copeland, 2000). *Newspaper Article, Milwaukee*

Particularly concerning in terms of equalizing the developmental enrichment of children across family income brackets, the elimination of funding for four-year-old kindergarten (Norman, 2003) reduces the likelihood of equalization for children like The Rock's sister, Baby Miracle Blessed.

Louisiana legislators also consider stripping extra education money from the budget. As one representative puts it, "We need to fund our needs, not our wants. We can't fund education at the expense of the health care of our citizens" (Hasten, 2003). With Louisiana state income down, plans to raise salaries and give stipends to teachers seeking National Board certification are scrutinized, and concern looms over the state's hesitancy to expand the kind of prekindergarten programs that Elizabeth Seabrook located to better ensure her four-and-a-half-year-old's academic future. In 2003 only twenty-one New Orleans teachers were National Board certified (New Orleans Public Schools, 2005). At a time when many states are reducing their investment in education, Louisiana is trying to increase funding but its resources are limited. With three jobs and a rigorous upgrade training regimen, Elizabeth Seabrook has neither time nor money to spend on another school search.

Finally, in Missouri a private management firm took over the St. Louis Public School District in May 2003, replacing the position of superintendent with a management consultant team. The team's analysis of the district's financial position projected a $73 million deficit by the following June. The action taken to reduce this projected deficit to $14.7 million violated state law that prohibits unbalanced budgets. Accordingly, the management team reduced expenditures and increased local property taxes which lowered the cash flow shortfall from a projected $99 million to an actual figure of $37.6 million (McCaskill, 2004). Given that the St. Louis city schools are so financially strapped, seven-year-old Chris Tucker is fortunate that his mother enrolled him in a county school where she successfully sought and secured special testing and reading instruction. However the state budget deficit may have contributed to the fact that when the family moved to the inner city, special instruction was delayed for a year.

SCHOOL DISTRICT MANAGEMENT POLICIES

As the aforementioned St. Louis example shows, management policies intersect with budget cutbacks to create an ever-changing school landscape for parents to negotiate, ultimately misaligning with the demands of parents' work schedules to threaten both intra- and intergenerational mobility. For example, massive reorganization of the Philadelphia School District results in a major management shift in seventy schools that are among 884 declared by the state as "failing" (Langland, 2002). In AY2002–03, three for-profit firms, two universities, and two nonprofit organizations run forty-five schools, and additional funding and resources are funneled to twenty-five schools under existing public management. The children in three of the five Philadelphia families attend externally managed schools.

The New Orleans School District Superintendent, an ex-marine described by state educators as a "classic tragic figure, a person of heroic proportion" (Thevenot, 2002a), resigns amidst accusations of audit improprieties, political crossfire, and concern over test scores. At least 41 percent of fourth-graders and at least 59 percent of eighth-graders in New Orleans fail the standardized Louisiana Educational Assessment Program (LEAP) test in AY2002–03, an increase over the previous year (Nelson, 2003). Two chief officers follow in quick succession. The administrative mission of the newest chief is to "manage our fiscal resources to direct maximum funds toward student achievement" (Amato, 2004). At the same time, the audit advisory committee for the district reports that the school system's major departments have not undergone an internal audit for over a decade (Thevenot, 2002b). This tumultuous managerial environment awaits the four New Orleans families whose children will soon enter public elementary schools.

Seattle's Superintendent, another private sector recruit hired largely for his financial acumen, resigns, leaving the district to address serious financial problems. The Seattle School District experienced serious budgetary shortfalls over the previous four years and projects a $12 million budget gap for 2005–06 (Seattle School District, 2005). These deficits have been attributed to accounting problems at the district level, cuts in federal and state funding, and the need to eliminate lead contamination in drinking fountains throughout district schools (Roberts, 2004). Teacher turnover negatively impacts district resources as the average elementary school loses one out of five teachers each year (Bhatt, 2005). Such managerial turbulence potentially threatens the academic stability of vulnerable children like Isabell Smith's early-elementary-age sons.

The Wisconsin Department of Public Instruction names more than one-third of Milwaukee public schools on its list of schools facing escalating sanctions if they fail to show better results. With the exception of Juan Shanks, the Milwaukee families' children attend near-sanctioned schools. Simultaneously, critics of Milwaukee's school voucher system charge that the policy diverts money and attention away from the city's neediest schools (Weintraub, 2000).

Each of the five districts has thus experienced significant management and policy turbulence in the recent past, making both the intergenerational mobility of the children and the intragenerational mobility of the parents vulnerable.

SCHOOL POLICIES ABOUT FAMILY-SCHOOL INTERACTION

In addition to the macro landscape of budget cutbacks and management turbulence, the children and their families are embedded in a micro terrain of school policy aimed at family–school interaction. Such "parent involvement" policies are increasingly viewed as an antidote to the woes of inner-city schools (Patchen, 2004). These policies may also illustrate a myopic focus on school improvement at the expense of overall family well-being. Both outcomes are evident in this ethnography.

On the more positive side and along the lines of the intersecting networks in local and regional workforce development systems (Chapter 5), for the past fifteen years the Seattle Public School District has operated the Family Support Workers Program, which is a collaborative effort of the Seattle public schools, United Way and city government. Family Support Workers serve fifty-six elementary schools and assist over six thousand families a year to increase parents' involvement in their children's school. Three of the five Seattle families are assisted by this program, receiving tutor referrals, help finding community-based after-school care, and provision of book bags. Such a resource might be a vital boost to any school district.

In contrast, lacking a district policy, a Milwaukee school administrator calls for a special staff liaison to reach parents:

> I'd like to see a liaison between school and parents. The MPS [Milwaukee Public Schools] has so many changes that have to be explained to parents. I'd like the liaison people to tell parents what they need to know to help their kids succeed. Parents have to get the school's angle on things. The kids go home and tell a story and then the parents get angry before coming to school. Then it's hard to talk to the parents. The parents have to know that schoolwork comes first. Parents should make sure that homework is done first. [Is there anything that a workforce program can do to help?] I don't know that they can do anything about the problems that teachers have with this community. *Middle School Administrator, Milwaukee*

At the same time, involving parents in schools can be a triple-edged sword. Although parent involvement policies are defensible if not ideal in the abstract, teachers' and school administrators' expectations show little to no understanding of the competing work demands and responsibilities faced by hard-working parents with low incomes. Such expectations involve extensive involvement with homework and family participation in school events, strategies teachers hope will compensate for insufficient school funding and staffing but all too often limit parents' ability to successfully perform in or advance in their jobs. *Startlingly, in hundreds of conversations, not one teacher or administrator expresses the view that the parents' "work responsibility" or "work ethic" is admirable.* They seem only to view parents' work as disruptive to the schools' or teachers' goals, which tends to turn an "involve the parent" policy into a "blame the parent" practice, as Kevin McDonalds's story typifies.

Parent Involvement Policy—Blame the Parent Practice:
Kevin McDonalds's Family Story (Milwaukee)

Kevin and Lynn McDonalds's three children are bright and articulate like their parents. They are well cared for and well behaved, saying, "Excuse me" when poised to interrupt adult conversation. For their age, both six-year-old Salina and five-year-old Christina use difficult vocabulary with facility—words like "probably, usually, normally, actually, and permission." All three children are in good health, except for three-year-old Fireman's occasional bouts of asthma. At home the roles of parent and child are clearly delineated and the children respond respectfully and with affection to both Kevin and Lynn, thrilled to have their father back after a three-year felony incarceration. Despite having what Lynn describes as "different parenting styles based on our upbringings," Kevin and Lynn seem to have sorted out how to parent together effectively. TV programs are monitored, the girls generally do an art activity alongside TV watching, and Lynn engages interactively with them in letter writing and cooking.

At school the picture becomes more complicated, which may suggest that the problem exists at school or is simply manifested there. Salina and Christina attend a distant, European-style public elementary school whose students are mostly African American and Latino. When we first met the McDonalds family in February 2000, Salina was in first grade and Christina was in Kindergarten. By the next fall, Salina was still in first grade and Christina had advanced to first grade. In early September 2000, Lynn had already been to one school conference with the girls' teachers who reported that "Salina seemed to be doing better than last year" and that "Christina has improved in the last few weeks." Kevin planned a follow-up conference. Both parents have demanding work schedules, including what we call a "serial two-parent" arrangement whereby Kevin works nights and Lynn works days to assure continuous oversight of the children. At the same time they hold somewhat different views about the solution to Salina's school difficulty, as Kevin notes:

> [Lynn] thinks Salina has the same problems this year as last year and that Salina should go to a different class or switch schools. Salina has the same teacher as last year—they're in the same class for three years. I tell [Lynn] not to be frustrated. I think if we start now changing schools, classes, we get the kid set to think "If I don't like it, I can act up and move on." I think we have to stay here and get it right. *Kevin McDonalds, Father of Salina and Christina*

By late September the parents' and school's perceptions about the girls' school performance reflect opposite poles. The parents and children report mostly acceptable performance, the teachers report both problems and improvements, and an administrator issues a critical, arguably stereotypical report. Different perceptions of "discipline" underlie these variations.

Christina's teacher is puzzled by Christina's behavior: "She doesn't stay on task. Her reading skills need improvement. I don't know what happens at home, if the children aren't disciplined or have consistency." In contrast, although an administrator characterizes the European-style school as "more relaxed than a lot of public schools," the research team found Christina's classroom somewhat rigid. Christina greeted one researcher by running to her and hugging her—not an unusual reaction of a six-year-old to a familiar adult. In response the teacher said sternly: "You know we do not bother guests, Christina. The guest sits in this chair and observes. I want you to go back to your work now."

Similarly, one of Salina's teachers characterizes her as "not so focused. She's a challenge to have in the class. She just doesn't seem to pay attention or to follow directions." Another teacher said that Salina "has a lot of problems. She had tantrums last year. [And this year?] No, not so much." This teacher also notes improvement after the conference with Lynn and the parents' follow-through on Salina's home-reading packets: "She seems to do better work now." Again in contrast, the teacher complained that, "It is difficult to get the kids to do as they are told." The researcher observed this teacher as "very tense and scolded the children frequently, telling them to be quiet," similar to Lynn's observation during the previous school year. The teacher's description of school policy could be construed as excessive for a six-year-old child:

> She had a three-day suspension about a month ago. I don't know all of the details. I was gone for the day. There was a substitute. I am rarely absent from school. But anyway, Salina hit a girl on the playground. She was given a three-day suspension. [In school?] No, we do not have in-school suspensions. When you're suspended, you go home. *First Grade Teacher of Salina McDonalds*

A school administrator also suggested that Salina perhaps did not receive enough discipline at home and therefore was not appropriate for the school environment, notwithstanding the school's mission statement that all children will benefit from its environment:

> I get the feeling that the parents just let her do what she wants to do and there is no order or discipline at home, that she isn't made to follow any rules. *Elementary School Administrator*

If anything were the case, the children are perhaps too disciplined at home, having to maintain a strict schedule based on the mandates of their parents' work schedules. Kevin exercises a consistent and authoritative parenting style, albeit from the command point of the living room couch, with comments such as: "No skateboard in the house"; "Beds are not meant to be walked on"; and to Christina's complaint about her brother's behavior, "When did you become a parent? Who gave you the power to parent him?" Kevin also models the ability to acknowledge his own mistakes, a developmentally important skill for children to learn from a parent. When Fireman broke a glass picture, Kevin followed an initial frustrated remark immediately by acknowledging his complicity in the breakage:

> No, it was really my fault. I shouldn't have left the package that way. Now we'll have to clean it all up. *Kevin McDonalds, Father of Three-Year-Old Fireman*

In response to the administrator's comment about insufficient discipline, the researcher related the disciplined, organized structure of Lynn's daily routine:

> [Researcher:] The mother gets up very early in the morning and has to have the children prepared to get to school and prepare herself to work a full day. In order to do this, she prepares the evening before by setting out the children's clothes and they are fed and groomed on a regular schedule with a system. *Research Field Notes, McDonalds Family*

> [As Lynn described her routine:] I can't get Fireman to brush his teeth. The other two do it as part of a routine. When they get up in the morning, I brush one of their hair, while the other one brushes her teeth and then we trade off. The night before I iron their clothes and set them out. They take their pile and get dressed and then we eat. We have to have a routine or I would be late for work. I have to be at work at seven. So I have to be up by five and get them to before-school care by six. So we have to do it like that. *Lynn McDonalds, Mother of Salina and Christina*

The administrator's response to this information suggested a limited and judgmental perspective about the McDonalds family:

> Well, that's surprising. It certainly is a surprise. I was sure there was no discipline in the home. You said she gets everything ready the night before? Doesn't that seem obsessive to you? *Elementary School Administrator*

Similarly, the administrator evidenced no understanding of the parents' employment rigors. After his overnight shift Kevin attends three hours of upgrade training for the printing trade. Lynn often works as a nurse aide on weekends as well as weekdays. Running a household of three small children, ferrying them to a carefully-selected but distant school before work, and trying to compensate for Kevin's years of no income, was not easy. Yet the administrator blamed the parents for not being 'interested' enough in their children's education to follow the school policy of parent involvement:

> We have a full calendar of events for the students, families, and teachers to join in. We take trips to the museum. We went to the Shedd Aquarium in Chicago, and to the apple farm. We are having an ethnic potluck this coming Wednesday. We have sock-hops, and a sleigh ride during the winter holidays. We have a Black History program in February. I have never seen the family here. I send home information on the trips with each child in the school. *Elementary School Administrator*

When parents perceive negative approbation from school personnel to whom they have entrusted their cherished children, opposing views of children's performance surface. In some cases parents also withdraw from the school (Furstenberg et al., 1999), severing relations that ideally are trust based, which likely furthers inadequate communication to the children's detriment. Such patterns of school-family relations are all too common in impoverished urban areas and are clearly one way that the relationship between the McDonalds family and the school could evolve.

Parent Involvement Policy—Overwhelm the Parent Practice:
Elizabeth Seabrook's Family Story (New Orleans)

In another example, although equally designed for enrichment, parent involvement policies in preschools often put parents "over the top" in terms of expectations and stress. At our final meeting in May 2003 Elizabeth Seabrook worked *three* jobs, spurred largely by the fact that her childcare subsidy had been cut one month earlier. At the new rate Elizabeth pays $129 per month for Joseph's after-school program and $109 per month for Abigail's preschool program. The $238 per month total is an increase of $163 per month for already-strapped Elizabeth. Although the staff at her earlier workforce development program advocated actively against the decrease in child-care assistance, Elizabeth's solution is in concert with the tenacity she shows consistently—get more work:

> How was I ever going to do that [pay childcare]? So what did I do? I got two more jobs. At the end of March, I got a job here [her mother's assisted living residence] putting a lady to bed every night. Aunt "M," I put her to bed every day and Sundays I get her up and put her to bed. I bathe her once a week. I get paid fifty dollars a week. My other job I began at the end of April. I clean my boss's house. I get forty dollars for that; I do it on Thursdays. Last time I got forty dollars. God always makes a way. I don't mind cleaning toilets. I'd even get out there with a jackhammer if I could. I'll do anything to earn money for my children and me. *Elizabeth Seabrook, Mother of Preschoolers Joseph and Abigail*

Although the children's carefully selected preschool is a good environment for their learning, it places continuing burdens on Elizabeth. Short of funds, the school holds regular fundraising drives, such as selling candy and other items. Elizabeth does not have time or energy to add "saleswoman" to her multifaceted life, but parents are not allowed to return unsold goods. As a result, Elizabeth's recently ill mother bought the children's candy boxes out of income that she could have used for her grandchildren's immediate needs or for her own medical needs. In another example Elizabeth reports that the last week of school is "Teacher Appreciation" week and believes that each day holds different requirements: "Monday's supposed to be a plant or card date, real simple things, but . . . " On the final day of the week, children are to bring a gift. Elizabeth plans to get each teacher a gift, but has no time to "go to the mall" for a plant or card because of the demands of work, medical technology study, her mother's illness, and her children's daily homework requirements. And although she downplays the cost aspect, apparently neither the school nor Elizabeth thinks that a hand-drawn card or flower would suffice.

Finally, Elizabeth faces the challenges of the school's "special days": "Purple day; funny sock day; and then they want a certain kind of mat and a certain kind of cover for all the mats." Couple these demands with the homework demands and one sees quickly why the children's homework often eclipses Elizabeth's own:

> A lot of nights I would like to do my homework ... but I had to spend time with Joseph's homework. I had to read to him; he had to read to me; he had to answer questions. And when you bring it in, you have another stack for the next week.
> *Elizabeth Seabrook, Mother of Preschoolers Joseph and Abigail*

Even Abigail, barely in preschool, has daily homework. While the school environment nurtures Elizabeth's children, fulfilling its parent involvement policy delays Elizabeth's academic and employment progress, indirectly slowing the children's progress as well by making their parent's wished-for enrichment opportunities, lessened daily stress, and higher income farther in the future.

One other school policy is misaligned with the work demands of many low-income parents: the requirement that parents pick up children's report cards at school. Most often parents are blamed for failing to comply with what is arguably a misguided policy. In a typical example, despite the fact that forty-year-old single-parent Rachel Quinn breaks her back, figuratively, to locate and enroll her son Miguel in a magnet high school far from the neighborhood school that serves the family's public housing project, and literally, to work construction to support her family, Miguel's teachers do not understand that the school's report card pick-up hours conflict with Rachel's work hours. Although Rachel technically has a full-time job, assignments in the tradeshow portion of the construction industry seldom offer forty-hour workweeks, which means that Rachel's annual income reaches about one-fourth of what it should. When she is working, however, picking up Miguel's report card at the school's convenience means that Rachel loses vital income and currency on the union queue for work.

A final pattern emerged from the intersection of school policy, school practices, beleaguered teachers, families and parents' work. During repeated interviews and observations in schools in all five cities, teachers and administrators commonly give the researchers negative reports about children's performance, express pessimism about the children's futures, and evidence resignation and exhaustion in their jobs. In contrast, teachers tell the same children's parents that their children's problems are improving, commend them for their efforts, and predict future achievement for the children. In one of many such examples, the guidance counselor of Ayesha's son Tom reveals to the researchers that Tom is at risk of being held back. Ayesha was completely uninformed about this concern. The same pattern occurred with the children of Randy Jackson, Kevin McDonalds, Aida Gomez, and of others across the country, especially in relation to reports of bad behavior and threats of grade retention (Iversen, 2002). One "sense" that the field team makes of this pattern is that it is a strategy that teachers use to cope with their impoverished school environments. In effect, teachers use researchers as a sounding board and complaint bureau, viewing them as "like-minded professionals" in contrast to their view of the parents as uninterested or ill-equipped to partner with them on behalf of the children. It is also possible that teachers and administrators in these inner-city schools use the research interview as an opportunity to emphasize negatives and "worst-case scenarios" about the study children as a tool to effect change in the families via the researchers as intermediaries.

As the stories of many parents including Ayesha Muhammad, Wendy Delvalle, Elizabeth Seabrook, and Kevin McDonalds typify, teacher's perceptions that parents are uninvolved in their children's education are frequently inaccurate and based on incomplete information. The views of teachers and policies of school administrators reveal obvious lack of awareness of the rigid firm policies and long work hours that make it impossible for some working parents to be active partners in their children's homework or at their children's schools. For schools in particular, parents' work and policy remain perceived as separate, unrelated spheres (Gartrell, 1991), which limits parents' intragenerational mobility in the short run and children's intergenerational mobility over time.

SCHOOL POLICIES AND OTHER SOCIAL INSTITUTIONS MOVING TOWARD ALIGNMENT

At the same time, examples of schools moving toward alignment with other social institutions are found in all five districts. Further, examples of firms moving toward alignment with family responsibilities, although rare, do exist. Public policy alignment with schools, firms, and families, although even rarer, also surfaces occasionally.

In New Orleans, LEAP testing introduced by the deposed superintendent leads to reduced 'social promotion' of students. Summer school is mandatory for students who fail the LEAP tests to be promoted. The same superintendent also creates a department to deal with the "largely ignored problems of students with learning disabilities" in the state (Thevenot, 2002a). Also at the state level, the Board of Elementary and Secondary Education agrees to the governor's request to increase teacher pay across Louisiana by $1,000 on average starting with the 2001–02 fiscal year, which is about one-third of the amount necessary for Louisiana teachers to reach the average salary for teachers across southern states (Wardlaw, 2001). This school-policy alignment may improve teacher retention for the New Orleans families' elementary school children.

In Philadelphia the school district CEO allocates $19 million to develop what some call "the most ambitious after-school program" in the city's history (Woodall, 2002). Sixteen thousand third- through eighth-graders who are below grade level in math and language arts are eligible to attend. Juan Gomez, retained in second grade, benefits from this program, as do Tom and Don Muhammad before their debacle. A limitation is that no bus transportation is provided at the end of the weekday program at 5:15 P.M.

Seattle developed a city Office of Community Learning designed to deepen or form partnerships with organizations that share their goals of minimizing children's obstacles to learning and engaging students' families (Office of Community Learning, 2002). This structure is much like that of local or regional workforce development networks (Chapter 5). The focus of this office on school readiness, better outcomes for out-of-school time, and transforming schools into lifelong learning centers makes it possible for many low-income and refugee and immigrant families to use school-sited community-based technology centers and become more engaged with their children's education.

As these stories and excerpts suggest and history documents, individuals and institutions under budgetary and management constraints both suffer and strategize. At the same time, they demonstrate that the intersection of school, family, work, and policy is extremely complex. This intersection requires attention to the horizontal and reciprocal influence of multiple institutions, recognizing that the mobility chances of hard-working parents and children are significantly thwarted by the old paradigm practice of funding and perceiving each domain as an isolated, un-networked silo.

SUMMARY AND CONCLUSIONS

In the course of more than 120 days spent in children's schools and preschools during the research period, observations and interviews with parents, teachers, and employers suggest that families, communities, firms, and school policies *all* influence student achievement and that no single individual or institution can be responsible for children's education. We see real problems with student learning and get the sense from teachers and parents that current testing and accountability practices detract from critical issues that both invade and transcend the school walls. We also see teachers and parents who feel powerless: teachers working in classrooms without adequate training, books, or staff support; and parents struggling to understand complex bureaucracies while making ends meet, without losing control or sight of their children's needs. The families' experiences underscore the need to raise the level of dialog about how relationships and interinstitutional reciprocity influence management policies, state and school policies, firm policies and practices, and children's futures.

Essentially, one or another of the institutional actors—family, school or parents' work—suffers under current policy structures. Two might be aligned, but the third is not. Most often, as Seattle parent Isabell Smith puts it, families are "between a hard place and a rock." When parents stay at unsafe jobs, as Hard Working Blessed does, children worry about their parents and their grades fall. Schools then demand more of parents who have to take time off work to meet these demands, and family income suffers. If parents work two jobs to increase financial well-being, children act out, often in school, to regain parental attention. Schools then demand more of the parents' attention, leading parents to quit one of the jobs and jeopardize economic mobility or lose sleep and risk injury, especially in physically demanding work environments. The intersection rapidly becomes a downward spiral, despite the efforts of each actor to do the best it can for the children.

Even in Ayesha Muhammad's situation, which seems closest to interinstitutional alignment, problems in the Philadelphia school system threaten the balance for the family. Although her firm's flextime policy allows Ayesha time to advocate for Don's deep dilemmas at school, the time it takes to navigate that system means that she has to postpone the upgrade training that could raise her family above 110 percent poverty.

One truth is evident in all the misalignments: when faced with conflicting choices between the proximal and distal needs of their children, these parents choose the proximal over the distal. As the new mobility paradigm holds, the parents' choice processes are both cognitive and emotional, especially when resolving conflicting goals. Meeting proximal needs may be the right choice for the children's immediate development but that choice may be at the expense of family economic mobility.

How might genuine school reform foster both intra- and intergenerational mobility? In brief, reaching beyond the school doors, such reform might start with well-subsidized early childhood readiness strategies and be supported later through high quality before- and after-school programs and summer schools. It might also question the costs of shaping school culture around traditional business models and ask the business world to be more responsive to the needs of working families. Finally, it might foster parental involvement in the academic performance of their children in ways that do not constrict family economic mobility. Such involvement might mitigate the impacts of budget cutbacks, school management turbulence, and teacher turnover. Schools cannot produce this change alone, however. If parents' firms become involved in supporting these changes and recognize their role in *both* intra- and intergenerational mobility, they might experience extended economic health now and in the future. Genuine reform in paradigm, policies and practices appears to be needed to ensure the future of millions of America's children, as Chapter 8 discusses next.

8   Jobs Aren't Enough

Toward an Agenda for Family Economic Mobility

> How can people know what the problem is for more than a hundred years, put a man on the moon, make planes fly, but not answer the question of why certain classes of people are behind? If people would put the same focus and energy in pumping more grant information, job programs, legal programs, and other different programs that is out there, minorities wouldn't be stuck. —*Kevin McDonalds, Milwaukee*

> Why can't we help a few poor families that are trying to pay off debts get a fresh start? We could help them by getting a wealthy person to pay off their debt and get a tax deduction for that. This would help families and help the economy. —*Hard Working Blessed, Milwaukee*

FAMILY ECONOMIC MOBILITY TODAY

We establish at the beginning of this book that social and labor market conditions make it difficult for at least one in four workers in the United States to support their families, much less move forward economically through work. Long-held myths about unlimited opportunity, merit-based attainment, and individual responsibility for choices and outcomes are firmly entrenched in at least four of our major social institutions—family, education, firms, and the state, forming what we describe in Chapter 2 as the old paradigm for economic mobility. The institutionalized policies and procedures of these entrenched myths coalesce to constrain the economic well-being of many families—those with low incomes in particular, but increasingly those earning moderate to middle incomes as well.

We argue that a new paradigm for economic mobility is needed to realize the foundational American principle of *real* opportunity in contemporary society and to solve the wage inequality and disparate employment conditions that Osterman and colleagues (2001, p. 181) call "the most pernicious labor-market problem of our time." Krueger (2003, p. 10) concurs that there is "less mobility in income across generations in the U.S. than in most other countries." A new paradigm recognizes that multiple intersecting institutions are implicated in economic mobility, that mobility is a thoroughly relational process, that choice making involves cognitive and emotional dimensions, and that mobility paths are increasingly dynamic and variable. Most important, instituting equity and real opportunity requires changes in what we call the "public will."

The twenty-five key parents in this book show us that in many ways they are similar to millions of other adults across the United States that do not earn a family-sustaining income through full-time work. Chapter 3 articulates personal and structural challenges to the families' mobility that stem from incomplete or poor-quality education, inadequate services for language acquisition and acculturation, or periods away from family and the labor market due to incarceration and rehabilitation.

However, Chapter 3 and later chapters also show that other social institutions play defining roles in the families' mobility efforts. For example, family and policy institutions are intimately related through the availability, accessibility, and adequacy of subsidies and work supports. Similarly, family and labor market institutions are intimately related through the adequacy of wages and the availability of employer-provided health insurance benefits, especially given the prevalence of chronic health conditions and, seemingly, symptoms of depression that fluctuate with labor market conditions.

Chapter 3 also shows that economically impoverished urban environments and fiscal challenges facing city and state governments across the nation overarch the influence of location or "place" in limiting economic mobility. At the same time, place matters through the particular ways that state and city characteristics intersect with families, workforce development institutions, firms, children's schools, and policy. Place tells us *how* families experience employment, unemployment, and insufficient wages, but these constraints on mobility are experienced universally across the five cities. Thus, although knowledge about place-based particularities is critical to the development of appropriate policies and programs, national policies are the key to greater economic mobility writ large.

The sixty-six children living with these parents then show us in Chapter 4 who they are and how they experience their families' histories, neighborhoods, communities, and mobility efforts. Their parents' new jobs result in a mixture of tangible benefits, such as enough money for food and clothing, and tangible challenges such as too little time together, devolution of care for younger siblings from parents to adolescents, and fear about parents' health and safety at work. Overall Chapter 4 shows that constrained economic mobility imposes intragenerational penalties on children's current well-being and intergenerational penalties on children's mobility potential. These penalties occur largely through insufficient family income during the children's early years (Duncan et al., 1998) and through insufficient accumulation of the human, cultural, and social capital needed by both generations for mobility, as Chapter 7 later amplifies. Notably, the prevailing belief that parents' work is an unadulterated "plus," in terms of modeling the work ethic and responsible civic behavior, is challenged by children's responses to the physical dangers, stresses, and contingency of their parents' low-wage jobs. Many children come to perceive the world of work as one of futility, not as one of opportunity.

In Chapters 5 through 7, the stories of the families incorporate the views of their employers, job training staff, friends, child-care providers, school teachers and administrators, neighbors, faith leaders, and others—at least one thousand in all to show that the siloed structure of social institutions constrains the efforts of many families to move ahead. Chapter 5 reveals that, contrary to earlier evaluation findings that job training is not effective for economic mobility, local or regional workforce development networks that are constituted by strategic partnerships among workforce intermediaries, education and job training programs, civic organizations, policymakers, and employers enable families to move into better jobs than they've held in the past. In effect these new arrangements turn what Burt (1992, 2002) refers to in market relations as "structural holes" into what we call *structured wholes* for job seekers and firms alike. Accordingly, the parents' wages increase by magnitudes over previous earnings and, for the first time for most, their jobs offer nonwage benefits and advancement opportunity. As Milwaukee parent Kevin McDonalds observes, "Without a start, there's no finish." At the same time the parents' gains, and those of their children, cannot be sustained by the lattice of workforce development programs and networks alone. These new systems need to be positioned to effect significant changes in firms and public policy. Getting in the door of a good job through initiative simply isn't enough to secure economic mobility.

Chapter 6 then illustrates the limits of old paradigm reliance on human capital attainment as the key to family mobility. The limitations result partly from the fact that many of the institutional structures and policies in the parents' seventy-four firms are lodged too solidly in the old paradigm to provide mobility-enhancing conditions for today's multiethnic, young- and middle-adult working parents. In short, the disconnect between today's workforce and yesterday's firms results in a *life-stage mismatch* (Iversen, 2002). Thus, although jobs are crucial for economic mobility, jobs aren't enough. Critically, the wage structure in most firms remains inadequate and excessively disparate, and aspects of firm organization and relations are often inhospitable or physically dangerous. Even when wages increase over time, which many do, they seldom reach levels adequate to support a family. Nor do they seem likely to in the coming decade. Persistent wage disparity and other current labor market practices, such as reliance on temporary workers like Loretta Lopez and the lessened firm-to-worker loyalty that Isabell Smith experiences, belie the myth that hard work pays off. Overall, only Ayesha Muhammad's and Sam Gates's firms approximate what we term "firm as partner" to families' mobility efforts, largely through organizational structures and practices built on the new mobility characteristics of trust, reciprocity, and interinstitutional cooperation.

Chapter 7 then reveals that children's schools are a stronger influence on economic mobility than is commonly recognized—horizontally as structures and policies in schools are misaligned with those of parents' firms, and vertically as schools prepare children to be productive citizens and workers. These influences are recursive as well. When parents' work is going well and is compensated adequately, even if not sufficiently, children's school performance and behavior often improve, such as fifteen-year-old Tank Blessed's does when his father retrieves him from violent and failed Chicago schools and is newly able to support his family through work. But when parents are not paid a living wage or work under harsh conditions, as many of the stories in Chapter 6 illustrate, children often reflect the family's stress in their school behavior and performance—as Tank Blessed does when his father later suffers herniated discs, pneumonia, and flu on the job and is demoted in responsibility and wage. In situations like Tank's, underresourced, understaffed urban schools demand that parents attend conferences during the regular school day and participate heavily in their children's remediation, not realizing or ignoring the fact that such conferences and demands on parents' time generally result in lost wages or lost upgrade opportunity and may even result in job loss, outcomes that further stress the family's children in turn. Worse yet, embattled schools in impoverished neighborhoods generally have insufficient material, energy, and teacher expertise to provide the human and cultural capital that children in low-income families need to have a real chance for future mobility. Moreover, as Chapter 5 underscores, workforce development networks and firms do not offer parents the academic remediation they need to augment their children's attainment. Misaligned social conditions and institutional intersections then, as well as the absence of reciprocity and trust, severely constrain the mobility efforts of parents and children alike.

CURRENT STRATEGIES FOR ECONOMIC MOBILITY

Given the realities facing contemporary families, workforce development institutions, firms, and children's schools, and the ways in which these spheres intersect with each other and with public policy, we anticipated concluding this book with a set of specific policy and program recommendations to increase economic mobility for low-income families. The more we interview, observe, and read, the more obvious it is that many creative and workable micro- and macrolevel strategies have already been offered by thoughtful policymakers, policy advocates, scholars, practitioners, and low-income workers—Kevin McDonalds and Hard Working Blessed among them, as their comments illustrate at the beginning of this chapter.

For example, one recent strategy for economic mobility is the creation of partnerships between welfare and workforce programs and community colleges to build a skill-based career pathways system that fosters human capital-based mobility (Alssid et al., 2002; Roberts, 2002; Stone & Worgs, 2004). Not surprisingly, women leaving welfare and other low-wage workers with a high school diploma, previous vocational training, and higher than an eighth-grade reading level gain greater traction toward mobility from human capital strategies than do those with more limited educational histories. However, the upgrade efforts of Elizabeth Seabrook, Tasha Tracy, Randy Jackson, and others mentioned in Chapter 5 illustrate that such two-dimensional partnerships are too easily derailed by the absence of concurrent supports from public policy and labor market institutions. Contributing to this derailment, skilled personnel and methods to comprehensively assess the varied and interrelated needs of *all* family members are generally missing in welfare and workforce programs, and the reliance of community colleges on human capital investment neglects the critical contribution of social and cultural capital to mobility.

A more expansive strategy to foster the economic mobility of low-income families and the simultaneous economic development of their communities emerges from local and regional workforce development networks that are explicitly constituted by partnerships between community service and job training organizations, area employers, legislators, and other relevant local actors (Blair, 2005; Bliss, 2000; Giloth, 2004b; Kazis & Miller, 2001; Stone & Worgs, 2004). Although such networks are still only one of the necessary components of economic mobility, the families' experiences evidence their importance (Chapter 5). Notably, these efforts, often spearheaded by what are called labor market or workforce intermediaries (Giloth, 2004b; 2004c; Meléndez, 2004; Osterman, 2005; Osterman et al., 2001), identify that institutional partnerships built on trusted and sustained relationships and active commitment of local firms are integral to the mobility calculus. As Chapter 7 illustrates, children's educational institutions are equally integral to the calculus. Unless or until the nation engages in comprehensive integration of public education, the labor market, and public policy institutions, federally funded and local workforce development systems and networks may remain the default strategy to increase economic mobility for at least some low-wage families.

A more targeted strategy related to the role that firms play in economic mobility emerges from the findings of welfare-to-work research (Berlin, 2000; Michalopoulos, 2001; Rangarajan & Novak, 1999; Strawn & Martinson, 2000; Wagner & Herr, 2003). This research finds that work-incentive strategies such as wage supplements, help with accessing food, housing, transportation, and child-care subsidies, and selective but sustained postemployment guidance, increase job attainment and retention for some welfare participants, alleviating poverty and putting them in position to get and keep a job that may lead to economic mobility. The range of mobility supports that the parents in this book draw on (Chapter 2), as well as their met and unmet needs for such supports (Chapter 6), underscore that these strategies are similarly necessary for low-income working families. Arguably, income and wage support strategies allow firms to use tax dollars to boost low wages rather than compress their wage structure. In addition, subsidy and work support strategies remain guided by the myth of individual responsibility rather than by the ways in which the labor market and firms could alter their structures and relations to foster sustained economic mobility for low-income families.

From the demand side of the labor market, a few corporate strategies for increasing economic mobility are notable (Perlmutter, 1997; Sutton, 2004). Most of these corporations partner with community-based workforce development organizations to enhance the ability of employers to retain skilled employees through the joint development of customized training curricula, provision of training-based internships, guaranteed job placement, and/or employee mentor programs. The active participation of employers in workforce development networks was spurred by the tight labor market of the late 1990s. Such strategic alliances work best if the participating actors hold mutual goals and if firms are "characterized by both strong external networks with community partners and the strong internal support of management and co-workers" (Meléndez, 2004, p. 28; Sutton, 2004). Tasha Jones's firm evidences this kind of alliance (Chapter 6). At the same time, employer participation in workforce development strategies seems to be curtailed by the slack labor market conditions of the early 2000s and by tax deferral policies that induce corporations to shift profits away from foreign nations back to the United States without penalty. Supposedly a job creation strategy, evidence suggests that the tax savings are being used for corporate buyouts and other purposes (Corporate welfare runs amok, 2005).

Finally, across the institutions of family, workforce development, firms and children's schools, legislators and policy advocates actively promote selected efforts based on research evidence that economic mobility for low-wage workers and their families may be a lengthy process that involves multiple intersecting components (Herr, 2003; Iversen, 2002). Advocacy efforts include changes in welfare and workforce legislation, encouragement of functional skill-building networks, development of asset-building strategies, incorporation of cultural competency and antiracism initiatives, use of technological advancements to facilitate access to public benefits, provision of sustained subsidy and work supports such as the Earned Income Tax Credit (EITC) and, after the recession of 2001, extended eligibility for unemployment insurance (Johnson, 2001; Levin-Epstein, 2002; Mathur, 2002; Patel & Savner, 2001; Savner, 1999). However, innovative ideas about how to better use tax expenditures and tax credits—a key policy influence on mobility—are either ignored or paid scant attention by most strategists, with the notable exceptions of Howard (1997), Howard and colleagues (Gitterman, Howard, & Cotton, 2003), and Kochan (2005), who cogently illuminate how tax policies foster the mobility of higher income families and suggest how tax credits and expenditures can foster the mobility of low-income families as well.

Moreover, these and other strategies are put forward within the current context of relatively unconnected, siloed program structures and funding streams—structural holes (Burt, 1992) that are not but could be effectively spanned to facilitate mobility through structured wholes. With few exceptions, strategies are not funded at a sustainable scale or power. In addition, few recommendations are put forward in a broad construction of what more truly democratic, egalitarian, and humane strategies could mean to low-income working families and, reciprocally, to their communities, neighborhoods, firms, and social institutions. Although perpetuating the status quo may be expedient, especially in a relatively conservative policy environment, existing but currently unconnected strategies for economic mobility might gain traction and leverage if they are knit into an inclusively structured whole.

In the end we keep bumping up against these questions: why haven't more of these ideas been implemented or adequately funded? Given that work is at the core of the American ethos, why aren't legislators and the populace more generous in thought and funding for remedial or postsecondary education, training, and workforce programs? Why is there so little strategizing about changing the wage structure in firms? Why do legislators and the populace continue to conceptually and practically bifurcate government tax and subsidy aid into private and public categories of the "deserving us" and the "nondeserving them"? What will happen if we do nothing about the continuing challenges to mobility that millions of families face?

Already one out of every four families does not earn enough to support its members through work and middle earners increasingly experience wage reductions and job insecurity. If this pattern continues, firms may be required to cover the cost of higher and longer unemployment insurance and taxes may need to be levied to cover the costs of increased returns to the welfare rolls and mushrooming health care. Children's life chances will remain constricted, now and in the future, and American confidence in work and market solutions may erode. Although we know that resources are limited, the economy is turbulent, and change is difficult, policy decisions in each of the institutional spheres in this book involve choice. Ultimately we conclude that what is needed to improve the economic well-being of millions of hard-working but low-income families in the United States is a revitalization of this country's foundational "public will" toward greater reciprocity and prosperity for all residents and citizens.

Others also address the intransigence of poverty and lack of economic mobility in the United States in concepts akin to the public will. As Edwards (1979) notes, we have known about the "working poor" for decades. Even in the 1960s and 1970s, slightly over one half of families with incomes below the poverty line have family heads who work and one-fifth of the families work full time. Also writing in the 1960s, Gans (1999, p. 108) holds that, "The real issue is not lack of money, but lack of political support to spend a share of American affluence to abolish poverty." More recently Miller (2003, p. 82) argues that "in economically developed societies it is quite feasible to meet every citizen's genuine needs and still have ample resources to devote to other purposes—that there are sufficient resources in these societies to meet (locally defined) needs everywhere, if the political will exists to do so." Estes's *Report Card of World Social Progress* concludes that "while the worldwide view on nations' progress to provide such basic needs as healthcare, education, political rights and freedom from social chaos is promising . . . the United States, despite its great wealth, continues to be indifferent to the struggles of the poor" (Hyland, 2004, p. 4). Osterman and colleagues (2001, p. 11) argue that "the rhetoric and (to an extent) the practices of the job market have lost their moral grounding," and Giloth (2004c) questions the lack of public will in the politics of workforce development. Rank (2004, p. 244) echoes similarly that "One of the reasons for the high prevalence of U.S. poverty is not a lack of resources, but rather a lack of a national will to truly address the issue." Most recently, Rep. Emmanuel Cleaver from Missouri reportedly said, "Will is the key word. . . . It will take a truckload of money to bring back the Crescent City. . . . If we have the will, we can pretty much do what we want" (Gyan, 2006). Finally, two centuries ago Tocqueville offered a similar perspective: "I cling with a firmer hold to the belief that, for democratic nations to be virtuous and prosperous, they require but to will it" (Strauss, 1971, p. 110). The idea of the public will is thus not new, but the way we conceptualize it and recognize its import for the major intersecting social institutions and for a new economic mobility paradigm may provide a direction for more equitable strategies to prevail.

WHAT DO WE MEAN BY THE "PUBLIC WILL"?

We mention first what we do *not* mean by the public will. We do not mean a unified, universal ethos such as the "collective or common consciousness" that Durkheim (1933/1984) posits in *The Division of Labor in Society*. We explicitly do not view "will" as a characteristic held or not held by individuals or persons. We *do* mean freedom and responsibility of choice and choice making that is based on the foundational American principles of fairness and real opportunity—in short, principled choice-making.

Specifically then, our notion of the public will applies to the spheres of our society in which members exercise or potentially have a voice: for example, the political and economic spheres, the intra- and interinstitutional spheres, and the nexus of persons and institutions. Our notion of the public will assumes that members of society hold varied beliefs and worldviews that lead to varied choices and decisions about their own and others' well-being. Thus the form our education and training institutions take, the form our firms take, the form our children's schools take, and the form our social policies take are within our power to determine; they are not predetermined by an autocratic government or by the prevailing economic milieu. In all cases we (the people) have choices to make (Miller, 2003).

For instance, we now choose to conceptually and practically separate "education" from "workforce development" strategies (Grubb, 1996), even though both aim to prepare youth and young adults for the labor market as well as for civil society. In 2001, the federal government designated about $3 billion for adult workforce development through various departments and pieces of legislation and around $50 billion through the Higher Education Act for federal student financial assistance, most of which goes to middle-income families. Why would we expect a two- to three-month job training program to adequately prepare a worker for mobility when it takes from two hundred hours (one full-time semester) to at least nine hundred hours (four and a half semesters; Carnevale & Desrochers, 1999) of compensatory education to translate into wages that can or nearly can sustain a family? Is that why we choose now to spend more on public assistance than on job training? We *could* choose to design and fund workforce development policies and programs as a learning continuum through life that encompasses employment and civic education. We also *could* adequately fund workforce intermediaries, as well as other new forms of regional labor market consortia (Appelbaum et al., 2005), with combined tax and employer dollars to provide sustained mediation to new workers who need it, customized employee relations strategies to firms, and other structured efforts aimed at upgrading entry-level workers *and* increasing firm productivity.

In terms of firm policies and strategies, we now choose a "hands-off" position toward the disparate wage structure facing low earners in most contemporary firms and a "hands-on" position toward income enhancement strategies. We subsidize low wages for individuals through tax credits such as the EITC and the Child Tax Credit (CTC) rather than impose regulations or set standards for reasonable wage differences in firms. We subsidize firms to hire low-income workers, but not long enough to lead to sustainable employment. Although the wage structure in firms is nominally tied to educational attainment, is it really reasonable that a high-level administrator or manager, even with more years of education than the machine operator, earns more than ten times the operator's wage: say, $250,000 versus $25,000? Or that top managers might earn one hundred times more? Is it reasonable that by 2000, CEO compensation is 310 times higher than the compensation of a typical worker (Kochan [2005] reports 400 times higher), or that CEO compensation in the United States is about three times higher than that of CEOs abroad (Mishel, Bernstein, & Allegretto, 2005, p. 112)?

Is the disproportionate wage structure in firms really based on educational merit? How can education alone explain why the wealthiest 1 percent of the nation owns more than the bottom 90 percent put together (Reich, 2004)? We *could* compress the wage structure in firms, using Norway as a model. Instead of (putatively) keying wages to human capital attainment, wages *could* be keyed to quality of job performance, as long as the wage floor for all workers is set to least 100 percent of the local self-sufficiency standard. Firms *could* achieve this by reducing the disproportionate wages of the highest earners to increase wages for the lowest earners. Whereas unions serve as the wage compression force in Norway (Barth, Roed, & Torp, 2002), the federal government or consortia of socially responsible corporations (*Business Ethics* magazine, 2005) *could* serve as wage compression forces in the United States.

We also choose to rely on the workforce development system for the advancement of low-wage employees rather than on firms to provide upgrade training on site. As Giloth (2004c, p. 3) underscores, employers in the United States invest approximately 2 percent of annual payroll expenses in training, mostly for higher level workers, compared to a 6 percent investment by employers in other advanced economies. We *could* choose to use tax policy to subsidize or fund employers to provide and financially reward expanded advancement training for frontline workers. As Streeck (1997, 205) argues, "Workplace training, while undoubtedly economically beneficial, flourishes only when its provision is largely removed from rational-economic calculation by a socially and legally obligatory training regime."

We also *could* choose to help firms, perhaps aided by business associations and the federal government, to understand their stake in society more generally. For example, every one percentage point decline in the aggregate unemployment rate is now associated with around a 2 percent increase in output (Ehrenberg & Smith, 203, p. 533). As Hart (2005, p. 10) finds, "in certain situations, preventing pollution through process or product redesign could actually save money, reduce risk, and even improve products for the firm." Crudely, improving economic and social conditions in local communities stands to improve the bottom line in local firms at the same time.

Perhaps we even need multiple "bottom line" metrics: financial, societal, and familial—in effect, *profit and household* writ broadly. As Streeck (1997, 216) cautions, "Where justice is pursued only insofar as it fits economic needs, it will very likely fail to generate the legitimacy and trust an advanced economy requires to perform well." More broadly still, improving the economic mobility of low-wage workers means more discretionary income to spend on consumption, more tax revenue, and less federal and community money and energy spent on income transfer solutions. Just as U.S. firms are now forced to engage outside their national boundaries to remain productive, maintenance of high productivity will increasingly require firms to engage outside company boundaries with the economic and social conditions of the communities in which they are embedded.

Regarding public education strategies and policies, we now choose to view schools as atomistic institutions that influence mobility solely through intergenerational processes. As such, we "reform" schools and students, blaming these actors for educational failure rather than understanding them to be integral parts of interinstitutional networks. School districts and schools *could* systematically engage local firms as partners toward realizing the short- and longer term benefits of retaining and preparing a viable workforce and informed citizenry. Such active engagement might improve working conditions such that Rachel Quinn would want to show her teenagers her work environment (Chapter 6). Representatives of school districts in alliance with local businesses also *could* advocate with policymakers to recognize that schools fundamentally influence intra- as well as intergenerational economic mobility. As such, state budgets for enriching or equalizing programs, such as Early Start, Head Start, and after-school programs for children and adolescents *could* be block-grant funded in a K–20 continuum.[1] Current funding for childcare and preschools through the Childcare and Development Block Grant does not adequately meet the needs of at least two hundred thousand children (McGarvey, 2004). Improved child care and preschool and after-school services, possibly through business and government funding as well as business involvement in programs and curricula, *could* thus foster the mobility efforts of parents as well as the academic futures of children.

Finally, we still choose to design public policy according to the stubbornly persistent, old paradigm categories of "deserving" and "not deserving," ignoring the fact that middle- and higher income families receive numerous welfare benefits through tax policies such as interest deduction on home mortgages and delayed taxation for pension funds until retirement when assessment rates are lower. Firms are the beneficiaries of similar welfare benefits. As Katz (2001, p. 179) reports, "Pension contribution deductions cost the government $69.6 billion in foregone revenue in 1996," half of which could have come from firms. We also still choose to design and fund social programs through the structure of disparate bureaucratic silos. We *could* choose to create structures that would provide integrated and fluid responses to persistent and emergent social needs. Along these lines, a few state governments have merged departments of welfare and labor into departments of working families. In Giloth's (2004c, p. 16) view, we *could* choose to forge policy according to "performance regimes" of institutions enmeshed in a "broader civic context of relationships, networks, and leadership" that respond to human needs rather than organizing policy around "employment regimes" that inherently perpetuate bureaucratic relations and the status quo.

Regarding principled choice making more broadly, political theorists Gutmann and Thompson (1996, p. 18) hold that moral disagreement about such choices typically revolves around the distribution of *perceived* scarce or limited resources and human generosity or lack thereof, but also around "incompatible values, and incomplete understanding." Miller (1999) similarly highlights the historic disagreement about whether the fundamental, guiding value of a democracy is social justice or personal freedom, and elsewhere (2003) emphasizes that the hard political decisions or judgments about what ought to be, when several options are open and there is disagreement about the best one, involve facts, preferences, and moral principles. According to Stone's urban regime analyses, "Adequate financial resources, access to authority, and common ideas are necessary for durable coalitions to form and last around particular policy issues" (Giloth, 2004c, p. 16). And as Wuthnow (2005, p. 355) maintains, "The most effective times of [democratic] renewal are ones in which policies and programs challenge fundamental assumptions about individual identities and responsibilities."

Choices about economic mobility strategies then must be made by locating or constructing shared meanings about justice and social justice, freedom, interdependence and community, and reciprocity and trust in democratic governance. The landmark economic success of the Tupelo, Mississippi community, as a result of its collective versus individualistic orientation to business, education, and the social environment (Putnam, 2000), may be a model to emulate more broadly. As Charles Tilly (2004, p. 3) argues, "partial integration of interpersonal trust networks into public policies is a necessary condition of democracy." Choices will also need to be directed at just processes *and* just outcomes.

FROM OLD MOBILITY MYTHS TO NEW
MOBILITY OUTCOMES

Given the notion of public will, we see that the myths we dissect in Chapter 2–opportunity, meritocracy, and individual responsibility–need to be countered by the philosophical and distributive principles underlying the new view of mobility: those of context and shared power, trust and reciprocity, equity and equality, and social relatedness and relational responsibility.

Opportunity, merit, and atomistic individual responsibility congeal in the old paradigm myths that persist in institutional policies and practices, including those of the state, as we discuss fully in Chapter 2 and illustrate through family experiences with workforce development programs and networks (Chapter 5), firms (Chapter 6), and children's schools (Chapter 7). Actually, the concept of the self-made, lone-wolf, independent man (generally a gendered concept) underlies all three myths. Although it is understandable that our country's frontier history and contemporary interest-oriented market economy both strongly influence our proclivity to think of ourselves as atomistic, personally free, and individually responsible, it is puzzling that other historical realities are underemphasized in popular and policy discourse. For example, considerable generosity, collaborative effort, and sharing of resources took place in frontier times. Life was hard and settlers banded together to ensure survival and prosperity alike. Somewhat later craft guilds and cooperatives developed as communal forms of production. Currently, social relations in firms, participation in community associations and groups (Putnam, 1995), and "civic capacity," as the "sustained ability to overcome local divisions and fragmentation to pursue an accepted social purpose" (Giloth, 2004c, p. 19), are similarly necessary to the survival and prosperity of all. Yet deleteriously for so many, the myths and manifestations of excessive individualism persist. As Katz (2001, p. 96) reports, "In 1989, Democratic pollster Mark Mellman's survey of Americans on family values concluded that 'the single most widely shared value in this country is that people ought to be responsible for their actions.'" The fact that an Internet search for "personal responsibility" in November 2005 results in 4,750,000 entries underscores this survey's findings.

Could we write this book or live our daily lives if the labor market does not include the kinds of jobs that the hard-working parents here, and millions like them across America, hold? We don't think so. Could you do your work and live your life as well without the existence and products of these jobs? Probably not. For example, Kevin McDonalds's job produces the magazines and books that we use. The jobs of Hard Working Blessed, Tasha Jones, Tisha Shanks, Mike Jeremy, Sam Gates, Micarla Stewart, Nasir Winters, and Lucky Miracle give us the steel parts, hoisting equipment, refrigerator and air-conditioning compressors, propane gas canisters, plumbing rivets and washers, and electronic equipment that we need for our homes and businesses. The construction jobs of Randy Jackson, Ahree Raca, Nasir Winters, Joseph Faithful, and Rachel Quinn result in the interiors and exteriors of buildings that house our families, stores to keep the economy going, and displays and meeting rooms at our professional and academic conventions and conferences. Teresa Russell's and Ahree Raca's jobs keep our rental cars in good order and Mike Jeremy's job results in well-managed parking lots for our vehicles while we work or shop. The customer service jobs of Isabell Smith, Wendy Delvalle, and Aida Gomez give us easy, time-saving Internet and phone management of our orders and bills. Shanquitta Tucker's and Rachel Quinn's grocery jobs and Hard Working Blessed's fast-food job provide meal alternatives when we haven't time to cook. When we receive indecipherable medical and indemnity bills or insurance statements, Maya Vanderhand's, Isabell Smith's, Aida Gomez's, Ayesha Muhammad's, Wendy Delvalle's, and Loretta Lopez's jobs enable us to navigate this perplexing terrain. Jane Jenkins's job provides horticultural advice and lawn service and Elizabeth Seabrook's biological research job contributes to improvements in our environment. Tasha Tracy's and Joseph Faithful's security service jobs provide safe environments for large events and Loretta Lopez's job helps to solve the mysteries of our annual income tax returns. Aida Gomez's job provides developmental childcare for our children while we work and Lucky Miracle's and Lynn Walker's jobs keep our children's schools and our office buildings clean and orderly. Finally, when we are ill or need an operation Shanquitta Tucker's and Tasha Tracy's hospital jobs provide us with night-and-day nurse's aide services and meals and Elizabeth Seabrook's job enables us to have follow-up home health care.

Is it fair that the parents in and like those in this book work full time in jobs that benefit society yet do not provide a family-sustaining income? Doesn't this fact really mean that it is not so much that there are low-wage jobs as jobs that just happen to pay low wages?[2] This conundrum leads us to ask again, What about reframing the idea of personal responsibility as "responsibility for persons"? What about further reframing "corporations," which Bowles and Gintis (1987, p. 16) define as "the most powerful form of collective organization in contemporary capitalism," as "communities"? Such reframing forces attention to the interdependence between the efforts of each of us in our jobs and the smoothness of everyone's daily life; in effect what Osterman and colleagues (2001, p. 11) describe as "a manifestation of service to the community for the common good." In the spirit of mutual responsibility and interdependence then, what do all families, including and perhaps especially low-income families, deserve? Enriching schools. Decent jobs. Family-supporting wages. Future mobility for their children. In short, real opportunity to be a full part of American democratic life.

We view this argument as a charge to each of us to make good on our basic American values, principles and humanity, as we find that Kochan (2005), Osterman and colleagues (2001) and Reich (2002) similarly suggest. We need to recognize that we are all vitally interrelated—that we *should be* the "United" States, not what one of our typos presciently identified—the "Untied" States. We need to recognize that we are able to build a strong country in the twenty-first-century world only if we base it on reciprocity and trust. And we need to consider retooling our iron ethos of individual freedom and responsibility into a more flexible, dynamic ethos of cooperation, collaboration, and mutuality: simply put, shifting assumptions, policies, and practices from personal responsibility to relational responsibility. Critically, the interdependent work of children, families, schools, firms, and communities defines the future productivity of our country and the future well-being of its inhabitants.

The complexity of the ways in which the policy choices of our social institutions influence family economic mobility becomes increasingly obvious. When any element of this intricately interwoven tapestry becomes diminished, so do the others. The outcomes of inequity in *Jobs Aren't Enough* trumpet the need to enact a thoughtful and sustained agenda for action.

TOWARD AN AGENDA FOR FAMILY ECONOMIC MOBILITY

In light of the current strategies, philosophical positions, and theoretical premises described previously, we recommend a series of actions toward making family economic mobility real. Each aspect of this series heeds the charge that we follow in this book "to build theory for the more general case where contexts, structure, and individual actions interact and change together" (Granovetter, 2002, p. 54), and builds action items into that charge. Each aspect thus expands on the goal of *household and profit*, or what Osterman and colleagues (2001, p. 24) describe as a process of policy reform that is "guided by and must balance concerns for economic efficiency, for equality, and for the welfare of the whole society."

How can we simultaneously catalyze public interest in and forge dynamic solutions to this problem? Given that the mobility paradigm of the past no longer applies and that replacing it is the mandate of a just and productive society, we pose the following actions:

- The president would convene a bipartisan Blue Ribbon Commission focused on family economic mobility. Because multiple institutions intersect to affect economic mobility, this commission would include the following members at a minimum: workforce and economic development professionals; child-care, transportation, and mental health professionals; legislators and cabinet officials; business and corporate leaders; officials at philanthropic foundations and faith-based organizations; educators and scholars; tax experts; union officials; and families representing all income categories, weighted more heavily by those with low incomes. International experts should also be consulted. The American Assembly (Giloth, 2004b), the Task Force on Reconstructing America's Labor Market Institutions (Osterman et al., 2001), the Aspen Institute Roundtable on Community Change, the Saguaro Seminars (Putnam, 2000), National Governors Association Summits, and, at the state level, formation of the Massachusetts Work-Family Council in the Executive Office of Economic Development (Kochan, 2005), are deliberate efforts in this direction that could serve as models for the commission.
- The commission would launch a series of town hall meetings across the nation moderated by a high-profile individual who could garner media attention for the issue of family economic mobility. The meetings would seek local input about the nature and scope of the challenges to family mobility and elicit possible solution strategies. Following these information-gathering, stakeholder-intensive town hall meetings, the commission, or other body if more appropriate, would create an action agenda for family economic mobility. At a minimum such an agenda might promote the following new directions:
  - Reorientation of current tax credit and tax expenditure policies to enhance the mobility goals and efforts of low- and middle-income families.

- o Reorganization of employee-employer relations in firms and compression of disparate wage policies, possibly along the lines of the Norwegian model discussed briefly earlier.
- o Identification of firms like Ayesha Muhammad's and Sam Gates's and others across the nation that have devised ways to be socially responsible *and* productive, toward reinforcing them and expanding their numbers.
- o Establishment of multiyear initiatives focused on ensuring family economic mobility, with the stated intent of using evaluation findings from these initiatives to guide realignment and restructuring of funding streams and public policies to better support all families.
- The commission would also consider the establishment of a federal interdepartmental body focused on the economic mobility needs of families. This crosscutting body would have both governance and research responsibilities. Modeling the trust and reciprocity of the new view of mobility, governance would be shared by high-level decision makers from the Internal Revenue Service and the departments of Education, Labor, Health and Human Services, Agriculture, Commerce, Housing and Urban Development, Justice, and Homeland Security. In terms of its research responsibility, this interdepartmental body would identify a set of relational, inter-institutional measures of the nation's progress on family economic mobility. It could use current efforts to develop common measures of adult educational and workforce development underway in the departments of Education, Labor, Housing, and Health and Human Services as a partial guide. The nascent collaborative work of these departments could be strengthened by designing comprehensive measures of economic mobility based on the ways in which families intersect with other major social institutions. Indexes such as the European Union's "Indicators for Social Inclusion" and the International Labor Organization's "Decent Work Development Index" and "Employment Quality Index" may provide more comprehensive models.
- The commission or interdepartmental body would then identify a clearinghouse that will share the research data, disseminate and publicize the findings, and develop policy advocacy strategies to ensure that the agenda for family economic mobility remains in the forefront of the minds, hearts and actions of policymakers, employers, state and federal officials and representatives, and the general public.

The ethnographic findings in *Jobs Aren't Enough* show what is needed from policy, public and philosophical spheres to create economic mobility for the far too many families in today's America without it. We urge others to use this information to forge further theory about economic mobility and use that theory to inform research, advocacy and action toward the development of democratic policies, programs, and institutions that will ensure economic security for all working families.

Afterword

What Lies Ahead for the New Orleans Families after Hurricane Katrina?

HURRICANE KATRINA STRUCK at the end of August 2005, just as we submitted *Jobs Aren't Enough* to the publisher. From the barrage of press information we knew that the New Orleans families in this book lived in parts of the city that were particularly hard hit. We also knew that despite steady efforts to work full time, attend upgrade schooling, pursue careers, and raise their children well, the families had few resources to draw on to weather daily challenges, much less a disaster like Katrina.

In the months following Katrina, although we received some secondhand information from our contacts in New Orleans, we were unable to reach the families by telephone. Their phone numbers were either disconnected, out of service, or yielded the repeated message that "all circuits are busy," consistent with the devastated infrastructure in the city. Thus in February 2006, five and one-half months after the hurricane, we returned to New Orleans to see firsthand how the families' homes, schools, and work environments had fared. We also hoped to learn more about the families' whereabouts.

As prepared as we thought we were by post-Katrina reports, we were awestruck at the widespread level of destruction throughout the city as we traversed most of New Orleans's 181 square miles. We traveled mile after mile after mile on deserted streets that consisted of wind- and flood-demolished homes, overturned cars and boats, uprooted trees, caved-in roofs, piles of debris, and gutting and mold-removal service ads on lampposts. The city's infrastructure still featured potholes, sinkholes, few working traffic lights, and according to a number of conversations, relief money and promises of work that do not reach the residents. Wires hung dangerously in some areas, street signs were missing or lopsided, and schools, child-care facilities, hospitals, restaurants, shopping malls, and grocery stores remained closed and deserted. Even the French Quarter, publicized as fully operational, evidenced many stores, eating establishments, and hotels not yet open. A few facilities with new "Now Open" signs, perhaps in hopes of Mardi Gras patronage, showed "Help Wanted" signs in the windows.

Perhaps most noticeable was the absence of people. Although 130,000 of the almost half-million residents have returned to the city (Katz, Fellowes, & Mabanta, 2006), many are students who live and take classes in downtown hotels, rather than permanent residents. Usually heavily trafficked streets were without pedestrians or vehicles, except for police patrol cars, and most neighborhoods were completely or almost completely empty. In some neighborhoods, lone buzz saws, bulldozers, backhoes, and cranes provided an almost eerie background hum. With heavy hearts at this unbelievably devastated landscape, we canvassed the families' home and work environments.

Hurricane Katrina uprooted Elizabeth Seabrook's eighteen-month medical technology program that was going to take her forty-eight months to complete, at best. She was living in her "dream" house, affordable because of a Section 8 housing subsidy. The house, in which Elizabeth and her two preschool-age children lived in a second-floor apartment, was declared "Right-of-Entry for Debris Removal" on February 6, 2006. Located on the elevated side of a Gentilly-area street, this was perhaps the only one of the families' homes that might eventually be reconstructed. However it is not certain whether the owner will be able to afford required repairs or continue to qualify for Section 8 housing status. The house across the street was completely demolished. Moreover, Elizabeth's neighbor told us she has been on the FEMA trailer waiting list for five months, despite the fact that she's a state employee and cares for a profoundly disabled daughter. As of February 9, 2006, 21,039 FEMA trailers had been requested for New Orleans; only 3,342 are occupied (Steinhauer & Lipton, 2006).

Elizabeth's medical technology program is holding classes, but we learned that she was not enrolled in fall 2005. Her children's preschools are closed, as are most public elementary schools in the city, and her mother's multi-story assisted living facility in the devastated eastern section of New Orleans was vacated. A lone rusting wheelchair sat on the pavement outside the facility entrance. Grass growing in the cement parking lot, downed light poles, and puddles of standing water announce that Elizabeth's "plum" worksite, which offered flexible part-time employment for full-time students, is closed.

Rachel Quinn's public housing project is blocked off and enclosed by a six-foot-high barbed wire fence. The Housing Authority of New Orleans (HANO; www.hano.org) reports that the facility sustained several feet of standing water damage, although one small part (not Rachel's part) experienced no unit flooding and little wind damage. We learned from a construction union contact that, as one of the 105,000 New Orleans residents without access to cars to leave the city (Muro et al., 2005), Rachel remained in her unit during the storm. She was later evacuated to the Superdome to join 25,000 others without food, water, or electricity (Knauer et al., 2005) and was eventually transported to an east coast city where her daughter is in military service. In terms of Rachel's pre-Katrina construction employment, as problematic as it was, it may be similarly problematic if she returns to New Orleans. The union contact told us that construction work is plentiful for residential, but not yet commercial, facilities, in part because few journeymen have returned to the city. Carpentry for trade show events, which was Rachel's work, is virtually nonexistent at present. The convention center expects to reopen in June 2006.

Nasir Winters was struggling mightily in the years before Katrina to pursue his passion—a welding career—and simultaneously care for his two preschool-age children. A neighbor told us that Nasir's mother, with whom he lived at our last contact, remained in her house during the hurricane but left for a southwestern state several days later. The neighbor was not sure whether Nasir accompanied her or not. A U.S. Army Corps of Engineers sign on the door of his mother's ground-floor apartment in a two-family rental house stated on October 22, 2005, that the house was a "Non-Qualifying Property" for the "Blue Roof Program," a federally funded temporary roofing program (www.fema.gov). The tenant in the upstairs apartment said that the owner announced he will begin to collect rent again on March 1, 2006, but she did not know if Nasir's mother intends to return. The tenant predicted that if Nasir's mother does not return by March 1, 2006, the owner will likely rent the downstairs apartment to someone else—with or without the refurbishment it needs because of severe roof and water damage. What employment possibilities await Nasir if he returns? Although the construction union contact reported that welding skills are in high demand because of the need to construct new flood wall sheeting on the levees, the school that he planned to attend went out of business.

Before Katrina, Joseph Faithful was in a precarious position as a newly self-employed construction worker with a wife and two infants to support, one of whom has serious health concerns. The family's half of a rental house in the Lower Ninth Ward was destroyed and the family can't return to the apartment complex in New Orleans East that they lived in earlier because it too is in ruins. Although residential construction work is ample in New Orleans, start-up firms like Joseph's are not likely to receive contracts. The family's church would likely be a resource for them, but as one of the first to reopen will be besieged with requests.

Tasha Tracy's father, in a neighboring Gulf state, informed us that Tasha, her children, and her extended family relocated first to live with relatives in Texas and more recently to another relative's small apartment in a coastal Louisiana town. Her mother's home in the Lower Ninth Ward, where Tasha lived with her two young children, was designated "No Entry" by the inspection team and appears unlivable. We saw no sign that other families in the notoriously devastated area have returned to their homes. In terms of Tasha's goal to get nursing training, the near future demand may be low as many of the nursing and convalescent homes are closed, and some of the training facilities will never reopen.

The stories in this book show that even before Katrina the environment in New Orleans often deterred or countered the productivity of families. A Brookings Institution report characterized pre-Katrina New Orleans as a "racially divided, low-wage metropolis built on a marsh in hurricane country" (Muro et al., 2005, p. 2) that has experienced a steady downward population trend since 1970 (p. 4). African Americans made up 84 percent of the New Orleanians who lived below the poverty line (Berube & Katz, 2005). The average neighborhood poverty rate for public housing residents in the city, like Rachel Quinn and her family, was 74 percent (Berube & Katz). The median household income in New Orleans before Katrina was just over $30,000 (Katz, Fellowes, & Mabanta, 2006).

Making matters worse, the city's economic infrastructure was also declining. New Orleans's share of metro area jobs dropped from 66 percent in 1970 to 42 percent in 2000, and the remaining jobs shifted from a substantial manufacturing sector to predominantly service and retail sectors (Muro et al., 2005). This shift disproportionately disadvantaged African Americans, such that career-building employment was less available as a route out of poverty. In 2003, the average annual pay in half the metro-area jobs fell below the national average (Muro et al., 2005). Closely related, the New Orleans educational system is extremely weak (see Chapter 7), further limiting access to jobs that do exist. And for the children, only 15 percent of the 117 public schools had reopened as of February 2006 (Katz,

Fellowes, & Mabanta, 2006). The New Orleans School District announced that most of the public schools scheduled to open before fall 2006 are high schools (www.nops.k12.la.us). The youngest children seemed most forgotten. Empty playgrounds and child-care programs were prominent features of the landscape.

Can New Orleans be a real home for the New Orleans families in this book? Can it provide them with the opportunities they sought and the supports they needed even before Katrina?

Considering the extensive and pervasive devastation we encountered almost six months after the storm, the amount of time it's taking for the city to rebound, and the fact that people need to have a place to live and schools for their children before they can hold and keep a job, returning to New Orleans may or may not be an option for them. Hurricane Katrina dramatized the ineptness of federal, state, and city governments (Knauer et al., 2005) and draws attention to the preexisting fragility of residents affected by this terrible storm and its bungled aftermath. Structural connections among "helping institutions" and residents both were and remain tenuous, too late, or nonexistent. As countless reports document, housing aid, school openings, and employment opportunities are not forthcoming for many families (DeParle, 2005).

In sum, although Hurricane Katrina may seem like a unique crisis, the pervasive institutional failures in New Orleans are not unlike the inequities and inequalities that all the families in this book confront. Even though we do not know for certain what lies ahead for the New Orleans families, *Jobs Aren't Enough* makes it clear that their advancement efforts, and those of others like them across the United States, need to be embedded in resource-rich environments that offer education, housing, employment, and wages that foster real economic mobility.

Roberta Rehner Iversen
Annie Laurie Armstrong
New Orleans, February 16–19, 2006

REFERENCES

Berube, A. & Katz, B. (2005). *Katrina's window: Confronting concentrated poverty across America.* Washington, DC: Brookings Institution.

Katz, B., Fellowes, M. & Mabanta, M. (2006). *Katrina index: Tracking variables of post-Katrina reconstruction.* Washington, DC: Brookings Institution.

Knauer, K., Fanning, E., Cadley, P., Bellovin, I., Fenton, M.M., & Carr, B.C. (2005). *Hurricane Katrina: The storm that changed America.* New York: Time Books.

Muro, M., Liu, A., Sohmer, R., Warren, D., & Park, D. (2005). *New Orleans after the storm: Lessons from the past, a plan for the future.* Washington, DC: Brookings Institution.

DeParle, J. (2005, October 11). Liberal hopes ebb in post-storm poverty debate. *The New York Times*, A1, 18.

Steinhauer, J. & Lipton, E. (2006, February 9). Storm victims face big delay to get trailers. *The New York Times*, A1, 24.

Appendix A

*Frequently Asked Questions about the
Research in this Book: Research Design*

**How did we come to study economic mobility through these
twenty-five families?**

We gained entrée to the families and auxiliaries in this book through an eight-year
five-city[1] workforce development demonstration called the *Jobs Initiative*, created and
funded by the Annie E. Casey Foundation. To counteract labor market problems such as
skills mismatch, spatial mismatch, and race discrimination (Holzer, 1996; Jargowsky,
1997; O'Connor, Tilly, & Bobo, 2001), the demonstration aims to improve the employment and retention of young-adult job seekers in impoverished inner-city communities,
thereby helping children as well. As such, the demonstration is organized around local
and regional particularities yet retains a national focus through its overarching design
(Giloth, 2004a; Giloth & Phillips, 2000). Five key components comprise each city's effort: (1) civic infrastructure, (2) an appropriate development intermediary (called here
a "workforce intermediary"), (3) a designated impact community, (4) job projects, and
(5) job policy reform (Hebert et al., 2002). In effect, the demonstration systematically
crafts new program designs and organizational partnerships in concert with local needs
and capacities toward the dual goal of poverty alleviation and economic development
at both individual and community levels (Giloth, 1995).

Specific to this book, a variety of existing and new job-training programs affiliate
with or are created in conjunction with the local workforce intermediaries because their
program services correspond to local industries and markets that analyses consider robust for "good jobs." Most of the programs the key parents attend are freestanding,
independent programs that serve job seekers beyond those associated with the demonstration. As Chapter 5 shows, these programs range from "rapid attachment" welfare-
to-work programs to short-term skill training to intensive, long-term skill training in
vocational institutes or community colleges. Still, given the "work first" orientation of
programs under the sole auspices of TANF and WIA, the programs here may offer job
seekers somewhat easier access to skill training.

Instead of establishing fixed "eligibility criteria," the job programs explicitly target
services to economically disadvantaged residents of the cities' impoverished neighborhoods: for example, women on welfare, incumbent workers, single men, or any
low-income resident in the region. The general criteria emphasize but are not limited
to younger workers, ages eighteen to thirty-five, because of the Foundation's interest
in improving the well-being of young children (Fleischer, 2001). The programs also
deliberately target job seekers of African American descent and others from underrepresented minority and immigrant groups whose previous job pathways may have been
constrained by discrimination or insufficient acculturation.

Reports from the national evaluation team provide informative demographic and
performance data about participants, rates of job placement, wages and benefits,
rates of job retention, and advancement across the five demonstration cities (Abt

Associates & New School University, 2000; Fleischer, 2001; Hebert et al., 2002; Hebert, St. George, & Epstein, 2003). These findings stimulated the Foundation to try to understand more deeply about how parents' work and children's welfare intersect. Ethnography is the method of choice for such exploration, as it can reveal the subjective, interpretive perspective of families as they live their lives over time. Roberta Iversen was awarded an initial grant from the Foundation[2] to conduct ethnographic research in two of the demonstration cities for a period of eighteen months (Iversen, 2002). Subsequent grants expanded the research to twenty-five families in five demonstration cities. The ethnographic research on which this book is based is explicitly *not* an evaluation of the demonstration. In *Jobs Aren't Enough*, the job-training programs simply provide a platform from which to explore and articulate processes of family economic mobility.

Who are "I" and "we"?[3,4]

After the research began in January 2000, I (Iversen) constructed a research team across the five cities that consisted of eight local field researchers from diverse backgrounds and disciplines that include anthropology, urban studies, social work and social welfare, public administration, and one who describes herself as "from the poverty community." I directed, led, and joined these eight in continuous fieldwork between January 2000 and summer 2003. Annie Laurie Armstrong also served as the Seattle field ethnographer, and we wrote Chapter 6 with one of the Philadelphia researchers and doctoral analysts, Michele Belliveau.

Ethnographers, as all researchers, bring different lenses to their field work. The theoretical and applied lenses of the multiethnic field ethnographers in this research include those of the critical resistance movement (New Orleans), housing, employment and child welfare (Seattle), lived poverty and state-level workforce development (Milwaukee), cultural anthropology (Milwaukee), child development and immigration (Philadelphia), and social welfare and urban poverty (St. Louis and Philadelphia). Three primary doctoral research analysts add the lenses of postmodernism and urban geography, institutionalism, and immigration theory. The authors add the lenses of institutionally and socially embedded service provision (Armstrong) and a sociostructural, institutionalist perspective on urban poverty and mobility (Iversen). The Foundation's historic focus on child well-being infuses the field and analytical work. Despite the stance that only "like" researchers are able to get the full story, our experience was similar to Whyte's (1981): that as long as one expresses genuine interest in a person's experience, the fact that the researcher is "different" is expected by the respondent, not alienating. Moreover the presence of multiple researchers in our research allows more rapid identification and questioning of the various biases. For example, one field researcher was hyper alert to potential child abuse in one family; in her words she has "a particular sensitivity to child abuse," whereas the doctoral analysts and I perceived less potential danger. Nevertheless we honored the researcher's caution and monitored transcripts and field notes for evidence that might otherwise be missed. Fortunately, over the years of active fieldwork no child abuse was substantiated, but heeding, as well as checking, the lens of each researcher is critical nonetheless.

Why do we use ethnography and how can we trust the findings?

Basic ethnography has its roots in the fields of cultural anthropology and structural sociology. Our research draws strongly on the sociological version of ethnography and is a blend of basic and applied ethnography. Applied ethnography yields not only new knowledge and theory that is characteristic of basic ethnography but also information with practical significance (Fetterman, 1998). The field study and methods characteristic of ethnography emphasize direct, systematic observation of social behavior in its natural setting. The term "field" itself signals that the scope of inquiry is broad, beyond a "subject," "informant" or "respondent." Moreover, ethnography is inherently interactive rather than unitarily or neutrally imposed (Burawoy et al., 1991).

As Burawoy (2003, p. 655) holds, ethnography "seeks to comprehend an external world both in terms of the social processes we observe and the external forces we discern." In Burawoy's "reflexive ethnography" and in Bourdieu's work (1977), reflexive signifies consciousness of the relation the researcher has to those she studies, as we discuss above, and also of the relation she has to a body of theory she shares with other scholars. Similarly, Burawoy conceptualizes field work as a "rolling revisit," whereby each visit is a conversation that is connected to earlier and portends subsequent ones. A rolling analysis thus results in a continuous dialog between theory and data.

Ethnography is a research method of choice when *how* questions are paramount. Ethnography is also indicated for the study of processes that develop and change over time (Yin, 1994). Whyte (1981) reinforces the importance of observing change or the absence of change over time. Accordingly, the key question for the ethnographic research was, *How does getting a "good job" affect parents, children, workforce programs, employers, and communities, and vice versa?* The key question for this book then evolved into, *What is economic mobility for low-income families in today's America and how do parents and children in such families experience it?*

Specific to the inquiry in this book, Leicht (1998) argues in a review of several "end of work as we know it" books from the 1990s that methods for collecting data on employees and the workplace need to change. Leicht recommends the detailed construction of individual work histories and careers, through both quantitative and qualitative means. He argues that "bottom-up" sampling techniques are most likely to capture the changing relationships among employers, subcontractors, and employees, while keeping individual work experiences intact in a tight empirical package. He recommends the same for new qualitative research in the workplace. Instead of going to organizations and studying who works for them, he suggests that qualitative researchers should concentrate on reconstructing individual workplace biographies, complete with accounts of the successes and failures associated with moves from one employer to the next (Leicht, 1998, pp. 43–4). As Becker (1998) holds, if we do not describe the full range of the *actual*, how can we imagine the full range of the *possible*?

Use of multiple sources and levels of data as well as multiple researchers and analysts, also called triangulation, increases the reliability of data (Marshall & Rossman, 1999). Use of ethnographic interviews and observations as reciprocal influences progressively and developmentally particularizes and deepens study findings. Becker (1996) argues that the merit of results reached through ethnographic research rest on their credibility and believability as well as on whether those results continue to command respect and belief over time. He emphasizes the importance of accurate data, in the sense of being based on close observation; precise data, in the sense of being close to the thing being discussed; and the breadth and depth of analysis, in the sense of knowing about a wide range of matters that impinge on the question under study. Padgett (1998) suggests likewise that rigor in qualitative research, including ethnography, is signified by "the degree to which a study's findings are authentic and its interpretations credible" (p. 88). Although our design is lodged in these research procedures, we discuss challenges and limits to the research method in the sections below.

How did we select the families and the relevant auxiliaries?

We began by identifying male and female respondents in the five cities, each of whom was participating or had participated in a job-training program affiliated with the work-force demonstration. Our sole determining criterion was that the key respondent, who we call "key parent," have one or more children. The key parents were selected purposively as follows: first, staff from the workforce intermediary and its program affiliates recommended potential informants who completed or were currently attending a training program, had located or were ready to look for jobs, and had resident children. Second, I culled this array of about twenty "potentials" per city for varied ages, ethnic backgrounds, education, training, employment sector, length of time employed, gender, and number of children, with the goal of enrolling five families per city. Third, after a staff member gained permission for me to contact them, I invited potential informants to participate in the study, aiming for as much demographic variation as possible. As the research progressed, we consciously selected respondents in varied positions on the mobility path. In effect, the selection process aimed to identify as full a range of cases as possible and to maximize the chance of the odd case turning up (Becker, 1998), as ethnography focuses on a diversity of cases rather than on variation in variables. Consistent with the ethnographic design, willingness to participate was the decisive factor for inclusion in the study (Stake, 1995). In fact, once "signed up" all twenty-five families remained in the research.

Although there is always the risk that the respondents were chosen to reflect well on the organizations that identified them (Becker, 1998), some organizations explicitly referred families to us whose pathways puzzled or worried them. One reason the organizations were able to refer these families is that they still had contact information for them. This indicator of relationship or sociability may have made the families more willing to engage in the ethnography. The status of the lead ethnographer as a university professor and the imprimatur of the Foundation also facilitated the participation of both organizations and respondents in the research. At the same time, the stance of partial "outsider" allowed the authors to probe the hard questions that emerged from the running contact between the local field researcher and participant(s). Regardless of the organization's view of the key respondent, the job-seeking parents here turn out to be similar to thousands of others placed in jobs by the training programs and to national samples as well (see Chapter 3). Families were given honoraria for their study participation in the form of a modest stipend for the first six months and periodic honoraria for follow-up contacts. They report using these honoraria for essentials or debt reduction. The key parents and their family members selected their own pseudonyms. The research team selected pseudonyms for the firms and organizations. Any resemblance of the pseudonyms to the real names of persons or organizations is unintended and coincidental.

To more fully understand the complex intersections between work and family well-being we sought the perspective of others beyond the key parents and their families. Thus we extended our inquiry to people and organizations that the parent, family members, and we identified as important to his or her family and work life: approximately forty per family, or over one thousand in all. These auxiliaries include, at a minimum, staff members and principals in the local intermediary organization; staff and principals in the affiliated or independent welfare-to-work and job-training programs; friends; neighbors; extended family; faith institutions; employers, work supervisors and coworkers; union representatives; city policy boards; and children's child care providers, school teachers and administrators. The University of Pennsylvania Institutional Review Board (IRB) approved a consent form for the key parents that gave the research team permission to talk with family members, organizations, and "anyone you identify as important to your family and work life." We needed additional "introductory" letters on Penn letterhead to gain access to children's schools but for other interviews verbal consent was sufficient for access.

The research team spent thousands of hours with the families and auxiliaries, over 120 days in children's schools, and a similar amount of time at or observing the parents' seventy-four firms. This inquiry is similar to what Duneier (1999) calls an extended place method, what Marcus (1998) calls multisited ethnography, and what Burawoy (2003) describes as a reflexive ethnography that is developed through synchronic comparisons in different spatial contexts. In its explicit attempt to link micro- with macro-processes (Burawoy et al., 2000; Willis, 2000), such inquiry begins with a core place or person and fans out organically to those in contact with, mentioned by, and relevant to the core person(s) along the dimension of interest—here, economic mobility and family well-being. In so doing, micro and macro intersect dynamically and reciprocally rather than deterministically. As Willis (2000) does, we locate the mediators of social processes and personal agency at the heart of this intersection.

How did we go about finding out what we found out?: Methods of data collection

The ethnographic team gathered prospective and retrospective data through both qualitative and quantitative methods, covering the time period from 1998 to mid-2003. We had continuous direct contact with the families from January 2000 to summer 2003, access to administrative data from 1998 onward, and historical reports from the families and auxiliaries covering earlier decades.

Qualitative methods include direct observation; participant observation, or firsthand involvement in the social world chosen for study; and informal interviews, sometimes called "hanging out," in person, by telephone, and occasionally by e-mail. We also conducted systematic in-depth and life-history interviews that addressed overarching as well as particularistic issues and questions with each participant at multiple time points. For example, we kept a running list of "puzzles" that emerged from our observations and interviews that we pursued in follow-up visits and conversations. We also listened for what we didn't think to ask. In addition, we conducted "elite" interviews with individuals who have particular expertise and perspective on the families or the phenomena of interest. We shadowed parents on their jobs and daily rounds and children in their schools, and we reviewed documents such as organization mission statements and program designs, informational and promotional material from organizations and firms, and media accounts. Life-history interviews and document review in particular yield retrospective data or what Burawoy (2003) calls the "archeological revisit," which is a method used to give historical depth to ethnography. We audiotaped and transcribed hundreds of hours of interviews and kept detailed field notes on the others.

We also used selected quantitative methods. At the initial, six-month, eighteen-month, and final family interviews we administered the Center for Epidemiological Studies Depression Scale (CES-D) to the key parent (Radloff, 1977; Radloff & Locke, 1986). The CES-D is an assessment tool for evaluating individuals' current levels of depressive symptomatology in relation to current levels within the general population. This short, noninvasive tool of twenty questions allowed us to examine the general emotional condition of these job seekers and new workers in relation to employment and family transitions. The CES-D is used increasingly in work and family research because depression and depressive symptoms are frequently identified as obstacles to finding a job or remaining employed, particularly among economically disadvantaged families (Ahluwalia et al., 2001; Danziger et al., 1998; Iversen & Armstrong, 2004; Wong, 2000). Although major (clinical) depression commonly acts as an obstacle to and during employment, depressive *symptoms* may not impede employment *unless* they are compounded by other challenges such as low levels of education; little work experience; insufficient wages; problems with transportation; health; or domestic violence; and correspondingly few mediating program or policy supports (Lennon, Blome, & English, 2001). Such multiple challenges are common among welfare recipients and other low-income workers such as the families in this book (Iversen & Armstrong, 2004). We hoped to administer the CES-D to the key parents' partners, but were unable to obtain a full set of responses during the first wave of the study and discontinued this effort in subsequent waves.

Program administrative data provided environmental background for the family context leading up to and during the period of study. Supplemental use of these data in the analyses ensured methodological triangulation. Quantitative cross-site data from the national evaluation (Abt Associates & New School University, 2000; Hebert et al., 2002; Hebert, St. George, & Epstein, 2003), a synthesis of evaluation and early ethnographic findings (Fleischer, 2001), and research and policy reports (Gewirtz, 2001; Gewirtz & Harrington, 2000; Giloth & Gewirtz, 1999) round out the demonstration's data sources. More broadly we drew on state-, district-, school-, and student-level performance data, OSHA data, Census data, and data from the Unemployment Insurance (UI) and Temporary Assistance for Needy Families (TANF) programs. In all, the dataset consists of more than ten thousand pages of transcribed audiotapes, field notes, and documents that yield "massive detailed descriptions" (Becker, 1998) for our analysis of the work and lives of the research families in their social, spatial, institutional, and policy contexts.

How did we figure out what we found out?: Analysis of the data

We organized the interview and observational data around the key parent respondent and his or her family. We conducted analyses throughout the study period to follow up on emergent themes and questions (Becker, 1998; Moffitt, 2000). A team of doctoral student research assistants and the authors analyzed the data using several techniques. We used a qualitative research software program called N-Vivo for initial categorical coding and retrieval of broad themes. We also constructed a SPSS file to calculate frequencies and simple comparisons (ANOVA) on descriptive variables. The core analytic strategy was mining the multiple data sources to develop narrative descriptions that document the range and complexity of the intersections between family-sustaining employment and family and community welfare. As we learned about the families' lives, we decided that a *diachronic narrative approach* (telling a story through time) best fit the purpose of the study, the initial conceptual framework, and the goal of expanded understanding about intersecting events and the dynamic importance of time. The theoretical argument in this book (see Chapter 2) also emerged out of the diachronic approach. The narrative constructions proceeded according to constant comparative analysis—an iterative process that begins inductively and includes the initial coding categories, becomes deductive through re-review of data to check codes and themes, and ends inductively with room for new themes to emerge. The narratives thus incorporate the "inside" perspectives of the respondents, or what institutional ethnographer Dorothy Smith calls their "constructed truths" (Campbell, 2003), and the "outside" reflections of the researchers and analysts. We call these twenty-five narratives the *Family*

Stories. Each family story is from twenty to forty single-spaced pages (references in Appendix C).

The local field researcher and I (Iversen) met with each family to review the written narrative in person before publication, a process that is called variously "member-checking" (Padgett, 1998), "valedictory revisiting" (Burawoy, 2003), "checking in" (Duneier, 1999), or the avoidance of "errors of attribution" (Becker, 1996). We asked families to check their story for both fact and interpretation. This step is a recent contribution to qualitative rigor (Duneier) that also forwards the conceptual premise that families are the primary experts on their lives. Changes resulted through a process of discussion and resolution. Where disagreement remained we identify it as such in the narrative. We struggle throughout the writing of the stories and this book to accurately render the complexity of the respondents' lives and environments (Anderson, 2002; Wacquant, 2002)—the unflattering and deviant alongside the admirable and normative—but to do so in ways that do not succumb to Pollyanna-ism on the one hand or "provide material for their regulation" (Burawoy et al., 2000, p. 15), invite labeling, or fuel simple categories of "deserving" and "undeserving" poor on the other hand.

The valedictory revisit was a remarkable intervention in itself—generally an empowering one. Many families told us that seeing their history over time and in one place led them to recognize their cumulative strengths and accomplishments and, for the first time, to recognize that some of their persistent challenges reside in social institutions and social policies outside themselves. In effect, the stories helped them to use what Mills (1959/2000) calls "the sociological imagination" to understand that personal troubles and public issues are inextricably interrelated. For some, reading the family story was a sobering experience as well, yet these parents reported that it was the truth, even if a bitter or hard truth. Serendipitously, reading her final narrative spurred Loretta Lopez to contact a therapist about depression—an action that earlier urging had not produced.

What is the public response to presenting the findings as "Family Stories?"

Anecdotal or journalistic stories are generally based on the "exception," which makes it easy for policymakers to dismiss them as anomalous or irrelevant to their broader constituencies. In contrast, when ethnographic analyses are reported in narrative form, the findings can be richly detailed, easily understandable, and compelling (Padgett, 1998). The "story" becomes an exemplar that reflects the range of human experience or the "rule," and thus may be harder to dismiss.

For example we learned that our research influenced policy efforts in each of the five cities, and possibly farther afield as well. New findings about family wage sufficiency led welfare-to-work and workforce program staff and policy advocates to press for living wage legislation. Amplified understanding about families' postemployment needs led to changes in housing policy favorable to families like those in this research. New information about education and mobility led to increased state funding for upgrade education and training.

At the implementation level, job-training programs added questions about debt and housing status to their assessment procedures based on our findings that debt accumulation and homelessness diminish the adequacy of new job incomes and threaten job retention. In turn, the national evaluator of the demonstration added questions about debt and housing to its randomized eighteen- and thirty-month follow-up surveys. Last, after learning how unpaid workdays and periodic layoffs diminish the adequacy of new workers' wages, training providers in several cities instituted more extensive postemployment support services and used the outcome data, together with narrative examples, to show legislators that sustained work supports can increase job retention and reduce returns to welfare.

Particular benefits of using narratives to influence policy seem to include the following. First, narratives are a particularly appropriate learning method for adults (Belenky et al., 1986), as evident in the long history of transmitting culture and knowledge through story (Maitino & Peck, 1996). Second, because stories are a mode of communication that uses lay rather than "scientific" language to convey complexity and diversity (Gans, 1999), the listener may find the reported experiences credible, which often produces an "Ahhhh, I didn't realize that" connection. The story's authenticity then may help to combat stereotypes and previously held myths or views. Finally, stories engage the listener's emotions and give the listener a cause. Personal narrative, in particular, demands the emotional engagement and sustained reflection (Hall, 1999) that are often precursors to action.

What challenges confront this ethnographic research?

Possible bias. Researchers are always on the lookout for possible bias. We used several methods to maximize authenticity and credibility in the face of the following threats or possible biases. First, time: prolonged contact helps to minimize reactivity or the effect of the researcher's presence in the field. In effect, the researcher becomes part of the woodwork over time. Second, use of multiple interviewers, analysts, reviewers, and the families help to counter researcher bias. Transcriptions helped us check for "leading" questions and identify possible bias emanating from a researcher's particular epistemology. The doctoral analysts, local researchers, and co-author of this book helped to identify my biases. Third, multiple interviews, interviewers, and informants help to counter respondent bias in the form of withholding or sharing information or, alternatively, agreeing with the perceived expectation of the researcher. For example, we learned from one of Wendy Delvalle's suggested auxiliary contacts that Wendy's husband had recently been in prison, which ultimately allowed us to probe the impact of this situation directly with Wendy, even though she had not previously revealed this information. Finally, time, engagement and reciprocity help to reduce the power imbalance that inheres in a research endeavor, even though nothing can completely eliminate it (Burawoy et al., 1991).

Possible methodological or ethical conflicts. Although asking questions is itself a form of intervention, respondents' needs often cry out for more active intervention that may raise methodological or ethical conflicts for the researcher. Most of our interventions involved simple provision of information, which is typical in ethnographic research. For example, a Philadelphia parent asked the researcher to locate information about subsidized diagnostic and counseling services for her learning-disabled son that the youth's beleaguered middle school was unable to provide. Small interventions also sometimes involved "in-kind" reciprocity such as helping the key parent or his or her spouse or partner with resumé construction or providing transportation to medical appointments. Heeding Monette, Sullivan, and DeJong's (2005) caution that intervention may at times be counterproductive to the research goal, we treated all interventions as emergent data, noting and reporting situations in which intervention was needed or given. In many cases these reports resulted in changes to program design, such as longer postemployment follow-up or adding questions to assessment materials. If research involves only occasional action or intervention and is reported as data, the rigor is not thought to be severely compromised (Monette, Sullivan, & DeJong).

Ethical conflicts are likely to emerge in ethnography in conjunction with the extended, intensive interaction with respondents. For example, in a few cases we learn vital information that we do not include in the family stories. We arrive at that decision through consultation with the local researchers, doctoral analysts, parents or auxiliaries, and the final narrative review. Finally, although many families wanted us to use their real names, we felt that pseudonyms would protect them, and especially their children, more fully.

Possible limits to policy and program influence. Most problematic for policy influence, ethnographic findings do not lend to "sound bites." The researcher needs time to convey the totality and complexity of findings and to engage the listener's mind and heart, but seldom has enough time in the political arena. A workforce specialist who was moved to legislative advocacy by Hard Working Blessed's family story at a research conference wished that the twenty- to forty-page family stories could be summarized in one or two pages to facilitate legislative attention, but this wish contradicted the reason he and others were influenced in the first place. Because narrative impact is cumulative and exponential, condensing risks hazards shared by statistical methods—loss of valuable information. At the same time, if a policy target will not read or hear the whole story, the onus is on the scholar to hone the narrative while losing the least amount of information possible.

Longitudinal ethnographic research is also resource intensive and time intensive. Unless the researcher—policymaker or researcher—program relationship is strong and sustained, such that emergent findings are shared and used iteratively, the lag time between the end of the research and the need to respond to constituents may be too great to influence volatile policies and programs. To provide real-time knowledge for use, it helps to use a "dialogical" approach that involves regular and formal written and verbal feedback to and from all relevant stakeholders throughout the research period (Ostrander, 1995), as we did.

Exiting the field. Although research texts and ethnographic monographs devote extensive attention to entering the field, exiting the field is seldom mentioned. Even though ethnographers attend closely to not becoming a full *part of* the culture they study, deep relationships form over time. We repeatedly reminded the key parents and their families, as well as the organizations with which we had repeated contact, that the research had a decisive end point. We created ending rituals that included small framed plaques[5] certifying participation in the "family study," books to the children, or gift certificates to the parents. We also sent each family its final, simply bound "Family Story" and disseminated the monograph (Iversen, 2002), even if the family had not participated in that wave of study. In every case, I included my business card so that I could be contacted in the future if need be, and some families have done so with tax questions, referral questions, or to update me on postresearch happenings. Still, several of the local researchers, who after all remain in the same city as the families, have experienced more protracted exits. They repeatedly clarify to the families that any information learned after June 2003 is *not* part of the research and is not included in this book. They have also endeavored to limit such contacts and in general have been successful in this. Departure may be psychically hard, however, on both parent and researcher, especially where strong relationships have been forged with the family's children. For this reason too we did not mandate an iron rule of "no further contact." We simply emphasized that further contact was not part of the research, and over time the families generally got too busy to pursue the research team.

Appendix B

Industry, Firm, Occupation, and Wage
Information and Projections

THE THREE TABLES in Appendix B provide detailed information about the industries, occupations (jobs), wages and wage adequacy in the seventy-four firms in which the key parents are employed during the research period, 1998 to mid-2003. The data presented in all three tables are discussed in full in Chapter 6.

Table B.1 presents descriptive data on characteristics of the parents' firms and jobs. Table B.1 also provides results of analyses of parents' wage adequacy in all seventy-four jobs, according to both federal poverty level (FPL) and Self-Sufficiency Standard (SSS) metrics.

Table B.2 hones in on wages and wage adequacy, providing data on change in both measures between each parent's first post-training job and last known job. Table B.2 also summarizes changes in wages and wage adequacy between the first and last jobs for the parent group as a whole. Taken together, Table B.1 and B.2 provide a wide-angle perspective on economic mobility in the context of the parents' jobs, firms, and industries.

Table B.3 looks at what the parents' mobility might be like in the future, through national and city data on projected employment patterns to 2012 and wage patterns in the parents' occupations and industries to 2003.

The data in the three tables are drawn from the ethnographic interviews, workforce program administrative records, firm information and promotional material, the North American Industry Classification System (NAICS 2002), the U.S. Census Bureau, and the Occupational Safety and Health Administration of the U.S. Department of Labor.

TABLE B.1. Characteristics of Parents' Firms and Jobs: 1998 to Mid-2003

NAICS industry[a] or firm [state] (parent)[b]	Parent's occupation	Parent's hourly wage[c]	Parent's wage adequacy[d]	Nonwage benefits	Type of firm	Size of firm[e]	Safety record[f]	Union presence	Firm issues
Manufacturing **Bindery** [WI] (McDonalds)	Floor person	'99: $9.76	105%FPL; 63%SSS	Comprehensive; variable eligibility	Private local company	80	No inspections found	Nonunion	No clear advancement path
Printing & Bindery [WI] (McDonalds)	Floor person	'99: $9.76 '01: $12.09	105%FPL; 63%SSS 142%FPL; 78%SSS	Comprehensive; cost share	Multinational corporation	360 local; 38,000 intl	3 "serious" violations in 2003	Union	Downsized 2000–03; closed 15 plants; cut 5000 jobs
Manufacturing Company [WI] (Jones)	Machine operator; Assembler (lateral)	'99: $9.84 '00: $10.01	145%FPL; 49%SSS 152%FPL; 50%SSS	Health insurance; not eligible for other benefits	Public company, national	123 local; 20,700 natl	1 "serious" violation in 2000	Union	Layoffs 2002; plant closed 2003
Product Manufacturing Company [WI] (Shanks)	Cell operator	'98: $7.86 '00: $9.71	84%FPL; 49%SSS 99%FPL; 61%SSS	Comprehensive; not enrolled	Subsidiary of multinational corporation	1900 natl	12 "serious" in 2001	Union	Layoffs; production decrease 2002
Steel Company [WI] (Shanks)	Spot welder	'00: $10.93 '01: $12.50	114%FPL; 69%SSS 157%FPL; 79%SSS	Comprehensive incl. funeral + child college; fully paid	Private company	824 local	7 "serious" in 2002	Nonunion	Layoffs 2002; plant closed 2003
Manufacturer [WI] (Shanks)	Spot welder	'02: $9.80	113%FPL; 62%SSS	Not known	Not known	Not known	No OSHA information	Not known	Layoffs 2003
Brass Co. [WI] (Shanks)	Not known	'02: $8.75 '03: $9.80	101%FPL; 55%SS 111% FPL; 62%SSS	No	Private company	205 local	2 "serious" 1998–2002	Nonunion	Company in downturn 2003

Company	Job	Wage	%FPL; %SSS	Insurance/Benefits	Company type	Employees	OSHA	Union	Notes
Steel Mill & Foundry [WI] (Blessed)	Crane & forklift operator; Grinder	'98: $11 '00: $13	118%FPL; 70%SSS 135%FPL; 82%SSS	Medical; self & family	Private company	Not known	4 "serious" in 1995	Nonunion	On-job injury & demotion; firm bankruptcy 2000–01
Printing Co. [WI] (Blessed)	Forklift operator; Supply superintendent	'00: $10.20 '00: $11	106%FPL; 65%SSS 115%FPL; 70%SSS	Comprehensive after 90 days	Private, employee-owned corporation	9000 state; 2000 intl	5 "serious" in 1992	Nonunion	Corporate art collection; perceived on-job racism
Metal Company [WI] (Blessed)	Material handler	'00: $12 '01: $13	125%FPL; 76%SSS 131%FPL; 82%SSS	Family plan; employee pay	Private company	Not known	7 "serious" in 2003	Some unions	Cutbacks 2001
Equipment Manufacturer [WA] (Jeremy)	Assembler	'99: $11.82^g '99: $11.50^h '00: $12.43	177%FPL; 55%SSS 140%FPL; 55%SSS 169%FPL; 54%SSS	Comprehensive	Public company; division of large public corporation (2002)	1800	15 "serious" and 1 "willful" in 1999; 2 "serious" in 2000	Nonunion	Local company had 390 permanent layoffs in 2001; on-job injury
Laser Company [PA] (Gates)	EDM operator	'99: $12.65	158%FPL; 77%SSS	Medical & life insurance only; cost share	Private company	46	No OSHA information	Nonunion	Company layoffs in 1999
Technology Management Co., Cable Division [PA] (Gates)	Machinist	'00: $14.25	174%FPL; 103%SSS	Comprehensive; cost share	Subsidiary of private foreign company	80 local; 900 natl	No OSHA information	Nonunion	Division dissolved 2001

(continued)

TABLE B.1. (*continued*)

NAICS industry[a] or firm|state|(parent)[b]	Parent's occupation	Parent's hourly wage[c]	Parent's wage adequacy[d]	Nonwage benefits	Type of firm	Size of firm[e]	Safety record[f]	Union presence	Firm issues
Technology Management Co., Electronics Division [PA] (Gates)	"Senior" machinist	'01: $16.90 '02: $17.50 '03: $18.10	240%FPL; 103%SSS 242%FPL; 106%SSS 241%FPL; 110%SSS	Comprehensive; co-pay	Subsidiary of private foreign company	100–130 local; 900 natl	"Serious" violations (1999–2003); 4 "other" violations (2003)	Nonunion	Globalized production & competition; parent corp. European; pays temps on par with permanent workers
Manufacturing Technology Company [PA] (Stewart)	Machine operator; Trainee	'00–'01: $11.70 '02: $15.70	166%FPL; 59%SSS 217%FPL; 79%SSS	Comprehensive	Public company	2800 intl	No OSHA information	Nonunion	Acquired by parent multinational in 2003; on-job injury
Beverage Company [PA] (Stewart)	Machine operator	'02: $13.50	187%FPL; 68%SSS	Not known	Local franchise of private regional company	200 local	No OSHA information	Not known	Offered job; laid off before began; economic downturn
Industry [LA] (Winters)	Welding helper	'01: $8.25	97%FPL; 111%SSS	Comprehensive; not eligible	Local subsidiary of large public corporation	6000 local	60 "willful" or "serious" violations (1996–2004)	Union	Largely dependent on Dept. of Defense contracts; serious safety concerns; global labor pool

Company	Position	Wage	%FPL; %SSS	Health insurance	Company type	Number	Violations	Union	Notes
Food Company [WA] (Miracle)	Assistant shipping & receiving manager	'99: $10.70 '03: $10.70i	131%FPL; 51%SSS 95%FPL; 39%SSS	Health insurance for self; full pay	Private company: wholesale & retail	41–50	Not known	Nonunion	No raises in 1999; allergens in job environment
Construction									
Construction Company-WI [WI] (Jackson)	Laborer; Office work	'00: $16.40 '01: $19	192%FPL; 70%SSS 224%FPL; 82%SSS	Union coverage (self + family)	Private, employee-owned company	600	33 "serious" violations since 1990; also job safety award	Union	
Construction Company- MO [MO] (Raca)	Dry-waller	'01: $13.18 '02: $14.38	138%FPL; 106%SSS 141%FPL; 100%SSS	Benefits available; did not use until second year	Private, employee-owned company	Not known	9 "serious" and "other" violations 1998–2002	Union	Seasonal layoffs
FFF Construction [WI] (Jackson)	Laborer; Office work	'01: $21.10	249%FPL; 91%SSS	Union coverage for family	Private company	100–200	5 "serious" since 2000	Union	
Construction Company-LA [LA] (Winters)	Laborer	'02: $10.25	118%FPL; 68%SSS	Not known	Private company	Not known	Not known	Not known	Fired; perceived racism
Church Construction Co. [LA] (Faithful)	Construction assistant	'02: $6.25 '03: $7.50	86%FPL; 41%SSS 86%FPL; 50%SSS	None	Church sponsored (private contractor)	>10	Not known	Nonunion	Informal arrangement; paid under table

(continued)

TABLE B.1. (*continued*)

NAICS industry[a] or firm [state] (parent)[b]	Parent's occupation	Parent's hourly wage[c]	Parent's wage adequacy[d]	Nonwage benefits	Type of firm	Size of firm[e]	Safety record[f]	Union presence	Firm issues
Stone Company [LA] (Winters) [Pretraining]	Helper	'00: $7	103%FPL; 46%SSS	Not known	Private company	Not known	Not known	Not known	Merger & name change 1997
Union [LA] (Faithful)	Hard carrier	'00: $10	147%FPL; 73%SSS	Ineligible for coverage	Trade union	Not known	Not known	Union	Insufficient work for the union tradesworkers
Union [LA] (Quinn)	Apprentice	'00: $10.76 '03: $13.56	154%FPL; 105%SSS 185%FPL; 136%SSS	Persistently ineligible for coverage	Trade union	Not known	Not known	Union	Insufficient work for the union tradesworkers
Events Company [LA] (Quinn)	Apprentice	See Union (above)	See Union (above)	Ineligible	Private company; union contractor	200	Not known	Union	Benefits only for company employees
Real Estate, Rental, & Leasing									
Rental Car Company [WA] (Russell)	Utility person	'00: $8.75 '03: $11.75	131%FPL; 63%SSS 202%FPL; 98%SSS	Comprehensive through Union	Subsidiary of public international corporation	11,400 intl; ~50 local	Not known	Union	Subsidiary bankrupt 2002; taken over by corporation
Rental Car Company [MO] (Raca)	Car detailer	'00: $8 '01: $8.50	98%FPL; 55%SSS 100%FPL; 59%SSS	Available; not used	Subsidiary of public international corporation	11,400 intl	Not known	Union; not belong	Subsidiary bankrupt 2002; taken over by corporation

Company	Job title	Wage	%FPL; %SSS	Benefits	Ownership	Employees	OSHA	Union	Notes
Retail Trade									
Tech Company [WA] (Smith)	Customer service rep I, II	'99: $10 '01: $13	125%FPL; 95%SSS 153%FPL; 123%SSS	Comprehensive; used medical + dental	Employee-owned public company; international	400+ local; 7800 intl	No OSHA violations	Nonunion; unsuccessful union drive	1300 layoffs in 2000–01; Branch closed 2001
Second Tech Company [WA] (Smith)	Data specialist	'01–'02: $13 (through Temp Agency)	149%FPL; 123%SSS	Not eligible for benefits	Private local company	100–200	No OSHA information	Not known	IT unemployment rate (2003) twice state average
Grocery-MO [MO] (Tucker)	Deli worker	'01: $7^i	49%FPL; 39%SSS	Not available (part time)	Private, family-owned company	17,000 state	4 "other" (2000–2002)	Union	Strike threat 2003
Oil Chain [WI] (McDonalds)		'01: <6 mo		Comprehensive; cost share; not eligible	Multinational corporation	53,000 intl	0.6 incidence	Not known	
Independent Pharmacy [PA] (Delvalle)	Pharmacy technician	'02: $10 '03: $14.25	138%FPL; 56%SSS 161%FPL; 80%SSS	Health insurance (only); after 3 mo	Independent business	Not known	No OSHA information	Nonunion	
Grocery-LA [LA] (Quinn)	Deli worker	'99: $7	105%FPL; 69%SSS	Not available	Independent family-owned grocery chain	325 local	No OSHA information	Nonunion	Owners operate several other chains too
Finance & Insurance									
Insurance Company [WA] (Vanderhand)	Personal lines operator	'99: $11.53 '03: $15	103%FPL; 94%SSS 122%FPL; 123%SSS	Comprehensive; cost share	Private company; local subsidiary	11,200 natl	No OSHA information	Nonunion	On-job injury; layoffs 2001, 2003; unit divestment 2003

(continued)

TABLE B.1. *(continued)*

NAICS industry[a] or firm [state] (parent)[b]	Parent's occupation	Parent's hourly wage[c]	Parent's wage adequacy[d]	Nonwage benefits	Type of firm	Size of firm[e]	Safety record[f]	Union presence	Firm issues
Safety Company [WA] (Smith)	Administrative assistant; (training for Office manager)	'02: $10.50[i] '03: $12	75%FPL; 31%SSS 136%FPL; 56%SSS	No benefits (part time); Comprehensive (full time); used medical/dental	Local branch of private national company	>10 local; 200 natl	3 "other" violations in 2004	Nonunion	Growth industry
Health Insurance Co. [PA] (Gomez)	Customer service rep	'01: $10 '02: $10.15	133%FPL; 56%SSS 116%FPL; 57%SSS	Comprehensive; remained on Medicaid	Local subsidiary of national corporation	2000 local	No OSHA information	Nonunion	Acquired by larger corporation (2002); lawsuit 2003
Financial Services Company [PA] (Muhammad)	Assistant, Bill distribution; Assistant, Group insurance	'01: $10.50[h] '03: $13.25	93%FPL; 34%SSS 112%FPL; 42%SSS	Comprehensive; self + family	Local subsidiary of national public company	30,000 natl	No OSHA information	Nonunion	Major industry restructuring 1980s to 2001; went public in 2001; quality company for minorities and women
Medical Billing Company [PA] (Delvalle)	Provider service rep	'01: $9.50	135%FPL; 53%SSS	Optional health insurance plan; full employee pay	Private company	500 natl	No OSHA information	Nonunion	Unusually strong employee focus
Medical Insurance Company [PA] (Delvalle)	Member service rep	'01: $12.31	175%FPL, 69%SSS	Comprehensive	Private company	10,000 natl	No OSHA information	Nonunion	

Collection Agency [MO] (Lopez)	Insurance collections	'01: $10.50	149%FPL; 76%SSS	Hospital-based agency; temp not eligible	Private nonprofit company	26,000 (parent company)	No OSHA information	Nonunion	
Information									
Military Facility [LA] (Tracy) [Pretraining]	Spreadsheet enterer	'01: $7	125%FPL; 53%SSS	No benefits	Federal, state, academic, & private industry consortium	Not known	No OSHA information	Not known	Temporary welfare-to-work internship
Library [MO] (Walker)	Tech I	'02: $8.75	86%FPL; 43%SSS	Comprehensive	State government	Not known	No OSHA Information	Nonunion	State funding cutbacks; layoffs
Administrative Support, Waste Management, & Remediation Services									
Temp Service-PA [PA] (Muhammad)	File clerk	'01: $8.25	72%FPL; 26%SSS	Some benefits	Temp agency branch	Branch of international temp service; 28,000 intl	No OSHA information	Nonunion	Financial probe & lawsuits in N. American affiliate
Temp Service-MO [MO] (Lopez)	Bank teller	'02: $8.08	112%FPL; 59%SSS	Not available	Temp agency branch	Branch of international temp service; 28,000 intl	No OSHA information	Nonunion	Financial probe & lawsuits in N. American affiliate
Lawn Service Company [MO] (Jenkins)	Customer service rep	'01: $8.50	86%FPL; 74%SSS	Not known; covered by husband's firm	Subsidiary of public company	<10 local; 4000 natl	Nonereported	Nonunion	Laid off just before 6-month eligibility period

TABLE B.1. (*continued*)

NAICS industry[a] or firm [state] [parent][b]	Parent's occupation	Parent's hourly wage[c]	Parent's wage adequacy[d]	Nonwage benefits	Type of firm	Size of firm[e]	Safety record[f]	Union presence	Firm issues
Medical Temp Agency [MO] (Lopez)	File clerk	'99: $8	120%FPL; 62%SSS	Not available	Subsidiary of public company	900 (parent company)	No OSHA information	Nonunion	*Forbes Magazine* acclaim for parent company
Second Medical Temp Agency [MO] (Lopez)	Clerical	'00: $11.50	169%FPL; 83%SSS	Not available	Branch of public company	380 natl	No OSHA information	Nonunion	Assignments were 3 months or less
Business Company[k] [MO] (Lopez)	Telemarketer	'01: $8	116%FPL; 58%SSS	Not available	Private company	Not known	No OSHA information	Nonunion	Work environment bad reputation
Research Co. Temp Service [MO] (Walker)	Computer-assisted telephone interviewer	'01: $8.50 '01: $8.50[i]	86%FPL; 42%SSS 43%FPL; 42%SSS	Not eligible	National staffing company	Not known	No OSHA information	Nonunion	Benefits only available to company employees
Cleaning Service [MO] (Walker)	Office cleaner	'01: $6.25[i]	31%FPL; 31%SSS	Not specified	Private company	4000 state; 1850 local	No OSHA record	Nonunion	
Security Firm [LA] (Tracy)	Security guard	'02: $6 '03: $7	105%FPL; 46%SSS 95%FPL; 53%SSS	Available; used after Medicaid expired	Multistate private company	Not known	No OSHA information	Not known	
Security Co. [LA] (Faithful)	Security guard	'01: Not known		Not available	Local private company	36	No OSHA information	Nonunion	
Communications Company [MO] (Raca)	Customer service trainee	'01: $8.75	103%FPL; 70%SSS	Not eligible; not complete probation period	Public international company	56,500 intl	2 "serious" violations in 2003	Nonunion	Restructuring; downsizing; outsourcing

Other Services

Church [MO] (Lopez)	Secretary	'02: $10^i	73%FPL; 73%SSS	Not available	Religious institution	Not known	No OSHA information	Nonunion	
Parking Company [WA] (Jeremy)	Parking attendant	'00: $8.50^i '03: $9.50^i	78%FPL; 30%SSS 51%FPL; 21%SSS	Not available	Private company	800	3 "other" violations (1993–2000)	Nonunion	Parking market downturn in 2001
Professional, Scientific, & Technical Services									
Tax Company [MO] (Lopez)	Tax preparer	'02: $6^i '03: $6^i	43%FPL; 44%SSS 41%FPL; 44%SSS	Not available	Private company; public filing in 2004	345	No OSHA information	Nonunion	Seasonal; 2002 acquired by multinatl corp (+ bought Rental Car Company)
Research Company [MO] (Walker)	Computer-assisted training interviewer	See **Research Co. Temp Services** (above)	See **Research Co. Temp Services** (above)	Not eligible; temp position	Branch of national nonprofit trust	100+ local (~80 temp); 7000–9000 natl	No OSHA information	Nonunion	Branch lost research funding (high dependence on federal research funds)
Research Facility [LA] (Seabrook)	Biological science technician	'01: $10.26^l '03: $10.26^l	102%FPL; 78%SSS 100%FPL; 78%SSS	Option to buy into a health insurance plan	Regional office of federal government department	2100 federal	No OSHA information	Nonunion	As part-time, no regular GS increases

(continued)

TABLE B.1. (*continued*)

NAICS industry[a] or firm[state](parent)[b]	Parent's occupation	Parent's hourly wage[c]	Parent's wage adequacy[d]	Nonwage benefits	Type of firm	Size of firm[e]	Safety record[f]	Union presence	Firm issues
Health Care & Social Assistance									
Childcare Center [PA] (Gomez)	Assistant teacher	'99: $6.75 '00: $6.75	101%FPL; 38%SSS 99%FPL; 38%SSS	Not available	Division of private company	~20 local; 200,000 multinatl	No OSHA records	Nonunion	Local corp owned until 2003; revenue fell; bought out by 2nd multinatl corp
Childcare, Inc. [PA] (Gomez)	Assistant teacher	'00: $7 '01: $7.50	100%FPL; 39%SSS 101%FPL; 42%SSS	Medical benefits; $50 cost share	Division of private company backed by venture fund	8 local	No OSHA records	Union	Division filed for bankruptcy in 2003; facility closed
Hospital-MO [MO] (Tucker)	Certified nursing assistant	'01: $10.20 '03: $11.12	120%FPL; 57%SSS 126%FPL; 62%SSS	Comprehensive; parent only + vision for kids	Private nonprofit hospital affiliate of multistate system	Not known	9 "serious" violations in 1995	Nonunion	Department of Commerce Quality Award
Hospital-LA [LA] (Tracy)	Dietary service worker	'01: $5.58 '02: $5.58	100%FPL; 43%SSS 97%FPL; 43%SSS	Available; not utilized	Community faith-based hospital	Not known	1 "serious" & 1 "other" violation in 1998	Nonunion	

Accommodation & Food Service

	Position	Wage	% FPL; % SSS	Health coverage	Ownership	Employees	OSHA	Union	Notes
FastFood [IL] (Blessed)	System manager	'02: $6.75	66%FPL; 43%SSS	Comprehensive; not eligible	Public franchise part of international corporation	39,000 natl + internatl	No violations	Nonunion	Litigation pending regarding unfair labor practices; wage/hour class action suits
Historic Hotel [LA] (Tracy)	Housekeeper	'02: $6.25	109%FPL; 48%SSS	Available; not utilized	Investment firm owns hotel	Not known	No OSHA information	Nonunion	
Boutique Hotel [LA] (Faithful)	Food & beverage service	'00: $10 '01: $10	147%FPL; 66%SSS 142%FPL; 66%SSS	Not available	Independent hotel owned by venture capital firm (1999)	Not known	No OSHA information	Nonunion	"Managed" [acquired] by out-of-state venture capital firm

Wholesale Trade

	Position	Wage	% FPL; % SSS	Health coverage	Ownership	Employees	OSHA	Union	Notes
Wholesale Company [WI] (Blessed)	Truck driver; Warehouse manager	'02: $10 '03: $12	115%FPL; 63%SSS 136%FPL; 76%SSS	Not known	Private company	12 million natl; 47 local	Not known	Not known	
Distribution Company [WI] (Jones)	Order picker	'00: $9.66 '00: $10.36	142%FPL; 48%SSS 152%FPL; 51%SSS	Comprehensive after 90 days; not used	Private company	Not known	No OSHA information	Not known	Mandatory overtime

(continued)

TABLE B.1. *(continued)*

NAICS industry[a] or firm [state] (parent)[b]	Parent's occupation	Parent's hourly wage[c]	Parent's wage adequacy[d]	Nonwage benefits	Type of firm	Size of firm[e]	Safety record[f]	Union presence	Firm issues
Education Services									
School District [WA] (Miracle) [2nd job concurrent with Food Co.]	Custodian	'00: $14.62 '01: 2 jobs '03: $15.70 '03: 2 jobs	178%FPL; 70%SSS 319%FPL; 116%SSS^m 177%FPL; 75%SSS 268%FPL; 114%SSS^m	Comprehensive; some mandatory, some optional	Public institution	Not known	2 "other" violations (1990)	Nonunion	Allergens in job environment; district financial problems 2002–03; staff cutbacks
Arts, Entertainment, & Recreation									
Video Casino [LA] (Winters)	Security guard	'02: $7^i	48%FPL; 94%SSS	Available; not used	Branch of private chain	Not known	No OSHA information	Nonunion	Target of anti-gambling activism
Transportation & Warehousing									
Courier Service [LA] (Faithful) [Pretraining]	Courier	'99: $4.25	107%FPL; SSS not applicable (single man)	Not available	Local private company	20	No OSHA information	Nonunion	Promotes minority business

Self-Employment

Trade-Export org. [WI] (McDonalds)	Start-up person	'02: No income	No income	Not available	Web-based self-employment	1	No OSHA information	Nonunion	Fragile self-employment
Maintenance Company [LA] (Faithful)	Start-up person	'03: No income	No income	Not available	Not yet incorporated	1	No OSHA information	Nonunion	Fragile self-employment

Key to typefaces: Italic typeface indicates an industry sector overall. Firm names in **bold** represent the initial post-training job.

[a] Industries are categorized according to the North American Industry Classification System (NAICS 2002). Available at www.census.gov/epcd/naics.html

[b] All firm and family names are pseudonyms. **Bold** firm names represent the initial post-training job; nonbold firm names represent subsequent jobs. Research states: [WI] = Wisconsin; [LA] = Louisiana; [PA] = Pennsylvania; [MO] = Missouri; [WA] = Washington.

[c] Wages given for each job are the parent's hourly starting wage and the ending or last-known wage. Unless specified otherwise, these are full-time wages.

[d] Wage adequacy relative to Federal Poverty Level (FPL; available at www.aspe.hhs.gov/poverty/figures-fed-reg.shtml) and Self-Sufficiency Standard (SSS; Wider Opportunities for Women, 2001, 2004). The SSS may *overestimate* sufficiency, as incomes are often not received for the full calendar year. The metric is based on full-time/full-year employment and also assumes that a spouse (if any) is working. Thus, even if the respondent's SSS score qualifies as "sufficiency," at or above 100%, unless the job is held for the year and/or unless the spouse or partner is earning a similar income, the family's total income *will not be sufficient.* Cautions in data interpretation include the following: (a) the second adult income is generally as precarious as the first; (b) the key parent's income is a useful and reliable "proxy" where two incomes are "possible," and an exact figure where only one income is possible; (c) the second parent's income is almost always more like the key parent's income than different from it (i.e., larger).

[e] Number of employees.

[f] Safety information based on OSHA records. Available at http://www.osha.gov/oshstats/index.html. Categories in descending order of severity: willful, repeat, serious, other-than-serious, unclassified, total.

[g] Temporary.

[h] Permanent.

[i] Part time.

[j] Second training program-related job.

[k] Third training program-related job.

[l] Part time during academic year; full time during summer.

[m] Wage adequacy of income from two jobs combined (70 hours/week).

General notes: (1) Many parents hold a second, or even a third, concurrent part-time job. These jobs are not included in this table or in the FPL or SSS calculations, as the critical point for mobility is how much a worker can earn at a single job. Having a second or third job generally precludes off-the-job advancement training. (2) In PA, WA, and WI, the SSS amounts to about one-third of the FPL advancement training. In MO and LA, the SSS amounts to about one-half the FPL. These differences illustrate the local inequalities created by setting the "poverty" metric at the federal level. (3) The SSS is not calculated annually in any of the states, and in many cases only one round of calculations has been completed. In states with multiple calculations, we use the one nearest to the year of research contact.

TABLE B.2. Changes in Parents' Wages and Wage Adequacy: 1998 to Mid-2003

Months worked[a]	Parent's name[a]	Hourly wage change[b]	Percent change in hourly wage[b]	Wage adequacy[c]	Percent change in wage adequacy[c]
≤11 months	Jenkins	8.50 (3/01) to 8.50 (8/01)	0%	86% to 86%	0%
	Winters	8.25 (11/01) to 7 (10/02)	−15%	97% to 48%	−49%
12–23 months	Jones	9.84 (8/99) to 10.36 (12/00)	+5%	145% to 152%	+7%
	Walker	8.50 (1/01) to 8.75 (6/02)	+3%	86% to 86%	0%
	Muhammad	8.25 (2/01) to 13.25 (1/03)	+61%	72% to 112%	+40%
	Delvalle	9.50 (7/01) to 14.25 (3/03)	+50%	135% to 161%	+26%
	Tracy	5.58 (10/01) to 7 (3/03)	+25%	100% to 95%	−5%
	Raca	13.18 (7/01) to 14.38 (8/02)	+11%	98% to 141%	+43%
24–35 months	Seabrook	10.26 (4/01) to 10.26 (4/03)	0%	102% to 100%	−2%
	McDonalds	9.76 (4/99) to 12.09 (6/01)	+24%	105% to 142%	+37%
	Jackson	16.40 (1/00) to 21.10 (3/02)	+29%	192% to 249%	+57%
	Stewart	11.70 (9/00) to 13.50 (11/02)	+15%	166% to 187%	+21%
	Faithful	10 (8/00) to 7.50 (3/03)	−25%	147% to 86%	−61%
	Quinn	10.76 (9/00) to 13.56 (5/03)	+30%	154% to 184%	+30%
	Tucker	10.20 (6/01) to 11.12 (6/03)	+9%	120% to 126%	+6%
36–47 months	Russell	8.75 (1/00) to 11.75 (2/03)	+34%	131% to 202%	+71%
	Smith	10 (10/99) to 12 (5/03)	+20%	125% to 136%	+11%
	Lopez	8 (7/99) to 6 (4/03)	−25%	120% to 41%	−79%
	Gomez	6.75 (4/99) to 10.15 (9/02)	+50%	101% to 116%	+15%
	Gates	12.65 (3/99) to 18.10 (1/03)	+43%	158% to 241%	+83%
	Miracle	10.70 (1/00) to 15.70 (1/03)	+47%	131% to 177%	+46%
48–60 months	Shanks	7.86 (9/98) to 9.80 (6/03)	+25%	84% to 113%	+29%
	Blessed	11 (6/98) to 12 (4/03)	+9%	118% to 135%	+17%
	Vanderhand	11.53 (1/99) to 15 (1/03)	+30%	103% to 122%	+19%
	Jeremy	11.50 (1/99) to 9.50 (1/03)	−17%	177% to 51%	−126%
Group Average			+18%	122% to 132%	+9%
Average Increase			+27%		+33%
Average Decrease			−21%		−54%

[a] All parent names are pseudonyms.
[b] Hourly wage change from initial post-training wage to last-known wage. Dates are given in parentheses.
[c] Wage adequacy relative to Federal Poverty Level (FPL), from initial post-training wage to last-known wage.

TABLE B.3. Employment and Wage Projections to 2012 by Parent's Industry, Occupation, and City

NAICS industry[a] or firm [city] (parent)[b]	Parent's occupation	Parent's hourly wage [2003 estimate]	Annual rate of change in employment (%)[c]	Mean hourly wage, 2003, national (industry/occupation)[d]	Mean hourly wage, 2003, city, occupation[e]	Projected or actual wage mobility[f]
Manufacturing			*−0.1*	*$15.74*		
Bindery [M] (McDonalds)	Floor person	'99: $9.76 ['03: $10.56]	−5.2	$15.74 / $11.81	$10.00	**Downward**
Printing & Bindery [M] (McDonalds)	Floor person	'99: $9.76 '01: $12.09 ['03: $12.57]	+4.6	$15.74 / $14.93	$15.37	Downward
Manufacturing Company [M] (Jones)	Machine operator; Assembler	'99: $9.84 '00: $10.01 ['03: $10.52]	−3.6	$15.74 / $13.09	—	**Downward**
Distribution Company [M] (Jones)	Order picker	'00: $9.66 '00: $10.36 ['03: $12.46]	—	$17.32 / $10.03	—	Upward
Product Manufacturing Company [M] (Shanks)	Cell operator	'98: $7.86 '00: $9.71 ['03: $12.50]	—	$15.74 / $12.36	—	**Upward**
Brass Co. [M] (Shanks)	Spot welder	'02: $8.75 '03: $9.80	+17	$15.74 / $15.06	$16.55	Downward
Steel Mill & Foundry [M] (Blessed)	Crane & forklift operator; Grinder	'98: $11 '00: $13 ['03: $16]	−2.8	$15.74 / $13.52	$14.24	**Upward**
Wholesale Company [M] (Blessed)	Truck driver; Warehouse manager	'02: $10 '03: $12	+18.4	$17.32 / $16.31	—	Downward

(continued)

TABLE B.3. (continued)

NAICS industry[a] or firm [city] (parent)[b]	Parent's occupation	Parent's hourly wage [2003 estimate]	Annual rate of change in employment (%)[c]	Mean hourly wage (industry/occupation)[d] national, 2003	Mean hourly wage, 2003, city, occupation)[e]	Projected or actual wage mobility[f]
Equipment Manufacturer [SE] (Jeremy)	Assembler	'99: $11.50 '00: $12.43 ['03: $15.22]	–3.6	*$15.74 / $16.31*	—	**Downward**
Parking Company [SE] (Jeremy)	Parking attendant	'00: $8.50 (30 hr/wk) '03: $9.50 (20 hr/wk)	+19.3	*$13.98 / $8.50*	$10.02	Downward
Laser Company [P] (Gates)	EDM operator	'99: $12.65	–16.3	*$15.74 / —*	—	—
Technology Management Co., Electronics Division [P] (Gates)	"Senior" machinist	'01: $16.90 '02: $17.50 '03: $18.10	+8.2	*$15.74 / $16.30*	$17.32	Upward
Manufacturing Technology Company [P] (Stewart)	Machine operator trainee	'00: $11.70 '02: $15.70 ['03: $17.70]	+21.1	*$15.74 / $11.40*	$11.84	**Upward**
Beverage Company [P] (Stewart)	Machine operator	'02: $13.50 ['03: $13.77]	+21.1	*$15.74 / $11.40*	$11.84	Upward
Food Company [SE] (Miracle)	Assistant shipping & receiving manager	'99: $10.70 '03: $10.70	+10.5	*$15.74 / $12.11*	—	**Downward**
School District [SE] (Miracle) [2nd job concurrent with Food Co.]	Custodian	'00: $14.62 '01: 2 jobs combined (70 hr/wk) '03: $15.70 '03: 2 jobs combined	+16.4	*$13.98 / $10.21*	$11.53	Upward

	Job	Wage history	%	Comparison	Amount	Direction
Industry [NO] (Winters)	Welding helper	'01: $8.25 ['03: $8.58]	+17	*$15.74 / $15.06*	$15.88	**Downward**
Video Casino [NO] (Winters)	Security guard	'02: $7 ['03: $7.14]	+31.9	$8.74 / $10.34	$8.34	Downward
Construction **Construction Company-WI [M]** (Jackson)	Laborer; Office staff	'00: $16.40 '01: $19	*+1.4* +14.2	*$18.75* $18.75 / $13.64	$10.31	**Upward**
FFF Construction [M] (Jackson)	Laborer; Office staff	'01: $21.10 ['03: $21.94]	+14.2	*$18.75 / $13.64*	$10.31	Upward
Construction Company-MO [ST] (Raca)	Drywaller	'01: $13.18 '02: $14.38 ['03: $14.96]	+21.4	*$18.75 / $17.56*	$25.56	**Downward**
Rental Car Company-MO [ST] (Raca)	Car detailer	'00: $8 '01: $8.50 ['03: $9.50]	—	— / $16.02	—	Downward
Union [NO] (Faithful)	Hard carrier (carpenter helper)	'00: $10 ['03: $11.66]	+13.7	*$18.75 / $10.93*	—	**Upward**
Church Construction Co. [NO] (Faithful)	Construction assistant	'02: $6.25 '03: $7.50	+13.7	*$18.75 / $10.93*	$10.31	Downward
Union [LA] (Quinn)	Apprentice	'00: $10.76 '03: $13.56	+13.7	*$18.75 / —*	—	**Downward—**

(continued)

TABLE B.3. (*continued*)

NAICS industry[a] or firm [city] (parent)[b]	Parent's occupation	Parent's hourly wage [2003 estimate]	Annual rate of change in employment (%)[c]	Mean hourly wage, 2003, national (*industry/occupation*)[d]	Mean hourly wage, 2003, city, occupation)[e]	Projected or actual wage mobility[f]
Other Services			*+1.5*	*$13.98*		
Rental Car Company-WA [SE] (Russell)	Utility person	'00: $8.75 / '03: $11.75	+26.3	$13.98 / $16.02	—	**Downward**
Retail Trade			*+1.3*	*$11.91*		
Tech Company [SE] (Smith)	Customer service rep I, II	'99: $10 / '01: $13 / ['03: $16]	+24.3	$11.91 / $13.73	$16.34	**Equivalent**
Safety Company [SE] (Smith)	Administrative assistant (training for Office manager)	'02: $10.50 / '03: $12	+4.5	$17.09 / $17.22	—	Downward
Finance & Insurance			*+1.2*	*$17.09*		
Insurance Company [SE] (Vanderhand)	Personal lines operator	'99: $11.53 / '03: $15	+24.3	$17.09 / $13.73	$16.34	**Downward**
Medical Billing Company [P] (Delvalle)	Provider service rep	'01: $9.50 / ['03: $9.98]	+24.3	$17.09 / $13.73	$14.16	**Downward**
Independent Pharmacy [P] (Delvalle)	Pharmacy technician	'02: $10 / '03: $14.25	+28.8	$11.91 / $11.47	$10.65	Upward

Administrative Support, Waste Management, Remediation Services			+3.2	—		
Temp Service-PA [P] (Muhammad)	File clerk	'01: $8.25 ['03: $8.58]	-.3	—/$10.43	$11.77	**Downward**
Financial Services Company [P] (Muhammad)	Assistant, Bill distribution; Assistant, Group insurance	'01: $10.50 '03: $13.25	+7	$17.09/$14.33	—	Downward
Lawn Service Company [ST] (Jenkins)	Customer service rep	'01: $8.50 ['03: $8.84]	+24.3	—/$13.73	$13.52	**Downward**
Medical Temp Agency [ST] (Lopez)	File clerk	'99: $8 ['03: $8.64]	+17	—/$10.43	$11.77	**Downward**
Tax Company [ST] (Lopez)	Tax preparer	'03: $6 (20 hr/wk)	+23.2	—/$15.69	$19.87	Downward
Research Co. Temp Service [ST] (Walker)	Computer-assisted telephone interviewer	'01: $8.50 '01: $8.50 (20 hr/wk) ['03: $8.84]	+28	*$17.24/$11.44*	$11.63	**Downward**
Library [ST] (Walker)	Tech I	'02: $8.75 ['03: $8.83]	+21.5	*$21.10/$10.23*	$8.88	Equivalent
Professional, Scientific, & Technical Services			+2.5	*$17.24*		
Research Facility [NO] (Seabrook)	Biological science technician	'01: $10.26 (PT during academic yr; FT summer) '03: $10.26 (same schedule)	+19.4	*$17.24/$16.62*	$13.05	**Downward**

(continued)

TABLE B.3. (*continued*)

NAICS industry[a] or firm [city] (parent)[b]	Parent's occupation	Parent's hourly wage [2003 estimate]	Annual rate of change in employment (%)[c]	Mean hourly wage, 2003, national (*industry/occupation*)[d]	Mean hourly wage, 2003, city, occupation)[e]	Projected or actual wage mobility[f]
Health Care & Social Assistance			*+2.8*	—		
Childcare Center [P] (Gomez)	Assistant teacher	'99: $6.75 / '00: $6.75 / ['03: $7.16]	+11.7	—/$8.37	$8.49	**Downward**
Health Insurance Co. [P] (Gomez)	Customer service rep	'01: $10 / '02: $10.15 / ['03: $10.30]	+24.3	*$17.09/$13.73*	$14.16	Downward
Hospital-MO [ST] (Tucker)	Certified nursing assistant	'01: $10.20 / '03: $11.12	+31.3	—/$10.12	—	**Upward**
Accommodation & Food Service			*+1.5*	*$8.74*		
Hospital-LA [NO] (Tracy)	Dietary service worker	'01: $5.58 / '02: $5.58 / ['03: $5.58]	+16.7	*$8.74/$7.76*	$6.66	**Downward**
Security Firm [NO] (Tracy)	Security guard	'02: $6 / '03: $7	+31.9	—/$10.34	$8.34	Downward

Key to typefaces: Italic typeface indicates data for an industry sector overall. Entries in **bold** are data from the initial post-training job.

[a] Industries are categorized according to the North American Industry Classification System (NAICS, 2002). Available at www.census.gov/epcd/www/naics.html.

[b] All firm and parent names are pseudonyms. **Bold** firm names represent the initial post-training job; nonbold firm names represent the last-known job at the end of the research period. Firms are grouped according to the industry of the parent's initial post-training job; the parent's last-known job follows immediately, even if it is located in a different industry sector. Research cities: [M] = Milwaukee; [NO] = New Orleans; [P] = Philadelphia; [ST] = St. Louis; [SE] = Seattle.

[c] Projected average annual rate of change in employment from 2002 to 2012. Rates shown in *italic* apply to an industry sector overall; rates that are not italic apply to the specific occupation.

[d] *Sources: Industry* wage figures for 2003 (U.S. Census Bureau, 2004b); *Monthly Labor Review*, February 2004, table 15, p. 134.

[e] *Sources:* Occupation wage figures for 2003: Department of Labor Standard Occupational Categories (SOC), available at http://stats.bls.gov/news.release/ocwage.t01.htm and www.bls.gov/oes.data.htm. Berman, J. M. (2004). Industry output and employment projections to 2012. *Monthly Labor Review*, 127(2), 58–79. Also, Hecker, D. E. (2004). Occupational employment projections to 2012. *Monthly Labor Review*, 127(2), 80–105.

[f] Projected or actual wage mobility is calculated according to city average. In the few cases that city average is not available, the national average for the occupation is used.

Appendix C

Resident Family Composition and
Family Story References

Key

Key Parent: Name (all names are pseudonyms), age at first contact, racial/ethnic
self-identification, city
> *Spouse/Partner:* Name in italics, (relationship status), racial/ethnic
> self-identification, age at first contact
> Children: Age at first contact
> Family Story Reference

Hard Working Blessed: Age 40, African American, Milwaukee
Mrs. Hard Working Blessed (wife): African American, age 37
Tank: Age 15
The Rock: Age 14
Baby Miracle: Age 1
Iversen, R. R., Turner, D. M., & Basta, M. (2002). The "Hard Working Blessed"
Family Story. In R. R. Iversen, *Moving up is a steep climb*. Baltimore, MD:
Annie E. Casey Foundation.

Wendy Delvalle: Age 32, Hispanic American, Philadelphia
Edwin, Sr. (resident partner, became husband): African American, age 33
Edwin, Jr.: Age 14
Marta: Infant born during research period
Iversen, R. R., Belliveau, M., & Fairbanks, R. P. II. (2003). The "Wendy Delvalle"
Family Story. Baltimore, MD: Annie E. Casey Foundation.

Joseph Faithful: Age 23, African American, New Orleans
Lisa (wife): African American, age 19
Joseph: Age $1^1/_2$
Faith: Infant born during research period
Iversen, R. R., Barrios, I., & Fairbanks, R. P. II. (2003). The "Joseph Faithful"
Family Story. Baltimore, MD: Annie E. Casey Foundation.

Sam Gates: Age 40, Caucasian, Philadelphia
Joyce (ex-spouse): Caucasian, age unknown
Bill: Age 14
Jill: Age 11
Rich: Age 9
Iversen, R. R., Saltzman, C., & Fairbanks, R. P. II. (2003). The "Sam Gates"
Family Story. Baltimore, MD: Annie E. Casey Foundation.

Aida Gomez: Age 26, Hispanic, Philadelphia
Marcos (became resident fiancé during study): Hispanic, age 23
Juan: Age 8

Luis: Age 3
Eva: Infant born during research period
Iversen, R. R., Saltzman, C., & Belliveau, M. (2003). The "Aida Gomez" Family
    Story. Baltimore, MD: Annie E. Casey Foundation.

Randy Jackson: Age 40, African immigrant, Milwaukee
Shawn (wife): African American, age 28
Junior: Age 5$^1/_2$
Roger: Age 4$^1/_2$
Iversen, R. R., Johnson, K., & Basta, M. (2002). The "Randy Jackson" Family
    Story. In R. R. Iversen, *Moving up is a steep climb*. Baltimore, MD: Annie E.
    Casey Foundation.

Jane Jenkins: Age 28, African American, St. Louis
George (husband): African American, age 35
Elroy: George's son; Jane's stepson, age 11
Kevin: Jane's son; George's stepson, age 10
Astro: Age 1
A.C.: Infant born during research period
Iversen, R. R., Morton, L., & Belliveau, M. (2002). The "Jane Jenkins" Family
    Story. Baltimore, MD: Annie E. Casey Foundation.

Mike Jeremy: Age 42, African refugee, Seattle
Christina: (wife), African immigrant, age 29
Tony: Age 2
Tonya: Infant born during research period
Iversen, R. R., Armstrong, A. L., & Belliveau, M. (2002). The "Mike Jeremy"
    Family Story. In R. R. Iversen, *Moving up is a steep climb*. Baltimore, MD:
    Annie E. Casey Foundation.

Tasha Jones: Age 24, African American, Milwaukee
Fiancé (boyfriend then husband): Middle Eastern refugee, age about 29
Nami: Age 2
Nicolette: Age 1
Baby Girl: Infant born during research period
Iversen, R. R., Turner, D. M., & Belliveau, M. (2002). The "Tasha Jones" Family
    Story. In R. R. Iversen, *Moving up is a steep climb*. Baltimore, MD: Annie E.
    Casey Foundation.

Loretta Lopez: Age 27, African American, St. Louis
Roberto Hernandez: Age 7
Placeta: Age 3
Iversen, R. R., Morton, L. & Fairbanks, R. P. II. (2002). The "Loretta Lopez"
    Family Story. Baltimore, MD: Annie E. Casey Foundation.

Kevin McDonalds: Age 29, African American, Milwaukee
Lynn (resident fiancée): Caucasian, Age 27
Salina: Age 6
Christina: Age 5
Fireman: Age 3
Iversen, R. R., Johnson, K., & Belliveau, M. (2002). The "Kevin McDonalds"
    Family Story. In R. R. Iversen, *Moving up is a steep climb*. Baltimore, MD:
    Annie E. Casey Foundation.

Lucky Miracle: Age 43, Asian refugee, Seattle
Fantastic (wife): Asian refugee, age 44
Special: Age 9
Awesome: Age 4
Iversen, R. R., Armstrong, A. L., & Basta, M. (2002). In R. R. Iversen, *Moving up is a steep climb*. Baltimore, MD: Annie E. Casey Foundation.

Ayesha Muhammad: Age 45, African American, Philadelphia
Christopher: Age 21
Fatimah: Age 19
James: Age 12
Don: Age 10
Tom: Age 10
Iversen, R. R., Saltzman, C., & Belliveau, M. (2003). The "Ayesha Muhammad" Family Story. Baltimore, MD: Annie E. Casey Foundation.

Rachel Quinn: Age 42, African American, New Orleans
Sadé: Age 16
Miguel: Age 15
Iversen, R. R., Burch, M., & Belliveau, M. (2003). The "Rachel Quinn" Family Story. Baltimore, MD: Annie E. Casey Foundation.

Ahree Raca: Age 18, African American, St. Louis
Ahrayl (resident partner): African American, age 18
Little Ahree: Age 1
Little Ahrayl: Age 4 months
Uriel: Infant born during research period
Iversen, R. R., Morton, L., & Fairbanks, R. P. II. (2002). The "Ahree Raca" Family Story. Baltimore, MD: Annie E. Casey Foundation.

Teresa Russell: Age 43, African American, Seattle
Tom: Age 10
Iversen, R. R., Armstrong, A. L., & Belliveau, M. (2002). In R. R. Iversen, *Moving up is a steep climb*. Baltimore, MD: Annie E. Casey Foundation.

Elizabeth Seabrook: Age 37, African American, New Orleans
Joseph: Age 4^1/$_2$
Abigail: Age 2^1/$_2$
Iversen, R. R., Burch, M., & Fairbanks, R. P. II. (2003). The "Elizabeth Seabrook" Family Story. Baltimore, MD: Annie E. Casey Foundation.

Tisha Shanks: Age 33, Hispanic American, Milwaukee
Maine (resident partner then separated): African American, age 31
Lita: Age 15
Juan: Age 14
Maria: Age 11
Iversen, R. R., Johnson, K., & Belliveau, M. (2002). The "Tisha Shanks" Family Story. In R. R. Iversen, *Moving up is a steep climb*. Baltimore, MD: Annie E. Casey Foundation.

Isabell Smith: Age 31, Hispanic American, Seattle
Domingo (resident partner): Hispanic, age 24
Pedro: Age 4^1/$_2$

Carlos: Age 2^1/$_2$
Iversen, R. R., Armstrong, A. L., & Belliveau, M. (2002). In R. R. Iversen,
Moving up is a steep climb. Baltimore, MD: Annie E. Casey Foundation.

Micarla Stewart: Age 24, African American, Philadelphia
Shalon: Age 6
Latice: Age 3
Iversen, R. R., Saltzman, C., & Fairbanks, R. P. II. (2003). The "Micarla Stewart"
Family Story. Baltimore, MD: Annie E. Casey Foundation.

Tasha Tracy: Age 21, African American, New Orleans
Rachel: Age 2^1/$_2$
David: Infant born during research period
Iversen, R. R., Barrios, I., & Belliveau, M. (2003). The "Tasha Tracy" Family
Story. Baltimore, MD: Annie E. Casey Foundation.

Shanquitta Tucker: Age 37, African American, St. Louis
Iesha: Age 13
Chris: Age 7
Kenyetta: Age 2
Iversen, R. R., Morton, L., & Fairbanks, R. P. II. (2002). The "Shanquitta Tucker"
Family Story. Baltimore, MD: Annie E. Casey Foundation.

Maya Vanderhand: Age 32, Hispanic, Seattle
Jesus (husband): Hispanic, age 48
Iesha: Age 13
Sahari: Age 11
Zimba: Age 8
Max: Age 7
Iversen, R. R., Armstrong, A. L., & Basta, M. (2002). The "Maya Vanderhand"
Family Story. In R. R. Iversen, *Moving up is a steep climb*. Baltimore, MD:
Annie E. Casey Foundation.

Lynn Walker: Age 36, African American, St. Louis
Waldo Aloysious: Age 13
Kelly: Age 9
Diamond: Age 5
Breion: Age 2
Iversen, R. R., Morton, L., & Belliveau, M. (2002). The "Lynn Walker" Family
Story. Baltimore, MD: Annie E. Casey Foundation.

Nasir Winters: Age 19, African American, New Orleans
Star Summers (resident partner then separated): African American, age 17
Damarius: Age 1^1/$_2$
Heavenly: Age 6 months
Iversen, R. R., Burch, M., & Belliveau, M. (2003). The "Nasir Winters" Family
Story. Baltimore, MD: Annie E. Casey Foundation.

Notes

CHAPTER ONE

1. The term "key parent" signifies the twenty-five parents who constitute the core research sample (see Appendix A, Research Design, for details).

CHAPTER THREE

1. Throughout this chapter and others, we generally refer to the parents' "job-training programs" or "workforce development programs" rather than to the demonstration, because this book is explicitly not an evaluation of the demonstration and most of the job programs affiliated with it function independently from it as well (see Appendix A, Research Design).

2. For some types of research, Zip Code Tabulation Areas (ZCTAS) replace U.S. Postal Service zip code service areas as the level of analysis (U.S. Census Bureau, 2000). In most cases, the conventional zip code and ZCTA are the same, especially as pertains to the densely populated inner cities in this book.

CHAPTER SIX

1. We acknowledge Andersson, Holzer, and Lane's (2005, p. 16) definition of firm as "establishment" or as "specific places of business and employment" and "the overall legal entity that sometimes encompasses multiple places of business," and DiPrete's (1993) definition of an "organization" as either. Because the examination in this chapter is more strongly focused on micro- and meso- than on macrolevels of interaction we use these terms interchangeably, prioritizing "firm" as is common in research on workers and employers (Andersson, Holzer, & Lane).

2. "Initial post-training job" signifies the job (i.e., position or firm) that the parent attains after attending one of his or her local workforce development network's job training programs. In a few cases the program or network intermediary contracts with firms to guarantee jobs for completers of the training program. In most cases, program staff helps the job seeker locate a job, using either network contacts or more traditional modes, such as newspaper ads, to identify employment opportunities.

3. The OSHA Web site (U.S. Department of Labor, 2004) issues the following disclaimer. "The Integrated Management Information System (IMIS) was designed as an information resource for in-house use by OSHA staff and management, and by state agencies which carry out federally approved OSHA programs. Access to this OSHA work product is being afforded via the Internet for the use of members of the public who wish to track OSHA interventions at particular work sites or to perform statistical analyses of OSHA enforcement activity. It is critical that users of the data understand several aspects of the system in order to accurately use the information. The source of the information in the IMIS is the local federal or state office in the geographical area where the activity occurred. Information is entered as events occur in the course of agency activities. Until cases are closed, IMIS entries concerning specific OSHA inspections are subject to continuing correction and updating, particularly with regard to citation items, which are subject to modification by amended citations, settlement agreements, or as a result of contest proceedings. THE USER SHOULD ALSO BE AWARE THAT DIFFERENT COMPANIES MAY HAVE SIMILAR NAMES AND CLOSE ATTENTION TO THE ADDRESS MAY BE NECESSARY TO AVOID MISINTERPRETATION.

The Integrated Management Information System (IMIS) is designed and administered as a management tool for OSHA to help it direct its resources. When IMIS is put to
new or different uses, the data should be verified by reference to the case file and confirmed by the appropriate federal or state office. Employers or employees who believe
a particular IMIS entry to be inaccurate, incomplete or out-of-date are encouraged to
contact the OSHA field office or state plan agency which originated the entry."

4. We use the standard Census Bureau formula to translate hourly wages into annual incomes in order to examine wage adequacy according to both federal poverty
level (FPL) and Self-Sufficiency Standard (SSS) metrics (Table B.1, Appendix B). That
formula is hourly wage × 40 hours per week × 52 weeks per year (Bonthius, 2004).
Annual income calculations for tax and subsidy purposes variably include income
from sources such as taxable interest, dividends, capital gains, rental real estate, unemployment compensation, or public assistance benefits. Because our central focus
is on economic mobility, in this book "annual income" signifies *wage income only*.
Few of the study families receive income from the aforementioned sources; for most,
wage income, periodically augmented by public subsidies or work supports, is the sole
source of money for the family.

Because the formula used to calculate annual income from hourly wage figures
assumes forty-hour work weeks and fifty-two weeks of income per year, the annual
incomes of some of the key parents may be slight overestimates. However, in many cases
thirty-five-hour weeks are compensated at a forty-hour rate. To some extent this may
counterbalance the fact that subsidy eligibility guidelines often include income from
sources we do not consider in our FPL and SSS calculations. Ultimately, the possibility
of overestimated annual incomes in this analysis suggests that the economic status and
mobility of the study families may be even *worse* than our discussion presents it to
be, thus discovering routes to economic mobility for low-income families seems even
more critical.

5. The number of jobs left involuntarily is underreported. One parent experienced
multiple short-term (one-week to three-month) jobs with involuntary exits from each,
but because her wage was virtually the same in each job, only one set of changes is
included in the calculation here.

CHAPTER SEVEN

1. Sources for school performance data are listed under Table 7.2 in this chapter.

CHAPTER EIGHT

1. We are grateful to Mary Jane Vujovic for this insight.
2. We are grateful to Sanford Schram for this insight.

APPENDIX A

1. A sixth city, Denver, participated in the demonstration program until 1999. It
withdrew before the ethnographic research began.

2. In toto, the ethnographic research was conducted under four independent grants
from The Annie E. Casey Foundation to Roberta Iversen. The contents of this book do
not necessarily reflect the opinions of the Foundation.

3. The pronouns "I" and "me" in this Appendix refer to the first author, Roberta
Iversen. When "we" is used, it refers variously to both authors—Roberta Iversen and
Annie Laurie Armstrong—or to the research team of nine as a whole.

4. Author contact information: Iversen: riversen@sp2.upenn.edu; and Armstrong:
bgcc@jetcity.com

5. Particular thanks to Dr. Susan Kinnevy for design and production of the plaques.

References

Abt Associates & New School University. (2000). *AECF Jobs Initiative: Evaluation report on the capacity building phase (March 1997–March 2000)*. Cambridge, MA: Abt Associates, Inc.

Acs, G., Phillips, K.R., & McKenzie, D. (2001). Playing by the rules, but losing the game: Americans in low-income working families. In R. Kazis & M.S. Miller (Eds.), *Low-wage workers in the new economy*, pp. 21–44. Washington, DC: Urban Institute.

Adler, P. S., & Kwon, S-W. (2000). Social capital: Prospects for a new concept. Unpublished paper.

AFL-CIO. (2004). Facts about working women. Washington, DC: Author. Retrieved July 24, 2004, from www.aflcio.org

Ahluwalia, S. K., McGroder, S. M., Zaslow, M. J., & Hair, E. C. (2001). Symptoms of depression among welfare recipients: A concern for two generations. *Child Trends Research Brief*. Washington, DC: Child Trends.

Albelda, R., & Tilly, C. (1997). *Glass ceilings and bottomless pits: Women's work, women's poverty*. Boston: South End.

Alssid, J. L., Gruber, D., Jenkins, D., Mazzeo, C., Roberts, B., & Stanback-Stroud, R. (2002). *Building a career pathways system*. New York: Workforce Strategy Center.

Althauser, R. P., & Kalleberg, A.L. (1990). Identifying career lines and internal labor markets within firms: A study in the interrelationships of theory and methods. In R.L. Breiger, *Social mobility and social structure*, pp. 308–356. New York: Cambridge University.

Amato, A. (2004). New Orleans public schools: Overview of 2004–2005 budget. Retrieved February 12, 2005, from www.nops.K12.la.us

American Lung Association. (2004). Asthma & children fact sheet. Retrieved February 2, 2005, from www.lungusa.org

America's Workforce Network. (2002). Discussion guide: WIA reauthorization issues. Washington, DC: Author.

Anderson, E. (1990). *Streetwise: Race, class, and change in an urban community*. Chicago: University of Chicago Press.

———. (2002). The ideologically driven critique. *American Journal of Sociology*, 107, 1533–50.

Andersson, R., Holzer, H. J., & Lane, J. I. (2005). *Moving up or moving on: Who advances in the low-wage labor market?* New York: Russell Sage Foundation.

Annie E. Casey Foundation. (1998). *When teens have sex: Issues and trends*. Baltimore, MD: Author.

———. (2001a). *City Kids Count 2001: Data on the well-being of children in large cities*. Baltimore, MD: Author.

———. (2001b). *Taking the initiative on jobs and race*. Baltimore, MD: Author.

———. (2004). *Kids count data book 2004: State profiles of child well-being*. Baltimore, MD: Author.

Ansberry, C. (2003, July 22). Some U.S. jobs are drying up for good. *The Asian Wall Street Journal*, M8.

Appelbaum, E., Bernhardt, A., & Murnane, R. J. (Eds.). (2003). *Low-wage America: How employers are reshaping opportunity in the workplace*. New York: Russell Sage Foundation.

Appelbaum, E., Bernhardt, A., Murnane, R. J., & Weinberg, J. A. (2005). Low-wage employment in America: Results from a set of recent industry case studies. *Socio-Economic Review*, 3, 293–310.

Armstrong, A. L. (1997). Indicators of abuse or neglect in preschool children's drawings. *Journal of Psychosocial Nursing and Mental Health Services,* 35 (4), 10–17.

———. (2002). Creating a HOPE VI education, training and employment system. *HOPE VI assisting public housing authorities in supporting families,* pp. 35–57. Washington, DC: CWLA Press.

Armstrong, A. L., Lord, C., & Zelter, J. (2000). Information needs of low-income residents in South King County. *Public Libraries,* 39 (6), 330–35.

Associated Press. (2003, March 8). U.S. shed jobs in February: Unemployment increased to 5.8%. *The International Herald Tribune*, 15.

Bach, D. (2003, January 16). Seattle Schools deficit just gets worse. *The Seattle Post Intelligencer*, A1, 13.

Barnett, W. S. (2003). Better teachers, better preschools: Student achievement linked to teacher qualifications. New Brunswick, NJ: National Institute for Early Education Research.

Baron, J. N. (1984). Organizational perspectives on stratification. *American Review of Sociology*, 10, 37–69.

Baron, J. N., Hannan, M. T., Hsu, G., & Kocak, O. (2002). Gender and the organization: Building process in young high-tech firms. In M. F. Guillen, R. Collins, P. England, & M. Meyer (Eds.), *The new economic sociology: Developments in an emerging field*, pp. 245–73. New York: Russell Sage Foundation.

Barth, E., Roed, M., & Torp, H. (2002). *Toward a closing of the gender pay gap: Country report Norway*. Oslo: Norwegian Centre for Gender Equality.

Bartik, T. J. (2001). *Jobs for the poor: Can labor demand policies help?* Kalamazoo, MI: W.E. Upjohn Institute for Employment Research.

Batt, R., Hunter, L., & Wilk, S. (1998). The quality of jobs and mobility opportunities for customer service and sales workers. Proposal. Philadelphia, PA: University of Pennsylvania, Wharton School.

Baumol, W. J., Blinder, A. S., & Wolff, E. N. (2003). *Downsizing in America: Reality, causes, and consequences*. New York: Russell Sage Foundation.

Beck, E. M., & Colclough, G. S. (1988). Schooling and capitalism: The effect of urban economic structure on the value of education. In G. Farkas & P. England (Eds.), *Industries, firms, and jobs: Sociological and economic approaches*, pp. 113–39. New York: Plenum.

Becker, G. S. (1976). *The economic approach to human behavior*. Chicago: University of Chicago Press.

Becker, G. S. (1993). *Human capital*, 3rd edition. Chicago: University of Chicago Press.

Becker, G. S. (2002). Lecture on human capital at the University of Pennsylvania, February 26, 2002.

Becker, H. S. (1996). The epistemology of qualitative research. In R. Jessor, A. Colby, & R. Schweder (Eds)., *Essays on ethnography and human development*, pp. 53–71. Chicago: University of Chicago Press.

Becker, H. S. (1998). *Tricks of the trade*. Chicago: University of Chicago Press.

Belenky, M. F., Clinchy, B. M., Goldberger, N. R., & Tarule, J. M. (1986). *Women's ways of knowing*. New York: Basic Books.

Belussi, F., & Garibaldo, F. (2000). Variety of pattern of the post-Fordist economy: Why are the 'old times' still with us and the 'new times' yet to come? In K. Grint (Ed.), *Work and society*, pp. 280–302. Cambridge, UK: Polity.

Bell, D. (1996). *The cultural contradictions of capitalism*, 20th anniversary edition. New York: Basic Books.

Berlin, G. L. (2000). *Encouraging work and reducing poverty: The impact of work incentive programs*. New York: MDRC.

Berman, J. M. (2004). Industry output and employment projections to 2012. *Monthly Labor Review*, 127 (2), 58–79.

Bernhardt, A., Morris, M., Handcock, M. S., & Scott, M. A. (2001). *Divergent paths: Economic mobility in the new American labor market*. New York: Russell Sage Foundation.

Berube, A. (2006). *The new safety net: How the tax code helped low-income working families during the early 2000s*. Washington, DC: Brookings Institution.

Berube, A., & Forman, B. (2001). A local ladder for the working poor: The impact of the Earned Income Tax Credit in U.S. metropolitan areas. Washington, DC: Brookings Institution.

Berube, A., & Tiffany, T. (2004). The "state" of low-wage workers. Washington, DC: Brookings Institution.

Bhatt, S. (2005, January 3). Schools struggle to reduce high teacher turnover. *The Seattle Times* [Online]. Retrieved February 2, 2005, from www.seattletimes.nwsource.com

Bielby, W. T., & Bielby, D. D. (2002). Telling stories about gender and effort: Social science narratives about who works hard for the money. In M. F. Guillen, R. Collins, P. England, & M. Meyer (Eds.), *The new economic sociology: Developments in an emerging field*, pp. 193–217. New York: Russell Sage Foundation.

Bingham, T. (2004). Imagine. Alexandria, VA: American Society for Training & Development.

Blair, A. (2005). How does business benefit from sectoral workplace development services? *Workforce Strategies Initiative Update*, Issue 3. Washington, DC: Aspen Institute.

Blau, P. M., & Duncan, O. D. (1967). *The American occupational structure*. New York: Wiley.

Bliss, S. (2000). *San Francisco Works: Toward an employer-based approach to welfare reform and workforce development*. New York: MDRC.

Bloom, H. S., Orr, L. L., Cave, G., Bell, S. H., & Doolittle, F. (1993). *The National JTPA Study: Title II-A impacts on earnings and employment at 18 months*. Washington, DC: U.S. Department of Labor.

Bonthius, B. (2004). Federal poverty guidelines in a nutshell. Cleveland, OH: Legal Aid Society of Cleveland.

Bourdieu, P. (1977). *Outline of a theory of practice*. Cambridge, UK: Cambridge University Press.

Bourdieu, P. (1998). *Practical reason*. Stanford, CA: Stanford University Press.

Bourdieu, P. (2001). The forms of capital. In M. Granovetter & R. Swedberg (Eds.), *The sociology of economic life*, pp. 96–111. Boulder, CO: Westview Press.

Bowles, S., & Gintis, H. (1987). *Democracy and capitalism: Property, community, and the contradictions of modern social thought*. New York: Basic Books.

Braverman, H. (1974). *Labor and monopoly capital: The degradation of work in the twentieth century*. New York: Monthly Review Press.

Breiger, R. L. (Ed.). (1990). *Social mobility and social structure*. New York: Cambridge University Press.

Briggs, X. S. (1998). Brown kids in white suburbs: Housing mobility and the many faces of social capital. *Housing Policy Debate*, 9(1), 177–221.

Brinton, M. C., & Nee, V. (1998). *The new institutionalism in sociology*. Stanford, CA: Stanford University.

Brooks-Gunn, J., Duncan, G. J., & Aber, J. L. (Eds.). (1997). *Neighborhood poverty*, Vol. 1. New York: Russell Sage Foundation.

Buck, M. L. (2002). *Charting new territory: Early implementation of the Workforce Investment Act*. Philadelphia: Public/Private Ventures.

Buck, M. L., Edin, K., Fink, B., Padilla, Y., Quint, J, Simmons-Hewitt, O., & Valmont, M. (1999). *Big cities and welfare reform: Early implementation and ethnographic findings from the Project on Devolution and Urban Change*. New York: MDRC. Retrieved September 29, 2004, from www.mdrc.org/publications/55/execsum.html

Buehlmann, B. (2003). Workforce development system employer survey. Washington, DC: Center for Workforce Preparation.

Burawoy, M. (2003). Revisits: An outline of a theory of reflexive ethnography. *American Sociological Review*, 68, 645–79.

Burawoy, M., Burton, A., Ferguson, A. A., Fox, K. J., Gamson, J., Gartrell, N., et al. (1991). *Ethnography unbound: Power and resistance in the modern metropolis*. Berkeley: University of California Press.

Burawoy, M., Blum, J. A., George, S., Gille, Z., Gowan, T., Haney, L., et al. (2000). *Global ethnography: Forces, connections, and imaginations in a postmodern world*. Berkeley: University of California Press.

Business Ethics. (2005, Spring). 100 best corporate citizens for 2005. *Business Ethics Online*. Retrieved June 19, 2005, from www.crswire.com/sfprint.cgi?sfArticleId=1734

Burt, R. S. (1992). *Structural holes*. Cambridge, MA: Harvard University Press.

Burt, R.S. (2002). The social capital of structural holes. In M. F. Guillen, R. Collins, P. England, & M. Meyer (Eds.), *The new economic sociology: Developments in an emerging field*, 148–90. New York: Russell Sage Foundation.

Cadena, B.C. & Sallee, J.M. (2005). Why did poverty rise in 2004? A preliminary analysis of the U.S. Census Bureau's poverty report. *Poverty Research Insights*, Fall, 1–3.

Campbell, M. (2003). Dorothy Smith and knowing the world we live in. *Journal of Sociology and Social Welfare*, 30(1), 3–22.

Cancian, M., & Reed, D. (2001). Changes in family structure: Implications for poverty and related policy. In S. H. Danziger & R. H. Haveman (Eds.), *Understanding poverty*, pp. 69–96. New York: Russell Sage Foundation, and Cambridge, MA: Harvard University.

Cappelli, P. (1999). *The new deal at work: Managing the market-driven workforce*. Boston, MA: Harvard Business School Press.

Cappelli, P. (2000). A market-driven approach to retaining talent. *Harvard Business Review*, January–February.

Carnevale, A. P., & Desrochers, D. M. (1999). *Getting down to business*. Princeton, NJ: Educational Testing Service.

Carnevale, A. P., & Rose, S. J. (2001). Low-earners: Who are they? Do they have a way out? In R. Kazis & M. S. Miller (Eds.), *Low-wage workers in the new economy*, pp. 45–66. Washington, DC: Urban Institute.

CBPP. (2004). Facts about the Child Tax Credit. Washington, DC: Center on Budget and Policy Priorities.

Chase-Lansdale, P. L., Moffitt, R. A., Lohman, B. J., Cherlin, A.J., Coley, R. L., Pittman, L. D., et al. (2003). Mothers' transitions from welfare to work and the well-being of preschoolers and adolescents. *Science*, 299, 1548–52.

Cherlin, A. (2004). The consequences of welfare reform for child well-being: What have we learned so far and what are the policy implications? Paper presented at the Annual Meeting of the American Sociological Association, August 2004.

Childhood Asthma Foundation. (2005). What is asthma? Retrieved February 2, 2005, from www.childasthma.com/about.html

Child Trends. (1999). *Children and welfare reform: A guide to evaluating the effects of state welfare reform policies.* Washington, DC: Author.

Child Trends. (2003). Children in working poor families. Retrieved March 1, 2003, from www.childtrendsdatabank.org/income/poverty/74workingpoor.htm

Clymer, C., Roder, A., & Roberts, B. (2005). *Promoting opportunity: Findings from the State Workforce Policy Initiative on retention and advancement.* Philadelphia: Public/Private Ventures.

Coleman, J. S. (1990). *Foundations of social theory.* Cambridge, MA: Belknap.

Coley, R. L., Chase-Lansdale, P. L., & Li-Grining, C. (2001). Childcare in the era of welfare reform: Quality, choices and preferences. Policy Brief 01–04. Baltimore, MD: Johns Hopkins University.

Conant, J., & Haugeland, J. (Eds.). (2000). *The road since Structure.* Chicago: University of Chicago Press.

Connolly, H., & Gottschalk, P. (2001). Stepping stone jobs: Theory and evidence. Working paper #427. Chestnut Hill, MA: Boston College, Economics Department.

Copeland, P.Y. (2000, May 28). Here's your homework, parents. *Milwaukee Sentinel Journal,* J-1.

Corcoran, M. (1995). Rags to rags: Poverty and mobility in the United States. *Annual Review of Sociology,* 21, 237–67.

Corporate welfare runs amok. (2005, January 30). *The New York Times,* Section 4, p. 16.

Council of the Great City Schools. (2004). Raising student achievement in the St. Louis public schools. Washington, DC: Author.

Crone, T. M. (2000). The region's economy: Setting a sustainable pace. Philadelphia: Federal Reserve Bank of Philadelphia.

Crutsinger, M. (2004, January 23). Group reexamines date recession began. *The Philadelphia Inquirer,* A16.

Danziger, S. H., & Haveman, R. H. (Eds.). (2001). *Understanding poverty.* New York: Russell Sage Foundation, and Cambridge, MA: Harvard University Press.

Danziger, S., Corcoran, M., Danziger, S., Heflin, C., Kalil, R., Levine, J., et al. (1998). *Barriers to the employment of welfare recipients.* Ann Arbor, MI: University of Michigan, Poverty Research & Training Center.

Dash, L. (1989). *When children want children.* New York: William Morrow.

Davey, M., & Leonhardt, D. (2003, April 27). Jobless and hopeless, many quit the labor force. *The New York Times,* pp. 1, 34.

DeNavas-Walt, C., Cleveland, R., & Roemer, M. I. (2001). *Money income in the United States: 2000.* Current Population Reports, P60-213. Washington, DC: U.S. Government Printing Office.

DeNavas-Walt, C., Proctor, B. D., & Mills, R. J. (2004). *Income, poverty, and health insurance coverage in the United States: 2003.* Current Population Reports, P60-226. Washington, DC: U.S. Government Printing Office.

DeParle, J. (2004). *American dream: Three women, ten kids, and a nation's drive to end welfare.* New York: Viking.

DiMaggio, P. (Ed.). (2001). *The twenty-first century firm: Changing economic organization in international perspective.* Princeton, NJ: Princeton University Press.

DiPrete, T. A. (1993). Industrial restructuring and the mobility response of American workers in the 1980s. *American Sociological Review,* 58, 74–96.

DiPrete, T.A. & Nonnemaker, K.L. (1997). Structural change, labor market turbulence, and labor market outcomes. *American Sociological Review,* 62(3), 386–404.

DiPrete, T. A., Goux, D., & Maurin, E. (2001). Internal labor markets and earnings trajectories in the post-Fordist economy: An analysis of recent trends. Retrieved September 22, 2004, from www.crest.fr/pageperso/dr/maurin/ssr.pdf

Dresser, L., & Wright, G. (2004). Data shows 205,136 Wisconsin children in poverty in 2003—Increase of more than 34,337 since 2000. News Release. Madison, WI: Center on Wisconsin Strategy.

DuGay, P., & Salaman, G. (2000). The cult[ure] of the customer. In K. Grint, *Work and society*, pp. 77–93. Cambridge, UK: Polity.

Duncan, G. J., Boisjoly, J., & Smeeding, T. (1996). Economic mobility of young workers in the 1970s and 1980s. *Demography*, 33 (4), 497–509.

Duncan, G. J., & Chase-Lansdale, P. L. (2001). *For better and for worse: Welfare reform and the well-being of children and families*. New York: Russell Sage Foundation.

Duncan, G. J., Yeung, W. J., Brooks-Gunn, J., & Smith, J. R. (1998). How much does childhood poverty affect the life chances of children? *American Sociological Review*, 63 (3), 406–23.

Duneier, M. (1999). *Sidewalk*. New York: Farrar, Straus and Giroux.

Durkheim, E. (1984). *The division of labor in society*. New York: Free Press. (Original work published 1933)

Dwyer, R. E. (2004). Downward earnings mobility after voluntary employer exits. *Work and Occupations*, 31 (1), 111–39.

Edin, K., & Lein, L. (1997). *Making ends meet*. New York: Russell Sage Foundation.

Edwards, R. (1979). *Contested terrain: The transformation of the workplace in the twentieth century*. New York: Basic Books.

EdWeek. (2005). Quality counts 2005: No small change: Targeting money toward student performance [Internet only]. Retrieved February 13, 2005, from www.edweek. org/we/qc/2005/multiple_state_data.html

Ehrenberg, R. G., & Smith, R. S. (2003). *Modern labor economics: Theory and public policy*, 8th edition. Boston: Addison-Wesley.

Eisenstadt, S. N. (1963/1993). *The political systems of empires*. New Brunswick, NJ: Transaction.

Employment and Training Administration. (2005). *WIA reauthorization and reform*. Washington, DC: U.S. Department of Labor, Author.

Entwisle, D., Alexander, K., & Olson, L.S. (1997). *Children, schools, and inequality*. Boulder, CO: Westview.

Esping-Anderson, G. (1990). *The three worlds of welfare capitalism*. Princeton, NJ: Princeton University Press.

Ewen, D., & Hart, K. (2003). *State budget cuts create a growing childcare crisis for low-income working families*. Washington DC: Children's Defense Fund.

Farber, N. (2003). *Adolescent pregnancy: Policy, programs, and prevention services*. New York: Springer.

Farber, N. B., & Iversen, R. R. (1996). Transmitting values about education: A comparison of black teen mothers and their nonparent peers. Discussion paper #1094-96. Madison, WI: University of Wisconsin-Madison, Institute for Research on Poverty.

Farber, N. B., & Iversen, R. R. (1998). Family values about education and their transmission among black inner-city young women. In A. Colby, J. James, & D. Hart (Eds.), *The development of competence and character through life*, pp. 141–67. Chicago: University of Chicago Press.

Fetterman, D. M. (1998). *Ethnography*, 2nd edition. Thousand Oaks, CA: Sage.

Fisher, G. M. (1997). The development and history of U.S. poverty thresholds: A brief overview. Washington, DC: U.S. Department of Health and Human Services.

FitzGerald, S. (2003, January 20). Another possible toxic effect of lead: Behavior problems. *The Philadelphia Inquirer*, C1, 12.

Fleischer, W. (2001). *Extending ladders: Findings from the Annie E. Casey Foundation's Jobs Initiative*. Baltimore, MD: Annie E. Casey Foundation.

Fligstein, N. (2002). Agreements, disagreements, and opportunities in the "new sociology of markets." In M. F. Guillen, R. Collins, P. England, & M. Meyer (Eds.), *The new economic sociology: Developments in an emerging field*, pp. 61–78. New York: Russell Sage Foundation.

Fogg, N. P., & Harrington, P. E. (2001). *Growth and change in the Louisiana and New Orleans labor markets*. Boston, MA: Northeastern University, Center for Labor Market Studies.

Freeman, E. W., & Rickels, K. (1993). *Early childbearing: Perspectives of Black adolescents on pregnancy, abortion, and contraception*. Newbury Park, CA: Sage.

Freeman, R. B., & Gottschalk, P. (Eds.). (1998). *Generating jobs*. New York: Russell Sage Foundation.

Fremstad, S., & Primus, W. (2002). Strengthening families: Ideas for TANF reauthorization. Report, January 22, 2002. Washington, DC: Center on Budget and Policy Priorities. Retrieved March 2, 2002, from www.centeronbudget.org/1-22-02tanf.htm

Friedlander, D., & Burtless, G. (1995). *Five years after: The long-term effects of welfare-to-work programs*. New York: Russell Sage Foundation.

Fronczek, P. (2005). *Income, earnings, and poverty from the 2004 American Community Survey*. Washington, DC: U.S. Census Bureau.

Fukuyama, F. (2003). Still disenchanted? The modernity of postindustrial capitalism. Working Paper #3. Ithaca, NY: Cornell University, Center for the Study of Economy & Society.

Furstenberg, F. F., Jr. (1976). *Unplanned parenthood: The social consequences of teenage childbearing*. New York: Free Press.

Furstenberg, F. F., Jr., Brooks-Gunn, J., & Morgan, P. (1987). *Adolescent mothers in later life*. New York: Cambridge University Press.

Furstenberg, F. F. Jr., Cook, T. D., Eccles, J., Elder, G., & Sameroff, A. (1999). *Managing to make it: Urban families and adolescent success*. Chicago: University of Chicago Press.

Furstenberg, F. F. Jr., & Hughes, M. E. (1997). The influence of neighborhoods on children's development: A theoretical perspective and a research agenda. In R.M. Hauser, B.V. Brown, & W.R. Prosser, *Indicators of children's well-being*, pp. 346–71. New York: Russell Sage Foundation.

Gans, H.J. (1999). *Making sense of America: Sociological analyses and essays*. Lanham, MD: Rowman & Littlefield.

Garsten, C. (1999). Loose links and tight attachments: Modes of employment and meaning-making in a changing labor market. In R. A. Goodman (Ed.), *Modern organizations and emerging conundrums: Exploring the postindustrial subculture of the third millennium*, pp. 281–92. New York: Lexington Books.

Gartrell, N. (1991). Coming together: An interactive model of schooling. In M. Burawoy et al. (Eds.), *Ethnography unbound: Power and resistance in the modern metropolis*, pp. 203–20. Berkeley: University of California Press.

Gelles, R. J., & Levine, A. (1999). *Sociology: An introduction*, 6th edition. Boston, MA: McGraw-Hill College.

Gephart, M. A. (1997). Neighborhoods and communities as contexts for development. In J. Brooks-Gunn, G. J. Duncan, & J. L. Aber (Eds.), *Neighborhood poverty*, Vol. 1, pp. 1–43. New York: Russell Sage Foundation.

Gerson, K. (1985). *Hard choices: How women decide about work, career, and motherhood*. Berkeley, CA: University of California Press.

Gerstel, N., & Clawson, D. (2001). Union's responses to family concerns. *Social Problems*, 48, 277–97.

Gewirtz, S. (2001). Retaining low-income residents in the workforce: Lessons learned from the Annie E. Casey Jobs Initiative. Policy Update. Baltimore, MD: Annie E. Casey Foundation.

Gewirtz, S., & Harrington, R. (2000). Developing effective Management Information Systems to support workforce development efforts. Research brief. Baltimore, MD: Annie E. Casey Foundation.

Giloth, R. (1995). Social investment in jobs: Foundation perspectives on targeted economic development during the 1990s. *Economic Development Quarterly*, 9, 279–89.

Giloth, R. (2004a). *Mistakes, learning, and adaptation: Philanthropy and the Jobs Initiative.* Baltimore, MD: Annie E. Casey Foundation.

Giloth, R. (Ed.). (2004b). *Workforce intermediaries for the twenty-first century.* Philadelphia, PA: Temple University Press in association with The American Assembly, Columbia University Press.

Giloth, R. (Ed.). (2004c). *Workforce development politics: Civic capacity and performance.* Philadelphia: Temple University Press.

Giloth, R., & Gewirtz, S. (1999). Retaining low-income residents in the workforce. Research brief. Baltimore, MD: Annie E. Casey Foundation.

Giloth, R., & Phillips, W. (2000). Getting results: Outcome management and the Annie E. Casey Foundation's Jobs Initiative. Policy brief. Baltimore, MD: Annie E. Casey Foundation.

Gitterman, D. P., Howard, C., & Cotton, K. D. (2003). *Tax credits for working families: The new American social policy.* Washington, DC: Brookings Institution.

Gotlib, I. H., & Cane, D. B. (1989). Self-report assessment of depression and anxiety. In P. C. Kendall & D. Watson (Eds.), *Anxiety and depression*, pp. 131–69. New York: Academic Press.

Gottlieb, P.D. (2004). *Labor supply pressures and the "brain drain": Signs from Census 2000.* Washington, DC: Brookings Institution.

Gottschalk, P. (2001). Wage mobility within and between jobs. Working Paper #486. Chestnut Hill, MA: Boston College, Economics Department.

Grall, T. S. (2005). Support providers: 2002. Current Population Reports. Washington, DC: U.S. Census Bureau.

Granovetter, M. (1973). The strength of weak ties. *American Journal of Sociology*, 78, 1360–80.

Granovetter, M. (1978). Threshold models of collective behavior. *The American Journal of Sociology*, 83 (6), 1420–43.

Granovetter, M. (1983). The strength of weak ties: A network theory revisited. *Sociological Theory*, 1, 201–33.

Granovetter, M. (1985). Economic action and social structure: The problem of embeddedness. *American Journal of Sociology*, 91, 481–510.

Granovetter, M. (1988). The sociological and economic approaches to labor market analysis: A social structural view. In G. Farkas & P. England (Eds.), *Industries, firms, and jobs: Sociological and economic approaches*, pp. 187–216. New York: Plenum.

Granovetter, M. (1995). *Getting a job: A study of contacts and careers*, 2nd edition. Chicago: University of Chicago Press.

Granovetter, M. (2002). A theoretical agenda for economic sociology. In M. F. Guillen, R. Collins, P. England, & M. Meyer (Eds.), *The new economic sociology: Developments in an emerging field*, pp. 35–60. New York: Russell Sage Foundation.

Granovetter, M., & Swedberg, R. (2001). *The sociology of economic life*, 2nd edition. Boulder, CO: Westview Press.

Grint, K. (1991). *The sociology of work: An introduction*. Cambridge, UK: Polity.

Grint, K. (Ed.). (2000). *Work and society: A reader*. Cambridge, UK: Polity.

Grubb, W.N. (1996). *Learning to work: The case for reintegrating job training and education*. New York: Russell Sage Foundation.

Gueron, J. M., & Pauly, E. (1991). *From welfare to work*. New York: Russell Sage Foundation.

Guillen, M. F., Collins, R., England, P., & Meyer, M. (Eds). (2002). *The new economic sociology: Developments in an emerging field*. New York: Russell Sage Foundation.

Gutmann, A., & Thompson, D. (1996). *Democracy and disagreement*. Cambridge, MA: Belknap.

Gyan, J. Jr. (2006, January 14). Congressional panel meets with Nagin. *Baton Rouge Advocate*. Retrieved January 15, 2006, from www.2theadvocate.com

Hachen, D. S. Jr. (1990). Three models of job mobility in labor markets. *Work and Occupations*, 17, 320–54.

Hakim, D. (2004, August 15). The jobs picture. *The New York Times*, p. 20.

Hall, J. C. (Ed.). (1999). *Approaches to teaching Narrative of the Life of Frederick Douglass*. New York: Modern Language Association of America.

Hall, P. A., & Soskice, D. (Eds). (2001). *Varieties of capitalism: The institutional foundations of comparative advantage*. Oxford, UK: Oxford University Press.

Harrison, B., & Weiss, M. (1998). Labor market restructuring and workforce development. In R. P. Giloth (Ed.), *Jobs and economic development: Strategies and practice*, pp. 19–41. Thousand Oaks, CA: Sage.

Hart, S. L. (2005). *Capitalism at the crossroads: The unlimited business opportunities in solving the world's most difficult problems*. Upper Saddle River, NJ: Pearson Education/Wharton School Publishing.

Hasten, M. (2003). Education a key legislative topic. *The Shreveport Times*. Retrieved March 31, 2003, from www.shreveporttimes.com

Hauser, R. M., Brown, B., & Prosser, W. R. (Eds.). (1997). *Indicators of children's well-being*. New York: Russell Sage Foundation.

Hayes, C. (Ed.). (1987). *Risking the future: Adolescent sexuality, pregnancy, and childbearing*, Vol.1. Washington, DC: National Academy Press.

Hebert, S., St. George, A., & Epstein, B. (2003). *Breaking through: Overcoming barriers to family sustaining employment*. Boston, MA: Abt Associates and the New School University.

Hebert, S., Welch, D., St. George, A., Berrien, J., Schwartz, A., Mueller, E., & Park, S. R. (2002). *AECF Jobs Initiative: Evaluation of the capacity building phase, April 1997–2000*. Boston, MA: Abt Associates and the New School University.

Heilbroner, R. L. (1999). *The worldly philosophers*, 7th edition. New York: Touchstone.

Herr, T. (2003). The challenge of integrating workforce development lessons into community-building initiatives. Paper presented at the Annie E. Casey Foundation Jobs Initiative Research Conference, February 28–29, Tampa, Florida.

Herr, T., & Halpern, R. (1994). *Lessons from Project Match for welfare reform*. Chicago: Erikson Institute.

Hirsch, A. E., Dietrich, S. M., Landau, R., Schneider, P. D., Ackelsberg, I. Bernstein-Baker, J., & Hohenstein, J. (2002). *Every door closed: Barriers facing parents with criminal records*. Washington, DC: Center for Law and Social Policy.

Hirst, P., & Zeitlin, J. (1997). Flexible specialization: Theory and evidence in the analysis of industrial change. In J. R. Hollingsworth & R. Boyer (Eds.), *Contemporary capitalism: The embeddedness of institutions*, pp. 220–39. New York: Cambridge University Press.

Holahan, J. & Cook, A. (2005). *Changes in economic conditions and health insurance coverage, 2000–2004*. Washington, DC: Urban Institute.

Hollingsworth, J. R., & Boyer, R. (Eds.). (1997). *Contemporary capitalism: The embeddedness of institutions.* New York: Cambridge University Press.

Hollister, M. N. (2004). Does firm size matter anymore? The new economy and firm size wage effects. *American Sociological Review,* 69, 659–76.

Holzer, H. J. (1996). *What employers want.* New York: Russell Sage Foundation.

Holzer, H. J., Stoll, M. A., & Wissoker, D. (2004). Job performance and retention among welfare recipients. *Social Service Review,* 78 (3), 343–69.

Howard, C. (1997). *The hidden welfare state: Tax expenditures and social policy in the United States.* Princeton, NJ: Princeton University Press.

Hunter, L. W. (1999). Customer differentiation, institutional fields, and the quality of jobs in nursing homes. Working paper. Philadelphia, PA: University of Pennsylvania, Wharton School.

Hyland, T. (2004, December 9). The state of nations: Interview with Richard Estes. *Penn Current,* p. 4.

Internal Revenue Service. (2004). IRS outlines EITC eligibility for 2003 tax year. Washington, DC: U.S. Department of the Treasury, Author. Retrieved September 6, 2004, from www.irs.gov/newsroom/article/0,,id=119793,00.html

Iversen, R. R. (1995). Poor African-American women and work: The occupational attainment process. *Social Problems,* 42, 554–73.

Iversen, R. R. (1998). Occupational social work for the 21st century. *Social Work: Special Centennial Issue,* 43, 551–66.

Iversen, R. R. (2000). TANF policy implementation: The invisible barrier. *Journal of Sociology and Social Welfare,* 27, 139–59.

Iversen, R. R. (2001). Occupational social work and job retention supports: An international perspective. *International Social Work,* 44(3), 329–42.

Iversen, R. R. (2002). *Moving up is a steep climb.* Baltimore, MD: Annie E. Casey Foundation.

Iversen, R. R. (2004). How do workers see advancement? In R. Giloth (Ed.), *Workforce intermediaries for the twenty-first century,* pp. 241–62. Philadelphia, PA: Temple University Press in association with The American Assembly, Columbia University.

Iversen, R. R., & Armstrong, A.L. (2004). Maternal depression, employment and child well-being. Research brief. Baltimore, MD: Annie E. Casey Foundation.

Iversen, R. R., & Farber, N. B. (2000). Transmission of family values, work and welfare among poor urban black women. In T. L. Parcel & D. B. Cornfield (Eds.). *Work and Family: Research Informing Policy,* pp. 249–73. Thousand Oaks, CA: Sage.

Iversen, R. R., Furstenberg, F. F., Jr., and Belzer, A.A. (1999). How much do we count?: Interpretation and error-making in the decennial census. *Demography,* 36, 121–34.

Jacobs, J. A. (1993). Careers in the U.S. service economy. In G. Esping-Anderson, *Changing classes: Stratification and mobility in post-industrial societies,* pp. 195–224. Newbury Park, CA: Sage.

Jacoby, S. M. (2004). *Employing bureaucracy.* Mahwah, NJ: Lawrence Erlbaum Associates.

Jargowsky, P. A. (1997). *Poverty and place.* New York: Russell Sage Foundation.

Jargowsky, P. A. (2003). Stunning progress, hidden problems: The dramatic decline of concentrated poverty in the 1990s. Washington, DC: Brookings Institution.

Johnson, M. (2000, September 11). Study challenges benefits of smaller class sizes. *Milwaukee Journal Sentinel,* A1, 8.

Johnson, S. H. (2001). *Public benefits portal.* Seattle, WA: Office of Economic Development, City of Seattle.

Joyce Foundation. (2002). *Welfare to work: What have we learned?* Chicago, IL: Author.

Kalil, A., Corcoran, M. E., Danziger, S. K., Tolman, R., Seefeldt, K. S., Rosen, D., & Nam, Y. (1998). *Getting jobs, keeping jobs, and earning a living wage: Can welfare reform work?* Ann Arbor, MI: University of Michigan, Center on Poverty, Risk, and Mental Health.

Kahneman, D. (2003). A perspective on judgment and choice. *American Psychologist,* 58 (9), 697–720.

Kalleberg, A.L. & Marsden, P.V. (2005). Externalizing organizational activities: Where and how U.S. establishments use employment intermediaries. *Socio-Economic Review,* 3(3), 389–416.

Kalleberg, A. L., & Mastekaasa, A. (2001). Satisfied movers, committed stayers. *Work and Occupations,* 28, 183–209.

Kalleberg, A. L., Reskin, B. F., & Hudson, K. (2000). Bad jobs in America: Standard and nonstandard employment relations and job quality in the United States. *American Sociological Review,* 65, 256–78.

Karger, H. J., & Stoesz, D. (2002). *American social welfare policy: A pluralist approach,* 4th edition. Boston: Allyn & Bacon.

Kasarda, J. (1995). Industrial restructuring and the changing location of jobs. In R. Farley (Ed.), *State of the union,* Vol. 1. New York: Russell Sage Foundation.

Katz, B. (2004). A progressive agenda for metropolitan America. Washington, DC: Brookings Institution.

Katz, M. (2001). *The price of citizenship: Redefining the American welfare state.* New York: Henry Holt and Company.

Kauff, J., Derr, M.K., & Pavetti, L. (2004). *A study of work participation and full employment strategies.* Washington, DC: Mathematica Policy Research.

Kazis, R., & Miller, M. S. (2001). *Low-wage workers in the new economy.* Washington, DC: Urban Institute.

Keith, K., & McWilliams, A. (1995). The wage effects of cumulative job mobility. *Industrial and Labor Relations Review,* 49, 121–37.

Kerckhoff, A. C. (Ed.) (1996). *Generating social stratification.* Boulder, CO: Westview.

King, C. T. (2004). The effectiveness of publicly financed training in the United States: Implications for WIA and related programs. In C. J. O'Leary, R. A. Straits, & S. A. Wandner (Eds.), *Job training policy in the United States,* pp. 57–99. Kalamazoo, MI: W.E. Upjohn Institute for Employment Research.

Kingsley, G. T., & Pettit, K. L. S. (2003). Concentrated poverty: A change in course. Washington, DC: Urban Institute.

Kinukawa, A., Guzman, L., & Lippman, L. (2004). National estimates of child care and subsidy receipt for children ages 0 to 6: What can we learn from the National Household Education Survey? Research brief. Washington, DC: Child Trends.

Koball, H. & Douglas-Hall, A. (2005). *Marriage not enough to guarantee economic security.* New York: Columbia University, National Center for Children in Poverty.

Kochan, T.A. (2005). *Restoring the American dream.* Cambridge, MA: MIT Press.

Kreider, R. M., & Fields, J. M. (2002). Number, timing, and duration of marriages and divorces: Fall 1996. Current Population Reports, P70-80. Washington, DC: U.S. Census Bureau.

Krippner, G., Granovetter, M., Block, F., Biggart, N., & Beamish, T. (2004). Polanyi Symposium: A conversation on embeddedness. *Socio-Economic Review,* 2, 109–35.

Krueger, A. B. (2003). Inequality, too much of a good thing. In J. J. Heckman & A. B. Krueger (Eds.), *Inequality in America: What role for human capital policies?,* pp. 1–75. Cambridge, MA: MIT Press.

Ku, L., Broaddus, M., & Wachino, V. (2005). Medicaid and SCHIP protected insurance coverage for millions of low-income Americans. Washington, DC: Center on Budget and Policy Priorities.

268   REFERENCES

Kuhn, T. (1970). *The structure of scientific revolutions*, 2nd ed. Chicago: University of Chicago Press.

Kurz, D. (2002). Poor mothers and the care of teenage children. In F. Cancian, D. Kurz, A. London, R. Reviere, & M. Tuominen (Eds.), *Child care and inequality: Re-thinking carework for children and youth*, pp. 23–36. Oxford: Routledge.

Lafer, G. (2002). *The job training charade*. Ithaca, NY: Cornell University Press.

Lane, J., Moss, P., Salzman, H., & Tilly, C. (2003). Too many cooks? Tracking internal labor market dynamics in food service with case studies and quantitative data. In E. Appelbaum, A. Bernhardt, & R. J. Murnane (Eds.), *Low-wage America: How employers are reshaping opportunity in the workplace*, pp. 229–69. New York: Russell Sage Foundation.

Langland, C. (2002, December 31). Pa. issues warnings to 884 schools. *The Philadelphia Inquirer*, B1, 6.

Lareau, A. (2003). *Unequal childhoods: Class, race, and family life*. Berkeley: University of California Press.

Laufer, J. K. & Winship, S. (2004). In R. P. Giloth (Ed.)., *Workforce intermediaries for the twenty-first century*, pp. 216–40. Philadelphia, PA: Temple University Press in association with The American Assembly, Columbia University.

Lawrence, S. (2002). Domestic violence and welfare policy: Research findings that can inform policies on marriage and child well-being. New York: Columbia University, National Center for Children in Poverty.

Leicht, K. T. (1998). Work (if you can get it) and occupations (if there are any)?: What social scientists can learn from predictions of the end of work and radical workplace change. *Work and Occupations*, 25, 36–48.

Leicht, K. T. (Ed.) (2002). *The future of market transition*. Oxford, UK: Elsevier Science Ltd.

Lennon, M. C., Blome, J., & English, K. (2001). *Depression and low-income women: Challenges for TANF and welfare-to-work policies and programs*. New York: Columbia University, National Center for Children in Poverty.

Levin-Epstein, J. (2002). *New study shows adolescents fare poorly under welfare reform: Reauthorization could worsen or improve teen well-being*. Washington, DC: Center for Law and Social Policy.

Levine, M. V. (2003, August 30). Rolled over by unemployment. *Milwaukee Journal Sentinel*. Retrieved September 22, 2004, from www.jsonline.com/news/editorials/aug03/166013.asp

Liebow, E. (1967). *Tally's corner*. Boston: Little Brown.

Lin, A. C. (2000). Interpretive research for public policy. In S. Danziger & A.C. Lin, *Coping with poverty*, pp. 1–23. Ann Arbor, MI: University of Michigan.

Lin, N. (2001). *Social capital: A theory of social structure and action*. Cambridge, UK: Cambridge University Press.

Lipsky, M. (1980). *Street-level bureaucrats*. New York: Russell Sage Foundation.

Louisiana Department of Education (2001, November). *Reaching for results: 2000–2001 school report card for parents*. Retrieved September 8, 2002, from www.lcet.doe.la.us

Mader, B. (2002). Trumpeting the tricks of the carpentry trade. *The Business Journal of Milwaukee*, September 23, 2002. Retrieved June 3, 2004, from http://milwaukee.bizjournals.com/milwaukee/stories/2002/09/23/focus3.html

Magura, S., & Moses, B. S. (1986). *Outcome measures for child welfare services*. Washington, DC: Child Welfare League of America.

Maitino, J. R., & Peck, D. R. (Eds.). (1996). *Teaching American ethnic literatures*. Albuquerque: University of New Mexico Press.

March, J. G., & Simon, H. A. (1958). *Organizations*. New York: Wiley.

Marcus, G. E. (1998). *Ethnography through thick and thin*. Princeton, NJ: Princeton University Press.

Marshall, C., & Rossman, G. B. (1999). *Designing qualitative research*, 3rd ed. Thousand Oaks, CA: Sage.

Marx, K. (1978). *Capital*, Vol. I. In R. C. Tucker (Ed.), *The Marx-Engels reader*, 2nd edition. New York: Norton. (Original work published 1867)

Mathur, A. (2002). *Credentials count*. Washington, DC: Center for Law and Social Policy.

Mathur, A., Reichle, J., Strawn, J., & Wisely, C. (2004). *From jobs to careers: How California community college credentials pay off for welfare recipients*. Washington, DC: Center for Law & Social Policy.

McCall, L. (2000). Gender and the new inequality: Explaining the college/non-college wage gap. *American Sociological Review*, 65, 234–55.

McCaskill, C. (2004). Yellow sheet. Jefferson City, MO: Office of the State Auditor General of Missouri.

McGarvey, A. (2004). Women and children last. *The American Prospect Online*, Aug. 13, 2004. Retrieved January 22, 2005, from www.prospect.org

McLanahan, S., & Sandefur, G. (1994). *Growing up with a single parent: What hurts, what helps*. Cambridge, MA: Harvard University.

Meléndez, E. (2002). Prospectus for *Communities and workforce development*. Submitted to the W.E. Upjohn Institute for Employment Research, Kalamazoo, MI.

Meléndez, E. (Ed.). (2004). *Communities and workforce development*. Kalamazoo, MI: W.E. Upjohn Institute for Employment Research.

Mezey, J., Greenberg, M., & Schumacher, R. (2002). The vast majority of federally eligible children did not receive child care assistance in FY 2000. Washington, DC: Center for Law and Social Policy.

Mezzacappa, D. (2002, November 15). PA moves to raise teacher standards. *The Philadelphia Inquirer*, A1, 16.

Michalopoulos, C. (2001). Sustained employment and earnings growth: Experimental evidence on earnings supplements and pre-employment services. In R. Kazis & M. S. Miller (Eds.), *Low-wage workers in the new economy*, pp. 135–50. Washington, DC: Urban Institute.

Michalopoulos, C., Edin, K., Fink, B., Landriscina, M., Polit, D.F., Polyne, J. C., et al. (2003). *Welfare reform in Philadelphia: Implementation, effects, and experiences of poor families and neighborhoods*. New York: MDRC.

Miller, D. (1999). *Principles of social justice*. Cambridge, MA: Harvard University Press.

Miller, D. (2003). *Political philosophy: A very short introduction*. Oxford, UK: Oxford University Press.

Mills, C. W. (1959/2000). *The sociological imagination*. New York: Oxford University Press.

Minehan, C. E. (2004). Labor markets: What we know and what we don't. Boston, MA: Federal Reserve Bank of Boston.

Mishel, L. (2004). A tale of two economies. *EPI Journal*, Winter 2004.

Mishel, L., & Bernstein, J. (1994). *The state of working America 1994/1995*. Armonk, NY: M.E. Sharpe.

Mishel, L., Bernstein, J., & Allegretto, S. (2005). *The state of working America 2004/2005*. Ithaca, NY: Cornell University Press.

Mishel, L., Bernstein, J., & Boushey, H. (2003). *The state of working America 2002/2003*. Ithaca, NY: Cornell University Press.

Moffitt, R. (2000). Perspectives on the qualitative-quantitative divide. *Poverty Research News*, 4, 5–8.

Moffitt, R., Chase-Lansdale, P. L., & Cherlin, A. (2004). *Explaining disparate findings from the Three-City and the MDRC Next Generation studies on the employment and welfare impacts on children and adolescents.* Retrieved October 13, 2004, from www.jhu.edu/~welfare

Moffitt, R., & Winder, K. (2002). The correlates and consequences of welfare exit and entry: Evidence from the Three-City Study. *Focus* 22(2), 70–72.

Monette, D. R., Sullivan, T. J., & DeJong, C. R. (2005). *Applied social research: Tool for the human services,* 6th ed. Belmont, CA: Brooks/Cole, Thomson.

Morris, M., & Western, B. (1999). Inequality in earnings at the close of the twentieth century. *Annual Review of Sociology,* 25, 623–57.

Moss, P., & Tilly, C. (2001). *Stories employers tell: Race, skill, and hiring in America.* New York: Russell Sage Foundation.

Mukamel, D. (2001). *From hard time to full time: Strategies to help move ex-offenders from welfare to work.* Washington DC: U.S. Department of Labor.

Mullahy, J., & Wolfe, B. L. (2001). Health policies for the non-elderly poor. In S. H. Danziger & R. H. Haveman (Eds.), *Understanding poverty,* pp. 278–313. New York: Russell Sage Foundation, and Cambridge, MA: Harvard University.

Murray, C. (1984). *Losing ground.* New York: Basic Books.

Musick, J.S. (1993). *Young, poor, and pregnant: The psychology of teenage motherhood.* New Haven, CT: Yale University Press.

Nafziger, R. (2000). The new economy and the future of work. Olympia, WA: Governor's Executive Policy Office.

National Center for Fair & Open Testing. (2002). ESEA: Ten percent of U.S. schools labeled "failing." Cambridge, MA: Author.

National Center for Public Policy and Higher Education. (2002). *Losing ground: A national status report on the affordability of American higher education.* San Jose, CA: Author.

National Governor's Association and National Association of State Budget Officers. (2002). *The fiscal survey of states: November 2002.* Washington, DC: Authors.

National Governor's Association and National Association of State Budget Officers. (2003). *The fiscal survey of states: December 2003.* Washington, DC: Authors.

National Low Income Housing Coalition. (2004). *Out of reach 2004.* Washington, DC: Author.

National Research Council. (1999). *The changing nature of work: Implications for occupational analysis.* Washington, DC: National Academy Press.

Nee, V. (2003). A new institutional approach to economic sociology. CSES Working Paper Series #4. Ithaca, NY: Cornell University, Center for the Study of Economy & Society.

Nee, V. & Swedberg, R. (2005). *The economic sociology of capitalism.* Princeton, NJ: Princeton University Press.

Needels, K., Corson, W., & Nicholson, W. (2001). *Left out of the boom economy.* Report #8573. Princeton, NJ: Mathematica Policy Research.

Nelson, R. (2003, May 10). Orleans scores stagnate. *The Times-Picayune,* A1, 12.

Newman, K. (1988). *Falling from grace.* New York: Vintage Books.

Newman, K. (2002). No shame: The view from the left bank. *American Journal of Sociology,* 107, 1577–99.

New Orleans Public Schools. (2005). The "new" New Orleans public schools. Retrieved February 12, 2005, from www.nops.K12.la.us

Norman, J. (2003, May 11). WI state disinvests in public education. *The Milwaukee Journal Sentinel.* Retrieved May 11, 2003, from www.jsonline.com

North, D. C. (1998). Economic performance through time. In M. C. Brinton & V. Nee (Eds.), *The new institutionalism in sociology,* pp. 247–57. Stanford, CA: Stanford University Press.

Nyhan, P. (2004, April 14). 'Help wanted' signs are scarce in Seattle. *Seattle Post-Intelligencer Reporter*. Retrieved September 22, 2004, from www.seattlepi.nwsource.com/business/168930_jobless14.html

O'Connor, A., Tilly, C., & Bobo, L. D. (Eds.) (2001). *Urban inequality: Evidence from four cities*. New York: Russell Sage Foundation.

Office of Community Learning. (2002). What is community learning? Retrieved July 14, 2002, from www.seattleschools.org

O'Leary, C. J., Straits, R. A., & Wandner, S. A. (Eds.). (2004). *Job training policy in the United States*. Kalamazoo, MI: W.E. Upjohn Institute for Employment Research.

Osterman, P (1999). *Securing prosperity*. Princeton, NJ: Princeton University Press.

Osterman, P. (2005). Employment and training policies: New directions for less-skilled adults. Conference paper, October 2005. Washington, DC: Urban Institute.

Osterman, P., Kochan, T. A., Locke, R., & Piore, M. J. (2001). *Working in America: A blueprint for the new labor market*. Cambridge, MA: MIT Press.

Ostrander, S. A. (1995). *Money for change*. Philadelphia: Temple University Press.

Padavic, I., & Reskin, B. (2002). *Women and men at work*, 2nd ed. Thousand Oaks, CA: Pine Forge Press.

Padgett, D. K. (1998). *Qualitative methods in social work research: Challenges and rewards*. Thousand Oaks, CA: Sage.

Parcel, T., & Menaghan, E. (1994). *Parents' jobs and children's lives*. Chicago: Aldine De Gruyter.

Parker, S. (2002, June 12). Vehicles per household in USA. *USA Today*, 1A.

Parsons, T. (Ed. & Trans. with Henderson, A. M.). (1947). *Max Weber: The theory of social and economic organization*. New York: Free Press.

Patchen, M. (2004). *Making our schools more effective: What matters and what works*. Springfield, IL: Charles C Thomas.

Patel, N., & Savner, S. (2001). *Implementation of Individual Training Account policies under the Workforce Investment Act*. Preliminary report. Washington, DC: Center for Law and Social Policy.

Pearce, D. (2000). *The Self-Sufficiency Standard for Wisconsin*. Madison, WI: Education Fund of the Wisconsin Women's Network.

Pearce, D. (2001). Personal communication about the Self-Sufficiency Standard for Washington, May 25 and June 28.

Perlmutter, F. D. (1997). *From welfare to work: Corporate initiatives and welfare reform*. New York: Oxford University Press.

Petit, B. (2004). Moving and children's social connections: Neighborhood context and the consequences of moving for low-income families. *Sociological Forum*, 19 (2), 285–311.

Philadelphia Citizens for Children and Youth. (2001). Counting on childcare: Information about childcare in Southeastern Pennsylvania. Philadelphia: Author.

Polanyi, K. (2001). The economy as instituted process. In M. Granovetter & R. Swedberg (Eds.), *The sociology of economic life*, pp. 31–50. Boulder, CO: Westview.

Poppe, N., Strawn, J., & Martinson, K. (2004). Whose job is it? Creating opportunities for advancement. In R. Giloth (Ed.), *Workforce intermediaries for the twenty-first century*, pp. 31–69. Philadelphia, PA: Temple University Press in association with The American Assembly, Columbia University.

Portes, A. (1998). Social capital: Its origins and applications in modern sociology. *Annual Review of Sociology*, 24, 1–24.

Price, L., & Fungard, Y. (2004). Understanding the severity of the current labor slump. Briefing Paper, February 19, 2004. Washington, DC: Economic Policy Institute.

Putnam, R. D. (1995). Bowling alone: America's declining social capital. *Journal of Democracy*, 6, 65–78.

Putnam, R. D. (2000). *Bowling alone: The collapse and revival of American community.* New York: Simon & Schuster.

Radloff, L. S. (1977). The CES-D scale: A self-report depression scale for research in the general population. *Applied Psychological Measurement,* 3, 385–401.

Radloff, L. S., & Locke, B. Z. (1986). The Community Mental Health Assessment Survey and the CES-D scale. In M. M. Weissman, J. K. Myer, & C. E. Ross (Eds.), *Community surveys of psychiatric disorders,* pp. 177–89. New Brunswick, NJ: Rutgers University Press.

Rainwater, L., & Smeeding, T. M. (2003). *Poor kids in a rich country.* New York: Russell Sage Foundation.

Rangarajan, A., & Novak, T. (1999). *The struggle to sustain employment: The effectiveness of the Postemployment Services Demonstration.* Princeton, NJ: Mathematica Policy Research.

Rangarajan, A. & Razafindrakoto, C. (2004). *Unemployment Insurance as a potential safety net for TANF leavers: Evidence from five states.* Princeton, NJ: Mathematica Policy Research.

Rangarajan, A., Meckstroth, A., & Novak, T. (1998). *The effectiveness of the Postemeployment Services Demonstration: Preliminary findings.* Princeton, NJ: Mathematica Policy Research.

Rangarajan, A., Schochet, P., & Chu, D. (1998). *Employment experiences of welfare recipients: Who find jobs: Is targeting possible?* Princeton, NJ: Mathematica Policy Research.

Rank, M. R. (2004). *One nation, underprivileged: Why American poverty affects us all.* New York: Oxford University Press.

Reform Journal. (2003, May 28). Teacher-building sessions stressful for staff and coach. *The Philadelphia Inquirer,* A13.

Reich, R. B. (2002). *I'll be short: Essentials for a decent working society.* Boston: Beacon.

Reich, R. B. (2004). Starting November 3. *The American Prospect Online,* Nov. 1, 2004. Retrieved January 22, 2005, from www.prospect.org

Reskin, B. F. (2002). Rethinking employment discrimination and its remedies. In M. F. Guillen, R. Collins, P. England, & M. Meyer (Eds.), *The new economic sociology: Developments in an emerging field,* pp. 218–44. New York: Russell Sage Foundation.

Roberts, B. (2002). *The best of both: Community college and community-based organizations partner to better serve low-income workers and employers.* Philadelphia: Public/Private Ventures.

Roberts, G. (2004, July 1). Schools' lead levels 'severe.' *Seattle Post-Intelligencer.* Retrieved February 2, 2005, from www.seattlepi.nesource.com

Rodman, H. (1971). *Lower-class families: The culture of poverty in Negro Trinidad.* New York: Oxford University Press.

Rosenbaum, J. E. (1990). Structural models of organizational careers: A critical review and new directions. In R. L. Breiger, *Social mobility and social structure,* pp. 272–307. New York: Cambridge University Press.

Rouse, C., Brooks-Gunn, J., & McLanahan, S. (2005). Introducing the issue. *The Future of Children,* 15(1), 5–14.

Runzheimer International. (2004). Runzheimer analyzes daycare costs nationwide. Retrieved February 2, 2005, from www.runzheimer.com/corpc/news/scripts/011604.asp

Savner, S. (1999). *Key implementation decisions affecting low-income adults under the Workforce Investment Act.* Kellogg Devolution Initiative Paper. Washington, DC: Center for Law and Social Policy.

Scheuren, F., & Wang, K. (1999). The National Survey of America's Families (NSAF): A mid-term status report. In D. Chandler, J. Meisel, & P. Jordan (Eds.), *Child well-being under welfare reform.* Washington, DC: American Enterprise Institute for Policy Research.

Schmitt, E. (2001, August 6). Census data show a sharp increase in living standard. *New York Times*, A-1, 10.

Schulman, K. (2000). The high cost of child care puts quality care out of reach for many families. Washington, DC: Children's Defense Fund.

Schulman, K., & Blank, H. (2004). Child care assistance policies 2001–2004: Families struggling to move forward, states moving backward. Issue brief. Washington, DC: National Women's Law Center.

Seattle Public Schools. (2001). Data profile: District summary: Student Information office. Retrieved March 2002, from www.seattleschools.org

Seattle School District. (2005). Potential school consolidation, student assignment and transportation plans. Retrieved February 20, 2005, from www.seattleschools.org

Seltzer, J. A., McLanahan, S., & Hanson, T. L. (1997). Will child support enforcement increase father-child contact and parental conflict after separation? MacArthur Research Network. Retrieved January 23, 2005, from www.olin.wustl.edu

Sen, A. K. (1977). Rational fools: A critique of the behavioral foundations of economic theory. *Philosophy and Public Affairs*, 6, 317–434.

Shapiro, I., Kogan, R., & Aron-Dine, A. (2005). *How does this recovery measure up?* Washington, DC: Center on Budget and Policy Priorities.

Shapiro, T. M., & Wolff, E. N. (Eds.). (2001). *Assets for the poor: The benefits of spreading asset ownership.* New York: Russell Sage Foundation.

Sherraden, M. (1991). *Assets and the poor: A new American social welfare policy.* Armonk, NY: M.E. Sharpe.

Sherraden, M., Zhan, M., & Williams, T. (2003). Assets, poverty, and children. The Fedele F. and Iris M. Fauri Memorial Lecture in Child Welfare. Ann Arbor, MI: University of Michigan School of Social Work.

Shipler, D. K. (2004). *The working poor: Invisible in America.* New York: Alfred A. Knopf.

Short, K. (2001). *Experimental poverty measures: 1999.* Washington, DC: U.S. Department of Commerce, Economic and Statistics Administration and U.S. Census Bureau.

Smith, H. (2004). National statistics: Snapshots of work and family in America. Retrieved September 6, 2004, from www.pbs.org/workfamily/discussion_snapshots.html

Smith, D. M., & Woodbury, S. A. (2000). *The low-wage labor market: Challenges and opportunities for economic self-sufficiency.* Washington, DC: U.S. Department of Health and Human Services, Assistant Secretary for Planning and Evaluation. Retrieved September 22, 2004, from www.aspe.hhs.gov/lwlm99/smithwood.htm

Smith, W., Wittner, J., Spence, R., & Van Kleunen, A. (2002). *Skills training works: Examining the evidence.* Washington, DC: The Workforce Alliance.

Snyder, S. (2002, September 4). Phila. vows tougher discipline in schools. *The Philadelphia Inquirer*, A1, 16.

Snyder, S. (2003, June 12). Loaded guns found at two city schools. *The Philadelphia Inquirer*, B9.

Stack, C. B. (1974). *All our kin: Strategies for survival in a Black community.* New York: Harper & Row.

Stack, C. B. (1996). *Call to home: African Americans reclaim the rural south.* New York: Basic Books.

Stake, R. E. (1995). *The art of case study research.* Thousand Oaks, CA: Sage.

Stone, C., & Worgs, D. (2004). Poverty and the workforce challenge. In R. Giloth (Ed.), *Workforce development politics: Civic capacity and performance*, pp. 249–280. Philadelphia: Temple University Press.

Strauss, A. L. (1971). *The contexts of social mobility: Ideology and theory.* Chicago: Aldine.

Strawn, J., & Martinson, K. (2000). *Steady work and better jobs*. New York: MDRC.

Streeck, W. (1997). Beneficial constraints: On the economic limits of rational voluntarism. In J. R. Hollingsworth & R. Boyer (Eds.), *Contemporary capitalism: The embeddedness of institutions*, pp. 197–219. New York: Cambridge University Press.

Sutton, S. A. (2004). Corporate-community workforce development collaborations. In E. Meléndez (Ed.), *Communities and workforce development*, pp. 439–71. Kalamazoo, MI: W.E. Upjohn Institute for Employment Research.

Swedberg, R. (2003). *Principles of economic sociology*. Princeton, NJ: Princeton University Press.

Swedberg, R. (2004). The toolkit of economic sociology. Working Paper #22. Ithaca, NY: Cornell University, Center for the Study of Economy and Society.

Swedberg, R. (2005). Hope and economic development: The case of 18th century Sweden. CSES Working Paper Series #28. Ithaca, NY: Cornell University, Center for the Study of Economy and Society.

Taylor, J. C., & Rubin, J. (2005). Engaging employers to benefit low-income job seekers: Lessons from the Jobs Initiative. Boston: Jobs for the Future.

The new protectionism: The great hollowing-out myth. (2004, February 21–27). *The Economist*, Vol. 370 (No. 8363), 27–29.

Thevenot, B. (2002a, June 30). About face. *The Times-Picayune*, A1, 8.

Thevenot, B. (2002b, October 17). Panel: Beef up schools audit office. *The Times-Picayune*, B1, 3.

Tilly, C. (1996). *Half a job*. Philadelphia: Temple University Press.

Tilly, C. (2004). Trust and predation. Paper written October 24, 2004 and presented at the University of Pennsylvania, February 10, 2005.

Uchitelle, L. (2003, July 12). Blacks lose better jobs faster as middle-class work drops. *The New York Times*, A1, C14.

U.S. Census Bureau. (2000). Census 2000 ZCTAs ZIP Code Tabulation Areas technical documentation. Washington, DC: Author.

U.S. Census Bureau. (2003). Average number of children per family and per family with children, by state: 2000 Census. Retrieved August 26, 2004, from www.census.gov/main/www/cen2000.html

U.S. Census Bureau. (2004a). Income stable, poverty up, numbers of Americans with and without health insurance rise. Census Bureau Reports. Washington, DC: Author. Retrieved August 26, 2004, from www.census.gov/Press-Release/www.releases/archives/income_wealth/002484.html

U.S. Census Bureau. (2004b). North American Industry Classification System (NAICS 2002). Washington, DC: Author. Retrieved August 4, 2004, from www.census.gov/epcd/www.naics.html

U.S. Department of Health and Human Services. (2001). *Fiscal year 2001: Characteristics and financial circumstances of TANF recipients*. Washington, DC: Author, Administration for Children & Families. Retrieved August 18, 2004, from www.acf.dhhs.gov/programs/ofa/character/FY2001/characteristics.htm

U.S. Department of Labor. (2001). OSHA Regional news release, May 15. Washington, DC: U.S. Department of Labor, Office of Public Affairs. Retrieved December 21, 2004, from www.osha.gov/pls/oshaweb/owadisp.show_document?p_table=NEWS_RELEASE.

U.S. Department of Labor. (2004). Establishment search page. Washington, DC: U.S. Department of Labor, Occupational Safety & Health Administration. Retrieved May-June 2004, from www.osha.gov/pls/imis/establishment.html

U.S. Department of Labor. (2005). Inflation calendar. Washington, DC: U.S. Department of Labor, Bureau of Labor Statistics. Retrieved April 9, 2005, from http://stats.bls.gov

Van Kleunen, A., & Spence, R. (2003). Analysis of Bush Administration's reauthorization proposal for the Workforce Investment Act (WIA). Chicago, IL: The Workforce Alliance.

Von Bergen, J. M. (2005, January 8). U.S. added 2.2 million jobs in 2004. *The Philadelphia Inquirer*, A1, 12.

Vroman, W. (2002). Unemployment Insurance primer: Understanding what's at stake as Congress reopens stimulus package debate. Research paper. Washington, DC: Urban Institute.

Wacquant, L. (2002). Scrutinizing the street: Poverty, morality and the pitfalls of urban ethnography. *American Journal of Sociology*, 107, 1468–1532.

Wagner, S. L., & Herr, T. (2003). "Something old, something new" revisited: Project Match experiments with retention incentives. *Research & Policy Update*, December. Chicago, IL: Project Match.

Wagner, S. L., Brooks, D., & Herr, T. (2004). Can we motivate people to become steady workers? 19-month findings from Project Match's retention incentives project. *Research & Policy Update*, November. Chicago, IL: Project Match.

Waldron, T., Roberts, B., & Reamer, A. (2004). *Working hard, falling short: America's working families and the pursuit of economic security*. Baltimore, MD: Annie E. Casey Foundation.

Wallin, B. (2005). *Budgeting for basics: The changing landscape of city finances*. Washington, DC: Brookings Institution.

Wardlaw, J. (2001, March 14). Are we on our way to being average? *The Times-Picayune*, B7.

Warren, J. R., Hauser, R. M., & Sheridan, J. T. (2002). Occupational stratification across the life course: Evidence from the Wisconsin Longitudinal Study. *American Sociological Review*, 67, 432–55.

Weber, M. (1946). Bureaucracy. In H. Gerth & C. W. Mills (Eds.), *From Max Weber*, pp. 196–252. New York: Oxford University Press. (Original work published 1915)

Weber, M. (1978). *Economy and society*, Volumes I and II. In G. Roth & C. Wittich (Eds.). Berkeley: University of California Press. (Original work published 1922)

Weber, M. (1949). *The methodology of the social sciences*. In E.A. Shills & H. A. Finch (Eds. & Trans.). New York: Free Press. (Original work published 1904)

Weicher, J. (1999). Housing conditions and living arrangements. In Proceedings of the "Child well-being under welfare reform" conference, December 8–9. Washington, DC: American Enterprise Institute for Public Policy Research.

Weintraub, J. (2000, September 11). The right choice? *Milwaukee Journal Sentinel*, E1, 3.

West, K. K., Hauser, R. B., & Scanlan, T. M. (Eds.). (1998). *Longitudinal surveys of children*. Washington, DC: National Academy Press.

Western, B. (2002). The impact of incarceration on wage mobility and inequality. *American Sociological Review*, 67, 526–46.

Whyte, W. F. (1981). *Street corner society*, 3rd edition. Chicago: University of Chicago.

Wider Opportunities for Women. (2001). The Self-Sufficiency Standard. Washington, DC: Author. Retrieved March 22, 2003, from www.sixstrategies.org/state

Wider Opportunities for Women. (2004). The Self-Sufficiency Standard. Washington, DC: Author. Retrieved August 5, 2004, from www.sixstrategies.org/state

Wilhelm, T., Carmen, D., & Reynolds, M. (2002). Connecting kids to technology: Challenges and opportunities. *Kids Count Snapshot*, June 2002. Baltimore, MD: Annie E. Casey Foundation.

Willis, P. (2000). *The ethnographic imagination*. Cambridge, UK: Polity.

Wilson, W. J. (1987). *The truly disadvantaged*. Chicago: University of Chicago Press.

Wilson, W. J. (1996). *When work disappears*. New York: Alfred A. Knopf.

Winston, P. (1999). *Welfare, children, & families: A three city study/overview and design.* Baltimore, MD: Johns Hopkins Press.

Wong, Y. I. (2000). Measurement properties of the Center for Epidemiologic Studies Depression scale in a homeless population. *Psychological Assessment, 12,* 69–76.

Woolcock, M. (1998). Social capital and economic development: Toward a theoretical synthesis and policy framework. *Theory and Society, 27,* 151–208.

Woodall, M. (2002, January 23). Low achievers catching up, thanks to after-school help. *The Philadelphia Inquirer,* A1, 7.

Workforce Alliance. (2005). *The Workforce Alliance "Washington update."* Washington, DC: Author.

Wuthnow, R. (2005). Democratic renewal and cultural inertia: Why our best efforts fall short. *Sociological Forum, 20*(3), 343–357.

Wysen, K., Pernice, C., & Riley, T. (2003). How public health insurance programs for children work. *The Future of Children, 13,* 171–91.

Yin, R. K. (1994). *Case study research: Design and methods,* 2nd ed. Thousand Oaks, CA: Sage.

Zedlewski, S. (2005). Five questions for Sheila Zedlewski. Washington, DC: Urban Institute.

Zelizer, V. (2002). Intimate transactions. In M. F. Guillen, R. Collins, P. England, & M. Meyer (Eds.), *The new economic sociology: Developments in an emerging field,* pp. 274–300. New York: Russell Sage Foundation.

Zhan, M., & Schreiner, M. (2004). Saving for post-secondary education in Individual Development Accounts (Working Paper No. 04–11). St. Louis, MO: Washington University, Center for Social Development.

Index